ACCA TX-UK

Taxation – United Kingdom
FA2022

(For exams between 1 June 2023 and 31 March 2024)

Welcome to Emile Woolf's study text for TX-UK *Taxation – United Kingdom FA2022* which is:

- Written by tutors
- Comprehensive but concise
- In simple English
- Used around the world by Emile Woolf Colleges including China, Russia and the UK

EW | EMILE WOOLF INTERNATIONAL
Developing Trusted Professionals

Sixteenth edition published by
Emile Woolf International Limited
Fielding House, Jubilee Road
Littlewick Green   SL6 3QU   United Kingdom
Email: info@ewiglobal.com
www.emilewoolf.com

© Emile Woolf International Limited, March 2023

All rights reserved. No part of this publication may be reproduced, stored in a retrieval system, or transmitted, in any form or by any means, electronic, mechanical, photocopying, recording, scanning or otherwise, without the prior permission in writing of Emile Woolf International Limited, or as expressly permitted by law, or under the terms agreed with the appropriate reprographics rights organisation.

You must not circulate this book in any other binding or cover and you must impose the same condition on any acquirer.

Notice

This study text has been written specifically for ACCA's TX-UK examination. Its contents should not be used to inform decisions regarding 'real life' tax scenarios. Emile Woolf International Limited has made every effort to ensure that at the time of writing the contents of this study text are accurate, but neither Emile Woolf International Limited nor its directors or employees shall be under any liability whatsoever for any inaccurate or misleading information this work could contain.

British Library Cataloguing in Publications Data
A catalogue record for this book is available from the British Library.

ISBN: 979-8-38911-062-5

Printed and bound in Great Britain.

Acknowledgements
The syllabus and study guide are reproduced by kind permission of the Association of Chartered Certified Accountants.

Taxation – United Kingdom
(TX-UK) FA2022

Contents

	Page
Syllabus and study guide	vii
Tax rates and allowances	xxvii
Chapter 1: The UK tax system	1
Chapter 2: Introduction to income tax	11
Chapter 3: Property and investment income	39
Chapter 4: Employment income	55
Chapter 5: Computing trading income	85
Chapter 6: Capital allowances	107
Chapter 7: Assessing the trading income of individuals	133
Chapter 8: Trading loss relief for individuals	145
Chapter 9: Partnerships	169
Chapter 10: Simpler income tax for small businesses	179
Chapter 11: Tax relief for pension contributions	187
Chapter 12: Residence	197
Chapter 13: National Insurance contributions	205
Chapter 14: Capital gains tax	215
Chapter 15: CGT on shares and securities	241
Chapter 16: Capital gains tax reliefs	251
Chapter 17: Self-assessment for individuals	273
Chapter 18: Inheritance tax on lifetime gifts	291
Chapter 19: Inheritance tax on the value of an estate	309

Chapter 20: Introduction to corporation tax	321
Chapter 21: Taxable total profits	333
Chapter 22: Chargeable gains of a company	353
Chapter 23: Company trading losses	371
Chapter 24: Group corporation tax	383
Chapter 25: Value added tax	401
Practice questions	431
Answers to practice questions	469
Index	523

Commentary on syllabus requirement G

A section called "**Employability and technology skills**" is included in the syllabus of each **Strategic Professional** paper and all **Applied Skills** papers **except for Corporate and Business Law.**

This is found in section G of the Taxation syllabus as follows:

G   EMPLOYABILITY AND TECHNOLOGY SKILLS

1. **Use computer technology to efficiently access and manipulate relevant information.**

2. **Work on relevant response options, using available functions and technology, as would be required in the workplace.**

3. **Navigate windows and computer screens to create and amend responses to exam requirements, using the appropriate tools.**

4. **Present data and information effectively, using the appropriate tools.**

The introduction to the syllabus contains the following guidance relating to this section.

> *Section G of the syllabus contains outcomes relating to the demonstration of appropriate digital and employability skills in preparing for and taking the examination. This includes being able to interact with different question item types, manage information presented in digital format and being able to use the relevant functionality and technology to prepare and present response options in a professional manner. These skills are specifically developed by practicing and preparing for the exam, using the learning support content for computer-based exams available via the practice platform and the ACCA website and will need to be demonstrated during the live exam.*

This text does not contain material to cover Section G. You must prepare by following ACCA's advice and using the learning support content for computer exams as stated above.

Your starting point is the CBE Practice Platform. This includes short video sessions including an introduction to the Practice Platform as well as practice exams.

It is imperative that you use the ACCA CBE Practice Platform to become as familiar as possible with the exam process and to develop an approach to using the tools.

The exam will allow you to access a series of exhibits and related requirements. Answers must be entered into "response options" as appropriate using tools such as the word processing package and spreadsheet package.

Calculations and workings must be entered into a spreadsheet response option and narrative answers into a word processing response option. You should use labelling to cross reference information from one package to the other, for example, if you need to provide a written commentary (in the word processing response option) on numbers calculated (in the spreadsheet resposne option).

Warning about spreadsheets

In order to use the spreadsheet tools you must be competent in their use (thus the need to practice).

You should not assume that the spreadsheet has calculated something correctly. Many students who use spreadsheet formulae to calculate answers misuse the spreadsheet tools and introduce errors into their answer. Remember the old adage – rubbish in leads to rubbish out.

Common errors include:

- Forgetting to use brackets or percentage signs correctly in formulae.
- Typing a figure in brackets and then setting the formula to deduct it. A bracketed number is seen as a negative by the software and deducting a negative number results in it being added. For example the sum of 10 – 7 should equal 3. However, a candidate might enter 10 into cell 1 and (7) into cell 2 and then set the formula to "Cell 1 minus Cell 2". This would result in a total of 17.
- Using the spreasheet tool to sum a column of numbers which already includes a subtotal, ending up with an answer larger than it should be.
- Referring to incorrect cell numbers. For example, wanting to add figures in Cells 1 and 2 but instead adding Cell 1 to Cell 3.

Be careful! Always look at the output of a calculation to see if it looks OK.

Although you are provided with a spreadsheet in which to input numerical answers you do not have to use the tools within that spreadsheet. You could simply type in figures and use a calculator to perform calculations in the usual way! This may be a better approach if your ability to use a spreadsheet is weak.

Taxation – United Kingdom
(TX-UK) FA2022

Syllabus and study guide
1 June 2023 to 31 March 2024

Guide to ACCA Examination Assessment

This syllabus and study guide is valid for exams from June 2023 to March 2024.

For UK tax exams, examinations falling within the period 1 June to 31 March will generally examine the Finance Act which was passed in the previous year. Therefore, exams falling in the period 1 June 2023 to 31 March 2024 will examine the Finance Act 2022 and any examinable legislation which is passed outside of the Finance Act before 31 May 2022.

For additional guidance on the examinability of specific tax rules and the depth in which they are likely to be examined, reference should be made to the relevant Finance Act article written by the examining team and published on the ACCA website.

None of the current or impending devolved taxes for Scotland, Wales, and Northern Ireland is, or will be, examinable.

Approach to examining the syllabus

The syllabus is assessed by a three-hour computer-based examination.

All questions are compulsory. The exam will contain both computational and discursive elements.

Some questions will adopt a scenario/case study approach.

Tax rates, allowances and information on certain reliefs will be given in the exam.

Section A

Section A comprises 15 objective test questions of 2 marks each.

Section B

Section B comprises three case style questions. These each contain five objective test questions of two marks each which are based around a common scenario.

Section C

Section C comprises one 10 mark question and two 15 mark constructed response questions.

The two 15 mark questions will focus on income tax (syllabus area B) and corporation tax (syllabus area E).

All other questions can cover any areas of the syllabus.

Total 100 marks

Introduction to the syllabus

The aim of the syllabus is to develop knowledge and skills relating to the tax system as applicable to individuals, single companies, and groups of companies.

The syllabus for Taxation - United Kingdom (TX-UK) introduces candidates to the subject of taxation and provides the core knowledge of the underlying principles and major technical areas of taxation as they affect the activities of individuals and businesses.

Students are introduced to the rationale behind – and the functions of – the tax system. The syllabus then considers the separate taxes that an accountant would need to have a detailed knowledge of, such as income tax from self-employment, employment and investments, the corporation tax liability of individual companies and groups of companies, the national insurance contribution liabilities of both employed and self-employed persons, the value added tax liability of businesses, the chargeable gains arising on disposals of investments by both individuals and companies, and the inheritance tax liabilities arising on chargeable lifetime transfers and on death.

Having covered the core areas of the basic taxes, students should be able to compute tax liabilities, explain the basis of their calculations, apply tax planning techniques for individuals and companies and identify the compliance issues for each major tax through a variety of business and personal scenarios and situations.

Section G of the syllabus contains outcomes relating to the demonstration of appropriate digital and employability skills in preparing for and taking the examination. This includes being able to interact with different question item types, manage information presented in digital format and being able to use the relevant functionality and technology to prepare and present response options in a professional manner. These skills are specifically developed by practicing and preparing for the exam, using the learning support content for computer-based exams available via the practice platform and the ACCA website and will need to be demonstrated during the live exam.

Main capabilities

On successful completion of this exam, students should be able to:

A   Explain the operation and scope of the tax system and the obligations of tax payers and/or their agents and the implications of non-compliance

B   Explain and compute the income tax liabilities of individuals and the effect of national insurance contributions (NIC) on employees, employers and the self employed

C   Explain and compute the chargeable gains arising on individuals

D   Explain and compute the inheritance tax liabilities of individuals

E   Explain and compute the corporation tax liabilities of individual companies and groups of companies

F   Explain and compute the effects of value added tax on incorporated and unincorporated businesses

G   Demonstrate employability and technology skills

The syllabus

A The UK tax system and its administration
1. The overall function and purpose of taxation in a modern economy
2. Principal sources of revenue law and practice
3. The systems for self-assessment and the making of returns
4. The time limits for the submission of information, claims and payment of tax, including payments on account
5. The procedures relating to compliance checks, appeals and disputes
6. Penalties for non-compliance

B Income tax and NIC liabilities
1. The scope of income tax
2. Income from employment
3. Income from self-employment
4. Property and investment income
5. The comprehensive computation of taxable income and income tax liability
6. National insurance contributions for employed and self-employed persons
7. The use of exemptions and reliefs in deferring and minimising income tax liabilities

C Chargeable gains for individuals
1. The scope of the taxation of capital gains
2. The basic principles of computing gains and losses
3. Gains and losses on the disposal of movable and immovable property
4. Gains and losses on the disposal of shares and securities
5. The computation of the capital gains tax
6. The use of exemptions and reliefs in deferring and minimising tax liabilities arising on the disposal of capital assets

D Inheritance tax
1. The basic principles of computing transfers of value
2. The liabilities arising on chargeable lifetime transfers and on the death of an individual
3. The use of exemptions in deferring and minimising inheritance tax liabilities
4. Payment of inheritance tax

E Corporation tax liabilities

1. The scope of corporation tax
2. Taxable total profits
3. Chargeable gains for companies
4. The comprehensive computation of corporation tax liability
5. The effect of a group corporate structure for corporation tax purposes
6. The use of exemptions and reliefs in deferring and minimising corporation tax liabilities

F Value added tax

1. The VAT registration requirements
2. The computation of VAT liabilities
3. The effect of special schemes

G Employability and technology skills

1. Use computer technology to efficiently access and manipulate relevant information
2. Work on relevant response options, using available functions and technology, as would be required in the workplace
3. Navigate windows and computer screens to create and amend responses to exam requirements, using the appropriate tools
4. Present data and information effectively using the appropriate tools

Detailed study guide

A   THE UK TAX SYSTEM AND ITS ADMINISTRATION

1   The overall function and purpose of taxation in a modern economy

(a) Describe the purpose (economic, social etc) of taxation in a modern economy.

(b) Explain the difference between direct and indirect taxation.

(c) Identify the different types of capital and revenue tax.

2   Principal sources of revenue law and practice

(a) Describe the overall structure of the UK tax system.

(b) State the different sources of revenue law.

(c) Describe the organisation HM Revenue & Customs (HMRC) and its terms of reference.

(d) Explain the difference between tax avoidance and tax evasion, and the purposes of the General Anti-Abuse Rule (GAAR).

(e) Appreciate the interaction of the UK tax system with that of other tax jurisdictions.

(f) Appreciate the need for double taxation agreements.

(g) Explain the need for an ethical and professional approach.

Excluded topics

Specific anti-avoidance legislation.

3   The systems for self-assessment and the making of returns

(a) Explain and apply the features of the self-assessment system as it applies to individuals.

(b) Explain and apply the features of the self-assessment system as it applies to companies, including the use of iXBRL.

4   The time limits for the submission of information, claims and payment of tax, including payments on account

(a) Recognise the time limits that apply to the filing of returns and the making of claims.

(b) Recognise the due dates for the payment of tax under the self-assessment system, and compute payments on account and balancing payments/repayments for individuals.

(c) Explain how large companies are required to account for corporation tax on a quarterly basis and compute the quarterly instalment payments.

(d) List the information and records that taxpayers need to retain for tax purposes.

Excluded topics

The payment of capital gains tax by annual instalments.

The calculation of payments on account for disposals of residential property where there is more than one residential property disposal during a tax year.

Simple assessments.

Quarterly accounting by companies for income tax.

Quarterly instalments for very large companies.

5 The procedures relating to compliance checks, appeals and disputes

(a) Explain the circumstances in which HM Revenue & Customs can make a compliance check into a self-assessment tax return.

(b) Explain the procedures for dealing with appeals and First and Upper Tier Tribunals.

Excluded topics

Information powers.

Pre-return compliance checks.

Detailed procedures on the carrying out and completion of a compliance check.

6 Penalties for non-compliance

(a) Calculate late payment interest and state the penalties that can be charged.

B INCOME TAX AND NIC LIABILITIES

1 The scope of income tax

(a) Explain how the residence of an individual is determined.

Excluded topics

The split year treatment where a person comes to the UK or leaves the UK.

Foreign income, non-residents and double taxation relief.

Income from trusts and settlements.

2 Income from employment

(a) Recognise the factors that determine whether an engagement is treated as employment or self-employment.

(b) Recognise the basis of assessment for employment income.

(c) Recognise the income assessable.

(d) Recognise the allowable deductions, including travelling expenses.

(e) Discuss the use of the statutory approved mileage allowances.

(f) Explain the PAYE system, how benefits can be payrolled, and the purpose of form P11D.

(g) Explain and compute the amount of benefits assessable.

(h) Recognise the circumstances in which real time reporting late filing penalties will be imposed on an employer and the amount of penalty which is charged.

Excluded topics

The calculation of a car benefit where emission figures are not available.

The calculation of a car benefit for cars which have emissions below 50g/km and are neither electric nor hybrid.

Tax free childcare scheme.

Share and share option incentive schemes for employees.

Payments on the termination of employment, and other lump sums received by employees.

Optional remuneration arrangements.

3   Income from self-employment

(a) Recognise the basis of assessment for self-employment income.

(b) Describe and apply the badges of trade.

(c) Recognise the expenditure that is allowable in calculating the tax-adjusted trading profit.

(d) Explain and compute the assessable profits using the cash basis for small businesses.

(e) Recognise the relief which can be obtained for pre-trading expenditure.

(f) Compute the assessable profits on commencement and on cessation.

(g) Recognise the factors that will influence the choice of accounting date.

(h) Capital allowances

 (i) Define plant and machinery for capital allowances purposes.

 (ii) Compute writing down allowances, first year allowances and the annual investment allowance.

 (iii) Compute capital allowances for cars.

 (iv) Compute balancing allowances and balancing charges.

 (v) Compute structures and buildings allowances.

 (vi) Recognise the treatment of short life assets.

 (vii) Recognise the treatment of assets included in the special rate pool.

- (i) Relief for trading losses
  - (i) Understand how trading losses can be carried forward.
  - (ii) Understand how trading losses can be claimed against total income and chargeable gains, and the restriction that can apply.
  - (iii) Explain and compute the relief for trading losses in the early years of a trade.
  - (iv) Explain and compute terminal loss relief.
  - (v) Recognise the factors that will influence the choice of loss relief claim.
- (j) Partnerships and limited liability partnerships
  - (i) Explain and compute how a partnership is assessed to tax.
  - (ii) Explain and compute the assessable profits for each partner following a change in the profit sharing ratio.
  - (iii) Explain and compute the assessable profits for each partner following a change in the membership of the partnership.
  - (iv) Describe the alternative loss relief claims that are available to partners.

Excluded topics

Change of accounting date.

Capital allowances for patents and research and development expenditure.

Enterprise zones.

Freeports.

Investment income of a partnership.

The allocation of notional profits and losses for a partnership.

Farmers averaging of profits.

The averaging of profits for authors and creative artists.

Loss relief following the incorporation of a business.

Loss relief for shares in unquoted trading companies.

The loss relief restriction that applies to the partners of a limited liability partnership.

Trading allowance of £1,000.

Non-deductible capital expenditure under the cash basis other than cars, land and buildings.

4 Property and investment income
- (a) Compute property business profits.
- (b) Explain the treatment of furnished holiday lettings.
- (c) Understand rent-a-room relief.
- (d) Compute the amount assessable when a premium is received for the grant of a short lease.

- (e) Understand and apply the restriction on property income finance costs.
- (f) Understand how relief for a property business loss is given.
- (g) Compute the tax payable on savings and dividends income.
- (h) Recognise the treatment of individual savings accounts (ISAs) and other tax exempt investments.
- (i) Understand how the accrued income scheme applies to UK Government securities (gilts).

Excluded topics

Premiums for granting subleases.

Junior ISAs.

The additional ISA allowance for a surviving spouse or registered civil partner.

Help-to-buy, innovative finance and lifetime ISAs.

Savings income paid net of tax.

The detailed rules for establishing whether higher or additional rate tax is applicable for the purposes of the savings income nil rate band.

Property allowance of £1,000.

Non-deductible capital expenditure under the cash basis other than cars, land and buildings.

The cap in respect of the property income finance costs tax reducer.

Carry forward of the property income finance costs tax reducer.

5 The comprehensive computation of taxable income and income tax liability

- (a) Prepare a basic income tax computation involving different types of income.
- (b) Calculate the amount of personal allowance available.
- (c) Understand the impact of the transferable amount of personal allowance for spouses and civil partners.
- (d) Compute the amount of income tax payable.
- (e) Understand the treatment of interest paid for a qualifying purpose.
- (f) Understand the treatment of gift aid donations and charitable giving.
- (g) Explain and compute the child benefit tax charge.
- (h) Understand the treatment of property owned jointly by a married couple, or by a couple in a civil partnership.

Excluded topics

Consideration of the most beneficial allocation of the personal allowance to different categories of income.

The blind person's allowance and the married couple's allowance.

Tax credits.

Maintenance payments.

The income of minor children.

6 National insurance contributions for employed and self-employed persons

    (a) Explain and compute national insurance contributions payable:

        (i) Class 1 and 1A NIC.

        (ii) Class 2 and 4 NIC.

    (b) Understand the annual employment allowance.

Excluded topics

The calculation of directors' national insurance on a month by month basis.

The offset of trading losses against non-trading income.

The exemption from employer's class 1 NIC in respect of employees aged under 21 and apprentices aged under 25.

Group aspects of the annual employment allowance.

7 The use of exemptions and reliefs in deferring and minimising income tax liabilities

    (a) Explain and compute the relief given for contributions to personal pension schemes, and to occupational pension schemes.

    (b) Understand how a married couple or a couple in a civil partnership can minimise their tax liabilities.

    (c) Basic income tax planning.

Excluded topics

The conditions that must be met in order for a pension scheme to obtain approval from HM Revenue & Customs.

The anti-avoidance annual allowance limit of £4,000 for pension contributions (the tapering of the annual allowance down to a minimum of £4,000 is examinable).

The threshold level of income below which tapering of the annual allowance does not apply.

The enterprise investment scheme and the seed enterprise investment scheme.

Venture capital trusts.

Tax reduction scheme for gifts of pre-eminent objects.

C CHARGEABLE GAINS FOR INDIVIDUALS

1 The scope of the taxation of capital gains

    (a) Describe the scope of capital gains tax.

    (b) Recognise those assets which are exempt.

Excluded topics

Assets situated overseas and double taxation relief.

Partnership capital gains.

2 The basic principles of computing gains and losses

(a) Compute and explain the treatment of capital gains.

(b) Compute and explain the treatment of capital losses.

(c) Understand the treatment of transfers between a husband and wife or between a couple in a civil partnership.

(d) Understand the amount of allowable expenditure for a part disposal.

(e) Recognise the treatment where an asset is damaged, lost or destroyed, and the implications of receiving insurance proceeds and reinvesting such proceeds.

Excluded topics

Assets held at 31 March 1982.

Small part disposals of land, and small capital sums received where an asset is damaged.

Losses in the year of death.

Relief for losses incurred on loans made to traders.

Negligible value claims.

3 Gains and losses on the disposal of movable and immovable property

(a) Identify when chattels and wasting assets are exempt.

(b) Compute the chargeable gain when a chattel or a wasting asset is disposed of.

(c) Calculate the chargeable gain when a private residence is disposed of.

Excluded topics

The disposal of leases and the creation of sub-leases.

The two year pre-occupation period exemption for private residence relief (PRR).

4 Gains and losses on the disposal of shares and securities

(a) Recognise the value of quoted shares where they are disposed of by way of a gift.

(b) Explain and apply the identification rules as they apply to individuals, including the same day and 30 day matching rules.

(c) Explain and apply the pooling provisions.

(d) Explain and apply the treatment of bonus issues, rights issues, takeovers and reorganisations.

(e) Identify the exemption available for gilt-edged securities and qualifying corporate bonds.

Excluded topics

The small part disposal rules applicable to rights issues, takeovers and reorganisations.

Gilt-edged securities and qualifying corporate bonds other than the fact that they are exempt.

5 The computation of capital gains tax

(a) Compute the amount of capital gains tax payable.

(b) Explain and apply business asset disposal relief.

(c) Explain and apply investors' relief.

Excluded topics

Business asset disposal relief for associated disposals.

Mixed use property being property with both commercial and residential parts.

Expanded definition of the 5% shareholding condition for business asset disposal relief.

Availability of business asset disposal relief where shareholding is diluted below the 5% qualifying threshold.

Business asset disposal relief lifetime limit prior to 6 April 2020.

6 The use of exemptions and reliefs in deferring and minimising tax liabilities arising on the disposal of capital assets

(a) Explain and apply capital gains tax reliefs:
   (i) rollover relief.
   (ii) gift holdover relief for the gift of business assets.

(b) Basic capital gains tax planning.

Excluded topics

Incorporation relief.

Reinvestment relief.

D INHERITANCE TAX

1 The basic principles of computing transfers of value

(a) Identify the persons chargeable.

(b) Understand and apply the meaning of transfer of value, chargeable transfer and potentially exempt transfer.

(c) Demonstrate the diminution in value principle.

(d) Demonstrate the seven year accumulation principle taking into account changes in the level of the nil rate band.

Excluded topics

Pre 18 March 1986 lifetime transfers.

Transfers of value by close companies.

Domicile, deemed domicile, and non-UK domiciled individuals.

Trusts

Excluded property.

Related property.

The tax implications of the location of assets.

Gifts with reservation of benefit.

Associated operations.

2 The liabilities arising on chargeable lifetime transfers and on the death of an individual

(a) Understand the tax implications of lifetime transfers and compute the relevant liabilities.

(b) Understand and compute the tax liability on a death estate.

(c) Understand and apply the transfer of any unused nil rate band between spouses.

(d) Understand and apply the residence nil rate band available when a residential property is inherited by direct descendants.

Excluded topics

Specific rules for the valuation of assets (values will be provided).

Business property relief.

Agricultural property relief.

Relief for the fall in value of lifetime gifts.

Quick succession relief.

Double tax relief.

Post-death variation of wills and disclaimers of legacies.

Grossing up on death.

Post mortem reliefs.

Double charges legislation.

Endowment mortgages.

The reduced rate of inheritance tax payable on death when a proportion of a person's estate is bequeathed to charity.

The tapered withdrawal of the residence nil rate band where the net value of the estate exceeds £2 million.

The protection of the residence nil rate band where an individual downsizes to a less valuable property or where a property is disposed of.

Nominating which property should qualify for the residence nil rate band where there is more than one residence.

3 The use of exemptions in deferring and minimising inheritance tax liabilities

(a) Understand and apply the following exemptions:

(i) small gifts exemption

(ii) annual exemption

(iii) normal expenditure out of income

(iv) gifts in consideration of marriage

(v) gifts between spouses

(b) Basic inheritance tax planning.

Excluded topics

Gifts to charities.

Gifts to political parties.

Gifts for national purposes.

4 Payment of inheritance tax

(a) Identify who is responsible for the payment of inheritance tax and the due date for payment of inheritance tax.

Excluded topics

Administration of inheritance tax other than listed above.

The instalment option for the payment of tax.

Interest and penalties.

E CORPORATION TAX LIABILITIES

1 The scope of corporation tax

(a) Define the terms 'period of account', 'accounting period', and 'financial year'.

(b) Recognise when an accounting period starts and when an accounting period finishes.

(c) Explain how the residence of a company is determined.

Excluded topics

Investment companies.

Close companies.

Companies in receivership or liquidation.

Reorganisations.

The purchase by a company of its own shares.

Personal service companies.

Freeports.

2 Taxable total profits

(a) Recognise the expenditure that is allowable in calculating the tax-adjusted profit.

(b) Recognise the relief which can be obtained for pre-trading expenditure.

(c) Compute capital allowances

(i) as for income tax.

(ii) the main pool super deduction of 130% and special rate pool first year allowance of 50% for expenditure incurred from 1 April 2021 to 31 March 2023.

(d) Compute property business profits and understand how relief for a property business loss is given.

(e) Understand how trading losses can be carried forward.

(f) Understand how trading losses can be claimed against income of the current or previous accounting periods.

(g) Recognise the factors that will influence the choice of loss relief claim.

(h) Recognise and apply the treatment of interest paid and received under the loan relationship rules.

(i) Recognise and apply the treatment of qualifying charitable donations.

(j) Compute taxable total profits.

Excluded topics

Research and development expenditure.

Non-trading deficits on loan relationships.

Relief for intangible assets.

Patent box.

Carried forward losses prior to 1 April 2017.

Restriction on carried forward losses for companies with profits over £5 million.

Disposals of assets for which a 130% main pool super deduction or 50% special rate pool first year allowance claim was made.

Apportionment in order to determine the amount of main pool super deduction where a period of account straddles 1 April 2023.

3 **Chargeable gains for companies**

(a) Compute and explain the treatment of chargeable gains.

(b) Explain and compute the indexation allowance available using a given indexation factor.

(c) Explain and compute the treatment of capital losses.

(d) Understand the treatment of disposals of shares by companies and apply the identification rules including the same day and nine day matching rules.

(e) Explain and apply the pooling provisions.

(f) Explain and apply the treatment of bonus issues, rights issues, takeovers and reorganisations.

(g) Explain and apply rollover relief.

Syllabus and study guide

Excluded topics

A detailed question on the pooling provisions as they apply to limited companies.

Substantial shareholdings.

Calculation of indexation factors.

Restriction on carried forward capital losses for companies with chargeable gains over £5 million.

4 The comprehensive computation of corporation tax liability

(a) Compute the corporation tax liability.

Excluded topics

The tax rates applicable to periods prior to financial year 2017.

Marginal relief.

Franked investment income.

5 The effect of a group corporate structure for corporation tax purposes

(a) Define a 75% group and recognise the reliefs that are available to members of such a group.

(b) Define a 75% chargeable gains group, and recognise the reliefs that are available to members of such a group.

Excluded topics

Relief for trading losses incurred by an overseas subsidiary.

Consortia.

Pre-entry gains and losses.

The anti-avoidance provisions where arrangements exist for a company to leave a group.

The tax charge that applies where a company leaves a group within six years of receiving an asset by way of a no gain/no loss transfer.

Overseas aspects of corporation tax.

Transfer pricing.

6 The use of exemptions and reliefs in deferring and minimising corporation tax liabilities

The use of such exemptions and reliefs is implicit within all of the above sections 1 to 5 of part E of the syllabus, concerning corporation tax.

F VALUE ADDED TAX (VAT)

1 The VAT registration requirements

(a) Recognise the circumstances in which a person must register or deregister for VAT (compulsory) and when a person may register or deregister for VAT (voluntary).

(b) Recognise the circumstances in which pre-registration input VAT can be recovered.

(c) Explain the conditions that must be met for two or more companies to be treated as a group for VAT purposes, and the consequences of being so treated.

2 The computation of VAT liabilities

(a) Calculate the amount of VAT payable/recoverable.

(b) Understand how VAT is accounted for and administered.

(c) Recognise the tax point when goods or services are supplied.

(d) List the information that must be given on a VAT invoice.

(e) Explain and apply the principles regarding the valuation of supplies.

(f) Recognise the principal zero rated and exempt supplies.

(g) Recognise the circumstances in which input VAT is non-deductible.

(h) Recognise the relief that is available for impairment losses on trade debts.

(i) Understand the treatment of the sale of a business as a going concern.

(j) Understand when the default surcharge, a penalty for an incorrect VAT return, and default interest will be applied.

(k) Understand the treatment of imports, exports and trade outside the UK.

(l) Understand postponed accounting for VAT on imports.

Excluded topics

VAT periods where there is a change of VAT rate.

Partial exemption.

In respect of property and land: leases, do-it-yourself builders, and a landlord's option to tax.

Penalties apart from those listed in the study guide.

The reverse charge for building and construction services.

Rules applying to imported goods with a value below £135.

Reform of the VAT penalties and interest regime for late filing and payment, which will apply from 1 January 2023.

3 The effect of special schemes

(a) Understand the operation of, and when it will be advantageous to use, the VAT special schemes:

  (i) cash accounting scheme.

  (ii) annual accounting scheme.

  (iii) flat rate scheme.

Excluded topics

The second-hand goods scheme.

The capital goods scheme.

The special schemes for retailers.

G EMPLOYABILITY AND TECHNOLOGY SKILLS

1 **Use computer technology to efficiently access and manipulate relevant information.**

2 **Work on relevant response options, using available functions and technology, as would be required in the workplace.**

3 **Navigate windows and computer screens to create and amend responses to exam requirements, using the appropriate tools.**

4 **Present data and information effectively using the appropriate tools.**

Taxation – United Kingdom
(TX-UK) FA2022

Tax rates and allowances

Contents
1   Tax rates and allowances
2   Abbreviations

Taxation - United Kingdom (TX-UK) FA2022

1 Tax rates and allowances

SUPPLEMENTARY INSTRUCTIONS

1. Calculations and workings need only be made to the nearest £.
2. All apportionments should be made to the nearest month.
3. All workings should be shown in Section C.

Income tax

		Normal rates	Dividend rates
Basic rate	£0 – £37,700	20%	8.75%
Higher rate	£37,701 to £150,000	40%	33.75%
Additional rate	£150,001 and over	45%	39.35%

Savings income nil rate band - Basic rate taxpayers	£1,000
Higher rate taxpayers	£500
Dividend nil rate band	£2,000

A starting rate of 0% applies to savings income where it falls within the first £5,000 of taxable income.

Personal allowance

Personal allowance	£12,570
Transferable amount	£1,260
Income limit	£100,000

Where adjusted net income is £125,140 or more, the personal allowance is reduced to zero.

Residence status

Days in UK	Previously resident	Not previously resident
Less than 16	Automatically not resident	Automatically not resident
16 to 45	Resident if 4 UK ties (or more)	Automatically not resident
46 to 90	Resident if 3 UK ties (or more)	Resident if 4 UK ties
91 to 120	Resident if 2 UK ties (or more)	Resident if 3 UK ties (or more)
121 to 182	Resident if 1 UK tie (or more)	Resident if 2 UK ties (or more)
183 or more	Automatically resident	Automatically resident

Child benefit income tax charge

Where income is between £50,000 and £60,000, the charge is 1% of the amount of child benefit received for every £100 of income over £50,000.

Car benefit percentage

The relevant base level of CO_2 emissions is 55 grams per kilometre.

The percentage rates applying to petrol cars (and diesel cars meeting the RDE2 standard) with CO_2 emissions up to this level are:

51 grams to 54 grams per kilometre	15%
55 grams per kilometre	16%

The percentage for electric cars with zero CO_2 emissions is 2%.

For hybrid-electric cars with CO_2 emissions between 1 and 50 grams per kilometre, the electric range of the car is relevant:

Electric range

130 miles or more	2%
70 to 129 miles	5%
40 to 69 miles	8%
30 to 39 miles	12%
Less than 30 miles	14%

Car fuel benefit

The base figure for calculating the car fuel benefit is £25,300.

Company van benefits

The company van benefit scale charge is £3,600, and the van fuel benefit is £688. Vans producing zero emissions have a 0% benefit.

Individual savings accounts (ISAs)

The overall investment limit is £20,000.

Personal scheme limits

Annual allowance	£40,000
Minimum allowance	£4,000
Income limit	£240,000
Lifetime allowance	£1,073,100

The maximum contribution which can qualify for tax relief without any earnings is £3,600.

Approved mileage allowances: cars

Up to 10,000 miles	45p
Over 10,000 miles	25p

Capital allowances: rates of allowance

Plant and machinery
Main pool	18%
Special rate pool	6%

Cars
New cars with zero CO_2 emissions	100%
CO_2 emissions between 1 and 50 grams per kilometre	18%
CO_2 emissions over 50 grams per kilometre	6%

Annual investmemt allowance
Rate of allowance	100%
Expenditure limit	£1,000,000

Enhanced capital allowances for companies
Main pool super deduction	130%
Special rate pool first year allowance	50%

Structures and buildings allowance
Straight-line allowance	3%

Cash basis accounting

Revenue limit	£150,000

Cap on income tax reliefs

Unless otherwise restricted, reliefs are capped at the higher of £50,000 or 25% of income.

Corporation tax

Rate of tax: Financial year 2022	19%
Financial year 2021	19%
Financial year 2020	19%
Profit threshold	£1,500,000

Value added tax

Standard rate	20%
Registration limit	£85,000
Deregistration limit	£83,000

Inheritance tax: tax rates

Nil rate band	£325,000
Residence nil rate band	£175,000
Rates of tax on excess	
- Lifetime rate	20%
- Death rate	40%

Inheritance tax: taper relief

Years before death	Percentage reduction
More than 3 but less than 4 years	20%
More than 4 but less than 5 years	40%
More than 5 but less than 6 years	60%
More than 6 but less than 7 years	80%

Capital gains tax: tax rates

	Normal rates	Residential property
Lower rate	10%	18%
Higher rate	20%	28%

Annual exempt amount	£12,300

Capital gains tax: business asset disposal relief and investors' relief

Lifetime limit – Business asset disposal relief	£1,000,000
– Investors' relief	£10,000,000
Rate of tax	10%

National Insurance contributions

Class 1 Employee	£1 – £12,570 per year	Nil
	£12,571 – £50,270 per year	13.25%
	£50,271 and above per year	3.25%
Class 1 Employer	£1 – £9,100 per year	Nil
	£9,101 and above per year	15.05%
	Employment allowance	£5,000
Class 1A		15.05%
Class 2	£3.15 per week	
	Lower profits limit	£12,570
Class 4	£1 – £12,570 per year	Nil
	£12,571 – £50,270 per year	10.25%
	£50,271 and above per year	3.25%

Rates of interest (assumed)

Official rate of interest	2.00%
Rate of interest on underpaid tax	3.25%
Rate of interest on overpaid tax	0.50%

Standard penalties for errors

Taxpayer behaviour	Maximum penalty	Minimum penalty - Unprompted disclosure	Minimum penalty - Prompted disclosure
Deliberate and concealed	100%	30%	50%
Deliberate but not concealed	70%	20%	35%
Careless	30%	0%	15%

Abbreviations

AIA	Annual investment allowance
AMA	Approved mileage allowances
ATPD	Actual tax point date
BA	Balancing allowance
BADR	Business asset disposal relief
BC	Balancing charge
BTPD	Basic tax point date
CAP	Chargeable accounting period
CGT	Capital gains tax
CTA 2010	Corporation Tax Act 2010
CYB	Current year basis
FA	Finance Act
FIFO	First in, first out
FY	Financial year
FYA	First year allowance
HMRC	Her Majesty's Revenue and Customs
IA	Indexation allowance
ICTA 1988	Income and Corporation Taxes Act 1988
ITA 2007	Income Tax Act 2007
ITEPA	Income Tax (Earnings and Pensions) Act 2003
ITTOIA	Income Tax (Trading and Other Income) Act 2005
LIFO	Last in, first out
NIC	National Insurance contributions
PA	Personal allowance
PAYE	Pay as you earn
POA	Payment on account
PPP	Personal pension plan
PRR	Private residence relief
QBA	Qualifying business asset
QCB	Qualifying corporate bond
SBA	Structures and buildings allowance
TCGA 1992	Taxation of Chargeable Gains Act 1992
TP	Total profits
TTP	Taxable total profits
TPD	Tax point date
TWDV	Tax written down value
WDA	Writing down allowance

Taxation – United Kingdom
(TX-UK) FA2022

CHAPTER 1

The UK tax system

Contents
1 The overall function and purpose of taxation in a modern economy
2 The different types of taxes
3 Principal sources of revenue law and practice
4 Tax avoidance and tax evasion

> **The overall function and purpose of taxation in a modern economy**
>
> - The economic function of taxation
> - The social justice purpose of taxation

1 The overall function and purpose of taxation in a modern economy

1.1 The economic function of taxation

The UK government raises billions of pounds in taxation every year and the system of taxation and spending by government impacts on the whole economy of a country.

Taxation policies have been used to influence many economic factors such as inflation, employment levels, imports/exports, etc.

Taxation policies can also influence the behaviour of individuals and businesses, which will then have an effect on the economy of the country.

Examples of this influence may be:

- Using interest rate changes to encourage either spending or saving.
- Encouraging individuals to save and invest, by offering tax incentives such as those for Individual Savings Accounts (ISAs) or personal pension plans (PPPs), etc.
- Encouraging charitable giving by offering tax relief on donations and gifts.
- Encouraging entrepreneurs to build their own businesses by offering capital gains tax reliefs such as business asset disposal relief and rollover relief.
- Encouraging businesses to invest in plant and machinery by offering capital allowances.
- Increasing car tax to try to cut down CO_2 emissions.
- Discouraging smoking and drinking alcohol by increasing tax on these goods.

1.2 The social justice purpose of taxation

The type of taxation structure imposed has a direct impact on the redistribution of the wealth of a country. The main ways of structuring the tax system are listed below.

Proportional taxation

As income rises, the proportion of tax remains constant. For example, a proportional tax is one that takes 20% of all earnings regardless of their level.

Progressive taxation

As income rises, the tax rate also rises. An example of this would be a tax rate of 10% on the first £100,000 of income, rising to a rate of 40% on the next £400,000 of income.

The UK's system of income tax is an example of a progressive tax system.

Regressive taxation

As income rises, the proportion of taxation paid falls. An example of this would be a tax on fuel that must be paid by both low and high earners. It would be described as regressive because the amount of tax represents a greater proportion of the lower earner's income.

Ad valorem principle

This is the percentage of tax added to the value of goods. An example of this would be 20% VAT on most goods sold in the UK. VAT is said to be a regressive tax as a low earner will spend more of their income on tax than a high earner.

> **The different types of taxes**
>
> - Income tax
> - National insurance contributions
> - Corporation tax
> - Capital gains tax
> - Inheritance tax
> - Value added tax
> - Stamp duty
> - Direct and indirect taxation

2 The different types of taxes

2.1 Income tax

Income tax is payable by individuals on their earned income, such as employment income, self-employment income and pension income.

It is collected from employees using the Pay As You Earn (PAYE) system, and from self-employed individuals using the self assessment system.

Income tax is also payable by individuals on their other income, such as bank interest, dividends and rental income.

2.2 National insurance contributions (NICs)

NICs are payable by most individuals who are either employed or self-employed. NICs are also payable by businesses in respect of their employees.

2.3 Corporation tax

Corporation tax is payable by companies on their income and gains.

2.4 Capital gains tax

Capital gains tax is payable by individuals on the disposal of chargeable assets, such as land, buildings and shares.

2.5 Inheritance tax

Inheritance tax is a tax on capital rather than income. It is charged when an individual's wealth or estate is given away. IHT can be charged during an individual's lifetime, for example on gifts of money or assets. It is also charged when an individual dies, on their death estate.

2.6 Value added tax

VAT is payable on most goods and services purchased by consumers.

2.7 Stamp duty

Stamp duty is payable on the purchase of land and buildings and shares.

2.8 Direct and indirect taxation

All of the above taxes can be classified as either direct or indirect taxation.

Direct taxation

This is where a taxpayer pays their tax directly to HM Revenue & Customs (HMRC). Examples of direct taxes include income tax, corporation tax, capital gains tax and inheritance tax.

Indirect taxation

This is where tax, such as VAT, is paid indirectly to HM Revenue & Customs. The consumer pays indirect taxes to the supplier, who then pays the tax to HMRC.

> **Principle sources of revenue law and practice**
> - The structure of the UK tax system
> - The different sources of revenue law
> - The interaction of the UK tax system with that of other tax jurisdictions

3 Principal sources of revenue law and practice

3.1 The structure of the UK tax system

The Chancellor of the Exchequer has the overall responsibility for the UK tax system and one of his roles includes producing the Budget each year.

The Treasury is the ministry responsible under the Chancellor for the imposition and collection of taxation.

HM Revenue and Customs (HMRC) is a single body that controls and administers all areas of UK tax law. It is also responsible for the administration of certain statutory payments, such as child benefit and statutory maternity pay.

3.2 The different sources of revenue law

Each year, following the Budget, the legislation is updated by passing a new **Finance Act**.

In addition to Acts of Parliament, the government issues **statutory instruments** which add detail, where needed, to any part of the legislation. Statutory instruments are also often used to make changes to the provisions of the Acts, particularly if an Act was introduced without adequate consultation or scrutiny.

Case law is introduced as a result of decisions made in tax cases taken before the courts. The results of cases that have been through the courts can set a precedent for the tax treatment of a particular item.

Statements of practice explain how HMRC believes the tax law should be applied in a particular situation.

Extra-Statutory Concessions are sometimes available to soften areas of tax law where it would seem to be unduly harsh or unfair. These concessions usually have to be claimed and sometimes taxpayers are unaware that they are available. No new concessions are being introduced. Existing concessions are in the process of being written into legislation or withdrawn.

3.3 The interaction of the UK tax system with that of other tax jurisdictions

The UK's tax system uses the concepts of residence and domicile to determine how an individual or business is taxed. However, overseas countries have their own tax laws and practices.

It is therefore possible for someone's income or gains to be liable to tax in more than one country at the same time, under completely different tax rules. As this is unfair, the countries concerned may draw up a double taxation agreement.

A double taxation agreement or treaty between two countries may over-rule the tax law of one or both of those countries. In this case, the individual or entity is taxed in accordance with the tax treaty.

A double taxation agreement will typically contain the following:

- exemption clauses whereby some income and gains are taxable in one country but exempt in the other
- an agreement on the level of taxation to be applied to some types of income in both countries, and
- a credit relief clause: this usually specifies that relief should be given for any overseas tax suffered. The credit is usually limited to the lower of the overseas tax suffered and the UK tax payable on the same income. This effectively ensures that, although the income is taxable in both countries, it only suffers tax once.

> **Tax avoidance and tax evasion**
>
> - The difference between tax avoidance and tax evasion
> - The General Anti-Abuse Rule (GAAR)
> - The need for an ethical and professional approach
> - Dishonest conduct by tax agents

4 Tax avoidance and tax evasion

4.1 The difference between tax avoidance and tax evasion

It is important to know the difference between tax avoidance and tax evasion, as the consequences of getting it wrong can be very different.

Tax avoidance

Tax avoidance is **legal**. It involves complying with the tax legislation in such a way as to minimise a taxpayer's tax liability.

- For example, an individual arranging their will in such a way as to minimise their inheritance tax liability is using tax planning opportunities and avoiding tax in a legal way in accordance with the tax law.

- Another example may be an individual making a capital gains tax election to tax the disposal of their business in such a way as to minimise their capital gains tax liability.

Tax evasion

Tax evasion is **illegal**. It involves reducing the tax liability in a way that is not following the tax legislation.

- For example, tax evasion is deliberately omitting some investment income from a tax return in order not to pay tax on that source of income.

- Another example of tax evasion is to overstate expenses, in order to reduce the tax liability.

Any taxpayer who carries out tax evasion could face criminal prosecution, including penalties, interest and sometimes imprisonment.

If a tax adviser believes that a client has been involved in tax evasion, they should advise the client of the implications of their actions and recommend that the client makes a full disclosure to HMRC. If the client refuses to do so, the tax adviser should consider ceasing to act for them.

If the tax adviser does cease to act, they must advise HMRC that they no longer act for this client, but they should not tell HMRC why they have ceased to act as this would break the client's confidentiality.

As tax evasion is a crime, the adviser should also make a report under the money laundering regulations.

4.2 The General Anti-Abuse Rule (GAAR)

Although tax avoidance is legal, there are occasions when taxpayers:

- behave in ways that were not anticipated at the time the legislation was enacted, or
- use loopholes in the legislation to reduce their liability.

This type of behaviour is sometimes referred to as 'aggressive' tax avoidance. It results in the Government losing tax that it had expected to be able to collect.

In the past, the Government has targeted aggressive tax avoidance and closed loopholes by using specific anti-avoidance legislation. The problem with this approach is that it takes place after the tax has been lost. It involves reacting to the action taken by taxpayers instead of anticipating it in advance. It also results in the tax system becoming more and more complicated, which may inadvertently result in the creation of more loopholes.

In order to provide a further deterrent, the tax system contains a General Anti-Abuse Rule (GAAR). This is intended to counteract **tax advantages** arising from **tax arrangements** that are **abusive**.

The terms used in the above definition have the following meanings:

- **'Tax advantages'** include increased tax deductions, reduced tax liabilities, deferral of tax payments and advancement of tax repayments.
- **'Tax arrangements'** are arrangements where the main purpose, or one of the main purposes, of the arrangements is obtaining a tax advantage.
- Arrangements are **'abusive'** where they cannot reasonably be regarded as a reasonable course of action, for example, where they include contrived steps or are intended to take advantage of shortcomings in the tax legislation. This is known as the double reasonableness test.

Where the GAAR applies, HMRC may counteract the tax advantages by, for example, increasing the taxpayer's tax liability by an amount that is just and reasonable. They must follow a specific procedure if they want to do this, which includes presenting their case to an independent Advisory Panel. The burden of proof rests with HMRC to show that the GAAR applies.

4.3 The need for an ethical and professional approach

ACCA expects its members to:

- Adopt an ethical approach to work, employers and clients.
- Acknowledge their professional duty to society as a whole.
- Maintain an objective outlook.
- Provide professional, high standards of service, conduct and performance at all times.

ACCA's 'Code of Ethics and Conduct' sets out five fundamental principles, which help members to meet these expectations:

- **Integrity** - Members should act in a straightforward and honest manner in performing their work.

- **Objectivity** - Members should not allow prejudice, or bias, or the influence of others to override objectivity.

- **Professional competence and due care** - Members should not undertake work that they are not competent to carry out. Members have an ongoing duty to maintain professional knowledge and skills. A member should carry out their work with due care having regard to the nature and scope of the assignment.

- **Confidentiality** - Members should respect the confidentiality of information acquired as a result of professional and business relationships and should not disclose any such information to third parties unless:

    - they have proper and specific authority; or

    - there is a legal or professional right or duty to disclose, e.g. to comply with Money Laundering regulations.

    Confidential information acquired as a result of professional and business relationships should not be used for the personal advantage of members or third parties.

- **Professional behaviour** - Members should refrain from any conduct that might bring discredit to the profession. They should not make exaggerated claims for the services they offer or make disparaging references to the work of others.

Example

You are an accountant. You have recently discovered that one of your clients has omitted a capital gain from their self-assessment tax return.

Required

Briefly explain what action you should take.

Answer

You should advise your client to disclose the gain to HMRC. If they refuse to do so, you should consider ceasing to act for them.

If you do cease to act, you must advise HMRC that you no longer act for this client, but you should not tell HMRC why you have ceased to act as this would break your client's confidentiality.

As your client's actions constitute tax evasion, which is a crime, you should also make a report under the money laundering regulations.

4.4 Dishonest conduct by tax agents

A single penalty regime applies to dishonest conduct by tax agents. Dishonest conduct occurs when a tax agent brings about a loss of tax by behaving in a dishonest manner.

HMRC can issue a dishonest conduct notice requiring access to all of an agent's working papers. They can apply a penalty of up to £50,000 where there has been dishonest conduct and the tax agent fails to supply the information or documents that HMRC has requested.

Taxation – United Kingdom
(TX-UK) FA2022

CHAPTER 2

Introduction to income tax

	Contents
1	Overview of income tax
2	Taxable income
3	The personal allowance
4	Tax rates
5	Gift Aid donations paid by individuals
6	Tax planning for married couples
7	Child benefit income tax charge
8	Summary

> **Overview of income tax**
> - Taxable income
> - The tax year
> - Preparing an income tax computation

1 Overview of income tax

1.1 Taxable income

Individuals are liable to:

- income tax on their taxable income, and
- a separate tax, capital gains tax, on their chargeable gains.

Taxable income is defined as:

- income generated from all sources which is not specifically exempt, **minus**
- deductible interest payments, trading losses and personal allowances.

Taxable income is listed in a taxable income statement according to its nature and source.

1.2 The tax year

Income tax rates and allowances are fixed for each tax year. A tax year is the period from 6 April in one year to the following 5 April.

Tax years are quoted as the calendar years in which the tax year begins and ends. For example, the tax year 2022/23 is the period from 6 April 2022 to 5 April 2023.

Income tax is based on the income relating to a particular tax year. For examinations during the period 1 June 2023 to 31 March 2024, questions will be based on the 2022/23 tax year, i.e. the provisions contained in Finance Act 2022.

The tax year is sometimes referred to as the **fiscal year** or the **year of assessment.**

1.3 Preparing an income tax computation

There are three key steps in the preparation of an income tax computation.

Step 1: Prepare a statement of taxable income for the tax year

The first step is to prepare a statement listing all the income that is chargeable to income tax in the tax year, after deducting allowable interest payments, trading losses and personal allowances.

This should be presented as follows:

Name of individual Income tax computation: 2022/23	See paragraph	£
Earned income		
Employment income	2.3	X
Trading income	2.4	X
Property income	2.5	
Savings income	2.6	
Building society interest received		X
Bank interest received		X
Dividends received	2.7	X
Total income		X
Minus Deductible interest	2.8	(X)
Net income		X
Minus Personal allowance (PA)		(X)
Taxable income		X

The items in this statement are explained in more detail in the following section.

Step 2: Calculate the income tax liability

The next step is to calculate the income tax liability on the taxable income. Income tax rates need to be applied carefully, as different types of income are taxed at different rates of tax.

Step 3: Calculate the income tax payable

The last step, which may be required in some examination questions, is to calculate how much of the income tax liability is still payable after taking account of any Pay As You Earn (PAYE) tax already deducted at source. If required, the due dates of payment of income tax still payable and the filing dates for self-assessment return forms need to be stated.

Each step involved in calculating the income tax payable is explained in more detail in the rest of this chapter. Self-assessment is explained in a later chapter.

> **Taxable income**
>
> - Classification of income
> - Exempt income
> - Employment income
> - Trading income
> - Property income
> - Savings income
> - UK dividend income
> - Deductible interest

2 The taxable income statement

2.1 Classification of income

Each source of income must be shown separately in the statement, because the rules to determine the amount of income that is taxable are different for each source.

In addition, it is important to group sources of income together, into non-savings income, savings income and dividend income. This is because different rates of tax apply to the different groups of taxable income.

2.2 Exempt income

The taxable income statement lists all taxable income that is not specifically exempt from income tax. There are many types of exempt income. Detailed knowledge of exempt income is not required for the examination, but a general awareness of the following main categories of exempt income might be useful.

The main types of exempt income to be aware of are:

- some social security benefits (e.g. child benefit, personal independence payment)
- the first £30,000 of compensation for loss of office
- competition prizes, national lottery and premium bond prizes, betting winnings
- income from ISAs (Individual Savings Accounts)
- interest on overpaid tax that has been repaid by HMRC
- interest on National Savings Certificates.

2.3 Employment income

Employment income is likely to be the primary source of income for an employed individual. The amount of income assessable under the employment income rules is the total gross remuneration (gross salary, plus benefits such as the use of a company car etc.) received in the tax year.

In examination questions, salaries and other remuneration are usually quoted as a gross amount. Gross means that the amount quoted is the amount of income **before** pay-as-you-earn (PAYE) income tax has been deducted at source by the employer.

The rules governing the computation of employment income are explained in detail in a later chapter.

2.4 Trading income

Trading income is likely to be the primary source of income for a self-employed individual. It covers the profits of a trade, profession or vocation of a self-employed individual. The taxable trading income is based on the accounting results of the business.

The rules applicable to the trading income of individuals are covered in later chapters.

2.5 Property income

The property income rules assess income received from land and buildings situated in the UK.

See the following chapter for details.

2.6 Savings income

Savings income consists mainly of interest income. Individuals are liable to income tax on the interest **received** in the tax year (i.e. a receipts basis of assessment). Interest is received on the date it is credited to the savings account.

Example

Gareth's building society account credits interest on 31 December annually. He received £1,200 interest on 31 December 2022 and £1,000 on 31 December 2023.

Required

Calculate Gareth's taxable interest for 2022/23.

Answer

Gareth's taxable interest for 2022/23 is £1,200, i.e. the amount received during 2022/23. The fact that the interest covered the period 1 January 2022 to 31 December 2022 rather than the tax year of 6 April 2022 to 5 April 2023 is irrelevant.

Exempt interest

Some types of interest are exempt from income tax. The main types of exempt interest are:

- Interest on ISAs (Individual Savings Accounts)
- Interest on National Savings Certificates.

2.7 UK dividend income

Individuals are taxed on the dividends **received** in the tax year (i.e. a receipts basis of assessment).

2.8 Deductible interest

Interest paid for *trading* purposes is deducted in calculating *trading* income.

The main types of interest payments deductible from *total* income are interest paid to:

- buy an interest in a partnership, employee-controlled company or co-operative
- buy plant or machinery for use in the individual's employment or partnership. Interest is allowed for three years and is apportioned if there is private use of the asset.

These types of interest are paid gross by an individual.

No relief is available for interest paid in respect of a mortgage to purchase the individual's residence or for credit card interest.

The personal allowance

- The personal allowance
- Withdrawal of the personal allowance
- The transferable amount of personal allowance

3 The personal allowance

3.1 The personal allowance

Every individual is entitled to a personal allowance (PA). This is an amount of income that can be received free of tax. The allowance is given in the tax rates and allowances table in the examination. For 2022/23 the PA is £12,570.

The PA is deducted from **net income**. Net income is defined as the total of income from all sources after the deduction of qualifying interest payments.

Use of the abbreviation PA is acceptable in the examination.

Note that if net income is less than the PA, the excess allowance is lost. For example, if an individual has net income of just £4,000 in 2022/23, the excess allowance of £8,570 is lost.

3.2 Withdrawal of the personal allowance

If an individual's adjusted net income exceeds £100,000 their PA is reduced by £1 for every £2 of excess income. Therefore, an individual with adjusted net income of £125,140 or more will receive no PA (£100,000 + (£12,570 x 2)).

Adjusted net income is net income as calculated above less the gross amount of:

- Personal pension contributions, and
- Gift Aid donations.

Personal pension contributions and Gift Aid donations are paid net of basic rate income tax. They are covered in more detail later in this text. For the time being you simply need to be aware that if an individual makes a personal pension contribution or Gift Aid payment of, say, £800, the payment is treated as a gross amount of £1,000 (= £800 × 100/80). The payments are not deducted in calculating the individual's taxable income.

An individual whose adjusted net income falls between £100,000 and £125,140 suffers an effective marginal rate of income tax of 60%. (This is the higher rate of 40% on income plus an additional 20% as a result of the withdrawal of the personal allowance.) It may therefore be beneficial for such individuals to make additional personal pension contributions or Gift Aid donations.

Example

Marilyn has net income of £105,000.

Required

Calculate Marilyn's personal allowance for 2022/23.

Answer

As Marilyn's net income exceeds £100,000 her PA is reduced by £2,500 ((£105,000 - £100,000) x ½) to £10,070 (£12,570 - £2,500).

Marilyn could avoid this reduction by making gross personal pension contributions or Gift Aid donations of £5,000 or more.

3.3 The transferable amount of personal allowance

£1,260 of the personal allowance can be transferred to an individual's spouse or civil partner. This transferable amount is known as the 'marriage allowance'.

The transfer is subject to the following conditions:

- The individuals concerned must be married or in a registered civil partnership for all or part of the tax year to which the election applies.

- Neither spouse must be liable to tax at more than the basic rate. The basic rate threshold for 2022/23 is £37,700. (This means that the marriage allowance cannot be used to save tax at the higher rates of 40% or 45%. It will only be of benefit where one spouse is unable to use their full personal allowance.)

- The election must be made within four years of the end of the tax year to which it applies. If an election is made before the end of the tax year to which it applies, it will remain in force for future tax years unless the election is withdrawn or the conditions are no longer met.

- An individual cannot give or receive more than one marriage allowance in a tax year, irrespective of whether they are a party to more than one marriage or civil partnership in that year.

The spouse who receives the marriage allowance does not deduct it from their income. Instead, it is converted into a tax reduction at the rate of 20%.

The marriage allowance therefore entitles the recipient to the following deduction from their income tax bill for 2022/23:

£1,260 x 20% = £252

The deduction cannot create a repayment, i.e. it cannot reduce the recipient's income tax liability below nil.

Example

(a) Kylie has employment income of £80,000. Her husband, Jason, has employment income of £8,000.

(b) Scott has employment income of £35,000. His wife, Charlene, has employment income of £8,000.

Required

Explain whether the marriage allowance is available to the above couples, assuming that neither of them has any other income.

Answer

(a) Jason cannot make an election to transfer part of his personal allowance as Kylie is a higher rate taxpayer.

(b) Charlene can elect to transfer £1,260 of her personal allowance to Scott. Her personal allowance will therefore become £12,570 - £1,260 = £11,310. This exceeds her income and her remaining personal allowance will be lost.

Scott's income tax liability will be as follows:

	£
Employment income	35,000
Minus PA	(12,570)
Taxable income	22,430

	£		£
Taxable income	22,430	at 20%	4,486
Less marriage allowance	1,260	at 20%	(252)
Income tax liability			4,234

> **Tax rates**
>
> - Overview of the income tax computation
> - The taxation of non-savings income
> - The taxation of savings income
> - The taxation of dividend income
> - Computing income tax payable

4 Tax rates

4.1 Overview of the income tax computation

Different rates of income tax apply to the different sources of income. Before calculating the income tax, it is first necessary to deduct from the appropriate sources of income:

- deductible interest, and
- the PA.

These deductions should be set-off in the following order:

(1) Non-savings income (i.e. income other than savings income and dividends), then
(2) Savings income (i.e. interest income), then
(3) Dividend income.

An easy method to ensure the correct allocation of the deductions is to lay out the taxable income computation as follows:

Name of individual Income tax computation: 2022/23	Total income	Non-savings income	Savings income	Dividend income
	£	£	£	£
Employment income	X	X		
Trading income	X	X		
Property income	X	X		
Interest income	X		X	
UK dividend income	X			X
Total income	X	X	X	X
Minus Deductible interest	(X)	(X)[1]	(X)[2]	(X)[3]
Net income	X	X	X	X
Minus Personal allowance (PA)	(X)	(X)[1]	(X)[2]	(X)[3]
Taxable income	X	X	X	X

Note that there are situations in which a different order of set off would be beneficial for the taxpayer. However, these are not examinable in the TX-UK paper.

To calculate an individual's income tax liability, the appropriate rate of tax must be applied to each category of taxable income.

The liability must be calculated in the following same strict order:

(1) Non-savings income (i.e. income other than savings income and dividends), then

(2) Savings income (i.e. interest income) then lastly,

(3) Dividend income.

4.2 The taxation of non-savings income

For 2022/23 non-savings income is taxed at the following rates:

Name of banding:	Non-savings income in the banding:	Tax rate
Basic rate band	£0 - £37,700	20%
Higher rate band	£37,701 - £150,000	40%
Additional rate band	£150,001 and over	45%

Example

Jing received employment income of £80,000 in 2022/23.

He paid deductible interest of £300 on 13 August 2022.

Required
Calculate Jing's income tax liability for 2022/23.

Answer

Jing: Income tax computation: 2022/23	Total income
	£
Employment income	80,000
Minus Interest payments	(300)
Net income	79,700
Minus Personal allowance (PA)	(12,570)
Taxable income	67,130

Income tax	Income		Tax
	£		£
Basic rate band:	37,700	at 20%	7,540
Higher rate band:	29,430	at 40%	11,772
Total taxable income	67,130		
Income tax liability			19,312

4.3 The taxation of savings income

Savings income is taxed after non-savings income.

Savings income may benefit from a nil rate band (sometimes referred to as a savings allowance). However, the amount chargeable at this nil rate depends on the taxpayer's marginal (i.e. top) rate of tax. The nil rate band is £1,000 for basic rate taxpayers and £500 for higher rate taxpayers. Additional rate taxpayers do not receive a nil rate band.

The key point to note is that an individual will be classed as a higher rate taxpayer even if they only have £1 of income in excess of the £37,700 threshold. Similarly, £1 of income above the £150,000 threshold will mean an individual is classed as an additional rate taxpayer.

For 2022/23 savings income is taxed at the following rates:

Name of banding:	Savings income in the banding:	Tax rate
Starting rate band (note)	0 - £5,000	0%
Basic rate band	£5,001 - £37,700	20%
Higher rate band	£37,701 - £150,000	40%
Additional rate band	£150,001 and over	45%

Note The starting rate band for savings income only applies where savings income falls within the first £5,000 of taxable income. As non-savings income is taxed first, if this exceeds £5,000 then this starting rate will not apply.

Example

Zan received the following income in 2022/23:

	£
Employment income	80,000
Interest income	5,000

She paid deductible interest of £300 on 13 August 2022.

Required

Calculate Zan's income tax liability for 2022/23.

Answer

Zan: Income tax computation: 2022/23

	Total income	Non-savings income	Savings income
	£	£	£
Employment income	80,000	80,000	
Interest income	5,000		5,000
Total income	85,000	80,000	5,000
Minus Deductible interest	(300)	(300)	
Net income	84,700	79,700	5,000
Minus Personal allowance (PA)	(12,570)	(12,570)	-
Taxable income	72,130	67,130	5,000

Income tax	Income		Tax
	£		£
Basic rate band: Non-savings	37,700	at 20%	7,540
Higher rate band: Non-savings	29,430	at 40%	11,772
Nil rate band: savings	500	at 0%	-
Higher rate band: Non-savings	4,500	at 40%	1,800
Total taxable income	72,130		
Income tax liability (note)			21,112

Notes:
(a) The calculation of the tax on the employment income is unchanged from the previous example. This is because the deductions and tax bands are applied to non-savings income first.
(b) As Zan is a higher rate taxpayer, her savings nil rate band is only £500.
(c) The starting rate band of £5,000 does not apply because the savings income falls into the higher rate band.

Example

Ming received the following income in 2022/23:

	£
Employment income	13,000
Interest income	6,000

She paid deductible interest of £300 on 13 August 2022.

Required

Calculate Ming's income tax liability for 2022/23.

a Answer

Ming: Income tax computation: 2022/23

	Total income	Non-savings income	Savings income
	£	£	£
Employment income	13,000	13,000	
Interest income	6,000		6,000
Total income	19,000	13,000	6,000
Minus Deductible interest	(300)	(300)	
Net income	18,700	12,700	6,000
Minus Personal allowance (PA)	(12,570)	(12,570)	-
Taxable income	6,130	130	6,000

Income tax	Income		Tax
	£		£
Basic rate band: Non-savings	130	at 20%	26
Starting rate band: Savings	4,870	at 0%	-
Nil rate band: Savings	1,000	at 0%	-
Basic rate band: Savings	130	at 20%	26
Total taxable income	6,130		
Income tax liability (note)			52

Notes:

(a) As Ming is a basic rate taxpayer, her savings nil rate band is £1,000.

(b) The starting rate band of £5,000 applies. However, because there is £130 of taxable non-savings income, only £4,870 of the starting rate band remains.

4.4 The taxation of dividend income

Dividend income is taxed after non-savings and savings income.

The first £2,000 of dividend income for the tax year 2022/23 benefits from a 0% rate of tax. This nil rate band applies to all taxpayers, irrespective of their marginal rate of tax.

For 2022/23 dividend income in excess of the dividend nil rate band is taxed at the following rates:

Name of banding:	Dividend income in the banding:	Tax rate
Basic rate band	0 - £37,700	8.75%
Higher rate band	£37,701 - £150,000	33.75%
Additional rate band	£150,001 and over	39.35%

Chapter 2: Introduction to income tax

Example

Barry, a self-employed plumber, received the following income in 2022/23:

	£
Building society interest	5,750
Dividends from a UK company	15,000

He paid deductible interest of £300 on 13 August 2022.

Required

Calculate Barry's income tax liability for 2022/23, assuming his trading income for 2022/23 was:

(a) £15,000

(b) £35,000

(c) £95,000

(d) £145,000

Answer

Barry: Income tax computation: 2022/23

(a) (Trading income = £15,000)	Total income	Non-savings income	Savings income	Dividend income
	£	£	£	£
Trading income	15,000	15,000		
Building society interest	5,750		5,750	
UK dividends received	15,000			15,000
Total income	35,750	15,000	5,750	15,000
Minus Deductible interest	(300)	(300)		
Net income	35,450	14,700	5,750	15,000
Minus Personal allowance (PA)	(12,570)	(12,570)		
Taxable income	22,880	2,130	5,750	15,000

Income tax		Income		Tax
		£		£
Basic rate band:	Non-savings	2,130	at 20%	426
Starting rate band:	Savings	2,870	at 0%	-
Nil rate band:	Savings	1,000	at 0%	-
Basic rate band:	Savings	1,880	at 20%	376
Nil rate band:	Dividends	2,000	at 0%	-
Basic rate band:	Dividends	13,000	at 8.75%	1,137
Total taxable income		22,880		
Income tax liability (note)				1,939

Notes:

(a) As the taxable amount of non-savings income was only £2,130, the remaining £2,870 of the starting rate band for savings income could be used.

(b) Barry is a basic rate taxpayer, so he is entitled to a savings nil rate band of £1,000.

(b) (Trading income = £35,000)	Total income	Non-savings income	Savings income	Dividend income
	£	£	£	£
Trading income	35,000	35,000		
Building society interest	5,750		5,750	
UK dividends received	15,000			15,000
Total Income	55,750	35,000	5,750	15,000
Minus Deductible interest	(300)	(300)		
Net income	55,450	34,700	5,750	15,000
Minus Personal allowance (PA)	(12,570)	(12,570)		
Taxable income	42,880	22,130	5,750	15,000

Income tax		Income		Tax
		£		£
Basic rate band:	Non-savings income	22,130	at 20%	4,426
Nil rate band:	Savings	500	at 0%	-
Basic rate band:	Savings	5,250	at 20%	1,050
Nil rate band:	Dividends	2,000	at 0%	-
Basic rate band:	Dividends	7,820	at 8.75%	684
		37,700		
Higher rate band:	Dividends (15,000 – 9,820)	5,180	at 33.75%	1,748
Total taxable income		42,880		
Income tax liability				7,908

Note: As Barry is a higher rate taxpayer, his savings nil rate band is only £500.

(c) (Trading income = £95,000)	Total income	Non-savings income	Savings income	Dividend income
	£	£	£	£
Trading income	95,000	95,000		
Building society interest	5,750		5,750	
UK dividends received	15,000			15,000
Total Income	115,750	95,000	5,750	15,000
Minus Deductible interest	(300)	(300)		
Net income	115,450	94,700	5,750	15,000
Minus Personal allowance (W)	(4,845)	(4,845)		
Taxable income	110,605	89,855	5,750	15,000

Income tax

		Income		Tax
		£		£
Basic rate band:	Non-savings	37,700	at 20%	7,540
Higher rate band:	Non-savings	52,155	at 40%	20,862
Nil rate band:	Savings	500	at 0%	-
Higher rate band:	Savings	5,250	at 40%	2,100
Nil rate band:	Dividends	2,000	at 0%	-
Higher rate band:	Dividends	13,000	at 33.75%	4,387
Total taxable income		110,605		
Income tax liability				34,889

Workings

	£
PA	12,570
Reduction based on Net Income (£115,450 - £100,000) × 50%	(7,725)
PA available	4,845

(d) (Trading income = £145,000)

	Total income	Non-savings income	Savings income	Dividend income
	£	£	£	£
Trading income	145,000	145,000		
Building society interest	5,750		5,750	
UK dividends received	15,000			15,000
Total Income	165,750	145,000	5,750	15,000
Minus Deductible interest	(300)	(300)		
Net income	165,450	144,700	5,750	15,000
Minus Personal allowance (PA)	(Nil)	(Nil)		
Taxable income	165,450	144,700	5,750	15,000

Income tax

		Income		Tax
		£		£
Basic rate band:	Non-savings income	37,700	at 20%	7,540
Higher rate band:	Non-savings income	107,000	at 40%	42,800
Higher rate band:	Savings	5,300	at 40%	2,120
Additional rate band:	Savings	450	at 45%	202
Nil rate band:	Dividends	2,000	at 0%	-
Additional rate band:	Dividends	13,000	at 39.35%	5,115
Total taxable income		165,450		
Income tax liability				57,777

Notes
(a) As Barry's adjusted net income exceeds £125,140 (£100,000 + (£12,570 x 2)) he will receive no PA.
(b) As Barry is an additional rate taxpayer, he does not receive a savings nil rate band.

4.5 Computing income tax payable

The computations so far show the **income tax liability** of an individual. This is the total amount of income tax which the individual is liable to pay to the tax authorities for the tax year. However, the **tax payable** is the amount of tax still outstanding. This is calculated as follows:

	£
Income tax liability	X
Minus PAYE tax	(X)
Income tax payable/(repayable) under self assessment	X / (X)

> **Gift Aid donations paid by individuals**
>
> - How the Gift Aid scheme operates
> - Relief for basic rate taxpayers
> - Relief for higher and additional rate taxpayers

5 Gift Aid donations paid by individuals

5.1 How the Gift Aid scheme operates

The Gift Aid scheme gives tax relief for cash donations made to registered charities.

Individuals are deemed to make Gift Aid donations **net of 20% tax**, which is recoverable by the charity from HMRC. Tax relief is available for the gross amount of the payment.

For individuals the scheme operates as follows:

- If an individual makes a Gift Aid payment of, say, £800, the gift is treated as a gross gift of £1,000 (= £800 × 100/80). The charity will receive £800 from the individual and a tax repayment of £200 from HMRC.

- The individual is entitled to tax relief for the gross donation of £1,000 at their highest marginal rate of tax.

5.2 Relief for basic rate taxpayers

A basic rate taxpayer is entitled to 20% tax relief. This relief is automatically obtained at source by making a net payment to the charity.

Gift Aid donations are therefore ignored in the individual's income tax computation as they have already obtained their tax relief at source.

5.3 Relief for higher and additional rate taxpayers

Higher rate taxpayers are entitled to 40% tax relief and additional rate taxpayers to 45%. This relief is obtained in two steps as follows:

- 20% tax relief is automatically obtained at source in the same way as for basic rate taxpayers.

- The additional relief is obtained by **extending the basic rate and higher rate bands** by the **gross** amount of the Gift Aid payment.

As a result, a sum equivalent to the gross Gift Aid payment will be taxed at the basic rate instead of the higher or additional rate.

Example

Carla is a higher rate taxpayer. In 2022/23 she had no income other than her employment income of £60,000.

Required

Calculate Carla's income tax liability for 2022/23 assuming:

(a) Carla did not make a Gift Aid donation

(b) On 16 March 2023 Carla made a donation of £1,760 to a charity under the Gift Aid scheme.

Answer

Carla : Income tax computation: 2022/23	(a) Total income £	(b) Total income £
Employment income = Net income	60,000	60,000
Minus PA	(12,570)	(12,570)
Taxable income	47,430	47,430

	Scenario (a)		Scenario (b)	
Income tax	Income	Tax	Income	Tax
	£	£	£	£
Basic rate band:	37,700 at 20%	7,540		
Extended basic rate band limit: (see working)			39,900 at 20%	7,980
Higher rate band	9,730 at 40%	3,892	7,530 at 40%	3,012
Total taxable income	47,430		47,430	
Income tax liability		11,432		10,992

Working

Gross Gift Aid donation = £1,760 × 100/80 = £2,200

Extended basic rate band = £37,700 + £2,200 = £39,900

Note that the tax saving as a result of extending the basic rate band

= £11,432 - £10,992 = £440

(i.e. additional 20% saving on the gross donation: £2,200 × 20% = £440).

> **Tax planning for married couples**
>
> - The concept of independent taxation
> - The taxation of married couples
> - Opportunities for minimising tax liabilities

6 Tax planning for married couples

6.1 The concept of independent taxation

The concept of independent taxation means that every individual (whether married, in a civil partnership or single) is treated as a separate taxable person. Each taxable person is liable to income tax on their own income.

6.2 The taxation of married couples

A separate income tax computation is produced for each spouse, but special rules apply for the allocation of joint income.

Where a married couple (or civil partners) jointly own assets that generate income, the income is *shared equally* between them, regardless of the actual ownership of the asset. (This is known as the 50:50 rule.)

For example, if a couple jointly own a house which generates £10,000 of taxable property income, each spouse will include £5,000 in their individual income tax computation. This will be the case whether the couple contributed to the purchase cost equally or whether one spouse contributed 75% and the other 25%.

However, if the couple enjoy the income in unequal proportions, they can make an 'actual entitlement declaration' to HMRC and ask to be taxed on the income in the proportion of their actual entitlement to that income (i.e. 75%:25% in the above illustration) rather than a 50:50 allocation.

It is important to note that the declaration:

- is optional, but once made it is irrevocable
- must be sent within 60 days of requiring it to be effective for tax purposes, and
- can only be made for a different allocation based on the facts of actual entitlement (i.e. the couple cannot choose to allocate in any proportion they wish to in order to minimise their tax liabilities).

Note that same-sex couples who acquire legal status for their relationship under the Civil Partnership Act 2004 are treated as married couples for taxation purposes.

6.3 Opportunities for minimising tax liabilities

A married couple (or civil partners) should ensure that each spouse (or civil partner) fully utilises their own:

- personal allowance,
- savings nil rate band,
- dividend nil rate band, and
- basic rate band

before either of them pays income tax at the higher or additional rates.

Using the full personal allowance

If one spouse is paying tax at the **basic rate** and the other spouse has not fully utilised their personal allowance, tax planning advice should be given to transfer £1,260 of the personal allowance from the non-taxpaying spouse to the other. If some of the personal allowance remains unused, the following advice about transferring income should also be followed.

Avoiding paying higher or additional rate tax

If one spouse is paying tax at the **higher or additional rate** and the other spouse has not fully utilised their personal allowance and/or basic rate band, tax planning advice should be given to:

- reduce the taxable income of the spouse paying the higher rate of tax, and
- increase the taxable income of the other spouse by an equivalent amount.

To achieve this, the following tax planning advice can be given:

- Gift income-producing assets from one spouse to the other spouse (see note below)
- Put assets into joint names so that the taxable income is split using the 50:50 rule
- Ensure that any allowable interest or Gift Aid donations are paid by the spouse paying the higher rate of tax.

Note:

To be effective for income tax purposes, any gift must be an outright gift of the legal ownership of the capital asset which gives rise to the source of income. The original spouse cannot retain any legal right to the asset or income in the future.

Note also that the gift will only affect the treatment of future income generated.

Tax planning with an unincorporated business

If the spouse paying the higher rate of tax has an unincorporated business, income can be transferred to the other spouse by:

- employing the spouse (see note below), or
- taking the spouse on as a partner.

It is important to note, however, that individuals employed by their spouse in an unincorporated business should be paid only at a level commensurate with their duties otherwise a tax liability may arise on the employing spouse.

Using the savings and/or dividend nil rate bands

The savings and dividend nil rate bands complicate the traditional advice to transfer income from a higher rate taxpaying spouse to a basic rate taxpaying spouse.

It is now necessary to consider the sources of income that each spouse has.

Example

Winston and Miriam are a married couple. Winston earns a salary of £75,000 a year. He has no other income.

Miriam earns a salary of £20,000 a year. She also receives interest of £1,500 a year.

Required

Explain how Winston and Miriam can minimise their 2022/23 income tax liability.

Answer

Winston is a higher rate taxpayer and Miriam is a basic rate taxpayer. However, as Winston is an employee and has no other income, it is not possible for him to transfer any of his income to make use of Miriam's basic rate band.

Miriam is a basic rate taxpayer, so her savings nil rate band is £1,000. The remaining £500 of her savings income will be taxable at the rate of 20%.

Winston is a higher rate taxpayer, so his savings income nil rate band is £500. At present he does not use any of this nil rate band therefore transferring sufficient savings to him so that he receives £500 of the savings income will save the couple income tax of £100 (500 at 20%) for 2022/23. This could perhaps be achieved by putting one of Miriam's savings accounts into joint names.

Child benefit income tax charge

- Child benefit
- Child benefit income tax charge
- Who is liable to pay the charge?

7 Child benefit income tax charge

7.1 Child benefit

Child benefit is a state benefit that can be claimed in respect of children. It is a tax free payment that can be claimed by anyone who qualifies for it, irrespective of the level of their income.

7.2 Child benefit income tax charge

Although child benefit is not classed as taxable income, an income tax charge removes the benefit from individuals on higher levels of income:

- Where adjusted net income is between £50,000 and £60,000, the income tax charge is 1% of the amount of child benefit received for every £100 of income over £50,000.
- Where adjusted net income exceeds £60,000, the income tax charge is equivalent to the full amount of child benefit received.

Adjusted net income is calculated in the same way as for personal allowance purposes. It is therefore possible for an individual to reduce their net income below the £50,000 threshold by making personal pension contributions or Gift Aid donations.

The child benefit income tax charge is added to the individual's income tax liability and collected through the self-assessment system.

Example

Margaret has adjusted net income of £65,000 for 2022/23. She receives child benefit of £1,885 in respect of her two children.

Jennifer has adjusted net income of £55,000 for 2022/23. She receives child benefit of £1,134 in respect of her son.

Required

Calculate the child benefit income tax charge for 2022/23 for both Margaret and Jennifer.

Answer

As Margaret's adjusted net income exceeds £60,000, her child benefit income tax charge will be equal to the amount of child benefit received, i.e. £1,885.

As Jennifer's adjusted net income falls between £50,000 and £60,000, her child benefit income tax charge will be £567, i.e. (£55,000 - £50,000)/100 x 1% = 50% x £1,134.

Remember that the charge is **added** to the income **tax liability**, not to the figure of taxable income.

7.3 Who is liable to pay the charge?

Where there are two partners in a household, the charge is payable by the partner who has the higher income. For example, if a husband and wife are entitled to child benefit in respect of their daughter, any child benefit income tax charge is payable by the spouse with the higher income irrespective of whether it is the other spouse who received the child benefit. The income of the lower earning spouse is irrelevant.

The term 'partner' in this context includes unmarried couples who are living together.

In order to avoid receiving child benefit and then having to repay it through the tax system, it is possible to elect not to receive the benefit. The election can be revoked if income subsequently falls below the level at which the child benefit will be clawed back.

Summary

- Proforma income tax computation

8 Summary

8.1 Proforma income tax computation

The full income tax computation is shown below. Some of the entries will be explained in later chapters, but are shown here for the sake of completeness.

	Total income	Non-savings income	Savings income	Dividend income
	£	£	£	£
Earned income				
Trading income	X	X		
Employment income (gross)	X	X		
Pension income	X	X		
Property business income (FHLs)	X	X		
Savings income				
Bank/Building society interest	X		X	
Dividend income				
UK dividends received	X			X
Total income	X	X	X	X
Less Deductible interest	(X)	(X) [1]	(X) [2]	(X) [3]
Net income	X	X	X	X
Less Personal allowance (PA)	(X)	(X) [1]	(X) [2]	(X) [3]
Taxable income	X	X	X	X

			£	£	£
Income tax					
Basic rate band:	Non-savings income		X	at 20%	X
	Savings		X	at 20%	X
	Dividends		X	at 8.75%	X
			37,700		
Higher rate band:	Non-savings income		X	at 40%	X
	Savings		X	at 40%	X
	Dividends		X	at 33.75%	X
			150,000		

	£	£	£
Additional rate band: Non-savings income	X	at 45%	X
Savings	X	at 45%	X
Dividends	X	at 39.35%	X
Total taxable income	X		
			X
Add Annual allowance charge on excess pension contributions (see chapter 11)			X
Less Marriage allowance at 20%			(X)
Less Tax reducers (see chapter 3)			
Property business finance costs at 20%			(X)
Income tax liability			X
Less Tax deducted at source:			
PAYE			(X)
Income tax payable			X

Notes

(1) If savings income falls within the first £5,000 of taxable income, it will be taxable at 0% to the extent that it does not exceed £5,000.

(2) A savings nil rate band of £1,000, £500 or nil applies depending on the taxpayer's marginal rate of tax.

(3) A dividend nil rate band of £2,000 applies to all taxpayers.

(4) The higher rate of tax is payable when taxable income exceeds £37,700 unless the basic rate band is extended due to gift aid donations or contributions into a personal pension scheme.

(5) The additional rate of tax is payable when taxable income exceeds £150,000 unless the higher rate band is extended due to gift aid donations or contributions into a personal pension scheme.

(6) An individual's **income tax liability** is the total amount of income tax which the individual is liable to pay to the tax authorities for the tax year. However, the **tax payable** is the amount of the tax still outstanding.

(7) Tax deducted at source may be refunded by HMRC.

Taxation – United Kingdom (TX-UK) FA2022

CHAPTER 3

Property and investment income

	Contents
1	Income derived from land and buildings in the UK
2	Individual Savings Accounts (ISAs)
3	Accrued income scheme

> **Income derived from land and buildings in the UK**
> - Introduction
> - Rental income
> - UK property income losses
> - Furnished holiday lettings
> - Rent-a-room relief
> - Premiums received on the granting of a short lease

1 Income derived from land and buildings in the UK

1.1 Introduction

The UK property income rules assess income received from land and buildings situated in the UK.

There are two key sources of property income:

- Rental income
- Lump sum premiums received on the granting of short leases.

1.2 Rental income

Rental income is assessed on an individual as 'non-savings income'. It is normally calculated on a cash basis. However, the accruals basis must be used if:

- property income receipts exceed £150,000 or
- an election is made for the accruals basis to apply. The election must be made by the 31 January which is 22 months from the end of the tax year.

(In the examination you should assume that the cash basis is to be used unless you are told otherwise.)

To calculate the rental income assessment:

- all **income received** from any rental property is pooled, and
- all **allowable revenue expenditure** paid wholly and exclusively in relation to the rental properties is deducted.

A single assessment is made on the net profits of all properties let by the individual, as if there is one property business with a year ended 5 April each year.

However, there are two exceptions to this rule. Profits/losses derived from the following properties are not pooled with the other properties but are calculated separately:

- 'furnished holiday lettings', and
- properties let at a nominal rent.

These are considered in detail in later sections of this chapter.

The proforma computation shown below can be used to calculate the rental income assessment for an individual.

(W) UK property income		
	£	£
Rents received in the tax year		X
Less Allowable revenue expenses paid *(see Notes below)*		
Accountant's fee	X	
Agent's management fees, advertising	X	
Council tax, water rates	X	
Gardener's wages, cleaner's wages	X	
Insurance for the property	X	
Insurance for the contents (if furnished)	X	
Repairs	X	
Painting and decorating	X	
Mileage allowances	X	
Interest relief *(see subsection below)*	X	
Replacement furniture relief *(see subsection below)*	X	
		(X)
Property income assessment		X

Notes

(1) Allowable expenses must be paid wholly and exclusively for the purposes of the property letting business and must be revenue, not capital, in nature.

(2) Allowable expenses include expenditure incurred in the seven years pre-letting, provided the expenses would normally be allowed if paid whilst letting property.

(3) Expenditure is allowable if the property is **available** for letting, therefore expenses are allowable if paid while the property is empty (e.g. repairs carried out in between old tenants moving out and new tenants moving in). However, if the owner occupies the property at any time, it may be necessary to time apportion some expenses and only allow those relating to the period that the property is **available for letting**.

(4) Security deposits are not treated as income as they are usually returned to the tenant on the cessation of the letting. However, if retained by the landlord, they would be treated as income at that point.

(5) Individuals and partnerships who incur mileage in respect of a property business can use HMRC's approved mileage allowances to calculate their deductible cost. This is as an alternative to claiming relief for the actual motor expenses incurred. (Approved mileage allowances are covered in more detail in the next chapter.)

Relief for interest

For income tax purposes, interest paid on any loan taken out to purchase, repair or improve the property (including incidental costs of obtaining the loan finance and any bank overdraft interest in respect of running the property business) is an allowable deduction in calculating the rental income.

However, relief for finance costs in respect of **residential** property is not deducted in calculating the rental income. Instead, relief is restricted to the basic rate of tax and deducted from the individual's income tax liability.

Example

Aston owns a couple of residential properties which he rents to students. The properties were purchased with the aid of a mortgage.

During 2022/23, Aston received rental income of £30,000 after the deduction of allowable expenses (excluding mortgage interest). He paid mortgage interest of £6,000.

The properties were Aston's only source of taxable income.

Required

Calculate Aston's income tax liability for 2022/23.

Answer

Aston's income tax liability – 2022/23

	£
Property income	30,000
Less personal allowance	(12,570)
Taxable income	17,430
Income tax:	
£17,430 x 20%	3,486
Interest relief (£6,000 at 20%)	(1,200)
Tax liability	2,286

Note that the basic rate restriction does not apply to:

- furnished holiday lettings (see section 1.4 below)
- non-residential property, such as offices
- property let by limited companies.

In those cases, the full amount of interest is deductible as an expense.

Replacement furniture relief

Replacement furniture relief (also known as replacement domestic items relief) allows the cost of **replacing** furniture and furnishings to be deducted when calculating the property income arising from renting out a **furnished** or partly furnished residential property.

The relief covers the cost of replacing items such as beds, televisions, fridges, carpets, curtains, crockery and cutlery. There is no relief for the initial cost of these items.

The amount of relief is reduced by any proceeds from selling the old asset. Any costs incurred in disposing of the old asset or acquiring the new one are deductible.

Relief is only given on a like-for-like basis. The cost of any improvement is not allowed. This means that, for example, if a landlord replaces a washing machine with a washer-dryer, only the cost of an equivalent washing machine will be deductible.

Example

Janette has rented out a furnished residential property for several years. During 2022/23 she incurred the following expenditure:

(a) £500 on the purchase of a new sofa. The new sofa was a similar size and style to the previous sofa. She sold the old sofa for £100.

(b) £400 on the purchase of a new double bed. This replaced a single bed. She paid £15 for the disposal of the single bed. A new single bed would have cost £200.

Required

Calculate the amounts deductible in calculating Janette's property income for 2022/23.

Answer

(a) The cost of the new sofa is deductible. However, the cost is reduced by the sale proceeds of the old sofa. The net deduction is therefore £400 (500 – 100).

(b) The double bed is not a like-for-like replacement of the single bed therefore relief is restricted to the equivalent cost of £200. The £15 incurred to dispose of the old bed is also deductible.

Note that replacement furniture relief is not available where the property is a furnished holiday letting (as capital allowances can be claimed instead) or where rent-a-room relief is claimed (see sections 1.4 and 1.5 below).

Relief for capital expenditure

Apart from the replacement furniture relief discussed above, as a general rule, capital expenditure is not an allowable deduction in calculating the taxable amount of property income. Capital allowances may, however, be available depending on the type of property concerned:

- If the property is **non-residential** (e.g. office or warehouse), capital allowances are available for plant and machinery provided with the property in the normal way.

- If the property is **residential** (e.g. dwelling house or flat), capital allowances cannot be claimed in respect of plant and machinery within the residential parts of the property, but may be available in respect of plant and machinery provided in any communal areas, such as entrance halls and gardens, as these may be regarded as being for the maintenance, repair or management of the property.

- If the property qualifies as a **furnished holiday let** (see later), capital allowances are available as normal.

- The costs of **renewing fixtures**, such as fitted kitchens and bathrooms, are regarded as a repair to the building rather than capital expenditure. Their cost is therefore deductible as a normal revenue expense.

Example

Hannah rented out two residential properties in 2022/23: Nos. 47 and 49 St. Peter's Boulevard.

No. 47 is a furnished property which Hannah purchased several years ago. It was let all year at a rent of £2,500 per month.

No. 49 is an unfurnished property. It was purchased on 1 January 2023. It was immediately let at a rent of £1,800 a month, payable on the first day of each month. However, the rental payments for March and April 2023 were not received until 10 April 2023.

In order to purchase this property, Hannah took out a £100,000 bank loan on 1 January 2023, at a fixed mortgage interest rate of 5% a year. The interest is paid monthly on the last day of each month.

The following additional expenses were paid during 2022/23:

	No. 47	No. 49
	£	£
Advertising for new tenants	Nil	920
Estate agent management fees	2,440	740
Council tax	860	150
Insurance (see below)	1,100	1,600
Repairs	3,200	Nil
Extension	15,000	Nil
Replacement double bed	500	-

The insurance paid in respect of property number 49 covers the period 1 January to 31 December 2023.

During 2022/23, Hannah drove 60 miles in her car in respect of her property business. The approved mileage allowance is 45 pence per mile.

Required

Calculate Hannah's property income assessment for 2022/23.

Answer

Hannah's property income – 2022/23

	£	£
Rents received in 2022/23 (£2,500 × 12) + (£1,800 × 2)		33,600
Less Allowable expenses		
Advertising	920	
Agents' management fees (£2,440 + £740)	3,180	
Council tax (£860 + £150)	1,010	
Insurance (£1,100 + £1,600)	2,700	
Repairs	3,200	
Extension (capital and therefore not allowable)	Nil	
Mileage allowance (60 miles at 45p)	27	
Interest on loan to purchase No.49 (see note)	Nil	
Replacement furniture relief	500	
		(11,537)
Property income assessment		22,063

Notes

(1) The rental payments due on 1 March and 1 April 2023 will be assessable in 2023/24 as they were received after the end of the 2022/23 tax year.

(2) The insurance paid in respect of property No. 49 is deductible in full as it was paid during 2022/23. The fact that it covers part of the 2023/24 tax year is irrelevant.

(3) Relief for the interest is given as an income tax reducer at the basic rate of tax, i.e. (£100,000 × 5% × 3/12) x 20% = £250.

1.3 UK property income losses

If the allowable expenditure exceeds the rents received on all properties pooled together, an overall net loss arises.

In this case, for income tax purposes:

- the UK property income assessment for the tax year is £Nil, and

- the loss arising can **only** be **carried forward** and set **against future UK property income**. It must be set off as soon as possible.

1.4 Furnished holiday lettings

Income from FHL is assessed separately from other UK property income and treated as earned income, not as investment income.

Therefore, profits of FHL are:

- not pooled with other UK property income

- treated as if profits of a separate **trade**

- assessed using the **trading income assessment rules**, not the property income rules – although the cash basis of computation can still apply, and
- included in the income tax computation as earned income along with employment income or other trading income, not as other investment income.

There are several key advantages in treating the income as earned income as opposed to investment income as outlined in the table below.

Tax	Advantage
Income tax	• instead of replacement furniture relief, normal capital allowances are available on *all* plant and machinery, including fixtures, fittings and furniture • the profits are treated as net relevant earnings for personal pension relief purposes
Capital gains tax	• the property is treated as a business asset rather than an investment asset therefore the following reliefs are available: – Rollover relief – Business asset disposal relief – Gift holdover relief

Losses from furnished holiday lettings

Losses from FHL can only be carried forward against future profits from furnished holiday lettings. They cannot be relieved against other types of property income.

Conditions for treatment as furnished holiday lettings

To be treated as FHL **all** of the following conditions must be satisfied:

- the property is situated in the **European Economic Area**, and
- is **furnished**, and
- is let on a **commercial** basis with a view to making profits, and
- is **available** for letting as holiday accommodation for at least **210 days** in the tax year, and
- is actually **let** for at least **105 days** in the tax year (see below), and
- is **not normally** occupied for periods of longer-term occupation (i.e. not normally occupied for **more than 31 consecutive days** by the **same** person).

If the **total** of all periods of longer-term occupation **exceeds 155 days** in any 12 month period, the property will **not** be treated as a FHL.

Note that the 105 day test may be satisfied by averaging the periods of letting of some or all of the FHL.

1.5 Rent-a-room relief

Where an individual rents out **furnished** accommodation which is **part of his main residence** (e.g. rents a furnished bedroom in his house or flat to a lodger), any rental income received is assessed to income tax as property income. However, rent-a-room relief is available.

The relief operates as follows:

Gross rental income (before expenses and allowances):	Property income assessment	If a loss arises
£7,500 or less	Nil – the income is exempt	No allowable loss arises **unless** an election is made for a normal property income loss to arise
		The election is only valid for the tax year of that loss
More than £7,500	Lower of: • Normal property income assessment • (Rents received less £7,500) but only if an election is made The election is binding until revoked, or gross rents received are £7,500 or less.	Normal property income loss arises

Any election must be made within 12 months after 31 January following the end of the tax year.

Note that the limit of £7,500 is halved to £3,750 if the income received from letting the room is shared with any other person(s).

Example

Ivor rented a furnished bedroom in his house to a lodger for the whole of 2022/23.

Required

Calculate Ivor's property income assessment for 2022/23 assuming the following four different situations:

	Rental income	Allowable expenses
		£
(a)	£800 per month	3,260
(b)	£800 per month	8,600
(c)	£400 per month	3,260
(d)	£400 per month	5,260

Answer

Ivor's property income assessment – 2022/23

(a)

Gross rents exceed £7,500	No election	With election
	£	£
Gross rents received (£800 × 12)	9,600	9,600
Less Allowable expenses/Rent-a-room relief	(3,260)	(7,500)
Assessed on the lower of	6,340	2,100

Ivor will be assessed on £2,100 but only if he makes an election by 31 January 2025 for the rent-a-room relief to apply. The election will remain in force until revoked by Ivor or until the gross rents in the future are £7,500 or less.

(b)

Gross rents exceed £7,500	No election	With election
	£	£
Gross rents received (£800 × 12)	9,600	9,600
Less Allowable expenses/Rent-a-room relief	(8,600)	(7,500)
Assessed on the lower of	1,000	2,100

Ivor will be assessed on £1,000 automatically. He will not wish to make the rent-a-room relief election.

(c)

Gross rents less than £7,500

Gross rents received (£400 × 12) = £4,800

Expenses are less than the rents received; therefore a profit is made but is exempt under the rent-a-room relief provisions.

Property income assessment is £Nil.

(d)

Gross rents less than £7,500	No election	With election
		£
Gross rents received (£400 × 12)	No allowable	4,800
Less Allowable expenses	loss arises	(5,260)
Allowable loss		(460)

Ivor will not be eligible for an allowable loss unless he makes an election for the normal property income loss of £460 to arise. He must elect by 31 January 2025 and the election is valid for 2022/23 only.

1.6 Premiums received on the granting of a short lease

A premium is a lump sum received by the landlord at the start of the lease in return for giving the tenant the **exclusive right to use** the property for the duration of the lease. When the lease terminates, the property reverts back to the owner.

A property income assessment arises on both:

- the **premium** received at the start of the lease, and
- the rent received for the actual use of the property.

The key points to remember are as follows:

- An assessment only arises on the **granting** of a **short** lease.
- A **short** lease is defined as a lease of **not more than 50 years** in duration.
- The assessable amount of premium is calculated as follows:

	£
Premium received	X
Less 2% × premium × (n – 1)	(X)
Property income assessment on the landlord	X
where: n = number of years of the lease	

- The number of years of the lease runs from the start of the lease to the **earliest date on which the lease may be terminated** by either the landlord or the tenant under the terms of the lease.

Example

Jacob granted a 35 year lease on a property to Karen on 6 October 2022 for a premium of £65,000. Jacob charges rent of £5,000 a year payable in advance on a quarterly basis starting on 6 October 2022.

Required

Calculate Jacob's property income assessment for 2022/23.

Answer

	£
Premium received	65,000
Less 2% × £65,000 × 34	(44,200)
Property income assessment on the premium received	20,800
Rental income received in 2022/23 (£5,000 × 6/12)	2,500
Total UK property income assessment for 2022/23	23,300

> **Individual Savings Accounts (ISAs)**
> - Individual Savings Accounts
> - The savings and dividend nil rate bands

2 Individual Savings Accounts (ISAs)

2.1 Individual Savings Accounts

An investment in an Individual Savings Account (ISA) has the following taxation advantages:

- All income is exempt from income tax (e.g. interest, dividends)
- All capital gains on the disposal of capital assets (e.g. shares) while in the ISA are exempt from capital gains tax.

The taxation exemptions are available even if the individual makes withdrawals from the account at any time.

Investment is allowed in accounts comprised of the following components:

- Cash products (e.g. bank and building society accounts)
- Qualifying stocks and shares.

Maximum annual investment:	£20,000 a year
Individual must be:	■ Aged 16 or over (for the cash component)
	■ Aged 18 or over (for the shares component)
	■ Resident in the UK

Notes

(1) Individuals can invest the full £20,000 in qualifying stocks and shares and insurance products, or £20,000 in a cash ISA, or £20,000 in any combination of the two.

(2) The cash and shares components can be invested with different providers or with the same provider, provided the overall limit of £20,000 is not exceeded.

(3) An individual can withdraw money from a cash ISA and replace it in the same year without the replacement counting towards their overall ISA limit.

(4) It is possible to transfer amounts from the stocks and shares component to the cash component and vice versa. However, it is important to make such transfers following the designated procedure; an individual cannot simply withdraw cash from an ISA and use it to purchase stocks and shares in another ISA as this would result in the funds losing their tax exempt status.

2.2 The savings and dividend nil rate bands

The availability of the savings nil rate band for basic and higher rate taxpayers means that there is little tax benefit of investing in cash ISAs for such individuals. However, cash ISAs are still advantageous for:

- additional rate taxpayers (as they are not entitled to a savings nil rate band), and
- individuals with savings income in excess of their nil rate band.

Similarly, the availability of the dividend nil rate band means that for many individuals there is little tax advantage of receiving dividend income within a stocks and shares ISA.

However, as chargeable gains made within a stocks and shares ISA are exempt from capital gains tax, ISAs are still advantageous for taxpayers who realise chargeable gains in excess of the annual exempt amount.

In addition, income and gains on investments held within an ISA do not need to be reported on a self-assessment tax return and are not counted as taxable income. This may help the individual to avoid breaching the various thresholds in the tax system (e.g. thresholds in respect of the child benefit charge, the withdrawal of the personal allowance, etc).

The accrued income scheme

- The accrued income scheme

3 The accrued income scheme

3.1 The accrued income scheme

The accrued income scheme applies to holdings of Government securities (i.e. gilts) and qualifying corporate bonds. These pay interest at a fixed date to the investor.

Gains arising on Government securities are exempt from capital gains tax. However, any interest is subject to income tax.

As interest payments are made on predetermined dates, it is possible for a vendor to sell securities shortly **before** the interest payment date **at an inflated price** to reflect the fact that they will not receive the next interest payment. The securities are being sold 'cum interest', i.e. at a price which includes accrued interest.

The interest element of the selling price is normally treated as a capital receipt so is not liable to income tax. There is also no capital gains tax liability on the sale as gilt-edged securities and qualifying corporate bonds are exempt assets for capital gains tax purposes.

However, anti avoidance legislation exists to prevent interest on marketable securities from escaping tax in this way.

If an individual owns securities with a total nominal value in excess of £5,000 at some time in the tax year, the accrued income scheme requires the selling price of those securities to be apportioned between an income element and a capital element.

The interest is deemed to accrue on a daily basis (although the monthly basis can be used in the examination). The amount accruing to the date of sale is assessed on the vendor as savings income in the normal way. The capital element is exempt from tax.

As far as the purchaser of cum interest stock is concerned, although they will receive the whole of the next interest payment, they will only be taxed on the amount of interest accruing since the purchase date. This is because any interest accruing prior to that date will be assessed on the vendor under the accrued income scheme.

Example

Tabitha holds 7% Treasury stock with a nominal value of £21,000. Interest on the stock is payable half yearly on 1 June and 1 December. She sold her stock on 1 November 2022. The stock went ex interest on 25 November 2022.

Required

(a) Calculate the interest income chargeable on Tabitha for 2022/23.

(b) Explain the treatment of the interest payable on 1 December 2022 in the hands of the purchaser.

Answer

(a) The amount of interest receivable on each payment date is:

£21,000 x 7% = £1,470 x ½ = £735.

Tabitha will be assessed on the interest of £735 received on 1 June 2022. She will also have an accrued income charge of £612, calculated as follows:

Months accruing from 1 June 2022 – 1 November 2022 = 5 months

Accrued income charge on Tabitha: £735 x 5/6 = £612

Tabitha will therefore have interest income of £1,347 (735 + 612) for 2022/23 in respect of this stock.

(b) The purchaser will receive the full amount of interest payable on 1 December 2022 (i.e. £735) as they purchased the stock cum interest.

However, they will only be subject to income tax on one month's interest as they purchased the stock on 1 November 2022, i.e. £123 (£735 - £612 assessed on Tabitha).

Taxation – United Kingdom
(TX-UK) FA2022

CHAPTER 4

Employment income

	Contents
1	Deciding whether an individual is employed or self-employed
2	Overview of the employment income assessment
3	Assessable benefits
4	Allowable deductions
5	The employment income computation

> **Deciding whether an individual is employed or self-employed**
>
> - The problem of deciding whether or not an individual is employed
> - The factors to determine the status of an individual

1 Deciding whether an individual is employed or self-employed

1.1 The problem of deciding whether or not an individual is employed

It is important to establish whether an individual is employed or self-employed as the status of the individual determines how they will be taxed on their income. An employed person is taxed under the employment income rules and a self-employed individual is taxed under the trading income rules for an unincorporated business.

In most cases the position is clear, but this is not always the case.

For example, it can be argued that an individual who provides consultancy services to two or three major clients is self-employed. However, it can also be argued that they have two or three part-time employments with different employers.

To determine the status of an individual, it is necessary to establish the terms of the relationship between the individual and the organisation paying for the work.

The tax legislation states that:

- an employee is deemed to have a contract **of** service with an employer, whereas
- a self-employed individual is deemed to have a contract **for** services, i.e. a supplier/client contract where the individual is contracted to provide their services to the client organisation which pays for the services.

Over many years cases have gone to court to decide whether a contract **of** service exists or whether the individual has been contracted **for** their services. As a result of court decisions, there is a list of factors that HMRC will consider in deciding whether an individual is employed or self-employed.

1.2 The factors to determine the status of an individual

In cases where there is doubt regarding the status of the individual, HMRC will consider the following factors:

- Degree of control
- Provision of the tools of the trade
- Degree of financial risk
- Ability to delegate work
- The client base
- Extent of enjoyment of normal employment rights.

There is no single factor that is more important than another, and no single factor will determine the treatment on its own. HMRC will look at all the facts of the given situation and make a decision.

Degree of control

A **self-employed individual** usually controls their own work, is not supervised in the performance of the work, and is contracted to produce a result. For example, a painter and decorator may be contracted to decorate a room.

Once the contract has been completed, a self-employed individual has no right to expect further work from the client, but equally has no obligation to take on further work with the client if they do not wish to do so.

However, an **employee** usually expects the employer to specify each task to be performed, to determine where, when and how it is to be performed, and to control and supervise the performance of each task. Once a task is completed, an employee has the right to expect further work and has an obligation to perform the work.

In summary, the exercise of a high level of control over an individual is a factor that may support the view that the individual is an employee. The exercise of a lesser degree of control over an individual may support the view that the individual has self-employed status.

Provision of the tools of the trade

A **self-employed individual** is usually expected to provide their own equipment and materials for the work to be performed. For example, a painter and decorator will bring their own ladders, dust sheets, paint brushes and so on.

However, an **employee** would expect the employer to provide the tools required to perform their tasks.

Intellectual assets (such as knowledge and experience) as well as physical assets may be considered in applying this test.

Degree of financial risk

A **self-employed individual** runs the risk of losing their own personal assets and capital if the business operates at a loss and/or fails. They are also personally responsible for the cost of their mistakes and the correction of sub-standard work.

However, an **employee** bears no personal financial risk. They will be paid whether or not the business is profitable and are not personally responsible for the cost of correction of mistakes.

Ability to delegate work

A **self-employed individual** is usually contracted to produce a result, but may subcontract and delegate work to others. This is often referred to as the ability to provide a substitute.

An **employee** has an obligation to perform the tasks personally. Delegation by an employee to another employee within the same organisation is, of course, normal business practice. However, an employee has no right to delegate work to others outside the organisation.

The client base

A **self-employed individual** will usually have a wide client base with a number of customers. However, an **employee** normally works for one employer only and is often prevented from working for others under the terms of their employment contract.

Extent of enjoyment of normal employment rights

An **employee** is entitled to normal employment rights, such as the receipt of an agreed remuneration package. In addition, the individual and the employer are protected by employment law. By law the individual has the right to claim holiday pay, statutory sick pay, etc. However, they are also subject to the disciplinary rules of the organisation. They are usually paid at regular intervals, and their tax and national insurance are deducted at source under the PAYE (pay-as-you-earn) scheme.

A **self-employed individual** (sometimes known as an independent contractor) is not entitled to the same rights as an employee and is not protected by employment law. They will not be paid unless the work is satisfactorily completed and have no entitlement to holiday pay or sick pay. To be paid they must issue an invoice for the work performed and will receive the income gross. It is their responsibility to self-assess the tax due on their trading profits.

> **Overview of the employment income assessment**
>
> - The scope of employment income
> - The receipts basis of assessment
> - Overview of assessing benefits of employment
> - Exempt benefits
> - Assessable benefits - the general rules

2 Overview of the employment income assessment

2.1 The scope of employment income

Employment income primarily includes income received by an individual from their employer in respect of their employment. An employed individual is assessed on all earnings received from their employment after allowable expenses and deductions.

Earnings in this context means not only cash received (such as salary, bonuses, commissions and termination payments) but **all** forms of remuneration **including benefits** derived from the employment.

The scope of the employment income rules is wider than just income from the employer. For income tax purposes, employment income also includes:

- any payments received as a result of the employment **regardless** of who pays them. (Payments by third parties such as tips and gifts are assessable if they are received as a result of the employment)
- pension income (for example state pensions and pensions received as a result of previous employment), and
- some taxable social security benefits, such as statutory sick pay (SSP), statutory maternity pay (SMP), carer's allowance, and jobseeker's allowance.

2.2 The receipts basis of assessment

Employment income is assessed on a receipts basis. This means that the individual is taxed on the income in the tax year (i.e. 6 April to 5 April) in which the cash or benefit is **received**, not necessarily when it is earned.

Date of receipt

Tax legislation provides a definition of the date of receipt. The date of receipt is the **earlier** of:

(1) the date that the employee becomes **entitled** to receive the income, and

(2) the date that the income is **actually received** by the employee.

Date of receipt for directors

Directors, as the senior management in an organisation, determine when employees – including themselves – will receive their remuneration. They are therefore in a position to manipulate their income tax liability by deliberately accelerating or delaying the receipt of income between tax years, to ensure they are taxed at the lowest possible rate of tax.

The date of receipt for directors is the same as for employees, but with three further rules, as follows. The date of receipt is the **earliest** of:

(1) the date that the director becomes **entitled** to receive the income

(2) the date that the income is **actually received** by the director

(3) the date that the **financial accounts are credited** with the director's earnings

(4) the **end of the company's period of account** if the earnings were determined by then; and

(5) the date the amount of earnings for that period is **determined** (for example, at a directors' board meeting) if **after** the end of the company's period of account.

PAYE: deduction of income tax on employment income at source

Usually, cash remuneration is received by an employee on a regular weekly or monthly basis, and income tax is deducted at source under the PAYE (pay-as-you-earn) scheme.

However, **the gross remuneration received in the tax year** must be brought into the employee's income tax computation in order to compute the income tax **liability**. Any PAYE deductions are an allowable tax credit in the income tax **payable** computation.

2.3 Overview of assessing benefits of employment

Benefits of employment are rewards to an employee that are not received in cash but in kind (i.e. in a form other than cash). For example, an employer may provide an employee with a company car or mobile phone and pay all the expenses relating to the asset. Benefits are often referred to as benefits-in-kind or BIKs.

Cash remuneration is straightforward to quantify and charge to tax. However, deciding the amount that should be charged to tax in respect of a benefit received from employment is more complex.

The tax legislation therefore provides a benefits code setting out:

- the general rules that must be applied to value a benefit for taxation purposes
- specific statutory rules to value some particular benefits, and
- which benefits are exempt from tax.

2.4 Exempt benefits

Exempt benefits are benefits that are not subject to income tax. There are many examples of exempt benefits. The most common examples are listed below.

- Employer's contributions to an approved pension scheme for the employee.
- Pension advice, provided it is available to all employees and costs no more than £500 per employee per tax year.
- Employee liability insurance.
- Subsidised canteen meals, provided they are available to all employees.
- Workplace childcare.
- Overnight expense allowance of up to £5 per night if working in the UK and £10 per night if working overseas. This is designed to cover small, incidental amounts of expenditure, such as laundry or newspapers. If the limit is exceeded the **full amount** is taxable.
- Overseas medical insurance and treatment, if the employee is working abroad.
- The provision of one mobile phone to the employee himself (but not the cost of the employee's own private mobile phone bill or top-up vouchers).
- The provision of a car parking space (or reimbursement of the cost of parking) at or near the place of work.
- Benefits aimed at encouraging employees to travel to work by means other than by car (for example the provision of bicycles, bicycle safety equipment).
- The cost of a works bus, or free or subsidised travel on public bus services used to travel between home and work.
- Car mileage allowances for the use of the employee's own car within statutory limits (Approved Mileage Allowances): this is explained later.
- Sporting and recreational facilities, provided they are available to all employees and not available to members of the public generally (for example membership at a public gym is not an exempt benefit).
- The provision of work-related training courses.
- Staff entertaining (such as the staff Christmas party, staff outings), provided this is available to all staff and the total cost, including VAT, in a tax year does not exceed £150 per head. (If there are two or more functions, the costs are aggregated. For example, if there were three functions each costing £60, the exemption would cover two of them. The third function could not be included within the exemption as the total cost would then exceed £150).
- Entertainment provided by a third party (such as a ticket to attend a sporting event or concert) to generate goodwill. (No monetary limit applies).
- Contributions towards the costs of working at home, up to £6 per week without the need for supporting documentation. Contributions in excess of £6 require supporting documentation in order to be tax-free.
- Relocation / removal costs of up to £8,000 if the employee does not already live within a reasonable daily travelling distance of their new place of work. The exemption covers all the expenses of disposing of the old property and buying

the new one, removal expenses, purchasing replacement goods such as carpets and curtains, and bridging loan costs. To qualify, the expenditure must be incurred by the end of the tax year following that in which the new job commenced.

- Counselling services for the welfare of employees (for example, outplacement counselling for redundant employees).

- Gifts from third parties of up to £250 per tax year if received as a result of employment. The figure of £250 includes VAT and if the £250 limit is exceeded, the full cost is taxable.

- Non-cash long service awards (e.g. a gold watch) with a value of up to £50 per year of service, provided the employee has had at least 20 years of service with the employer and has received no similar award in the previous 10 years.

- One health screening and one medical check-up per tax year.

- Where an employer pays for medical treatment, up to £500 per tax year per employee is exempt. In order to qualify for the exemption, the medical treatment must be provided in order to assist the employee to return to work after a period of absence due to ill-health or injury.

- The provision of eye care tests and corrective glasses in connection with an employee's use of visual display units.

- Awards under a staff suggestion scheme. The scheme must be open to all employees. Awards must not exceed £25 unless the suggestion is implemented and the reward reflects the suggestion's net financial benefit to the organisation. If an award exceeds £5,000, the excess is taxable.

- Assets used in performing the duties of the employment, provided any private use is insignificant. For example, occasional personal use of a company laptop.

- Trivial benefits. These are benefits that do not cost more than £50 per employee. A trivial benefit cannot be cash or cash vouchers.

- Workplace charging points for hybrid or electric cars used by employees.

2.5 Assessable benefits – the general rules

In general, employees are assessed on benefits provided to them, or to a member of their family or household, regardless of whether the benefit can be converted into cash.

The value of a benefit for income tax purposes is the cost to the employer of providing the benefit. **Cost to the employer** means the marginal cost or incremental cost to the employer providing the benefit.

When measuring the taxable amount of a benefit, two further rules generally apply:

- **Contributions made by the employee.** Where the employee pays a contribution to their employer towards the provision of the benefit, the value of the benefit is **reduced by the amount of the employee's contribution** provided it is paid by 6 July following the end of the relevant tax year. The only exception to this general rule is the provision of private fuel (explained later).

Chapter 4: Employment income

- **Provision of a benefit for only part of the tax year.** Where a benefit is provided for only part of the tax year, the general rule is that the benefit is **time-apportioned** according to the number of months the benefit has been received during the tax year.

Example

George has been employed by Harris Ltd throughout 2022/23. He received wages of £26,700 and the following benefits of employment:

- Free meals in the works canteen, costing the company £575
- A place at the company's nursery for his daughter, costing £4,000
- An annual season ticket to travel on the local buses and trains which would have cost George £1,050, but which Harris Ltd negotiated at a discount and paid only £960
- Attendance at an internal training course which cost the company £450 per employee.

Required

Calculate George's employment income for 2022/23.

Answer

		£
Wages		26,700
Benefits of employment:		
Free meals	Exempt	Nil
Workplace nursery	Exempt	Nil
Season ticket	Cost to employer	960
Provision of work related training courses	Exempt	Nil
Employment income		27,660

Season tickets for use on train or tram services are not exempt benefits. A bus-only season ticket would qualify as an exempt benefit.

> **Assessable benefits**
>
> - Company cars
> - Private fuel
> - Vans
> - Approved mileage allowances
> - Living accommodation benefits
> - The private use and gift of business assets
> - Beneficial loans
> - Miscellaneous benefits
> - Payrolling of benefits

3 Assessable benefits

3.1 Company cars

A car provided to an employee by an employer is often referred to as a company car.

An employee who is provided with a company car that can be used for both business and private use will be assessed on the benefit of the private use. The value of this benefit is based on a percentage applied to the list price of the car.

The assessable benefit for each car is calculated separately as follows:

Assessable benefit of a car		£		£
Manufacturer's list price (MLP)		X		
Minus Employee's capital contribution	(max £5,000)	(X)		
		X	at appropriate %	X
Minus Employee's contribution for the private use of the car				(X)
Car benefit				X

The manufacturer's list price (MLP) is the published price of the car when it was new and first registered, including:

- VAT
- delivery charges
- standard accessories provided with the car
- optional accessories provided with the car
- optional accessories provided at a later date which cost in excess of £100.

Any contribution by the employee towards the capital cost of the car, including qualifying accessories, can be deducted from the MLP, subject to a maximum deduction of £5,000.

The **appropriate percentage** to apply depends on the car's CO_2 emissions and the type of car (i.e. petrol, diesel, electric or hybrid-electric). The percentages for 2022/23 are as follows:

Electric cars

The percentage for electric cars with zero CO_2 emissions is 2%.

Hybrid-electric cars

For hybrid-electric cars with CO_2 emissions between 1 and 50 grams per kilometre, the electric range of the car is relevant:

Electric range

130 miles or more	2%
70 to 129 miles	5%
40 to 69 miles	8%
30 to 39 miles	12%
Less than 30 miles	14%

Example

Ella was provided with a hybrid-electric car throughout the tax year 2022/23. The car has a list price of £35,000, an official CO_2 emission rate of 20 grams per kilometre and an electric range of 60 miles.

Required

Calculate the car benefit assessable on Ella for the tax year 2022/23.

Answer

As the car is a hybrid-electric with CO_2 emissions between 1 and 50 grams per kilometre, the electric range is relevant. This is between 40 and 69 miles, so the relevant percentage is 8%. The car was available throughout 2022/23, so the benefit is £2,800 (35,000 × 8%).

Petrol cars

For petrol cars, the CO_2 emissions are relevant:

CO_2 emissions	
51 - 54 g/km	15%
55 g/km	16%

The base percentage (16%) increases by 1% per annum for each additional 5 g/km of emissions above the base figure of 55 g/km, up to a maximum percentage of 37%.

Diesel cars

The percentages for diesel cars are the same as for petrol cars. However, diesel cars are subject to an additional 4% charge, up to a maximum percentage of 37%, unless they meet the real driving emissions 2 (RDE2) standard.

The appropriate annual percentage for petrol and diesel cars with CO_2 emissions of more than 55 g/km is therefore calculated as follows:

	g/km	Petrol %	Diesel %
The car's CO_2 emissions in g/km (rounded down to the nearest 5 g/km)	X		
Minus Base level of CO_2 emissions (i.e. 55 g/km for 2022/23) (See tax rates and allowances)	(55)		
	X ÷ 5 g/km X	X
Plus Minimum percentage		16	16
Plus Diesel surcharge (if not RDE2)		-	4
Appropriate annual percentage		X	X

Restricted to a maximum of 37%

Rules applicable to all company cars

If an employee does not have the use of the car for the whole tax year, the benefit is time-apportioned.

- This applies if the car is acquired or disposed of during the year.
- It also applies if the car is made unavailable to the employee for at least 30 consecutive days during the year.

Payments towards the private use of the car (as opposed to payments towards the capital cost or payments towards the cost of private fuel) reduce the taxable benefit. However, such payments must be made by 6 July following the end of the tax year concerned.

Example

Harry and Janice are provided with the following company cars:

	Harry	Janice
Type of car	Petrol	Diesel
Date car was made available	6 April 2022	6 September 2022
Manufacturer's list price	£20,235	£19,600
CO_2 emissions	107 g/km	122 g/km
Capital contribution	£5,900	Nil
Contribution for the private use of the car	£55 per month	£20 per month

Required

Calculate the benefits assessable on Harry and Janice for the tax year 2022/23, assuming that Janice's diesel car does not meet the RDE2 standard.

Answer

	Harry g/km	Janice g/km		Harry Petrol %	Janice Diesel %
CO_2 emissions (rounded down to nearest 5 g/km)	105	120			
Base level of CO_2 emissions	(55)	(55)			
	50	65	÷ 5 g/km	10	13
Minimum percentages				16	16
Diesel surcharge				-	4
Appropriate percentages				26	33
Number of months car available in 2022/23				12	7

Harry's car benefit

	£		
Manufacturer's list price	20,235		
Minus Harry's capital contribution (restricted)	(5,000)		
	15,235	at 26%	3,961
Minus			
Contribution for the private use of the car (£55 × 12)			(660)
Car benefit			3,301

Janice's car benefit

	£		£
Manufacturer's list price	19,600		
Minus Capital contribution	(Nil)		
	19,600	at 33% × 7/12	3,773
Minus			
Contribution for the private use of the car (£20 × 7)			(140)
Car benefit			3,633

Note that the assessable benefit is for the **private use** of the car. There is no assessable benefit if the car is used **entirely for business** purposes.

Costs covered by the car benefit

The benefit is intended to cover all the capital and running costs incurred by an employer in providing the use of the car (for example, car tax, insurance, repairs and maintenance).

You should therefore ignore any information about these associated costs in an examination question, as they have already been taken into account in the calculation of the car benefit.

However, the car benefit does not take into account the provision of private fuel.

Pool cars

There is no benefit arising if the employee has the use of a pool car.

A pool car is defined as a car which is:

- **not** allocated to a particular employee and which is available for use by more than one employee, **and**
- **not** normally garaged at or near any employee's home overnight, **and**
- used primarily for business purposes, any private use by an employee being incidental to its use for business purposes.

3.2 Private fuel

An additional benefit arises if an employee is provided with **a company car** and is also provided with fuel for private mileage. (Note that there is no private fuel benefit if an employee is provided with a pool car and is also provided with private fuel.)

The provision of **private fuel for a company car** is a common scenario in practice and in examination questions.

An employee with the use of a company car is **automatically taxed** on fuel benefit, **unless**:

- the employee pays for all fuel and the employer only reimburses the business mileage cost, or
- the employer pays for all fuel and the employee reimburses the employer for the cost of **all** private mileage.

In both these situations, the employer does not bear the cost of any private fuel, and the employee does not receive a private fuel benefit.

However, where the employer pays for the private fuel and the employee makes a contribution towards the cost of private mileage but **does not pay for all of the private mileage costs**, the fuel benefit will be assessed on the employee **in full** with no deduction allowed for the employee's contributions.

This is the exception to the general rule that contributions paid by an employee to an employer in respect of a benefit will reduce the taxable amount of that benefit.

Calculating the private fuel benefit

The private fuel benefit is based on the percentage used to calculate the car benefit and a base figure set by HMRC each year. The base figure for 2022/23 is £25,300 and is given in the tax rates and allowances table provided in the examination.

The private fuel benefit is therefore calculated as follows:

| Private fuel benefit | = | £25,300 | × | Appropriate percentage (same as car benefit percentage) |

If an employee does not have the use of the car for the whole tax year, the fuel benefit as well as the car benefit is time-apportioned.

- This applies if the car is acquired or disposed of during the year.
- It also applies if the car is made unavailable to the employee for at least 30 consecutive days during the year.

The fuel benefit can also be time-apportioned where the employee opts out of private fuel provision by the employer or where the fuel itself is only provided for part of the year. Time-apportionment in these situations is only available provided that the withdrawal from the provision of fuel is a **permanent** rather than a temporary withdrawal.

Example

The facts are the same as in the previous example – Harry and Janice.

Required

Calculate the assessable fuel benefits for Harry and Janice in 2022/23.

Answer

The appropriate percentage, calculated in the previous example, is 26% for Harry and 33% for Janice.

	£		Benefit £
Harry's fuel benefit (full year)	25,300	at 26%	6,578
Janice's fuel benefit (7 months of the year)	25,300	at 33% × 7/12	4,870

3.3 Vans

Employees who are provided with a van that can be used for both business and private use will be assessed on the benefit of the private use **unless** the only private use is ordinary commuting (i.e. from home to work).

The assessable benefit is a fixed annual scale rate of £3,600. However, vans producing zero CO_2 emissions have a zero benefit charge.

There is also a separate private fuel benefit if fuel is provided for private mileage in a van. This is £688 a year. However, there is no fuel benefit for zero emission vans.

Note that these scale rates are annual rates therefore if the van and/or the fuel are only available for part of the tax year, the scale rates are time-apportioned. (The benefit is split where employees share the use of a van.)

3.4 Approved mileage allowances

As an alternative to an employer providing an employee with a company car, the employee may buy and run their own car and claim a mileage allowance from the employer for business travel.

Approved mileage allowances are statutory tax-allowable mileage rates for the use of privately-owned cars, vans, motor cycles and bicycles. In addition, there is a tax-free allowance for payments made to an employee who carries one or more colleagues as passengers in their own car or van to make the same business trip.

The rates for a car, van, motor cycle and bicycle are different. For example, the approved mileage allowance for 2022/23 for the first 10,000 business miles in a privately owned car is 45p and 25p thereafter. The approved mileage allowances for cars are given in the table of tax rates and allowances. If required in the examination, the approved mileage rates for other vehicles will be given in the question.

The consequences of approved mileage allowances are as follows:

If the mileage allowance received is:	Consequence:
- Equal to the approved mileage allowance	- The allowance received is tax-free - No benefit arises
- In excess of the approved mileage allowance	- An assessable benefit arises - Benefit = excess allowance received
- Less than the approved mileage allowance	- An allowable deduction from employment income is available. - Deduction = shortfall of allowances received

Example

Kevin uses his own car for business travel. During 2022/23 his business mileage was 14,000 miles, for which his employer paid him 50p per mile. Included in this mileage was a trip to Glasgow to a business conference, totalling 460 miles. Kevin took his colleague Len to the conference in his car as Len could not drive, and received £45 from his employer for taking Len as a passenger.

The approved mileage allowance (AMA) for a car is 45p for the first 10,000 miles and 25p thereafter. The passenger rate is 5p per passenger per mile.

Required

Calculate the assessable benefit, if any, arising on Kevin as a result of receiving the mileage allowances.

Answer

		£	£
Mileage allowance received	14,000 × 50p		7,000
AMA for the car	10,000 × 45p	4,500	
	4,000 × 25p	1,000	
			(5,500)
			1,500
Passenger allowance received		45	
AMA for passengers	460 × 5p	(23)	
			22
Assessable benefit			1,522

3.5 Living accommodation benefits

The amount of the assessable benefit in respect of living accommodation varies according to whether the living accommodation is job-related accommodation or not.

Definition of job-related accommodation

Job-related accommodation is accommodation provided by the employer for one of the following reasons:

- It is necessary for the employee to live in the accommodation **for the proper performance of their duties** (e.g. a school caretaker).

- It is not necessary, but it is customary for such accommodation to be provided in that type of employment and it **assists the better performance of the duties** (e.g. vicar, hospital employee, hotel employee, police officer).

- It is provided as **part of security arrangements** as there is a special threat to the employee's security (e.g. the Prime Minister's official residence).

Living accommodation that is not job-related

When the living accommodation is **not** job-related accommodation, there may be four separate elements to calculate in order to arrive at the total amount of living accommodation benefits. These are listed in the table below.

Living accommodation that is job-related

If the living accommodation is job-related accommodation, there are potentially only two benefits arising and these are subject to a maximum limit:

Potential benefits arising:	Not job-related accommodation	Job-related accommodation	
1. Annual value	✓	X	
2. Expensive accommodation benefit	✓	X	
3. Running costs	✓	✓*	*subject to
4. Provision of furniture	✓	✓*	max limit

Living accommodation provided by employers is usually not job-related accommodation, therefore all four associated benefits are potentially taxable.

In the examination, always assume that the accommodation is **not** job-related unless it is clearly stated or shown that it satisfies the definition of job-related accommodation.

(1) The annual value

This is the charge for the basic provision of the property to the employee, assuming an unfurnished property with no services.

The annual value of the property is a notional rental value. The annual value depends on whether the property has been purchased by the employer or rented by the employer on behalf of the employee. It is calculated as the greater of:

- the annual (i.e. rateable) value of the property
- the rent paid by the employer on behalf of the employee.

(2) The expensive accommodation benefit

Where the property has been purchased by the employer and the cost of providing the accommodation is in excess of £75,000, an **additional** benefit arises.

This additional benefit is calculated as follows:

	£
Cost of acquiring the property (see note (a) below)	X
Plus:	X
Capital improvements incurred before the **start** of the tax year	
Minus: Capital contributions made by the employee	(X)
Cost of providing accommodation	X
Minus: Limit	(75,000)
	X
× Official rate of interest at the start of the tax year (see note (c))	= £XX

Notes

(a) If the property was purchased by the employer more than six years before the employee first occupied it and the cost of providing the accommodation is in excess of £75,000, the market value of the property when the employee first occupied it should be used in the above formula instead of the original cost.

(b) Only capital improvements from the date the employee occupied the property to the start of the tax year should be brought into the computation, after deducting any capital contributions made by the employee, if any.

(c) The official rate of interest at the start of the tax year (i.e. 6 April) is the rate specified by HMRC. For 2022/23 the rate is 2%.

Example

Linda was first provided by her employer with unfurnished living accommodation on 5 June 2019. She pays all the running costs and a monthly contribution of £200 towards the provision of the accommodation.

Her employer purchased the property in 2018 for £300,000 and built an attached garage in July 2021 for £2,800. The annual value of the property is £6,700.

Required

Calculate the assessable benefits arising on Linda for the accommodation in 2022/23.

Answer

	£	£
Annual value of the property		6,700
Cost of acquiring the property	300,000	
Plus: Capital improvements incurred before the **start** of the tax year	2,800	
Minus: Capital contributions made by the employee	(Nil)	
Cost of providing accommodation	302,800	
Minus: Limit	(75,000)	
	227,800	
× Official rate of interest at the start of the tax year	2%	4,556
		11,256
Minus: Employee contributions towards the benefit: (£200 × 12)		(2,400)
Total assessable accommodation benefits		8,856

(3) **Running costs**

Any running costs relating to the accommodation paid by the employer for the employee are assessable.

For example, gas, electricity, cleaning, repairs and maintenance (but not structural alterations) would be assessed on the employee at the cost to the employer.

(4) Provision of furniture

If furniture is provided with the accommodation, the assessable benefit is calculated using the rules applicable to the use of assets, which are explained later.

Job-related accommodation: running costs and the provision of furniture

If the accommodation is job-related, the total of the running costs and the benefit for the provision of furniture is subject to a maximum amount. This is calculated as follows:

	£	£
Employee's employment income assessment **excluding** the accommodation benefits		Y
10% of this amount		X
Minus: Employee contribution		(X)
Maximum total benefit for job-related accommodation		X

3.6 The private use and gift of business assets

If an employee is provided with the private use of a business asset (other than a car or van), the assessable benefit is calculated as the **higher of:**

- 20% × Market value of the asset when **first** made available to **any** employee, and
- the rent or hire charge paid by the employer on behalf of the employee.

If the asset is later sold or gifted to the employee, a **further benefit** arises. This is calculated as the **higher of:**

		£
(1)	Market value at the date of sale/gift	X
	Minus: Price paid by employee, if any	(X)
		X
(2)	Market value when first provided to any employee	X
	Minus: Benefits already assessed	(X)
	Minus: Price paid by employee, if any	(X)
		X

However, **the outright gift of a new asset** acquired by an employer for an employee would be assessed as a benefit using the general rule of cost to the employer.

The above rules do not apply to the sale or gift of a company car. In this case, the assessable benefit is calculated as follows:

	£
Market value at the date of sale/gift	X
Minus Price paid by employee, if any	(X)
Assessable benefit	X

Example

On 6 August 2020, a company provided one of its directors, Yuma, with a home entertainment system for his own use. The system had cost £5,500 in December 2019 and was used by the company until 5 August 2020 when its market value was estimated to be £5,000.

On 6 April 2022 Yuma purchased the system from the company for £1,200. Its market value was estimated to be £2,800 at the date of sale.

Required

Calculate the assessable benefits arising on Yuma each year.

Answer

		£	£
2020/21	20% × £5,000 × 8/12 (private use for only 8 months)		667
2021/22	20% × £5,000		1,000
2022/23			
	Higher of:		
(1)	MV at the date of sale	2,800	
	Minus: Price paid by employee	(1,200)	
		1,600	
(2)	Market value when first provided to any employee	5,000	
	Minus: Benefits already assessed	(1,667)	
	Minus: Price paid by employee, if any	(1,200)	
		2,133	2,133
	Total assessments		3,800

3.7 Beneficial loans

When an employer provides an employee or any of the employee's relatives with a loan and does not charge a commercial rate of interest (i.e. when the employer provides a cheap loan to an employee), a taxable benefit arises as follows:

	£
Interest on the loan at the official rate of interest	X
Minus: Interest paid by the employee (or relative), if any	(X)
Assessable benefit	X

However, an assessable benefit arises on a loan only if the total loans outstanding for that employee (and/or their relatives) at any time during the tax year are in excess of £10,000.

The official rate of interest on beneficial loans is set by HMRC each tax year. The rate for the tax year 2022/23 is 2%.

Calculating the interest on the loan at the official rate of interest

The interest on the loan at the official rate of interest can be calculated in one of two ways, using:

- the average method or
- the strict basis of calculation.

(1) **The average method**

The interest is calculated on the average amount of the loan outstanding. The average is calculated as follows:

(Balance at start of tax year + balance at end of tax year) divided by 2

If the loan was taken out part way through the year, the opening balance of the loan is used instead of the balance at the start of the tax year. Similarly, if the loan was repaid part way through the year, the balance of the loan at the date of repayment is used instead of the balance at the end of the tax year.

(2) **The strict basis calculation**

The interest is calculated on the actual loan outstanding during each month of the year.

Example

Nigel's employer lent him £50,000 on 6 June 2022. Nigel repaid £10,000 on 6 December 2022. His employer charged him £600 interest in 2022/23.

Required

Calculate the assessable benefit on Nigel for 2022/23.

Answer

Average method - Interest at the official rate

Loan taken out part-way through the year = £50,000

Balance outstanding at the end of the tax year = £40,000

Average loan outstanding = £45,000 ((50,000 + 40,000)/2)

Length of time loan outstanding = 10 months

Interest at the official rate:

£45,000 x 2% x 10/12 = £750

Strict basis – Interest at the official rate

Balance outstanding from 6 June 2022 to 6 December 2022 (6 months) = £50,000

Balance outstanding from 6 December 2022 to 6 April 2023 (4 months) = £40,000

Interest at the official rate:

	£
Interest from 6 June 2022 to 6 December 2022 (6 months) £50,000 × 2% × 6/12	500
Interest from 6 December 2022 to 6 April 2023 (4 months) £40,000 × 2% × 4/12	267
	767

	Average method	Strict basis
	£	£
Interest on the loan at the official rate of interest	750	767
Minus Interest paid	(600)	(600)
Assessable benefit	150	167

Note that the two methods give slightly different benefit values.

The benefit is usually calculated using the average method, but the individual can elect for the strict basis if preferred. This option will be chosen if the strict basis calculation gives a lower benefit.

However, HMRC also have the right to insist on the strict basis if they so wish. They will only do so if:

- they believe that the individual has deliberately manipulated the loan payments and repayments during the year to minimise the assessable benefit by using the average method, **or**
- the difference between the two methods is material (i.e. significant in amount).

Finally in relation to beneficial loans, **if any part of the loan is written off** by the employer, the amount written off is assessed as a further benefit.

3.8 Miscellaneous benefits

Vouchers

Vouchers exchangeable for goods or services (such as gift vouchers and travel season tickets) are assessable benefits unless they are specifically exempt.

(Exempt items include car parking vouchers.)

Employees are assessed on the cost to the person providing the vouchers.

Company credit cards

Where an employee uses a company credit card, they will be assessed on whatever has been charged to the card, but not any charges in relation to acquiring the card or in respect of late payment (e.g. interest).

However, any expenditure satisfying the wholly, exclusively and necessarily tests can then be claimed as a deductible expense. (These tests are explained in the next section).

Air miles or points obtained as a result of business expenditure but used for private purposes are an exempt benefit.

Scholarships

Employees are taxable on the cost of any scholarship given to members of their family unless scholarships awarded by reason of employment do not exceed 25% of the scholarship fund's total payments.

3.9 Payrolling of benefits

Employers can choose to include most taxable benefits within their normal payroll by pro-rating the assessable amount of benefit over the number of pay days in the tax year.

This approach enables the employee's income tax liability to be collected under PAYE. Payrolled benefits do not then have to be reported on form P11D. However, employers must provide their employees with an annual statement showing the total taxable benefits on which PAYE has been operated.

Employers who wish to payroll benefits must register to do so before the start of the tax year.

If taxable benefits are not payrolled, they must be reported on form P11D. Income tax will then normally be collected by an adjustment to the employee's PAYE tax code.

> **Allowable deductions**
>
> - Overview of allowable expenses
> - Travel expenses
> - Entertaining expenses
> - Reporting of expenses

4 Allowable deductions

4.1 Overview of allowable expenses

The legislation specifically allows the following deductions from employment income:

- Employee contributions into an occupational pension scheme up to a maximum of 100% of earnings. (Pension contributions are dealt with in more detail in a later chapter.)

- Donations to charity under an approved payroll giving scheme (known as Give As You Earn). The employer deducts the donations from the employee's salary before calculating PAYE (thus giving tax relief for the donation) and pays them to an approved agent. The agent distributes the funds to charities selected by the employee.

- Subscriptions to approved professional bodies, if the subscription is relevant to the employment.

In addition, where an employee uses their own car and claims a mileage allowance, any shortfall in allowance received compared with the approved mileage allowances is an allowable deduction from employment income. (This was illustrated earlier.)

Expenses other than those referred to above are only allowable deductions if they satisfy the general rule and are incurred wholly, exclusively and necessarily in the performance of the employee's duties. This general rule for an employee is more rigorous than the wholly and exclusively rule for a self-employed individual that we will look at in the next chapter.

- The expense must be wholly and exclusively incurred such that only the business benefits from the expenditure. Any personal benefit that the employee gains as a result of the expenditure must be incidental to the primary purpose of the expense.

- The expense must also be necessarily (i.e. unavoidably) incurred by the employee in order for him to carry out his duties. To satisfy the necessarily test the employee must be able to show that it is necessary for **any** employee to have to incur the expense in order to perform the task. Expenses are not allowable if they are necessary for that individual to perform the task but would not be necessary for another employee.

- The expense must also be incurred **in** the performance of the duties. Therefore, any expenses incurred in order to prepare the individual to be able to perform the duties (e.g. ordinary commuting costs) are not allowable.

4.2 Travel expenses

Travelling and subsistence expenses are allowable provided that:

- they are not expenses of ordinary commuting
- they are not expenses of private travel, and
- they are necessary in the performance of duties (i.e. the job cannot be performed unless the employee travels to that location). For example, sales representatives and service engineers have to travel to clients in order to perform their duties.

Expenses of journeys from home to a temporary workplace (e.g. an associated office in another town) will be allowable provided the attendance at that work place lasts, or is expected to last, for no more than 24 months.

4.3 Entertaining expenses

The treatment of third party entertaining expenses depends on how the expense is paid for.

If the entertaining is paid for by the employee and reimbursed by the employer (or if it is paid for with a specific entertainment allowance):

- The reimbursement/specific entertainment allowance will be treated as exempt income in the hands of the individual as the expense is allowable under the wholly, exclusively and necessarily rule. It can therefore be ignored when calculating the employee's income.
- The expense is **disallowed** in the employer's adjustment of profit computation.

If the entertaining is paid for with a general round sum allowance or out of an increased salary:

- The individual is assessed on the amount of the general allowance or increased salary, but he **cannot** claim a deduction for the expenses under the wholly, exclusively and necessarily rule.
- In this instance, the expenses **are allowed** in the employer's adjustment of profit computation.

4.4 Reporting of expenses

Allowable business expenses that are paid or reimbursed by the employer do not have to be reported on form P11D. They are treated as exempt income.

Expenses will therefore only appear in an employee's income tax computation if they are met by the employee personally and not reimbursed by the employer.

5 The employment income computation

5.1 A proforma for the employment income computation

The following proforma can be used to compute employment income.

	£
Wages / salary	X
Bonuses / commissions	X
Assessable benefits	X
	X
Allowable deductions:	
Employee pension contributions	(X)
Donations to charity under an approved payroll giving scheme	(X)
Subscriptions to professional bodies	(X)
Expenses incurred wholly, exclusively and necessarily by the employee and not reimbursed by the employer	(X)
AMA deduction	(X)
Employment income	X

5.2 Example of an employment income calculation

Olga is employed by Pacific Enterprises plc. In 2022/23 she received a salary of £60,000 and a bonus of £15,000 paid on 15 January 2023.

She also received the following benefits:

(a) A diesel car costing £23,000, with a list price of £26,500 and CO_2 emissions of 158 g/km. The car does not meet the RDE2 standard. She contributed £4,600 towards the purchase of the car and £60 per month towards the use of the car. The company paid the car tax of £160, insurance of £550, and repairs in the year which cost £1,350.

(b) Private fuel which cost the company £2,400.

(c) Vouchers for a car park next to the Pacific Enterprises plc offices which cost £900.

(d) Private medical insurance which cost £1,300.

(e) Employer contributions into the occupational pension scheme of 5% of salary.

(f) Use of a new laptop computer and software for private use which cost the company £500.

Olga paid the following amounts during 2022/23:

(a) 3% of her salary into the company's occupational pension scheme.

(b) £2,250 on entertaining clients and suppliers, which Pacific Enterprises plc reimbursed as they were genuine business expenses.

(c) £400 donation to charity under the approved payroll giving scheme administered by Pacific Enterprises plc.

Required

Calculate Olga's employment income for 2022/23.

Answer

	£
Salary	60,000
Bonus	15,000
Assessable benefits	
Car benefit (W1)	7,383
Fuel benefit (£25,300 × 37%)	9,361
Car parking vouchers = exempt	Nil
Private medical insurance	1,300
Employer contributions to pension scheme = exempt	Nil
Use of laptop (£500 × 20%)	100
	93,144
Allowable deductions:	
Employee pension contributions (£60,000 × 3%)	(1,800)
Donations to charity under an approved payroll giving scheme	(400)
Employment income	90,944

Workings

(W1) Car benefit	g/km		Diesel
			%
CO_2 emissions (rounded down to nearest 5 g/km)	155		
Base level of CO_2 emissions	(55)		
	100	÷ 5	20
Minimum percentage			16
Diesel surcharge			4
Appropriate percentage = restricted to maximum 37%			40

	£	£
Manufacturer's list price	26,500	
Minus: Capital contribution towards the car	(4,600)	
	21,900 at 37%	8,103
Minus:		
Contribution for the use of the car (£60 × 12)		(720)
Car benefit		7,383

Notes

(a) The car tax, insurance and repairs are ignored as they are covered by the car benefit.

(b) The entertaining expenses are omitted from the computation. They are allowable business expenses reimbursed by the employer and are therefore classed as exempt income.

Taxation – United Kingdom
(TX-UK) FA2022

CHAPTER 5

Computing trading income

	Contents
1	Does a trade exist?
2	Overview of the trading income assessment for an unincorporated business
3	The adjustment of profit computation
4	Disallowable expenditure
5	Specifically allowable expenditure
6	Amounts credited in the accounts that are not taxable as trading income
7	Proforma adjustment of profit computation

> **Does a trade exist?**
>
> - Deciding whether or not a trading activity exists
> - The badges of trade
> - The principles of assessing trading income

1 Does a trade exist?

1.1 Deciding whether or not a trading activity exists

Before starting to compute the trading income assessment of an individual, it is important to establish that the income should be taxed as trading income. Income should only be taxed as trading income if a trading activity exists.

What constitutes a trade is widely defined by UK tax law as 'every trade, manufacture, adventure or concern in the nature of trade'.

In most cases it is clear that a trading business has been established and the profits should be taxed accordingly. However, in some cases the decision as to whether or not a trade exists is not clear-cut.

If a profit is made on the disposal of an asset, it can be argued that:

- it is a one-off capital disposal and so should be liable to capital gains tax and
- it does not constitute a trading activity.

Alternatively, depending on the type of asset, the disposal may be exempt from tax.

However, the conclusion might not be the same if another similar disposal were to take place six months later, or one week later, or every four months. It could be argued that the profits from these disposals should be liable to income tax as trading income, and that they are not capital gains from a non-trading activity.

Over many years cases have gone to court to decide whether or not a trading activity exists. As a result of court decisions, there is a list of factors (known as the badges of trade) which HMRC will consider in deciding:

- whether a trading activity exists, and therefore
- whether the profits derived from the activities should be taxed as trading income.

1.2 The badges of trade

In cases where there is doubt as to whether or not a trading activity exists, HMRC will consider six factors to decide the appropriate tax treatment.

No single factor is more important than another and no single factor will determine the treatment on its own. HMRC will look at all the facts of the given situation in making a decision.

The badges of trade (i.e. factors to consider) are as follows:

(1) The subject matter of the transaction and the motive at the time of purchase
(2) The reason for the disposal
(3) The length of ownership
(4) The frequency of transactions
(5) Altering the asset before resale
(6) Other general circumstances.

The subject matter of the transaction and the motive at the time of purchase

The intentions of the individual at the time of purchase are important. It is considered that there are only three reasons for the purchase of an asset:

- for personal use
- as a long-term investment, to sell ultimately at a gain and possibly produce income during ownership (e.g. investment property, shares, paintings)
- for resale at a profit.

Only the last of these three reasons suggests that a trading activity exists.

However, there must be a profit motive **at the time the asset is acquired** to suggest that an individual is trading. The asset must be acquired with the intention of selling it at a profit at a later date.

Acquiring an asset as a gift or by inheritance from a relative suggests that any profit made on the sale does not constitute a trading transaction.

The reason for the disposal

The motive behind the disposal is also considered.

If the individual is forced to sell the asset in order to raise funds and alleviate personal financial problems, the transaction is unlikely to be treated as a trading transaction. However, if the sale is not a forced sale, it is more likely to be considered part of a trading activity.

The length of ownership

In general, the shorter the length of the period of ownership before disposal, the more likely that HMRC will consider the transaction to be in the nature of a trading activity.

The frequency of transactions

Similarly, the more frequent the number of similar transactions, the more likely the transactions will constitute a trading activity.

Altering the asset before resale

If an individual purchases an asset and then alters the asset in some way, HMRC is likely to treat the profit on disposal as a trading profit.

Therefore, any manufacturing process or repairs that enhance the value of the asset, or simply repackaging an asset to increase its attractiveness in the market place, will signify a trading activity.

Other general circumstances

Other circumstances suggesting that a trading activity exists include evidence of the setting up of a business vehicle, advertising expenditure to promote the business, registering for VAT, and printing business stationery.

If an individual raises finance to purchase and/or process the asset before resale, the raising of finance also suggests that a trading activity exists.

The extent to which the individual relies on the profit as a source of income is also a factor to consider.

1.3 The principles of assessing trading income

Once it has been established that a trade is being carried on, any profits arising from trading are assessed under the trading income rules. This chapter considers the trading income rules that apply to unincorporated businesses.

An unincorporated business is a business owned and managed by an individual (i.e. a sole trader) or by two or more individuals operating in partnership.

The trading income assessment for an individual with an unincorporated business is based on the financial accounting results of the business.

The net profit in the financial accounts must be adjusted for taxation purposes because the treatment of some items for tax purposes differs from accepted accounting practice:

- Some items of expenditure in the financial accounts cannot be deducted as an expense in calculating the taxable profit.

- Some items of expenditure are allowable for taxation purposes, but the amount of expenditure that is allowable must be calculated under special tax rules rather than by following accounting rules. An important example is the calculation of how much capital expenditure is allowable for tax purposes. Under the tax rules, capital allowances are calculated. The amount of these capital allowances is different from the depreciation charges in the financial accounts.

Overview of the trading income assessment for an unincorporated business

- Calculation of the trading income assessment for income tax
- Proforma trading income computation

2 Overview of the trading income assessment for an unincorporated business

2.1 Calculation of the trading income assessment for income tax

There are three key steps in the calculation of a trading income assessment for a sole trader:

Step 1: Prepare an adjustment of profit computation

The first step is to prepare a computation adjusting the net profit of the business (as shown in the financial accounts) in order to calculate the adjusted trading profit before capital allowances for tax purposes. These rules are explained in this chapter.

Step 2: Calculate the capital allowances available

The next step is to calculate the capital allowances available for plant and machinery and/or structures and buildings. These rules are explained in the next chapter.

Step 3: Calculate the trading income assessment for the correct tax year

The last step is to apply special basis of assessment rules to the figure of adjusted profit after capital allowances, in order to decide in which tax year the profits will be taxed. These rules are explained in a later chapter.

2.2 Proforma trading income computation

A proforma for the computation of trading income is shown below.

	£
Net profit in the accounts	X
Add/Deduct: Required adjustments of profit (**Step 1**)	X/(X)
Adjusted profits before capital allowances	X
Minus Capital allowances (**Step 2**)	
Plant and machinery	(X)
Structures and buildings	(X)
Adjusted profit after capital allowances	X

> **The adjustment of profit computation**
>
> - Preparing an adjustment of profit computation
> - Basic adjustment of profit computation
> - The principles of allowable expenditure
> - The wholly and exclusively test
> - Private use by the owner
> - Appropriations of profit by the owner of the business

3 The adjustment of profit computation

3.1 Preparing an adjustment of profit computation

There are two key steps for calculating the adjusted profit figure.

Step 1: Review the expenditure charged in the financial accounts

The first step is to review the items of expenditure charged in the financial accounts, in order to identify the items that are not allowable for tax purposes under the trading income rules. These items of expenditure are often referred to as disallowable expenditure and must be added back to the net profit as shown in the financial accounts.

Step 2: Review the amounts credited to the financial accounts

The second step is to review the amounts credited to the financial accounts to identify any items that are not assessable as **trading** income. These amounts are deducted from the net profit to leave only the profits that relate to the trading business.

3.2 Basic adjustment of profit computation

A proforma for calculating the adjusted profits figure is shown below.

		£
Net profit in the accounts		X
Add	Items of expenditure charged in the accounts that are not allowable for tax under the trading income rules	X
Add	Trading income not recorded in the accounts	X
Minus	Amounts credited in the accounts that are not taxable as trading income	(X)
Minus	Amounts not charged in the accounts that are allowable for trading income purposes	(X)
Adjusted profits before capital allowances		X

3.3 The principles of allowable expenditure

In order to be an allowable expense for tax purposes, the expenditure:

- must be revenue expenditure (not capital expenditure), and
- must be incurred **wholly and exclusively for the purposes of the trade**, and
- must not be specifically disallowed by statute law.

Most items charged as expenses in the accounts satisfy this rule and are allowable expenditure, therefore no adjustment is required.

3.4 The wholly and exclusively test

The wholly and exclusively test requires that an item of expenditure, to be tax-allowable, must be:

- incurred for the purposes of the trade and
- incurred wholly and exclusively for trading purposes.

For example, the cost of sales, and the normal direct production and distribution costs of a business are incurred wholly and exclusively for the purposes of the trade.

3.5 Private use by the owner

The requirement for expenditure to be for the purposes of the trade means that any expenditure that is far removed (remote) from the purposes of the trade is not allowable. This principle is often referred to as the **remoteness test**.

Accordingly, when a business pays for personal expenditure of the owner that is not related to the trade, the expenditure is not allowable. For example, the personal income tax liability and national insurance contributions of the owner are not allowable. If the business pays for these items, they must be added back to the profit in the adjustment of profit computation.

If expenditure is not incurred **wholly and exclusively** for trade purposes it is also not allowable. Therefore, where a business incurs expenditure that is partly for business and partly for the private purposes of the owner:

- the expenditure is not incurred wholly and exclusively for the purposes of the trade and so
- is not allowable.

Examples of expenditure not incurred wholly and exclusively for the purposes of the trade include:

- expenses incurred in running the owner's car, when the car is used partly for business and partly for private mileage, and
- expenditure on telephones used partly for business and partly for private calls.

In theory, all this type of expenditure should be disallowed because the expenditure has a dual purpose (business use and private use). However, HMRC will allow an **apportionment** of the associated costs, provided that there is an identifiable part of the expense which is incurred wholly and exclusively for the trade.

The appropriate percentage of the associated costs of providing an asset with an element of private use **by the owner** must therefore be adjusted for (i.e. added to profit) in the adjustment of profit computation.

Note that adjustments are only made for private use **by the owner**. The private use of assets **by employees** is irrelevant and is ignored in the adjustment of profit computation. This is because the expenditure is incurred wholly and exclusively for the purposes of the trade from the business point of view.

All the costs associated with providing assets for both business and private use **by employees** are allowable for trading income purposes. The individual employee is assessed to income tax on the private use under the employment income rules.

3.6 Appropriations of profit by the owner of the business

Any amounts taken out of the business by a sole trader or by a partner in a partnership are known as appropriations of profit. They include drawings, salary or wages for the owner or partner, and interest on capital introduced to the business.

The owner of an unincorporated business is liable to income tax on **all** the tax-adjusted profits of the trade, not just on the amount he chooses to draw from the business.

Accordingly, any appropriations of profit are not allowable deductions for income tax purposes. Since they are not allowable, they must be added back to profit in the adjustment of profit computation.

This rule applies **only** to appropriations of profit **by the owner**.

Where the business employs the spouse or a child of the owner, the normal costs of employment of the spouse or child (for example, gross wages or salary, employee's and employer's national insurance contributions, and the employer's contributions into the employee's pension scheme) are allowable deductions for the business, **provided that they are reasonable** in relation to the services provided to the business.

> **Disallowable expenditure**
>
> - Items specifically disallowed or specifically allowed for tax purposes
> - Capital expenditure versus revenue expenditure
> - Provisions and allowances against asset values
> - Donations and subscriptions
> - Interest and royalties
> - Legal and professional fees
> - Leasing costs
> - Gifts
> - Entertaining expenses
> - Fines and penalties
> - Employee-related costs
> - Trading income not recorded in the accounts

4 Disallowable expenditure

4.1 Items specifically disallowed or specifically allowed for tax purposes

There are some items of business expenditure that are specifically disallowable for tax under the trading income rules. There are other expenses which are specifically allowable. The main examples are explained here.

If an item of expenditure does not fall into one of the categories explained here, you should apply the general principles of revenue expenditure or capital expenditure and then apply the wholly and exclusively test to make a decision about whether the expenditure should be allowable or not.

4.2 Capital expenditure versus revenue expenditure

In the financial accounts, the cost of purchasing non-current assets is usually taken to the balance sheet, and depreciation is charged against the profit for the period.

However, if the cost is not significant the purchase may be charged in full against profit. In addition, the costs of repairs and maintenance of non-current assets are usually charged against profit.

Any capital purchase, or other capital-related expenditure, that is charged against profit is disallowed in the adjustment of profit computation. The amount of the expense must be adjusted for by adding it back to profit. This is because the trading income rules only allow revenue expenditure to be charged against profit for tax purposes.

Capital expenditure

Capital expenditure is expenditure incurred on an asset which provides an enduring benefit to the business and, as a result of the expenditure, there is an element of improvement or enhancement in the value of the asset.

Capital expenditure therefore includes:

- the cost of purchasing non-current assets, and the cost of improvements, enhancements, extensions, etc
- incidental costs, including legal and professional fees, relating to the purchase, improvement, etc of a non-current asset
- **depreciation** and other equivalent write off of capital cost against profit (e.g. amortisation of leases)
- losses on the disposal of non-current assets.

Since they are capital expenditure, all these items are not allowable and must be added back to profit in the adjustment of profit computation.

(**Note**: For many businesses, **depreciation** is a major expense in the financial accounts. Depreciation and amortisation are capital-related expenses and are not allowable, so they must be added back to profit. However, there are **capital allowances** on items of capital expenditure for trading purposes. Capital allowances can be thought of as tax-allowable depreciation.)

Revenue expenditure

Revenue expenditure is expenditure incurred in running the business, maintaining the value of the assets or returning an asset to its original condition. Revenue expenditure is an allowable cost for trading income purposes.

Revenue expenditure therefore includes:

- repair costs
- maintenance costs
- re-decoration, re-plastering costs, etc.

However, if a business purchases an asset in such a condition that it is not usable and the purchase price reflects the poor condition of the asset, any expenditure incurred in bringing the asset into use in the business should be treated as capital-related expenditure and the expense will be disallowed.

4.3 Provisions and allowances against asset values

In the financial accounts, in accordance with generally accepted accounting principles (e.g. International Accounting Standards (IAS) and International Financial Reporting Standards (IFRS)), a business may reflect in the profit figure the movement in provisions or allowances made against the value of assets at the end of the period. For example, there may be provisions in the financial accounts against inventory values or allowances against amounts owed by customers.

If accounted for in accordance with generally accepted accounting principles, the movement in the provision or allowance in the financial accounts is **allowable** for trading income purposes.

Similarly, provisions for future costs are allowable against trading income provided the provision can be estimated accurately and is accounted for in accordance with generally accepted accounting principles.

Normal trade debts that are written off or recovered, and which are reflected in the accounts, do not need to be adjusted for. This is because they are items wholly and exclusively relating to the purposes of the trade.

However, the write off of **non-trade** debts such as a loan to a customer, supplier or an employee, must be adjusted for by adding back to the net profit.

4.4 Donations and subscriptions

Subscriptions to professional and trade associations (for example, subscriptions to ACCA and the Chamber of Commerce) **are allowable** against trading income provided they are incurred wholly and exclusively for the purposes of the trade. Therefore, no adjustment is required to the profit figure.

However, **donations** are **usually not allowable** against trading income. They must be added back to the profit, with the exception of small donations to local charities.

In summary:

- **small** donations to **local** charities are, by concession, usually allowable
- **any political** donation or subscription is not allowable
- **any** donation to a **national charity** is not allowable, and
- **any** donation made under the **Gift Aid scheme**, regardless of size, is not allowable under the trading income rules.

4.5 Interest and royalties

Interest payable in respect of loans for trading purposes (e.g. bank overdraft interest, hire purchase interest and loan interest) is allowable against trading income. Therefore, no adjustment is required.

Interest payable on underpaid tax is not allowable for income tax purposes and must therefore be added back.

In the examination, all royalties payable and receivable, such as patent royalties and copyright royalties, will be treated as trading expenditure or trading receipts. Therefore, no adjustment for royalties is required.

In addition, although they are of a capital nature, any costs incurred in relation to the registration of a patent or copyright for the purposes of the trade are specifically allowable.

4.6 Legal and professional fees

Legal and professional fees relating to capital expenditure are, in principle, not allowable against trading income.

However, legal and professional fees relating to revenue expenditure are allowable. These include legal and professional fees incurred in relation to:

- the collection of debts
- employment issues
- claims for breach of contract (including damages paid, if any, provided the court action relates to the trade and it is not proven that the business had broken the law)
- preparing and auditing the financial accounts and normal tax compliance work.

Costs in relation to **tax planning advice** and appealing against assessments and investigations are **not tax allowable**. However, the additional accountancy costs arising from an HMRC investigation are allowable provided the investigation does not result in additional tax, interest or penalties.

Legal and professional costs **relating to leases** are capital in nature and therefore not allowable. Thus, the costs associated with the setting up of a new lease, regardless of the length of the lease, would need to be added back in the adjustment of profit computation.

However, tax rules specifically allow against trading income any legal costs in relation to the **renewal** of a **short** lease (i.e. a lease with a life of ≤50 years remaining).

4.7 Leasing costs

If a business hires, rents or leases capital assets such as plant and machinery, the associated costs are allowable for trading income purposes, as they have been incurred wholly and exclusively for the purposes of the trade.

However, 15% of the leasing cost relating to a car with CO_2 emissions of more than 50 g/km is specifically disallowed for trading income purposes.

Example

Queenie leased a car for a rental cost of £6,600 per annum.

Required

Calculate the amount to add back to profit in the adjustment of profit computation assuming:

(a) The car has CO_2 emissions of 60 g/km

(b) The car has CO_2 emissions of 40 g/km.

Answer

(a) £6,600 x 15% = £990 will be disallowed.

(b) As CO_2 emissions are less than 50 g/km, none of the leasing cost will be disallowed.

4.8 Gifts

The treatment of gifts in an adjustment of profit computation depends on the recipient of the gift and nature of the gift.

Special rules apply as follows:

- Gifts to customers are not allowable for trading income purposes unless they carry a conspicuous advertisement for the business and the total cost per recipient does not exceed £50.
- Gifts of food, drink, tobacco or vouchers exchangeable for goods are not allowable under any circumstances, whatever the cost, with or without an advertisement.
- Gifts to employees are allowable for trading income purposes for the business (but the employee may be taxed on the receipt of a benefit from employment).

4.9 Entertaining expenses

Expenses incurred in **entertaining existing or potential customers or suppliers** are **not allowable** against trading income and therefore need to be added back in the adjustment of profit computation.

However, expenses incurred in **entertaining staff** are **allowable**, provided the entertainment is only for staff and the cost is not part of the cost of entertaining others (who are not staff).

4.10 Fines and penalties

Any costs associated with breaking the law, such as fines and penalties, are not allowable for tax purposes and therefore need to be added back to the net profit. However, parking fines incurred by an employee (but not the proprietor) while on a business activity are, by concession, allowable against trading income.

4.11 Employee-related costs

The gross salaries of employees and other employee-related costs are allowable as they are incurred wholly and exclusively for the purpose of the trade. Other employee-related costs include expenditure such as:

- the costs of providing benefits such as cars, accommodation, removal expenses, etc
- employer's national insurance contributions
- employer's pension contributions
- compensation for loss of office and redundancy pay

- counselling services provided for redundant employees, etc.

The business can claim **all** these employee-related costs **in full** as tax-allowable expenditure, even if the employee enjoys the benefit of private use of assets (for example, using a company car for both business and private mileage or a laptop for both business and personal use).

Since these employee-related costs will have been deducted in full in arriving at the figure of net profit, no adjustment will be required. However, the individual employee may be personally assessed to income tax for the element of private use.

If earnings have been charged in the accounts but have not been paid within nine months of the end of the period of account, the earnings are only deductible when actually paid.

4.12 Trading income not recorded in the accounts

Most sources of trading income are correctly reflected in the financial statements of the unincorporated business.

However, where the owner takes inventory out of the business for personal use or for use by family or friends, the treatment in the accounts must be considered. The transaction may not have been processed through the accounts at all, or may have been accounted for only at cost.

In both of these circumstances, an adjustment of profit is required because the tax rules state that the owner must be taxed on the profit of the transaction **as if** the goods had been sold to a third party at full market value.

- If not recorded in the accounts, the full market value of the goods must be added to profit.
- If recorded in the accounts but accounted for at cost, the gross profit that would have been made on the transaction must be added to profit.

This rule does not apply to the supply of services from the business to the owner.

> **Specifically allowable expenditure**
>
> - Specific allowable items
> - Pre-trading expenditure
> - Short leases on a property
> - Expenditure paid personally by the owner and not recorded in the accounts

5 Specifically allowable expenditure

5.1 Specific allowable items

Many items of expenditure which are **specifically allowed** against trading profits have already been mentioned in the explanations of specifically disallowable items.

There are, however, two other types of specific allowances available against trading profits which have not yet been mentioned in detail. These relate to:

- pre-trading expenditure, and
- short leases.

5.2 Pre-trading expenditure

Expenditure incurred prior to the business's first day of trading is, in principle, not incurred *wholly and exclusively for the purposes of the trade*, as a trade does not exist at that time.

However, tax law specifically permits pre-trading expenditure to be allowable under the trading income rules, and treated as if incurred on the first day of trading, provided the expenditure:

- was incurred within the seven years prior to the first day of trading, and
- would be allowable expenditure if incurred after the first day of trading.

5.3 Short leases on a property

Where a landlord grants a short lease on a property and receives a premium, this is treated for tax purposes partly as property income of the landlord and partly as a capital receipt.

The tenant who is granted the lease pays the premium to the landlord and in addition is usually required to pay rent on a monthly or quarterly basis.

If the tenant uses the property for the purposes of a trade, in the financial accounts the lease will be treated as follows:

- The premium is shown in the balance sheet as the cost of the lease.

- The premium is written off over the life of the lease against profit in each accounting period (i.e. depreciation of the premium is charged against profit, and is referred to as amortisation of lease in the accounts).
- Any rent payable is charged against profit for the period.

In the tenant's adjustment of profit computation, the following treatment must be applied:

- The rent payable is allowable for trading income purposes as wholly and exclusively incurred; therefore, no adjustment is required for the rent.
- The amortisation of the lease is capital-related and therefore is not allowable; it must be added back to profit.
- A specific allowable deduction is available against trading profit instead of the amortisation charge.

The **annual allowable deduction** is the landlord's property income assessment in respect of the premium received spread over the length of the lease. It is calculated as follows:

	£
Premium paid to landlord	X
Minus 2% × premium × (n – 1)	(X)
Property income assessment on the landlord (re the premium only)	A
Annual allowable deduction against profit for the tenant = (A ÷ n)	X
where: n = number of years of the lease	

The allowable deduction against profit is sometimes called **notional rent**.

If the tenant obtained the lease part-way through their accounting period, the notional rent must be time-apportioned according to the number of months the lease was held by the tenant in the accounting period.

Example

Rupert owns a property which he decided to lease on 1 January 2023. He granted a 25-year lease to Susan for a premium of £98,000 and quarterly rent of £6,800 payable in advance starting on 1 January 2023.

Susan prepares her accounts to 30 June each year. She has capitalised the lease on her balance sheet and, in addition to the rent payable, she has charged amortisation of £1,960 against her profit for the year ended 30 June 2023.

Required

Calculate the adjustments Susan needs to make to her profit for the year ended 30 June 2023 for trading income purposes.

Answer

Adjustment of profit – Susan: year ended 30 June 2023

Add back	Amortisation charge	£1,960
Deduct	Allowable deduction (see working below)	£1,019

No adjustment is required in respect of the rent payable because:

- it has been charged against the profit, and
- it is tax allowable since it is incurred wholly and exclusively for the purposes of the trade.

Property income assessment for Rupert in 2022/23:

	£
Premium paid to Rupert	98,000
Minus 2% × £98,000 × 24	(47,040)
Property income assessment re lease	50,960

Allowable deduction for lease for Susan in year ended 30 June 2023:

	£
Annual allowable deduction against profit (£50,960 ÷ 25 years)	2,038
Allowable deduction for year ended 30 June 2023: £2,038 ÷ 6/12 (leased for 6 months of Susan's accounting period)	1,019

5.4 Expenditure paid personally by the owner and not recorded in the accounts

If an owner incurs a business expense and pays for it personally, the expense is still allowable for income tax purposes (provided it complies with the normal rules for allowable expenses). The expense can therefore be deducted in the adjustment of profit computation.

A common example occurs where a sole trader uses a room in his home as an office for business purposes. The business proportion of expenses incurred in heating and lighting the room and a proportion of telephone calls etc is allowable expenditure, even if paid for personally by the sole trader.

> **Amounts credited in the accounts that are not taxable as trading income**
> - Income taxed under other assessment rules
> - Exempt income
> - Capital profits

6 Amounts credited in the accounts that are not taxable as trading income

6.1 Income taxed under other assessment rules

In the adjustment of profit computation, the aim is to adjust the figure of net profit recorded in the financial accounts and to identify the profit arising from the trading activities of the business.

The figure of net profit in the accounts may include income receivable from non-trading sources. It is therefore necessary to deduct any income credited in the accounts that is not assessable as trading income. This includes items such as:

- interest income
- dividend income
- UK property income
- foreign income.

This income is then included separately in the individual's income tax computation, applying the assessment rules for that source of income.

6.2 Exempt income

The net profit figure may also include income receivable that is exempt from income tax. This must be deducted in the adjustment of profit computation.

The main types of exempt income which could appear in the accounts of an unincorporated business are:

- competition prizes, national lottery and premium bond prizes, betting winnings
- income from ISAs (Individual Savings Accounts)
- repayment interest in respect of overpaid tax.

6.3 Capital profits

Capital profits on the disposal of assets also need to be deducted in the adjustment of profit computation, as these profits are not taxed as trading income. Capital profits are either liable to capital gains tax or not taxable at all.

Chapter 5: Computing trading income

> **Proforma adjustment of profit computation**
>
> - Detailed proforma adjustment of profit computation

7 Proforma adjustment of profit computation

7.1 Detailed proforma adjustment of profit computation

The proforma below sets out some of the adjustments that may be required to calculate the figure of adjusted trading profit.

(W1) Proforma computation: Adjustment of profit	£
Net profit as shown in the accounts	X
Add Items of expenditure charged in the accounts that are not allowable for tax under the trading income rules	
Capital expenditure (may be eligible for capital allowances)	X
Legal or professional fees relating to capital expenditure (including leases, except fees relating to the renewal of a short lease)	X
Depreciation/amortisation charges for non-current assets	X
Loss on the disposal of a non-current asset	X
Non-trade debt written off	X
Political donations and subscriptions	X
Charitable donations under Gift Aid	X
Appropriations of profit by the owner	X
Private expenditure by the owner	X
Goods taken out of the business by the owner	X
Professional fees in relation to tax advice	X
Disallowable portion of lease rental on car with CO_2 emissions over 50 g/km	X
Gifts to customers (if > £50 and no advertisement, or if a gift of alcohol, food, tobacco, or vouchers exchangeable for goods)	X
Fines and penalties	X
Remuneration not paid within nine months of the end of the period of account	X
Entertaining expenses (except entertainment of employees)	X
	X
Minus Amounts credited in the accounts that are not taxable as trading income	
Income taxed under other assessment rules (e.g. income taxed as property income, interest income)	(X)
Exempt income (e.g. ISA interest, repayment interest)	(X)
Capital profits (may be assessed as a chargeable gain instead) (e.g. profit on the disposal of a non-current asset, profit on the sale of shares etc)	(X)
Minus Amounts not credited in the accounts that are allowable for trading income purposes	
Allowable deduction for short leases	(X)
Adjusted profits before capital allowances	X

Example

David runs a printing business. He produces accounts to 31 March each year. The net profit for the year ended 31 March 2023 is £82,200 after taking account of the following:

	Notes	£
Stationery	1	9,200
Salaries and wages	2	109,000
National insurance	3	5,400
Depreciation		14,800
Repairs and maintenance	4	7,400
Gas, electricity, water		5,800
Royalties payable	5	4,000
Motor vehicle expenses	6	17,925
Lease of car for an employee	7	4,300
Bank overdraft interest and charges		3,900
Sundry expenses	8	2,300
UK dividends received		2,700
Bank deposit interest received		4,800

Notes

(1) During the year David had some stationery specially designed and printed by the firm for his daughter's wedding. David did not reimburse the business, but the goods were taken out of inventory in the accounts at their cost of £300. If sold to a customer the stationery would have been invoiced at £450.

(2) Salaries and wages comprised:

	£
Staff wages (including £8,500 salary to David's wife, who is employed as a part-time administrator)	66,250
Salary to David	40,000
Staff Christmas party	450
Agency fees for hiring of temps	2,300
	109,000

(3) National insurance includes Class 2 NICs of David at £164. The remainder of this expense relates to the employer's NI contributions on staff salaries.

(4) Repairs and maintenance include £3,100 relating to the repair of the office roof following a violent storm and £2,000 relating to alterations needed for the installation of a new printing press.

(5) Royalties of £4,000 were paid on 28 February 2023 to another printing firm for the use of a logo on a customer's product.

(6) Motor expenses consist of the following:

	£
Running costs of staff cars	9,105
Running costs of David's car	8,320
Loss on the sale of a car	500
	17,925

Chapter 5: Computing trading income

David's annual mileage was as follows:	Miles
Home to work	3,500
Visits to customers and suppliers	4,500
Private journeys	12,000
	20,000

(7) The leased car has a retail price of £24,000 and CO_2 emissions of 75 g/km. The employee uses the car 30% for business purposes.

(8) Sundry expenses include £145 paid to a charity under the Gift Aid scheme and a £20 donation to the local church appeal.

Required

Calculate David's adjusted profit before capital allowances for the year ended 31 March 2023. Your answer should list all of the items referred to in notes (1) to (8), indicating by the use of zero (0) any items which do not require adjustment.

Answer

David – year ended 31 March 2023	Notes	£
Net profit		82,200
Add Goods taken for own use		
– profit on wedding stationery (£450 – £300)		150
Depreciation		14,800
Staff wages	1	0
Salary to David	1	40,000
Staff Christmas party		0
Agency fees		0
Class 2 NICs of David	1	164
Repair of office roof		0
Alterations relating to the installation of the press	2	2,000
Royalties	3	0
Running costs of staff cars		0
Motor expenses (15,500/20,000 × £8,320)	4	6,448
Loss on the sale of car		500
Disallowable portion of lease charge on employee's car	5	645
Gift Aid donation	6	145
Donation to local church	7	0
		147,052
Minus Dividends received		(2,700)
Bank deposit interest received		(4,800)
Adjusted profits before capital allowances		139,552

Notes

The examiner will normally just ask you to 'calculate' the adjusted profit therefore there is no need to explain the reasons for your adjustments. The explanations shown here are to help you to understand the answer. Do not waste time in the examination giving explanations that have not been required.

(1) The wages paid to David's wife will probably be allowed as they appear to be reasonable remuneration for the services provided to the business. However, David's salary and his personal national insurance contributions are not allowable.

(2) The installation costs relating to the new printing press are capital-related and are not allowable. However, capital allowances will be available on the cost of the new printing press, including the installation costs.

(3) No adjustment is needed in respect of the royalties as they are regarded as a trading expense.

(4) Ordinary commuting from home to work is deemed to be private mileage therefore David's total private mileage is 15,500 out of his total annual mileage of 20,000.

(5) As the leased car has CO_2 emissions of more than 50g/km, 15% of the leasing cost is disallowed. The disallowable portion is £4,300 x 15% = £645.

(6) The Gift Aid donation is not allowable as a trading expense. The amount charged in the accounts must be added to profit. If a basic rate taxpayer, no further adjustment is required as basic rate tax relief will automatically be obtained in paying the donation net of 20% tax. If a higher rate taxpayer, the higher rate relief is obtained by extending the basic rate band by the gross amount of the Gift Aid donation.

(7) The gift to the local church appeal will be allowable as a small donation to a local charity.

Taxation – United Kingdom
(TX-UK) FA2022

CHAPTER 6

Capital allowances

	Contents
1	An overview of capital allowances
2	The definition of plant and machinery
3	The system of capital allowances for plant and machinery
4	The main pool
5	The special rate pool
6	Cars
7	Short life assets
8	Capital allowances for unincorporated businesses
9	Structures and buildings allowance

> **An overview of capital allowances**
> - The primary aim of capital allowances
> - The types of capital allowance available

1 An overview of capital allowances

1.1 The primary aim of capital allowances

Capital purchases and other capital-related expenditure, such as depreciation charges and legal fees incurred in making purchases of capital items, are not allowable deductions in the adjustment of profit computation. However, businesses may be able to claim capital allowances instead. Capital allowances can be thought of as tax depreciation allowances.

The depreciation charges in the financial accounts are calculated on a subjective basis. Depreciation charges are therefore not allowed as a deduction in calculating trading income. Instead, tax relief is given for the purchase cost of certain non-current assets and subsequent capital expenditure (such as extensions and improvements) using a standardised set of rules for capital allowances.

The primary aim of the capital allowance rules is to give tax relief for the **net cost** of non-current assets by means of deductions from the adjusted profits figure over one or more accounting periods.

The **net cost** of a non-current asset means the actual cost of using the asset in the business over its useful life, after taking account of any sale proceeds received. In other words, net cost is the original cost less any eventual sale/disposal proceeds.

(If a business is VAT-registered and can reclaim VAT on its purchases, the cost and sale proceeds for capital allowances purposes will be net of VAT. However, if the business is not VAT-registered or if the VAT is irrecoverable (for example, on cars) the cost and sale proceeds will include VAT. For exam purposes, you should ignore VAT unless the question specifically mentions it.)

Capital allowances are calculated for each chargeable period separately and deducted in the calculation of the trading income assessment.

1.2 The types of capital allowance available

For the purposes of the examination, the only relevant rules for capital allowances are those that apply to:

- plant and machinery and
- structures and buildings allowance.

> **The definition of plant and machinery**
> - The source of the definition of plant and machinery
> - Case law

2 The definition of plant and machinery

2.1 The source of the definition of plant and machinery

Tax legislation does not provide a comprehensive definition of plant and machinery.

Case law provides some guidance on items which have been held to be plant and machinery in the courts in the past, and some of these decisions have been brought into the tax legislation.

Statute law contains lists of some items of expenditure which are to be classified as plant and machinery and others which are specifically not to be classified as plant and machinery. However, statute law does not provide a formal all-inclusive definition of plant and machinery.

Deciding whether or not an item is plant and machinery is important because, in some cases, if an item is not deemed to be plant and machinery, there may be no allowances available.

2.2 Case law

From case law a key test, known as the functional test, has been applied to decide whether or not an item is to be treated as plant and machinery.

The functional test looks at the role the asset plays in the business as follows:

- If the asset is apparatus **with which** the business is carried on (i.e. the asset performs an active function and is used in the trade), it should be treated as plant and machinery

- If the asset is the setting **in which** the business is carried on, the asset performs a passive function in the business and should not be treated as plant and machinery.

Applying this functional test, it should be clear that plant and machinery includes the typical non-current assets used by a business such as motor vehicles, machines, computers, office furniture, equipment, fixtures and fittings, and so on. It also includes assets creating an atmosphere for the public appropriate to the business (such as pictures and artefacts in a hotel or restaurant).

> **The system of capital allowances for plant and machinery**
>
> - The different categories of plant and machinery
> - Allowances available for plant and machinery
> - Preparation of a capital allowances computation
> - Proforma capital allowances computation

3 The system of capital allowances for plant and machinery

3.1 The different categories of plant and machinery

For the purpose of capital allowances, plant and machinery must be grouped into different categories. This is because different rates of allowances are available for different types of asset.

All items of plant and machinery are included in the **main pool unless** they are:

- Short life assets = plant and machinery, other than cars, with a useful life of **less than** 8 years and for which an election has been made
- Private use assets = assets with an element of private use by the proprietor
- Integral features, long life assets, thermal insulation and cars with CO_2 emissions of more than 50 g/km. These go into the special rate pool.

3.2 Allowances available for plant and machinery

The types of capital allowances available are as follows:

- **Annual investment allowance**: this is available in the chargeable period in which an asset is purchased
- **Writing down allowances**: these are available in every chargeable period
- **First year allowances**: these are given in respect of certain types of expenditure in the chargeable period in which it is incurred
- **Balancing allowances and charges**: these are only applicable on the eventual disposal of an asset.

The rules for each allowance are explained in detail later in this chapter.

This text uses the following abbreviations:

- AIA = annual investment allowance
- WDA = writing down allowance
- FYA = first year allowance
- BA = balancing allowance
- BC = balancing charge

- TWDV = tax written down value: this represents the cost of the assets less the capital allowances claimed on them so far. It is their written down value for tax purposes.

3.3 Preparation of a capital allowances computation

There are seven key steps in preparing a computation of capital allowances. To ensure that the rules for capital allowances are applied correctly, it is important to follow these steps in the strict order shown below, and to set out the computations for capital allowances using the proforma that is given here.

Step 1: Review additions to non-current assets in the accounting period

Decide whether the purchased asset is plant and machinery and therefore eligible for capital allowances. Then decide the appropriate category of the asset and therefore to which column the addition should be allocated.

If the asset does not qualify for the AIA or FYA, add the cost of the asset to the tax written down value brought forward from the previous period (TWDV b/f) in the appropriate column of the proforma.

The TWDV b/f, if applicable, will be given in the examination question.

Step 2: Bring in additions that qualify for the AIA and calculate the AIA available

The cost of assets qualifying for the AIA should be entered as an addition in the appropriate column, and the AIA entered as a deduction.

Step 3: Deal with disposals of plant and machinery in the chargeable period

Capital allowances are given on the **net cost** of an asset. Therefore, when an asset has been disposed of, the sale proceeds are deducted from the TWDV. This deduction should be entered in the appropriate column of the proforma.

There are two exceptions to this rule:

- If the asset was sold for more than its original cost, deduct the original cost instead of the sale proceeds. (Never take out from a column more than the amount that was originally put in.)
- If the asset was given away (gifted) or sold for less than it was worth, the amount of the deduction is the lower of:
  - the full market value on the disposal date, and
  - the original cost.

When a building is sold, the vendor and purchaser make a joint election to determine how much of the sale proceeds is to be allocated to any fixtures included within the building. However, the amount allocated to the fixtures cannot exceed their original cost.

Step 4: Calculate balancing allowances (BAs) and balancing charges (BCs)

Next, the balancing allowances and balancing charges should be calculated and entered in the appropriate column of the proforma. The calculation of BAs and BCs is explained later.

Step 5: Calculate the writing down allowances (WDAs) available

Next, the writing down allowances should be calculated, and entered (as a deduction) in the appropriate column of the proforma. The calculation of WDAs is explained later.

Step 6: Bring in additions that qualify for FYAs and calculate the FYAs available

Enter the qualifying cost as an addition to the main pool and enter the FYA as a deduction.

Step 7: Calculate the total capital allowances for the period

There is a column in the proforma for capital allowances for the period. The amount of balancing allowances and balancing charges, WDAs, FYAs and the AIA are recorded in this column. The capital allowances available for the period should be totalled. (Total = BAs + WDAs + FYAs + AIA − BCs). This total should then be deducted from the adjusted profits before capital allowances to calculate the trading income assessment.

The TWDV is then calculated for each column and carried forward to the next period.

Study the proforma carefully. It may seem complicated initially. You should keep returning to the proforma as you learn more about calculating capital allowances.

3.4 Proforma capital allowances computation

Note: This proforma is the same as for corporation tax, except for the private use assets which are specific to income tax

	Main pool	Special rate pool	Short life assets A	Short life assets B	Private use assets C	Private use assets D	Total allowances
	£	£	£	£	£	£	£
TWDV b/f	X	X	X	X	X		
Acquisitions qualifying for AIA:							
Additions X							
AIA (X)	X						X
Acquisitions *not* qualifying for AIA:							
Car used privately					X		
Cars (depending on CO$_2$ emissions)	X	X					
	X	X	X	X	X		
Disposals: Lower of (i) sale proceeds, or (ii) original cost	(X)	(X)	(X)		(X)		
	X	X	X	X	X		
Balancing charge			(X)		(X)		
Balancing allowance			Nil	X	Nil	X	× Bus % (X) X
WDA (scale up or down re-the length of the chargeable period)							
18%	(X)			(X)	(X)		X
6%		(X)					X × Bus %
	X	X		X		X	
Acquisitions qualifying for FYA							
Additions X							
FYA (100%) (X)	–						X
TWDV c/f	X	X	X	X		X	
Total capital allowances							XX

> **The main pool**
>
> - The calculation of the AIA on main pool items
> - The calculation of WDAs on main pool items
> - Balancing allowances and balancing charges
> - Successions
> - Small pools

4 The main pool

4.1 The calculation of the AIA on main pool items

The annual investment allowance (AIA) gives 100% relief for the first £1,000,000 of capital expenditure on plant and machinery, **excluding cars,** in a chargeable period.

A chargeable period is:

- an accounting period for corporation tax purposes
- a period of account for income tax purposes.

The AIA is given in the chargeable period in which the asset is purchased. The £1,000,000 limit is proportionally reduced or increased where a chargeable period is shorter or longer than 12 months. For example, the AIA for a nine-month chargeable period would be £750,000 (1,000,000 × 9/12) and for a 15-month period would be £1,250,000 (1,000,000 × 15/12).

Any expenditure in excess of the £1,000,000 limit will qualify **immediately** for writing-down allowances (WDA).

If the full AIA is not used, the balance is lost. It cannot be carried forward or back.

Date of expenditure

As a general rule, capital expenditure is treated as incurred on the date on which the obligation to pay becomes unconditional. However, if payment is not due until four months or more after that date, the expenditure is treated as incurred on the date on which payment is due.

Pre-trading expenditure is generally treated as incurred on the date on which trade commences.

4.2 The calculation of WDAs on main pool items

WDAs are given in each chargeable period. They are calculated **after** bringing in additions (apart from additions qualifying for FYAs) and **after** taking account of asset disposals.

The rate of WDAs on main pool items is **18% for a 12-month chargeable period**, calculated on the balance in the pool.

The length of ownership of the asset in the chargeable period is irrelevant. However, for WDAs the length of the chargeable period is very important. If the chargeable period is less than 12 months, the WDA must be time-apportioned.

Example

Ulrika prepared her accounts for the three months ended 31 August 2022. In the period, she purchased the following items of plant and machinery:

		£
Purchases	Office furniture on 25 June 2022 – cost	100,000
	Factory equipment on 30 June 2022 – cost	175,000

On 1 June 2022 the tax written down value on the main pool was £75,000.

Required

Calculate the capital allowances available for the three months ended 31 August 2022.

Answer

Ulrika - Capital allowances for the three months ending 31 August 2022

		Main pool (TWDV)	Total allowances
	£	£	£
TWDV b/f		75,000	
Acquisitions qualifying for AIA			
Office furniture	100,000		
Factory equipment	175,000		
	275,000		
AIA (1,000,000 x 3/12)	(250,000)		250,000
		25,000	
		100,000	
Writing down allowance (WDA)			
(100,000 x 18% × 3/12)		(4,500)	4,500
TWDV c/f		95,500	
Total allowances available			254,500

4.3 Balancing allowances and balancing charges

A balancing allowance (BA) is the tax equivalent of a loss on disposal in the financial accounts. It will **increase** the capital allowances available in the chargeable period.

A balancing charge (BC) is the tax equivalent of a profit on disposal in the financial accounts. It is additional taxable trading profit and is usually recognised by **reducing** the capital allowances available in the chargeable period.

BAs and BCs are usually referred to collectively as **balancing adjustments**.

Where a main pool asset is disposed of, deduct the following disposal value from the pool:

> Disposal value =   Lower of:
> - Sale proceeds (or market value if gifted)
> - Original cost

(This is the application of Step 3, as explained earlier.)

Disposal value more than the balance in the pool

If the disposal value exceeds the balance on the pool, a balancing charge arises (i.e. a negative figure). A balancing charge means that allowances claimed in the past exceed the **net cost** of the asset. These excess allowances are clawed back in the year of disposal, by reducing the capital allowances in the year of disposal. A balancing charge is therefore a negative allowance.

A balancing charge can arise in any chargeable period. It reduces the capital allowances claim for that period.

Example

In the year ended 31 March 2023, Vera sold for £23,000 some plant and machinery which originally cost £26,000 on 31 January 2022.

The TWDV b/f on the main pool on 1 April 2022 was £18,000. Additions not qualifying for the AIA totalled £3,000, and those qualifying for the AIA totalled £25,000.

Required

Calculate the capital allowances available for the year ended 31 March 2023.

Chapter 6: Capital allowances

a Answer

Vera - Capital allowances – y/e 31 March 2023	£	Main pool £	Total allowances £
TWDV b/f		18,000	
Acquisitions not qualifying for AIA		3,000	
		21,000	
Acquisitions qualifying for AIA			
Cost	25,000		
AIA	(25,000)		25,000
		Nil	
Disposals - Lower of (i) sale proceeds, or (ii) original cost		(23,000)	
		(2,000)	
Balancing charge		2,000	(2,000)
		Nil	
Writing down allowance (WDA)		(Nil)	Nil
TWDV c/f		Nil	
Total allowances available			23,000

Disposal value less than the balance in the pool

If the disposal value is less than the balance on the pool, this means that allowances claimed in the past have been less than the **net cost** of the asset. The rest of the net cost can therefore be claimed as a capital allowance.

However, for the main pool assets, a balancing allowance does not arise at the time of the disposal. Instead, the shortfall in the allowances claimed for the asset will be claimed in the future by WDAs, in the normal way, on a reducing balance basis.

A BA **will only arise in the main pool in the period in which the business ceases to trade**, (i.e. the last chargeable period) when all the assets of the business are being disposed of. In this case, all the shortfall of allowances is claimed in the final period as a BA. This increases the capital allowances claim for the period.

e Example

William ceased trading on 31 December 2022 and produced a three-month final set of accounts. On 1 October 2022 the TWDV b/f on William's main pool was £64,000. There were no additions in the final three months of trading.

On cessation William sold his plant and machinery for scrap, and realised proceeds of £20,000.

Required

(a) Calculate the capital allowances available for the three month period to 31 December 2022.

(b) Show how your answer would differ had William continued to trade.

Answer

William - Capital allowances on cessation of trade – 3 months ending 31 December 2022	Main pool	Total allowances
	£	£
TWDV b/f	64,000	
Disposals - Lower of (i) sale proceeds, or (ii) original cost	(20,000)	
	44,000	
Balancing allowance	(44,000)	44,000
TWDV c/f	Nil	
Total allowances available		44,000

Note that no WDAs are given in the final period of trading.

William - Capital allowances if continuing to trade – 3 months ending 31 December 2022	Main pool	Total allowances
	£	£
TWDV b/f	64,000	
Disposals - Lower of (i) sale proceeds, or (ii) original cost	(20,000)	
	44,000	
WDA (44,000 x 18% x 3/12)	(1,980)	1,980
TWDV c/f	42,020	
Total allowances available		1,980

4.4 Successions

Where a trade passes from one connected person to another, balancing adjustments can be avoided by making a succession election. This election allows assets to be transferred to the purchaser at their TWDVs.

The election must be made within two years of the date the trade is transferred. If it is not made, the assets are deemed to be sold to the successor at their market values.

(The definition of a connected person is covered in chapter 14.)

4.5 Small pools

Where the balance of unrelieved expenditure in the main/special rate pool is less than £1,000, it can be written off immediately.

The £1,000 limit is reduced or increased proportionately if the chargeable period is less than or more than 12 months.

> **The special rate pool**
>
> - Introduction
> - Integral features
> - Long life assets
> - The AIA
> - WDAs in the special rate pool
> - Balancing adjustments

5 The special rate pool

5.1 Introduction

The special rate pool contains the following categories of asset:

- Features that are integral to a building
- Long life assets
- Thermal insulation of a building used for a qualifying activity (e.g. a trade)
- Cars with CO_2 emissions of more than 50 g/km.

5.2 Integral features

The following items are treated as being integral to a building:

- Electrical and lighting systems
- Cold water systems
- Space or water heating systems
- Powered systems of ventilation, cooling or air purification
- Lifts and escalators.

5.3 Long life assets

Long life assets are defined as plant (other than cars, ships, and plant and machinery used in shops, showrooms, offices and hotels) with:

- an expected working life of at least 25 years, and
- a total purchase cost of more than £100,000 in a 12-month period.

The expected working life relates to the capability of the plant and machinery, not just the expected useful life for the current owner.

The £100,000 limit is reduced (or increased) proportionately if the chargeable period is less than (or more than) 12 months, and is divided equally where a company has related 51% group companies (see chapter 24).

If the definition is satisfied, long life assets must be put into the special rate pool.

If the definition of a long life asset is not satisfied, the item of plant and machinery is treated as a normal main pool asset.

5.4 The AIA

The AIA **is** available on assets qualifying for inclusion in the special rate pool, with the exception of cars. This presents a business with a valuable tax planning opportunity.

If the business has incurred capital expenditure in excess of £1,000,000, the AIA should first be allocated to assets within the special rate pool as the rate of WDA for these assets is lower than that available for main pool items. (In other words, the business can allocate the AIA to whichever assets it chooses.)

5.5 WDAs in the special rate pool

The WDA in the special rate pool is calculated using the reducing balance method in the same way as for the main pool, except that the rate of **WDA is 6% for a 12-month period** (not 18%).

5.6 Balancing adjustments

The method of calculating balancing adjustments in the special rate pool is the same as for the main pool:

- A balancing charge can occur in any chargeable period.
- A balancing allowance can only occur on the cessation of trade.

Example

Felicity prepared her accounts to the 31 March 2023.

On 1 April 2022 the TWDVs brought forward were as follows:

	£
Main pool	24,000
Special rate pool	134,400

During the year Felicity made the following acquisitions:

	£
New packing machine (May 2022)	66,800
Delivery van (June 2022)	14,500
Car (July 2022) (CO_2 emissions of 75 g/km)	18,000

Disposals made in the year were as follows:

	£
Fork lift truck (sold for less than cost)	3,600

The new packing machine is expected to have a useful working life of 30 years.

Required

Calculate the capital allowances available for the year ended 31 March 2023.

Answer

Capital allowances – y/e 31 March 2023		Main pool	Special rate pool	Total allowances
	£	£	£	£
TWDV b/f		24,000	134,400	
Acquisitions (66,800 + 14,500)	81,300		18,000	
AIA	(81,300)			81,300
		-		
Disposals		(3,600)	(Nil)	
		20,400	152,400	
WDA (18%)		(3,672)		3,672
WDA (6%)			(9,144)	9,144
TWDV c/f		16,728	143,256	
Total allowances available				94,116

Notes

The packing machine has a life of ≥ 25 years. However, it cost < £100,000 and therefore is not treated as a long life asset.

The AIA covers both of the qualifying acquisitions. The balance of the AIA is lost.

The car does not qualify for the AIA.

Cars
■ The different categories of cars
■ Private use

6 Cars

6.1 The different categories of cars

The capital allowances system for cars depends on the car's CO_2 emissions. The following thresholds apply to cars acquired on or after 6 April 2021 (1 April 2021 for companies).

- New cars with zero CO_2 emissions are treated as main pool items, but qualify for a 100% FYA. (The length of ownership of the car in the chargeable period is irrelevant. The length of the chargeable period is also irrelevant. The full FYA is available simply for incurring qualifying expenditure within the relevant period.)
- Cars with CO_2 emissions between 1 and 50 g/km qualify for an 18% WDA and should therefore be allocated to the main pool.
- Cars with CO_2 emissions of more than 50 g/km qualify for a 6% WDA and should therefore be allocated to the special rate pool.

Note that the term 'car' does not include lorries, vans, taxis and motorcycles. These will be treated as main pool items unless there is an element of private use (see later). They will also qualify for the annual investment allowance.

Example

Ena prepared her accounts to the 31 March 2023.

On 1 April 2022 the TWDVs brought forward were as follows:

	£
Main pool	44,000
Special rate pool	155,400

During the year Ena made the following acquisitions:

	£
Car (April 2022) (zero CO_2 emissions)	12,000
Car (May 2022) (CO_2 emissions of 40 g/km)	14,500
Car (July 2022) (CO_2 emissions of 90 g/km)	18,000

Disposals made in the year were as follows:

	£
Plant (sold for less than cost)	3,600

Required

Calculate the capital allowances available for the year ended 31 March 2023.

Answer

Ena - Capital allowances – y/e 31 March 2023		Main pool	Special rate pool	Total allowances
	£	£	£	£
TWDV b/f		44,000	155,400	
Acquisitions		14,500	18,000	
Disposals		(3,600)	(Nil)	
		54,900	173,400	
WDA (18%)		(9,882)		9,882
WDA (6%)			(10,404)	10,404
Addition	12,000			
FYA (100%)	(12,000)			12,000
TWDV c/f		45,018	162,996	
Total allowances available				32,286

6.2 Private use

Private use of a car by an employee is irrelevant and has no effect on the WDA available.

Private use of a car by the proprietor of the business is covered later.

> **Short life assets**
>
> - The definition of a short life asset
> - The treatment of short life assets
> - The allowances available for short life assets
> - Balancing adjustments
> - The tax planning opportunities of making the de-pooling election

7 Short life assets

7.1 The definition of a short life asset

Short life assets are defined as plant and machinery with a predicted useful economic life of less than **eight years** (i.e. when they are purchased, the intention of the business is to dispose of them within the following eight chargeable periods).

In the examination, the most common examples of short life assets are computers and computer software. Cars and assets qualifying for inclusion within the special rate pool cannot be treated as short life assets.

7.2 The treatment of short life assets

Short life assets are treated as normal main pool items **unless a de-pooling election is made.**

If the de-pooling election is made, a separate record is maintained for that asset. This means that there must be a separate column for the asset in the capital allowances computation proforma.

The purpose of making the de-pooling election is to obtain a balancing allowance when the asset is sold.

Companies must make the election within two years of the end of the accounting period in which the expenditure was incurred. Individuals must make the election within one year after the 31 January following the end of the period of account in which the expenditure was incurred. For example, if the expenditure is incurred on 13 March 2022 and the sole trader has a 31 December 2022 year end, the election should be made by 31 January 2025 (12 months from the 31 January after the end of 2022/23).

If elections are made to de-pool several short life assets, a separate record is maintained for each individual short life asset.

7.3 The allowances available for short life assets

Short life assets qualify for the AIA in the same way as main pool items. However, if the AIA covers the full cost of the asset, a de-pooling election will not be beneficial as it would result in a balancing charge when the asset was eventually sold.

WDAs are claimed on short life assets in the same way and at the same rate as in the main pool.

7.4 Balancing adjustments

If the short life asset is disposed of within eight years of the end of the chargeable period in which it is acquired, a BA or a BC will arise.

- If the disposal value is higher than the TWDV for the short life asset, a balancing charge arises, which is a negative capital allowance.

- If the disposal value is less than the TWDV for the short life asset, a balancing allowance arises, which is added to the total capital allowances available for the period.

However, if the asset is not disposed of within eight years of the end of the chargeable period in which it is acquired, the TWDV of the asset must be transferred to the main pool.

7.5 The tax planning opportunities of making the de-pooling election

The de-pooling election is optional and should **only** be made where it is anticipated that the asset will be **sold for less than its TWDV** while it is being treated as a separate short life asset.

The aim of de-pooling is to accelerate the capital allowances available on that asset (i.e. allow the allowances to be claimed earlier), but the benefit does not crystallise until the period of disposal.

Up to the disposal of the asset, the same amount of allowances will be claimed whether or not the asset is de-pooled. However, on its disposal:

- if de-pooled and sold for less than its TWDV, a balancing allowance will arise

- if not de-pooled, the disposal value is deducted in the main pool and the allowances for the remaining net cost of the asset will be claimed as WDAs on an 18% reducing balance basis over several years; no balancing allowance arises.

It is important to note that the de-pooling **election would not be advantageous** where it is anticipated that the asset will be **sold for more than its TWDV**. This is because the disposal would crystallise a balancing charge early, whereas the deduction of the disposal value of this one asset from the main pool (which includes the TWDVs of many other assets) would be unlikely to give rise to a balancing charge.

Example

Yvonne is self-employed. She prepares her accounts to 31 March each year. On 1 November 2020 she purchased a computer for £3,200.

She disposed of the computer on 31 October 2022 for £950.

Required

Calculate the capital allowance claims in respect of the computer for the four accounting periods ending on 31 March 2024, both with and without the short life asset (de-pooling) election. Assume that there is a substantial balance brought forward on the main pool and that the AIA is not available.

a Answer

Yvonne Capital allowances	Short life election made		Short life asset election not made	
	Short life asset	Total allowances	Main pool	Allowances re the computer
	£	£	£	£
y/e 31 March 2021				
TWDV b/f			X	
Acquisitions	3,200		3,200	
WDA (18%)	(576)	576	(576)	576
TWDV c/f	2,624		2,624	
y/e 31 March 2022				
WDA (18%)	(472)	472	(472)	472
TWDV c/f	2,152		2,152	
y/e 31 March 2023				
Disposal	(950)		(950)	
	1,202		1,202	
Balancing allowance	(1,202)	1,202		
WDA (18%)			(216)	216
TWDV c/f	Nil		986	
y/e 31 March 2024				
WDA (18%)	Nil	Nil	(177)	177
TWDV c/f	Nil		809	
Total allowances claimed to date		2,250		1,441

The net cost of the computer is £2,250 (£3,200 - £950).

The full net cost is allowed by 31 March 2023 if the short life asset election is made.

If the election is not made, only £1,264 will have been allowed by 31 March 2023 and £1,441 by 31 March 2024. The remaining £809 of net cost will be relieved, but over several years on an 18% reducing balance method.

The election therefore accelerates the capital allowances claim.

Note that had the AIA been available to cover the full cost of the asset, a short life asset election would not have been beneficial as it would have given rise to a balancing charge of £950 on the disposal of the asset. In that situation, it would be better to leave the asset in the main pool.

> **Capital allowances for unincorporated businesses**
>
> - The treatment of private use assets
> - Short periods of account
> - Long periods of account

8 Capital allowances for unincorporated businesses

8.1 The treatment of private use assets

Full capital allowances are available to a company, even if there is an element of private use of an asset by a director or employee. The benefit of private use will be assessed on the individual as a benefit of employment; but it is irrelevant for calculating the capital allowances available to the company.

However, as regards an unincorporated business, where **any** business asset is used partly for business use and partly for private use **by the owner**, a separate record of that asset must be kept. This is because capital allowances are only available on the business proportion of the expenditure.

The most common example of a private use asset is a car used by the owner of the business.

(You should refer to the Proforma capital allowances computation when reading the following rules.)

(1) **WDA on private use assets**. The WDA on private use assets is calculated in the normal way using the reducing balance basis. The full WDA is deducted from the tax written down value in the appropriate private use asset column in the proforma. However, **only the business proportion of this WDA** can be claimed as a tax deduction and entered in the total allowances column in the proforma.

(2) **Disposal of private use assets**. On the disposal of a private use asset, a balancing adjustment is calculated in the normal way. However, in the case of assets with a private use element, **only the business proportion of the BA or BC** is entered in the total allowances column in the proforma.

(3) **Annual investment allowance (AIA) on private use assets**. If a private use asset is purchased in the period of account and the AIA is available, the AIA is calculated in the normal way and deducted from the cost in the appropriate private use asset column in the proforma. However, **only the business proportion of the AIA** calculated can actually be claimed and entered in the total allowances column.

These rules only apply to assets with an element of private use **by the owner**. Private use by an employee of the business is irrelevant. The assets are treated as normal additions and disposals, and allowances are available in full.

Example

Francis is a self-employed electrician. He prepares his accounts to 31 March each year. On 1 November 2021 he bought a car for £11,500 and sold it for £8,000 on 30 January 2023. The car has CO_2 emissions of 45 g/km. His private mileage in the car is 5,000 out of his annual total of 25,000. The TWDV b/f on the main pool on 1 April 2021 was £16,500.

Required

Calculate the capital allowances available for the years ended 31 March 2022 and 31 March 2023.

Answer

The private use of the car is 20% (5,000/25,000). The business use is therefore 80%.

Francis – Capital allowances, year ended 31 March 2022	Main pool	Car (80% business use)	Total allowances
	£	£	£
TWDV b/f	16,500		
Acquisitions not qualifying for AIA		11,500	
WDA (18%)	(2,970)		2,970
- Business % claim only		(2,070) x 80%	1,656
TWDV c/f	13,530	9,430	
Total allowances			4,626

Francis - Capital allowances, year ended 31 March 2023			
	£	£	£
TWDV c/f	13,530	9,430	
Disposals	(Nil)	(8,000)	
	13,530	1,430	
Balancing allowance		(1,430) x 80%	1,144
WDA (18%)	(2,435)		2,435
TWDV c/f	11,095		
Total allowances			3,579

8.2 Short periods of account

When there is a short period of account, the tax rules for capital allowances for unincorporated businesses and companies are the same. As explained above, the WDA is scaled down according to the length of the accounting period. For example, if a 7-month set of accounts is produced, the WDA for plant and machinery is 18% × 7/12.

8.3 Long periods of account

If an unincorporated business changes its accounting date and produces a set of accounts in excess of 12 months, the WDA is scaled up according to the length of the accounting period. For example, if a 17-month set of accounts is produced, the WDA for plant and machinery is 18% × 17/12. **Note that companies can never have an accounting period of more than 12 months (see later chapter).**

Note that only the AIA and WDA are scaled up. FYAs and balancing adjustments are not subject to time-apportionment.

Example

Gwen started to trade as a self-employed dressmaker on 6 April 2022 and prepared her first set of accounts to 31 July 2023. In the 16 month period she made the following capital purchases:

Purchases		£
6 April 2022	Two sewing machines	6,200
15 June 2022	Office equipment	2,000
1 July 2022	Computer equipment and software	5,500
1 July 2022	Second hand car	15,800
	(60% private use and CO_2 emissions of 45 g/km)	

Gwen has no asset disposals in the period.

Required

Calculate the capital allowances for the 16 month period ended 31 July 2023.

Answer

Gwen – Capital allowances, 16 months ended 31 July 2023	Main pool	Second hand car (40% business use)	Total allowances
	£	£	£
Acquisitions not qualifying for AIA	Nil	15,800	
Acquisitions qualifying for AIA			
Sewing machines £6,200			
Office equipment 2,000			
Computer equipment 5,500			
13,700			
AIA (13,700)			13,700
	Nil		
WDA (18% × 16/12)	(Nil)	(3,792) × 40%	1,517
TWDV c/f	Nil	12,008	
Total allowances			15,217

> **Structures and buildings allowance**
>
> - Introduction
> - Qualifying expenditure
> - The allowances
> - Disposal of a building

9 Structures and buildings allowance

9.1 Introduction

Structures and buildings allowance (SBA) is available where a qualifying structure or building is constructed on or after 29 October 2018.

9.2 Qualifying expenditure

SBA applies to the cost of:

- Offices, retail and wholesale premises, factories and warehouses
- Walls, bridges and tunnels.

The SBA is available in respect of:

- the initial cost of the qualifying building or structure, including fees for design and preparing the site for construction, and
- the cost of any subsequent improvements, renovations or conversions (whether or not the original building was purchased prior to 29 October 2018).

SBA does not apply to the cost of:

- Land
- Obtaining planning permission
- Dwelling houses (including any part of a building used as a dwelling house)
- Assets qualifying as plant and machinery for capital allowance purposes (such as integral features).

Where an unused building is purchased from a builder or developer, the qualifying expenditure will be the price paid less the value of the land.

9.3 The allowances

An annual straight-line allowance of 3% is given over a period of 33 years and 4 months.

The SBA must be time-apportioned if the business has a short accounting period (or scaled up if the period of account is more than 12 months).

SBAs are only available from the time when the building (or structure) is brought into qualifying use (or the date on which the qualifying expenditure is incurred, if later). Therefore, in the year of first use, the SBA will need to be time-apportioned.

Qualifying use means use in a qualifying activity such as a trade, profession or vocation, which is taxable in the UK.

A separate SBA is given for each qualifying building or structure.

Example

Belinda prepares her accounts to 31 March each year. On 1 August 2021 she purchased a newly constructed factory from a builder for £590,000 (including land of £90,000). She brought the factory into use on 1 December 2021.

Required

Calculate the SBAs available to Belinda for the years ended 31 March 2022 and 31 March 2023.

Answer

	£
y/e 31 March 2022	
Qualifying cost (£590,000 - £90,000)	500,000
SBA (3% x £500,000 x 4/12)	5,000
y/e 31 March 2023	
SBA (3% × £500,000)	15,000

9.4 Disposal of a building

No balancing adjustments arise on the disposal of a qualifying building or structure. Instead, the purchaser continues to claim the 3% allowance on the **original qualifying cost** for the remainder of the qualifying 33 years and 4 months.

For chargeable gains purposes, the disposal proceeds are increased by the allowances claimed. This effectively enables HMRC to recover the SBA from the vendor. (Chargeable gains are covered in more detail in later chapters.)

Example

Continuing with the above example.

On 31 July 2023 Belinda sold the factory to Damian for £625,000 (including land of £90,000). Damian brought the factory into qualifying use on 1 August 2023. Damian also makes up his accounts to 31 March each year.

Required

(a) Calculate the SBAs available to Belinda and Damian for the year ended 31 March 2024.

(b) Calculate Belinda's chargeable gain in respect of the factory.

Answer

(a) Belinda

y/e 31 March 2024	£
SBA (3% x £500,000 x 4/12)	5,000

Damian

y/e 31 March 2024	
SBA (3% × £500,000 x 8/12)	10,000

(b) Belinda's chargeable gain

	£
Disposal proceeds	625,000
Plus SBAs (5,000 + 15,000 + 5,000)	25,000
	650,000
Less cost	(590,000)
Chargeable gain	60,000

Note that the cost of the land is taken into account when calculating the chargeable gain.

Taxation – United Kingdom (TX-UK) FA2022

CHAPTER 7

Assessing the trading income of individuals

Contents
1 Overview of the basis of assessment rules
2 The opening year rules
3 The closing year rules
4 Choice of accounting date

> **Overview of the basis of assessment rules**
> - The need for basis of assessment rules
> - The current year basis of assessment

1 Overview of the basis of assessment rules

1.1 The need for basis of assessment rules

Sole traders and partnerships can prepare their accounts to any date they choose. They are not obliged to produce accounts to the end of the tax year (i.e. with a year ending 5 April). However, it is important to know in which tax year the tax-adjusted profits will be assessed to tax.

Tax legislation therefore needs rules for matching the adjusted profits after capital allowances of an unincorporated business with tax years. These rules are known as the basis of assessment rules.

1.2 The current year basis of assessment

The normal basis of assessment for trading income is the current year basis (CYB):

| Basis period for a tax year = | the 12-month **accounting period ending in the current tax year** |

The term **basis period** refers to the time period which is assessed for a particular tax year.

Example

Chen has been trading for many years preparing accounts to 31 December each year. He has recently received an enquiry from HMRC regarding the trading income figures he entered into his tax return for 2022/23.

Required

Which set(s) of accounts must Chen find to check the facts of the enquiry from HMRC?

Answer

The accounts which **end** in the 2022/23 tax year = Year ended 31 December 2022.

Chapter 7: Assessing the trading income of individuals

> **The opening year rules**
>
> - The need for special opening year rules
> - Calculating the opening year assessments

2 The opening year rules

2.1 The need for special opening year rules

When an individual starts to trade, they must choose a convenient ending date for their accounting period. Having chosen their accounting period closing date, their first set of accounts may be of any length.

If the CYB rule explained above is applied, it would be possible for a trader to avoid paying tax in the first tax year of trading. For example, if a trader commences trade on 1 January 2023 and prepares the first set of accounts to 31 December 2023, they will have commenced trading in the tax year 2022/23. However, as there are no accounts which end in that tax year, application of the normal CYB rule would mean there is no assessment to tax for 2022/23.

To ensure that some profits of the business are taxed in every tax year in which the individual is in business, the **CYB rule is not used**:

- in the opening year itself, and
- usually the next few years as well.

Instead, special opening year rules are applied.

2.2 Calculating the opening year assessments

The opening year assessment rules are summarised below.

Tax year	Basis period
First tax year	Assess on an actual tax year basis
	(i.e. from the date the trade started to the following 5 April)
Second tax year	See the decision table below
Third tax year	Assess the 12 months to the accounting date ending in the third tax year
Fourth tax year onwards	Assess using CYB rules as described above

The rules for the second tax year are set out in the following decision table. The approach is based on the answers to two questions

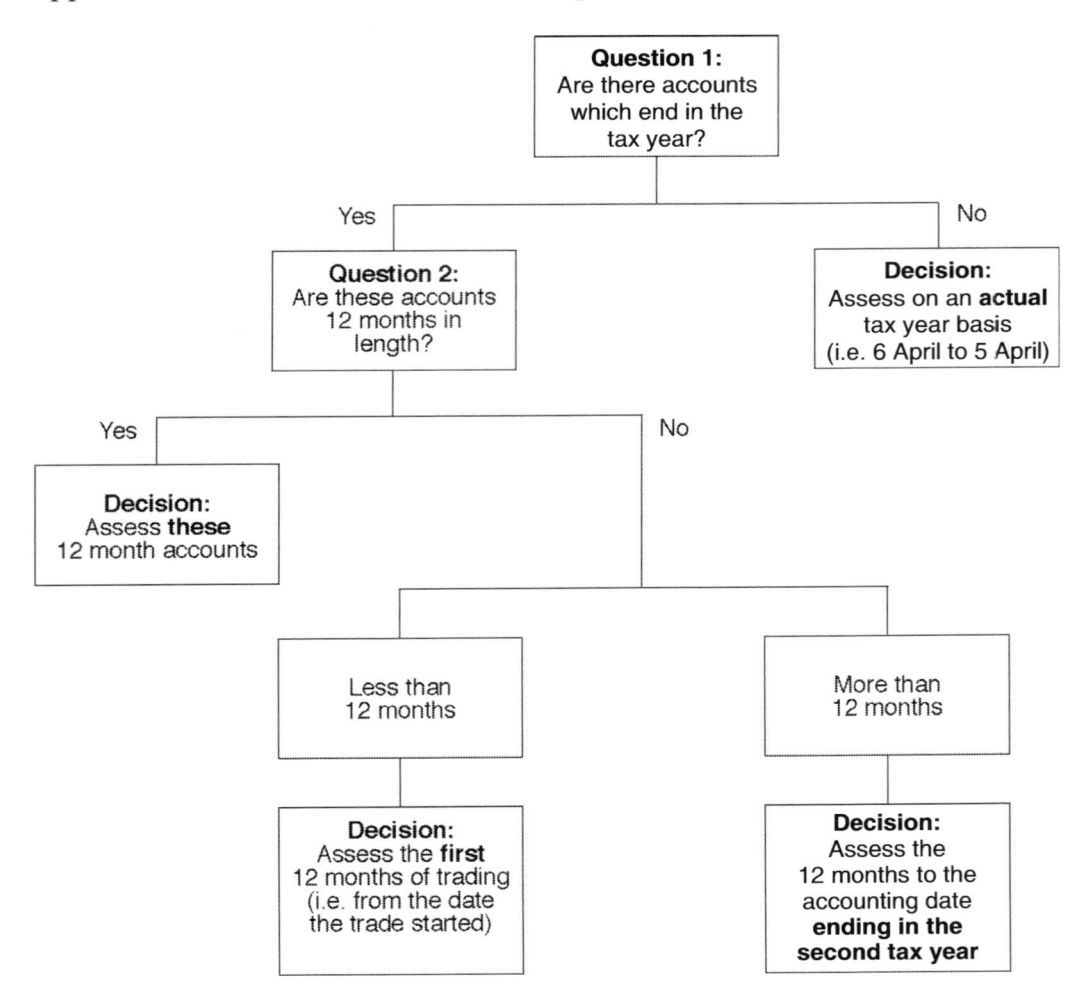

```
                    Question 1:
                  Are there accounts
                   which end in the
                      tax year?
           Yes    ┌──────┴──────┐    No
                                
    Question 2:                    Decision:
   Are these accounts           Assess on an actual
     12 months in                  tax year basis
       length?                 (i.e. 6 April to 5 April)
   Yes ┌──┴──┐ No
                
 Decision:
 Assess these
 12 month accounts
         ┌─────────┴─────────┐
     Less than            More than
     12 months             12 months
         │                     │
     Decision:              Decision:
   Assess the first        Assess the
  12 months of trading    12 months to the
   (i.e. from the date    accounting date
   the trade started)      ending in the
                           second tax year
```

In applying these assessment rules, it is assumed that profits accrue evenly over time. Therefore, where calculations to obtain an assessment require profits to be taken from more than one set of accounts, the profits must be time-apportioned.

The tax legislation requires apportionment in days, but in the examination calculations should be made to the nearest month.

A consequence of applying the opening year rules is that some profits will be assessed to tax more than once. These profits are known as **overlap profits**.

Relief is given for overlap profits in the final tax year on the cessation of trade, or possibly earlier if the business changes its accounting date.

Second tax year

From the decision table above, it can be seen that there are four possible scenarios for the second tax year.

Each of the four possible scenarios is illustrated on the following examples.

Example 1

Katie started to trade on 1 October 2020 and decided to prepare her accounts to 30 September each year. Her results for the first two years are as follows:

Year ended	Adjusted profit before capital allowances	Capital allowances
	£	£
30 September 2021	21,600	5,600
30 September 2022	64,800	6,500

Required

Calculate Katie's trading income assessments for the first three tax years, and the overlap profits arising from the application of the opening year rules.

Answer

Step 1. Calculate the adjusted profit after capital allowances for each accounting period

Year ended		Adjusted profit after capital allowances
		£
30 Sept 2021	(£21,600 - £5,600)	16,000
30 Sept 2022	(£64,800 - £6,500)	58,300

Step 2. Work out the basis period for the first tax year of trading

Trading starts on 1 October 2020 = In tax year 2020/21 = First tax year.

Tax year 1: Tax the profits from 1 October 2020 to 5 April 2021.

Step 3. Work out the basis period for the second tax year

Second tax year = 2021/22 Ask two questions:

Are there accounts which end in the tax year?	Yes = Year ended 30 September 2021
Are these accounts 12 months in length?	Yes
Decision	Assess the profits of those 12 months

Step 4. Summarise and calculate the trading income assessments

Tax year	Basis of assessment	Basis period	Workings	Trading income assessment
				£
2020/21	Actual	1.10.2020 – 5.4.2021	6/12 × £16,000	8,000
2021/22	12 months ending in second year	Year ended 30.9.2021		16,000
2022/23	12 months ending in third year	Year ended 30.9.2022		58,300

Step 5. If required, calculate the overlap profits

Profits are assessed more than once for the period 1.10.2020 – 5.4.2021.

Overlap profits = 6/12 × £16,000 = £8,000.

Example 2

Len started to trade on 1 November 2020 and decided to prepare his accounts to 31 May each year. His results for the first two accounting periods are as follows:

Period ended	Adjusted profit after capital allowances
	£
31 May 2021	13,400
31 May 2022	51,470

Required

Calculate the trading income assessments for Len for the first three tax years and calculate the overlap profits.

Answer

Trading starts on 1 November 2020 = In tax year 2020/21 = First tax year.

First tax year: Assess profits from 1 November 2020 to 5 April 2021.

Second tax year = 2021/22. Ask two questions:

Are there accounts which end in the tax year?	Yes = 7 months ended 31 May 2021
Are these accounts 12 months in length?	No: less than 12 months
Decision	Assess the profits of the first 12 months

Tax year	Basis of assessment	Basis period	Workings (nearest month)	Trading income assessment
				£
2020/21	Actual	1.11.2020 – 5.4.2021	5/7 × £13,400	9,571
2021/22	First 12 months	1.11.2020 – 31.10.2021	£13,400 + (5/12 × £51,470)	34,846
2022/23	12 months ending in third year	Year ended 31.5.2022		51,470

Overlap profits

		£
1.11.2020 – 5.4.2021	5/7 × £13,400	9,571
1.6.2021 – 31.10.2021	5/12 × £51,470	21,446
		31,017

Example 3

Cai started to trade on 1 June 2020 and decided to prepare her first accounts to 31 August 2021 and then to 31 August each year. Her results for the first two accounting periods are as follows:

Period ended	Adjusted profit after capital allowances
	£
31 August 2021	20,110
31 August 2022	77,200

Required

Calculate Cai's first three years' trading income assessments and the overlap profits.

Answer

Trading starts on 1 June 2020 = In tax year 2020/21 = First tax year.

First tax year: Assess the profits from 1 June 2020 to 5 April 2021.

Second tax year = 2021/22. Ask two questions:

Are there accounts which end in the tax year?	Yes = 15 months ended 31 August 2021
Are these accounts 12 months in length?	No: More than 12 months
Decision	Assess profits for the 12 months ending on 31 August 2021

Tax year	Basis of assessment	Basis period	Workings (to nearest month)	Trading income assessment
				£
2020/21	Actual	1.6.2020 – 5.4.2021	10/15 × £20,110	13,407
2021/22	12 months ending in second year	1.9.2020 – 31.8.2021	12/15 × £20,110	16,088
2022/23	12 months ending in third year	Year ended 31.8.2022		77,200

Overlap profits

1.9.2020 – 5.4.2021: 7/15 × £20,110 = £9,385.

Example 4

Nicholas started to trade on 1 January 2020 and decided to prepare his first accounts to 30 April 2021 and thereafter to 30 April each year. His results for the first two accounting periods are as follows:

Period ended	Adjusted profit after capital allowances
	£
30 April 2021	34,140
30 April 2022	51,250

Required

Calculate Nicholas' first four years' trading income assessments and the overlap profits.

Answer

Trading starts on 1 January 2020 = In tax year 2019/20 = First tax year.

First tax year: Assess the profits from 1 January 2020 to 5 April 2020.

Second tax year = 2020/21. Ask two questions:

Are there accounts which end in the tax year?   No

Decision   Assess the actual profits of the tax year: from 6 April 2020 to 5 April 2021

Third tax year = 2021/22. The 16-month accounts to 30 April 2021 end in the third tax year.

Decision = Assess the 12 months running up to the accounting end date that ends in the third tax year (i.e. the 12 months to 30 April 2021).

Tax year	Basis of assessment	Basis period	Workings (to nearest month)	Trading income assessment
				£
2019/20	Actual	1.1.2020 – 5.4.2020	3/16 × £34,140	6,401
2020/21	Actual	6.4.2020 – 5.4.2021	12/16 × £34,140	25,605
2021/22	12 months ending in third year	1.5.2020 – 30.4.2021	12/16 × £34,140	25,605
2022/23	CYB	Year ended 30.4.2022		51,250

Overlap profits

1.5.2020 – 5.4.2021: 11/16 × £34,140 = £23,471.

The closing year rules

- The need for special closing year rules
- Calculating the closing year assessments

3 The closing year rules

3.1 The need for special closing year rules

The primary aim of the basis of assessment rules is that the business should be taxed on the exact amount of adjusted profits after capital allowances earned over the entire life of the business.

In the opening years, overlap profits are assessed to tax more than once. To ensure that no more than the exact amount of adjusted profits is assessed to tax, relief is given for the overlap profits in the final tax year.

3.2 Calculating the closing year assessments

The closing year rules and approach are summarised as follows:

- **Step 1.** Work out which tax year is the final tax year.
- **Step 2.** Work out the trading income assessment of the **penultimate** year using the normal CYB rules.
- **Step 3.** Work out the final trading income assessment as follows:

	£
All profits not yet assessed (i.e. profits from the end of the accounting period ending in the penultimate year to the date of cessation)	X
Minus: Overlap relief	(X)
Closing year trading income assessment	X

Example

Owen has been trading for many years preparing accounts to 31 May each year. His overlap profits are £3,650. Owen ceased to trade on 30 September 2022 and has provided the following results for the last three accounting periods:

Period ended	Adjusted profit before capital allowances	Capital allowances
	£	£
31 May 2021	38,610	13,160
31 May 2022	23,200	10,000
30 September 2022	15,300	12,350

Required

Calculate Owen's last two trading income assessments.

Answer

The adjusted profit after capital allowances for each accounting period

Year ended		Adjusted profit after capital allowances
		£
31 May 2021	(£38,610 - £13,160)	25,450
31 May 2022	(£23,200 - £10,000)	13,200
30 Sept 2022	(£15,300 - £12,350)	2,950

Step 1: Work out the final tax year

Cessation of trade: 30 September 2022 = In tax year 2022/23 = Last tax year.

Step 2: Work out the trading income assessment of the penultimate year

| 2021/22 | CYB | Year ended 31.5.2021 | £25,450 |

Step 3: Work out the final trading income assessment

	£
Profits not yet assessed (1.6.2021 – 30.9.2022)	
Year ended 31 May 2022	13,200
Period ended 30 September 2022	2,950
Minus overlap relief	(3,650)
Closing year trading income assessment	12,500

> **Choice of accounting date**
> - A date early in the tax year
> - A date late in the tax year

4 Choice of accounting date

4.1 A date early in the tax year

Traders have a choice of accounting date. If they pick a date early in the tax year, for example 30 April, this will have the advantage of maximising the gap between earning profits and paying the tax on them. In 2022/23, for example, the assessment will be based on the profits of the year ended 30 April 2022. If profits are rising, this will produce a lower assessment than an accounting date of 31 March 2023.

A date early in the tax year will also make it possible to calculate taxable profits in advance of the end of the tax year. This will make tax planning easier.

However, a date early in the tax year will make the application of the basis period rules more complicated. It may also result in the assessment of more than 12 months' profits in the final year. See the previous example in which Owen was assessed on the profits of both the year ended 31 May 2022 and the period ended 30 September 2022 in 2022/23.

4.2 A date late in the tax year

A date late in the tax year, for example 31 March, will avoid the bunching of profits in the final tax year. So, in the previous example, if Owen had had an accounting date of 31 March instead of 31 May, his final tax year would have been based only on the profits of the period ended 30 September 2022 as the profits for the year ended 31 March 2022 would have been assessed in the penultimate year.

Choosing 31 March as the accounting date would also avoid overlap profits under the commencement rules. In addition, it has the advantage of being easy for the taxpayer to understand. However, its drawback is that it minimises the gap between earning profits and paying tax on them.

Taxation – United Kingdom
(TX-UK) FA2022

CHAPTER 8

Trading loss relief for individuals

Contents	
1	Overview of trading losses
2	The carry forward of trading losses
3	Relief against general income
4	Loss relief in the opening years
5	Loss relief in the closing years
6	Tax planning

> **Overview of trading losses**
> - The calculation of trading losses
> - The loss relief available

1 Overview of trading losses

1.1 The calculation of trading losses

A trading loss occurs when a business has:

- an adjusted trading loss before capital allowances that is increased by the addition of capital allowances, or
- an adjusted trading profit before capital allowances that becomes a loss when capital allowances are deducted.

If a trading loss occurs, the trading income assessment for the appropriate tax year is £Nil.

1.2 The loss relief available

A range of loss reliefs is available to individuals who incur a trading loss.

The reliefs available depend on whether or not the business is:

- in its opening years,
- in its closing years, or
- neither starting to trade nor closing down (an ongoing business).

An individual will choose to make use of their trading loss in the best way, by applying the tax planning principles described at the end of this chapter.

Ongoing business

The following reliefs for trading losses are available to an ongoing unincorporated business.

(1) Carry forward the trading loss and set it off against the first available profits from the trade that produced the loss.

(2) Make a claim to set off the trading loss against the total income of the individual:
   - in the tax year of the loss, **and/or**
   - in the preceding tax year.

(3) Make a claim to extend the relief in 2 above to set off the trading loss against the net gains of the individual:
- in the tax year of the loss, **and/or**
- in the preceding tax year.

Business in its opening years

In addition to the options for an ongoing business, an individual whose business is in its opening years can claim the following relief.

(4) Make a claim to set off the trading loss against the total income of the three tax years preceding the tax year of the loss.

Business in its closing years

The following reliefs for trading losses are available to an individual whose business is in its closing years:

(1) Make a claim to set off the trading loss against the total income of the individual:
- in the tax year of the loss, **and/or**
- in the preceding tax year.

(2) Make a claim to extend the relief in 1 above, to set off the trading loss against the net gains of the individual:
- in the tax year of the loss, **and/or**
- in the preceding tax year.

(3) Make a claim to set off the trading loss against the trading income of the individual:
- in the tax year of the loss **and**
- in the preceding three tax years.

These rules are explained in the rest of this chapter, except for relief against net gains which is explained in a later chapter.

> **The carry forward of trading losses**
>
> - Carry forward trading loss relief

2 The carry forward of trading losses

2.1 Carry forward trading loss relief

The income tax trading losses of an unincorporated business can be carried forward indefinitely, but the following rules apply.

The trading loss must be set off against:	Explanation:
The first available	- They must be set off in the next tax year if possible. - An individual cannot choose to miss out a tax year, for example to obtain a higher rate of tax relief.
Trading profits	- Set-off is against trading income only. - Trading losses carried forward cannot be set off against other income or gains.
Of the trade which produced the loss	- If an individual operates more than one type of trading activity, trading losses carried forward can only be set off against future profits from the activity that produced the loss. They cannot be set off against profits of a different trading activity.

Using as much as possible of the trading loss	- In each future tax year, the maximum amount of trading loss must be set off until relief has been given for the total trading loss.
	- The effect of this is that the loss to be relieved in any tax year is the lower of:
	  - the loss available, and
	  - the trading profit of the tax year.

Trading losses will be carried forward **automatically** and relieved in this way, unless the individual claims another type of loss relief.

The amount of trading loss available to carry forward must be agreed with HMRC within four years of the end of the tax year in which the loss was incurred.

Example

Anne has traded for many years, preparing her accounts to 31 March. She has supplied the following information regarding her adjusted trading profits/(losses):

	£
Year ended 31 March 2021	(12,000)
Year ended 31 March 2022	8,000
Year ended 31 March 2023	60,000

Anne's other income is as follows:

	2020/21 £	2021/22 £	2022/23 £
Bank interest	2,500	3,750	2,250
Dividends	600	700	1,000

Required

Calculate the taxable income for each tax year assuming losses are carried forward, and calculate the unrelieved loss, if any, at 6 April 2023. Assume the 2022/23 personal allowance applies in each year.

Answer

Step 1

Apply the basis of assessment rules to determine the trading income assessments. A nil assessment arises in the tax year in which the loss-making accounts end. Here the loss-making accounts end on 31 March 2021, which is in 2020/21.

Year ended	Basis of assessment	Tax year	Trading income assessment
31 March 2021	CYB	2020/21	Nil
31 March 2022	CYB	2021/22	£8,000
31 March 2023	CYB	2022/23	£60,000

Step 2

Prepare the income tax computations for each tax year affected.

Anne: Income tax computations	2020/21 £	2021/22 £	2022/23 £
Trading income	Nil	8,000	60,000
Minus: trading losses b/f	Nil	(8,000)	(4,000)
	Nil	Nil	56,000
Bank interest	2,500	3,750	2,250
Dividend income	600	700	1,000
Total income	3,100	4,450	59,250
PA (part wasted in 2020/21 and 2021/22)	(3,100)	(4,450)	(12,570)
Taxable income	Nil	Nil	46,680

Working: Record of trading losses	2020/21	2021/22	2022/23
	£	£	£
Unrelieved trading loss b/f	12,000	12,000	4,000
Set-off	0	(8,000)	(4,000)
Trading loss c/f	12,000	4,000	0

There is no loss left to carry forward at 6 April 2023.

Notes

(1) Losses brought forward can only be set against trading profits, not other income. The maximum amount possible must be deducted each year.

(2) A better rate of tax saving would be achieved if the full loss could be set off in 2022/23 as Anne is a higher rate taxpayer in that year. However, losses brought forward must be set against the first available future trading profits (i.e. 2021/22). It is not possible to skip a year.

(3) Unrelieved personal allowances are lost. Loss relief may therefore result in the wastage of personal allowances.

(4) It is not possible to make a partial claim in 2021/22 to maximise the use of personal allowances and save more loss for 2022/23. In any tax year the loss to be relieved is the lower of:

- the loss available, and
- the trading profit of the tax year.

(5) It may be possible to avoid the wastage of personal allowances by not claiming the maximum capital allowances in the accounting period. Tax planning issues are considered later.

Relief against general income

- Claiming relief against total income
- Proforma income tax loss relief computation
- Restriction on relief against non-trading income

3 Relief against general income

3.1 Claiming relief against total income

The objective of this form of loss relief is to allow an individual relief for a trading loss immediately the loss is incurred, rather than waiting to obtain the relief in the future years.

An individual can make a claim to set off losses against their total income:

- in the tax year of the loss, **and/or**
- in the preceding tax year.

In effect, this means that the individual can make a current year and carry back claim.

The basic rule allows a claim to be made:

- in both years in any order,
- in neither year, or
- in either year in isolation.

Therefore, with this form of loss relief, an individual has four options as follows:

(1) Set off in the current year only (i.e. the year of the loss).

(2) Carry back and set off in the preceding year only.

(3) Set off in the current year first, then carry back and set off in the preceding year.

(4) Carry back and set off in the preceding year first, then set off in the current year.

Note also that **a claim against total income is optional**; therefore, a fifth option is available:

(5) Make no specific loss relief claim and the trading losses will be automatically carried forward, as explained earlier.

When setting off the trading loss against general income in the current or preceding year, the following rules apply:

Rule:	Explanation:
Set off against total income	- Total income is all other income **after deducting** allowable interest payments, but **before the PA**.
Must set off as much as possible in the tax year	- It is an all or nothing relief. - The claim is optional. However, if the claim is made, the maximum amount must be deducted from the total income. - Loss relief may reduce the total income to £Nil, so that relief for the personal allowance is lost. - The personal allowance cannot be carried forward, or carried back; if unused, it is wasted/lost. - If total income is reduced to nil, the savings and dividend nil rate bands will also be wasted.

A claim for relief against total income must be made within one year of the 31 January following the end of the tax year of the loss (i.e. the 31 January immediately prior to the second anniversary of the end of the tax year of the loss).

If an individual claims relief against their total income, any trading losses left unrelieved are **automatically** carried forward and set off against future trading profits, unless a claim is made to set the loss against capital gains. (This claim is considered in a later chapter.)

3.2 Proforma income tax loss relief computation

A proforma for an income tax loss relief computation is set out below. This proforma assumes that the trading loss arises in the accounting period that forms the basis of the 2021/22 tax year.

Income tax computations	2020/21	2021/22	2022/23
	£	£	£
Trading income	X	Nil	X
Minus: trading losses b/f	-	-	(X)
	X	Nil	X
Other income	X	X	X
Minus: Deductible interest	(X)	(X)	(X)
Total income before loss relief	X	X	X
Minus:			
- current year claim		(X)	
- carry back claim	(X)		
	-	-	X
Minus: Personal allowance	Lost	Lost	(X)
Taxable income			X

Chapter 8: Trading loss relief for individuals

Working: Record of trading losses	2021/22	2022/23
	£	£
Trading loss in the tax year	X	
Set off against general income		
- in year of loss (i.e. 2021/22)	(X)	
- in preceding year (i.e. 2020/21)	(X)	
Trading loss c/f	X	
Trading loss b/f		X
Set off against future trading profits		(X)
Trading loss c/f		X

Example

Burton prepares his accounts to 31 March each year and has supplied the following information regarding his adjusted trading profits/(losses):

	£
Year ended 31 March 2021	35,500
Year ended 31 March 2022	(32,000)
Year ended 31 March 2023	16,250

Burton's other income and expenses are as follows:

	2020/21	2021/22	2022/23
	£	£	£
Building society interest	2,000	800	1,100
Dividends	300	70	900
Deductible interest	500	500	500

Required

Calculate the taxable income for each tax year assuming losses are relieved as soon as possible, and calculate the unrelieved loss available to carry forward, if any, at 6 April 2023. (Assume the 2022/23 personal allowance applies to all years.)

Answer

Trading income assessments

Year ended	Basis of assessment	Tax year	Trading income assessment
31 March 2021	CYB	2020/21	£35,500
31 March 2022	CYB	2021/22	Nil
31 March 2023	CYB	2022/23	£16,250

2021/22 = tax year of the loss

Burton: Income tax computations	2020/21	2021/22	2022/23
	£	£	£
Trading income	35,500	Nil	16,250
Building society interest	2,000	800	1,100
Dividend income	300	70	900
	37,800	870	18,250
Minus: Deductible interest	(500)	(500)	(500)
Total income before loss relief	37,300	370	17,750
Minus loss relief	(32,000)	(Nil)	(Nil)
Total income after loss relief	5,300	370	17,750
PA	(5,300)	(370)	(12,570)
Taxable income	Nil	Nil	5,180

(W) Record of trading loss	2021/22
	£
Trading loss in tax year	32,000
Loss relief claimed in 2020/21	(32,000)
Trading loss c/f	Nil

There is no loss left to carry forward at 6 April 2023.

Notes on this example

The claim has resulted in the loss of most of the personal allowance for 2020/21. Burton also loses the benefit of the savings and dividend nil rate bands for 2020/21.

The requirement in this example was that relief should be set off as soon as possible. This means that a loss relief claim is made in the preceding year and then the current year, if possible.

If the requirement had been for losses to be set off in the most tax-efficient manner, the answer would have been the same in this example. This is because:

- the total income in the year of the loss (i.e. 2021/22) is covered by the PA
- carrying forward the loss would waste more personal allowances. In addition, the individual would have to wait for the tax relief for his loss.

Therefore, even though some personal allowances and nil rate bands are lost with a carry back claim, the relief is obtained as soon as possible and, in this example, the claim saves the individual the most amount of tax. It may also be possible to avoid the wastage of personal allowances by not claiming full capital allowances.

3.3 Restriction on relief against non-trading income

There is a cap on the amount of loss that can be set against a person's total income. The cap is the **higher** of:

- £50,000 or
- 25% of total income after deducting the gross amount of any personal pension contributions.

The cap does not restrict the amount of loss that can be claimed against profits of the same trade in the preceding tax year.

Any loss remaining after the restriction can still be carried forward against future profits of the same trade (or claimed against the individual's chargeable gains).

Example

Yuki makes up her accounts to 31 March annually. Her recent results are as follows:

Period ended	Adjusted profit/(loss) after capital allowances
	£
31 March 2022	5,000
31 March 2023	(110,000)

Yuki also has employment income of £120,000 a year.

Required

Calculate Yuki's taxable income for 2021/22 and 2022/23 assuming she claims relief for her trading loss against her total income.

Answer

Yuki: Income tax computations	2021/22	2022/23
	£	£
Trading income	5,000	Nil
Employment income	120,000	120,000
Total income before loss relief	125,000	120,000
Minus loss relief (W1)	(55,000)	(50,000)
Total income after loss relief	70,000	70,000
PA	(12,570)	(12,570)
Taxable income	57,430	57,430

(W1) Record of trading loss	2022/23
	£
Trading loss in tax year	110,000
Loss relief claimed in 2022/23 (W2)	(50,000)
Loss relief claimed in 2021/22 (W3)	(55,000)
Trading loss c/f	5,000

(W2) Loss relief for 2022/23

Higher of:
£50,000 and
£120,000 x 25% = £30,000

Therefore £50,000

(W3) Loss relief for 2021/22

Higher of:
£50,000 and
Non trading income £120,000 x 25% = £30,000

Therefore £50,000

Plus an additional £5,000 as there is no restriction on the amount that can be set off against the trading income.

Note

The restriction has actually operated in Yuki's favour as it has allowed her to claim relief at the rate of 40% in both years. If the restriction had not applied, the full £110,000 would have been set off in either 2021/22 or 2022/23. This would have resulted in some of the relief being at the rate of 20%.

Chapter 8: Trading loss relief for individuals

> **Loss relief in the opening years**
>
> - Relief against general income in the opening years
> - The procedure for dealing with losses in the opening years
> - Early years' loss relief

4 Loss relief in the opening years

4.1 Relief against general income in the opening years

The rules for relieving a loss against general income in the opening years are exactly the same as the rules applying in the ongoing years. However, there are three issues to consider when claiming relief in the opening years:

- working out the trading income assessments in the opening years where a loss is involved
- deciding the tax year of the loss, and
- calculating the amount of loss relief available.

It is possible for a loss arising in one accounting period to be split into two separate losses for relief against general income in different years.

Where consecutive losses arise, the losses should be dealt with in date order; first loss first, then the second loss. If applicable, any current year loss set off takes priority over losses carried back to that year.

4.2 The procedure for dealing with losses in the opening years

The procedure to adopt for dealing with an opening year loss is as follows:

Step 1: Trading income assessments for each tax year

The opening year basis of assessment rules are applied to both profits and losses in the normal way. However, where an overall net loss arises (i.e. where the calculations give a negative figure), the trading income assessment for that tax year is £Nil.

Note that a loss may only be relieved once. There is no such thing as overlap losses. It is not possible to obtain relief for an amount greater than the loss that is actually incurred. Therefore, if a loss (or part of a loss) is brought into the calculation of an assessment in one tax year, it cannot also be taken into account in the next tax year's calculation. (See the example below.)

© Emile Woolf International Limited

Step 2: The loss relief available, the tax year(s) to which the loss(es) relate and the options available for loss relief

If an overall net loss is calculated in Step 1, this net loss is the amount available for relief against general income. The tax year of the loss is the tax year in which the net loss occurs and the trading assessment is £Nil.

Step 3: Prepare the income tax computations and keep a record of the losses

In answering an examination question, read the requirements carefully. Some questions require losses to be claimed in a specified way; other questions require losses to be utilised in the most tax-efficient manner. Tax planning is considered later.

Example

Debbie started to trade on 1 November 2020 and decided to prepare her accounts to 30 September each year. Her results for the first two years are as follows:

Period ended	Adjusted profit/(loss) after capital allowances
	£
30 September 2021	(22,000)
30 September 2022	60,000

Required

Calculate Debbie's trading income assessments for the first three tax years. State the amount of loss relief available to set against general income, and identify the years against which a claim can be made.

Answer

Step 1: Trading income assessments for each tax year

(a) Work out the **first tax year** of trading:

Trading starts on 1 November 2020 = In tax year 2020/21 = First tax year

i.e. 1 November 2020 to 5 April 2021

(b) Make the **second tax year** decision:

Second tax year = 2021/22. Ask two questions:

Are there accounts which end in the tax year?	Yes = period ended 30 September 2021
Are these accounts 12 months in length?	No = less than 12 months
Decision	Assess the first 12 months' profit/(loss)

(c) **Third tax year** = the 12 months ending in the third tax year

i.e. 1 October 2021 to 30 September 2022

Summarise and calculate the trading income assessments

Tax year	Basis period	Workings (nearest month)		Assessable trading income
			£	£
2020/21	**Actual**: 1.11.2020 – 5.4.2021	5/11 × £22,000 loss = Net loss	(10,000)	Nil
2021/22	**First 12 months**: 11 months ended 30.9.2021	Loss in the period	(22,000)	
		Loss already used in 2020/21 calculation	10,000	
			(12,000)	
	1 month 30.9.2022	Profit (1/12 × £60,000)	5,000	
		Net loss	(7,000)	Nil
2022/23	**12 months ending in third year** Year ended 30.9.2022			60,000

Step 2: Work out the loss relief available if relief against total income is claimed

For the £22,000 adjusted loss after capital allowances arising in the 11 months' accounting period ended 30 September 2021, the following loss relief is available:

Tax year of loss	Amount of loss	Loss relief available
	£	
2020/21	10,000	Relief available against total income in: (1) 2020/21 and/or (2) 2019/20
2021/22	7,000	Relief available against total income in: (1) 2021/22 and/or (2) 2020/21
Remaining loss	5,000 22,000	Used in calculating the 2021/22 assessment

Note

The 2021/22 assessment is nil. However, as £5,000 of profit was allocated to that year, £5,000 of loss must have been used in order to reduce the £5,000 profit to nil. This is referred to as relieving losses in aggregation.

4.3 Early years' loss relief

Early years' loss relief is available if the normal opening year rules result in a net loss arising in one or more of the **first four tax years of trading**.

Calculating the amount of loss relief available under the early years' rules is the same as for a claim against general income. However, early years' loss relief is given in different tax years from those used in a claim against general income.

A trading loss incurred in one of the **first four tax years** of assessment can be **carried back against total income** in the **three preceding tax years** on a first-in-first-out (FIFO) basis.

When setting off the trading loss under the early years' rules, the following rules apply:

Rule:	Explanation:
Set off against total income	- Total income is all other income **after deducting** allowable interest payments, but **before the PA**.
Strict order of set off	- Relief is on a FIFO basis (i.e. the earliest year must be relieved first and then the next year and the year after that, in date order).
All three years must be relieved, if possible	- An early years' claim is a single claim that applies to all three years. - The claim is optional. However, if the claim is made, the total income of **all three years** must be relieved as much as possible. - It is not possible to relieve in one or two years only, unless there is insufficient loss to relieve all three years.
Must set off as much as possible in each tax year	- It is an all or nothing relief. - The maximum amount must be deducted from the total income. - Loss relief may reduce the total income to nil, so that the relief for personal allowances is lost. - If total income is reduced to nil, the savings and dividend nil rate bands will be wasted.

A claim for early years' relief must be made within the same time limit as a claim against general income, i.e. within one year of the 31 January following the end of the tax year of the loss (i.e. the 31 January which is 22 months after the end of the tax year of the loss).

Example

The facts are the same as the previous example involving Debbie.

Required

State the amount of loss relief available and the years against which a claim for early years' loss relief can be made.

Answer

The trading income assessments are calculated in the same way as in the previous answer.

If early years' loss relief is claimed

For the £22,000 adjusted loss after capital allowances arising in the 11 month accounting period ended 30 September 2021 the following early years' loss relief is available:

Tax year of loss	Amount of loss	Loss relief available
	£	
2020/21	10,000	Early years' relief is available against total income in: (1) 2017/18 and then (2) 2018/19 and then (3) 2019/20 - in that strict order - as much as possible each year
2021/22	7,000	Early years' relief is available against total income in: (1) 2018/19 and then (2) 2019/20 and then (3) 2020/21 - in that strict order - as much as possible each year
Remaining loss	5,000	Used in calculating the 2021/22 assessment
	22,000	

Note that early years' loss relief is also subject to the cap on the amount of loss that can be set against an individual's total income, but the cap will not be examinable in this context.

> **Loss relief in the closing years**
>
> - Terminal loss relief
> - The procedure for dealing with a closing year loss

5 Loss relief in the closing years

5.1 Terminal loss relief

Terminal loss relief is available **if a trading loss is incurred in the last twelve months of trading**. An individual can make a claim to set off the loss:

- in the last tax year and then
- carry back the loss against **trading income in the three preceding tax years** on a last-in-first-out (LIFO) basis.

When setting off the trading loss the following rules apply:

Rule:	Explanation:
Set off against trading income	- The loss can only be set against trading income, not against other types of income or gains.
Strict order of set-off	- Relief is on a LIFO basis. The most recent year must be relieved first and then the previous year, and so on, in reverse date order.
All three years must be relieved, if possible	- A terminal loss claim involves a single claim which applies to all three years. - The claim is optional. However, if the claim is made, as much as possible of the trading income of **all three years** must be relieved. - The individual will want to claim as much relief as possible, because the business has ceased and there is no carry forward relief available.
Must set off as much as possible in each tax year	- It is an all or nothing relief. - The maximum amount must be deducted from trading income.

A claim must be made for terminal loss relief within four years of the end of the tax year in which the cessation occurs.

Note that closing year loss relief is **not** subject to the £50,000 cap as relief is given against **trading** income rather than total income.

Chapter 8: Trading loss relief for individuals

Calculating the available loss

The terminal loss is the **loss of the last twelve months of trading**. This calculated in two parts as follows:

	£
Last tax year	
1. Trading loss in the last tax year	
(i.e. from 6 April before cessation to the date of cessation)	X
Plus any overlap profits not yet relieved	X
(Ignore if a profit)	X
12 months before cessation to 5 April before cessation	
(the length of this period is y)	
2. Actual trading loss in period y	
(Ignore if a profit)	X
Terminal loss of the last 12 months trading	X

Note that a loss can only be relieved once therefore the terminal loss cannot include a loss that has been relieved under another provision. In other words, any losses claimed against total income or capital gains must be excluded.

5.2 The procedure for dealing with a closing year loss

The procedure to adopt for dealing with a closing year loss is as follows:

Step 1: Identify the last tax year. Work out the trading income assessments for the final year and preceding three tax years

The closing year basis of assessment rules are applied to both profits and losses in the normal way. However, where an overall net loss arises from applying the rules (i.e. the calculations give a negative figure), the trading income assessment for that tax year is £Nil.

Step 2: Set up the income tax loss computations in columnar format, for all the tax years affected

There should be a separate column for each tax year. Insert all the known figures into each column, i.e. the trading income assessments from Step 1, other income, allowable interest payments and personal allowances.

Step 3: Work out the amount of loss relief available, the tax year(s) to which the loss(es) relate, and the options available

If an overall net loss is calculated in Step 1, this net loss is the amount available for relief against general income. Consideration should be given as to whether claims against total income and capital gains are desirable.

For a decision, look at the income tax computations set up in Step 2 and determine whether a higher rate of relief is obtained by making a claim against total income and possibly a claim against capital gains, rather than carrying back the loss under the terminal loss relief rules.

The terminal loss then needs to be calculated, taking account of any losses claimed against general income and capital gains. This calculation should be done in a separate working.

Step 4: Complete the income tax computations

Relieve the terminal loss on a LIFO basis, and keep a record of the utilisation of losses for all tax years involved.

Example

Eva has been trading for many years preparing accounts to 31 January each year. On 30 September 2022 she ceased to trade. Her results for the last years are as follows:

	Adjusted profit / (loss) after capital allowances
	£
Year ended 31 January 2020	42,000
Year ended 31 January 2021	14,000
Year ended 31 January 2022	12,000
Eight months ended 30 September 2022	(8,000)

Eva received interest of £1,000 on a building society account on 31 December each year and paid deductible interest of £1,200 on 30 June each year. She also received a dividend of £3,000 from a UK company on 14 May 2021.

Her overlap profits not yet relieved total £32,000.

Required

Calculate Eva's taxable income for all tax years affected assuming a terminal loss relief claim is made. Assume the 2022/23 personal allowance applies to all years.

Answer

Step 1: Identify the last tax year and work out the trading income assessments for this and the preceding three tax years

Cessation of trade: 30 September 2022 = In tax year 2022/23 = Last tax year.

Penultimate year: 2021/22 = CYB basis of assessment = Year ended 31 January 2022.

Last tax year assessment – 2022/23	£
Profits not yet assessed (1.2.2022 – 30.9.2022)	
Period ended 30 September 2022 - loss	(8,000)
Minus: Overlap relief	(32,000)
Net loss = Loss relief available to set against general income	(40,000)
Final tax year assessment for 2022/23	Nil

Summary of assessments:

Tax year	Basis of assessment	Basis period	£
2019/20	CYB	Year ended 31 January 2020	42,000
2020/21	CYB	Year ended 31 January 2021	14,000
2021/22	CYB	Year ended 31 January 2022	12,000
2022/23	as above		Nil

Step 2: Set up the income tax loss computations in columnar format, for all the tax years affected

Set out the income tax computations in columnar form, as follows, inserting all known figures. Note that at this stage, the terminal loss figures and therefore the final result are not known.

Income tax computations	2019/20	2020/21	2021/22	2022/23
	£	£	£	£
Trading income	42,000	14,000	12,000	Nil
Minus: terminal loss relief	(?)	(?)	(?)	Nil
				Nil
Building society interest	1,000	1,000	1,000	1,000
Dividend income	Nil	Nil	3,000	Nil
				1,000
Minus: Deductible interest	(1,200)	(1,200)	(1,200)	(1,200)
Total income				Nil
Minus: Personal allowance	(12,570)	(12,570)	(12,570)	Wasted
Taxable income				Nil

The final year (2022/23) can be completed:

- there will be no claim against total income as there is no total income
- there is £200 of unrelieved interest in the last year and
- the personal allowance is wasted.

Step 3: Work out the amount of loss relief available and the tax year(s) to which the loss(es) relate

	£	£
Last tax year		
1. Actual trading loss in last tax year		
Period 6.4.2022 to 30.9.2022: (6/8 × £8,000 Loss) = £6,000 loss		6,000
Plus overlap profits not yet relieved		32,000
		38,000

		£	£
12 months before cessation to 5 April before cessation			
1.10.2021 to 5.4.2022 = 6 months			
2.	Actual trading loss in this 6 month period		
	Period 1.10.2021 to 31.1.2022: (4/12 × £12,000) profit	4,000	
	Period 1.2.2022 to 5.4.2022: (2/8 × £8,000 loss) loss	(2,000)	
	Net profit for the period	2,000	
	– Ignore profit in loss calculation		Nil
Terminal loss of the last 12 months trading			38,000

Step 4: Complete the income tax computations

Complete the income tax computations, carrying back the terminal loss on a LIFO basis. The loss should be deducted from trading income.

Income tax computations	2019/20	2020/21	2021/22	2022/23
	£	£	£	£
Trading income	42,000	14,000	12,000	Nil
Minus: terminal loss relief	(12,000)	(14,000)	(12,000)	Nil
	30,000	Nil	Nil	Nil
Building society interest	1,000	1,000	1,000	1,000
Dividend income	Nil	Nil	3,000	Nil
	31,000	1,000	4,000	1,000
Minus: Allowable interest payments	(1,200)	(1,200)	(1,200)	(1,200)
Total income	29,800	Nil	2,800	Nil
Minus: Personal allowance	(12,570)	wasted	(2,800)	wasted
Taxable income	17,230	Nil	Nil	Nil

Working: Record of trading losses	£
Terminal loss	38,000
Set off	
- in tax year of loss 2022/23	Nil
- carry back to 2021/22	(12,000)
- carry back to 2020/21	(14,000)
- carry back to 2019/20	(12,000)
	Nil

> **Tax planning**
>
> - Choosing the optimum loss relief
> - Making a reduced capital allowances claim

6 Tax planning

6.1 Choosing the optimum loss relief

When using trading losses, the primary aim of an individual should be to save the maximum amount of tax.

The rates of tax the individual is likely to pay in each tax year and the personal allowances available, including projected future rates of tax and allowances, are therefore a key factor in deciding the optimum loss relief claim.

However, cash flow could also be an important consideration. An individual may wish, for cash flow purposes, to claim relief as soon as possible, and carry back losses to obtain a cash repayment, and possibly repayment interest. This may be more important to the individual than obtaining a higher rate of relief at a later date.

If possible, the individual should prefer not to use losses where income is already covered by personal allowances or where any taxable income is covered by the savings or dividend nil rate bands. However, the individual may be prepared to waste personal allowances and nil rate bands in order to achieve a higher overall tax saving.

It may be possible to avoid the wastage of personal allowances by not claiming the maximum capital allowances available.

6.2 Making a reduced capital allowances claim

Loss relief is available for the adjusted loss **including** capital allowances.

It is not possible to treat the adjusted loss and the capital allowances as two separate losses. Therefore, an individual **cannot** set off only the adjusted loss **before** capital allowances against total income to maximise the tax savings and also carry forward the unrelieved capital allowances as a separate loss.

However, an individual does not have to claim the maximum amount of capital allowances for an accounting period. They can claim any amount up to the maximum available. Therefore, it may be advantageous to reduce a trading loss by not claiming any or all of the capital allowances available.

If a reduced capital allowances claim is made, the actual allowances claimed are deducted from the appropriate columns in the capital allowances computation. The TWDVs carried forward will therefore be higher, resulting in higher capital allowances being available in the future.

Taxation – United Kingdom (TX-UK) FA2022

CHAPTER 9

Partnerships

	Contents
1	Overview of the trading income assessment for a partnership
2	The treatment of partnerships
3	Partnership losses

> **Overview of the trading income assessment for a partnership**
>
> - Preparation of the trading income assessment

1 Overview of the trading income assessment for a partnership

1.1 Preparation of the trading income assessment

There are four key steps in the calculation of a trading income assessment for a partnership:

Step 1: Prepare an adjustment of profit statement

The first step is to prepare a statement adjusting the net profit of the business (in the financial accounts) to calculate the adjusted trading profit before capital allowances.

Step 2: Calculate the capital allowances available

The next step is to calculate the capital allowances available for plant and machinery and/or structures and buildings.

Step 3: Allocate the adjusted trading profit after capital allowances between the partners

Each partner in a partnership is taxed separately, in their own income tax computation, on their share of the partnership profits. The partnership is not treated as a separate entity and the partnership itself does not pay income tax.

Each partner is responsible for paying income tax at the appropriate rate on their share of the profits of the partnership, based on their own personal circumstances. It is therefore necessary to determine the amount of profits that relate to each partner.

The adjusted trading profits after capital allowances of the partnership are allocated between the individual partners in accordance with the profit-sharing agreement of the partners during the accounting period. The detailed rules governing the allocation of profit between partners are explained later.

Step 4: Calculate the trading income assessment for the correct tax year

The last step is to apply the basis of assessment rules to each partner's adjusted trading profit after capital allowances figure, in order to decide in which tax year the trading profits will be taxed.

> **The treatment of partnerships**
>
> - The adjustment of profit computation
> - The allocation of partnership profits
> - Allocation where there is a change in the partnership agreement
> - Calculating the trading income assessments
> - Limited liability partnerships

2 The treatment of partnerships

2.1 The adjustment of profit computation

Partners in a business partnership are treated as a group of individual sole traders. The calculation of the trading income assessments for partners is therefore the same as for a sole trader.

The adjusted trading profit (or loss) after capital allowances of the partnership is calculated first. In this calculation it is important to remember to add to profit any appropriations by the partners that have been charged through the accounts (such as salaries paid to partners and interest on partners' capital introduced).

2.2 The allocation of partnership profits

The adjusted trading profit (or loss) after capital allowances of the partnership is then allocated between the partners. This allocation is made in accordance with the terms of the **partnership agreement in the accounting period** in which the profit (or loss) arises.

A partnership agreement will specify the allocation rules that must be followed. Typically, an agreement will allocate the partnership trading profits in three ways:

- a fixed salary for some or all of the partners
- a fixed rate of interest on capital introduced to the partnership
- a profit-sharing ratio for the balance of the trading profits after any salary and interest is allocated.

Despite the terms used to describe the method of allocation between partners, the total share allocated to each partner is then assessable on that partner as trading income (**not** as employment income and interest income). Partnership 'interest' will therefore **not** qualify for the savings nil rate band.

Taxation - United Kingdom (TX-UK) FA2022

Example

Henry and Ivan are in partnership. The partnership agreement provides for the following:

	Henry	Ivan
	£	£
Salary per annum	50,000	30,000
Capital introduced	100,000	100,000
Interest on capital (rate per annum)	10%	10%
Profit sharing ratio	45%	55%

The adjusted trading profit of the partnership after capital allowances for the year ended 31 March 2023 was £246,000.

Required

Allocate the partnership trading profits for the year ended 31 March 2023 between Henry and Ivan.

Answer

	Total	Henry	Ivan
	£	£	£
Salary	80,000	50,000	30,000
Interest on capital introduced (10% × £100,000)	20,000	10,000	10,000
Balance of profits (45%: 55%)	146,000	65,700	80,300
Allocation of trading profits	246,000	125,700	120,300

2.3 Allocation where there is a change in the partnership agreement

If a partner leaves, or a new partner joins, or the partners change the partnership agreement part-way through an accounting period:

- the adjusted trading profit after capital allowances must be time-apportioned according to the date of change, and
- the appropriate partnership agreement rules should be applied to each period separately.

Example

Assume that Henry and Ivan from the previous example had changed their partnership agreement on 1 January 2023 and the new arrangement was as follows:

	Henry	Ivan
	£	£
Salary per annum	50,000	50,000
Interest on capital (rate per annum)	10%	10%
Profit sharing ratio from 1 January 2023	50%	50%

The adjusted trading profit of the partnership after capital allowances for the year ended 31 March 2023 was £246,000.

Required

Allocate the partnership trading profits for the year ended 31 March 2023 between Henry and Ivan.

Answer

	Total	Henry	Ivan
9 months to 31 December 2022	£	£	£
Salary (£50,000 × 9/12 : £30,000 × 9/12)	60,000	37,500	22,500
Interest on capital introduced			
(10% × £100,000 × 9/12)	15,000	7,500	7,500
Balance of profits (45%: 55%)	109,500	49,275	60,225
Allocation of profits (£246,000 × 9/12)	184,500	94,275	90,225
3 months to 31 March 2023			
Salary (£50,000 × 3/12)	25,000	12,500	12,500
Interest on capital introduced			
(10% × £100,000 × 3/12)	5,000	2,500	2,500
Balance of profits (50%: 50%)	31,500	15,750	15,750
Allocation of profits (£246,000 × 3/12)	61,500	30,750	30,750
12 months to 31 March 2023			
Total allocation of trading profits	246,000	125,025	120,975

2.4 Calculating the trading income assessments

When a partnership is originally set up:

- the opening year rules are applied in the normal way to each partner's share of the trading profits in the opening tax years
- the overlap profits of each individual partner are calculated separately.

If an existing partnership takes on a new partner, or a sole trader takes on a partner and the business becomes a partnership, the following consequences arise:

- The existing partners (or sole trader) continue to be assessed on their share of the trading profits on a normal current year basis as if there had been no change.
- The new partner is assessed on their share of the trading profits using the opening year rules and assuming the partner had their own accounting period **starting on the date they joined the firm**. The overlap profits of that partner are calculated.

When the partnership business ceases to trade:

- The closing year rules are applied in the normal way to each partner's share of the trading profits in the closing accounting periods.
- Each partner can deduct their own overlap relief.

If a partner leaves the partnership (e.g. retires or dies) and the existing business continues either as a partnership or as a sole trader business, the following consequences arise:

- The continuing partners (or sole trader) are assessed on their share of the trading profits on a normal current year basis as if there had been no change.

- The partner leaving the firm is assessed on their share of the trading profits, using the closing year rules and assuming the partner had their own accounting period ending on the date they left the firm. They will use their overlap relief in the final tax year.

Example

Tina and Vincent are partners and have been trading as a firm of solicitors for many years preparing accounts to 31 March each year. They have agreed to share profits equally. On 1 December 2021 Wang joined the firm on the agreement that the three partners (Tina, Vincent and Wang) would share profits in the ratio 3:2:1.

The adjusted trading profits after capital allowances of the partnership are as follows:

	Adjusted profit after capital allowances
	£
Year ended 31 March 2022	24,000
Year ended 31 March 2023	30,000

Required

Calculate the trading income assessments of each partner for 2021/22 and 2022/23 and Wang's overlap profits.

Answer

(1) **Allocate the adjusted trading profits after capital allowances between the partners in accordance with the partnership agreement in the accounting period**

Year ended 31 March 2022:	Total	Tina	Vincent	Wang
(1) 8 months to 30 November 2021	£	£	£	£
Profit share (50%: 50%)	16,000	8,000	8,000	Nil
(2) 4 months to 31 March 2022				
Profit share (3/6: 2/6: 1/6)	8,000	4,000	2,667	1,333
Allocation of profits	24,000	12,000	10,667	1,333
Year ended 31 March 2023				
Profit share (3/6: 2/6: 1/6)	30,000	15,000	10,000	5,000

(2) **Work out the trading income assessments of the existing partners using normal CYB**

			Tina	Vincent
			£	£
2021/22	CYB	Year ended 31 March 2022	12,000	10,667
2022/23	CYB	Year ended 31 March 2023	15,000	10,000

(3) **Work out the trading income assessments of the new partner**

Wang's share of profits:	£
4 months to 31 March 2022	1,333
Year ended 31 March 2023	5,000

Wang started to trade: 1 December 2021 = In tax year 2021/22 = His first tax year.

First tax year: Assess Wang's profits from 1 December 2021 to 5 April 2022

Second tax year = 2022/23. Ask two questions:

Are there accounts which end in the tax year?	Yes = year ended 31 March 2023
Are these accounts 12 months in length?	Yes
Decision	Assess those 12 months' profits

Tax year	Basis of assessment	Basis period	Trading income assessment £
2021/22	Actual	1.12.2021 – 5.4.2022	1.333
2022/23	12 months ending in second year	Year ended 31.03.2023	5,000

(4) **Work out the overlap profits of the new partner**

There are no overlap profits as the accounting date is 31 March.

2.5 Limited liability partnerships

A limited liability partnership (LLP) is a partnership in which the partners' liability to contribute towards the partnership debts and losses is limited in the partnership agreement.

A partner in an LLP is taxed in the same way as a partner in a normal partnership.

> **Partnership losses**
>
> - The loss relief options available to each partner
> - Restrictions on loss relief for non-active partners

3 Partnership losses

3.1 The allocation of partnership losses

If a partnership makes a trading loss, it is allocated between the partners in accordance with the partnership agreement in the accounting period in which it arises.

The allocation of partnership losses is therefore the same as for profits. Any fixed salary or interest on partners' capital must be allocated first. These items are classed as trading income for the partners. The balance of the loss is then allocated in accordance with the profit-sharing ratio.

Example

Frank and Wendy are in partnership and have the following partnership agreement:

	Frank	Wendy
	£	£
Salary (per annum)	45,000	25,000
Capital introduced	70,000	70,000
Annual interest on capital	8%	8%
Profit sharing ratio	40%	60%

The adjusted loss of the partnership after capital allowances for the year ended 31 March 2023 was £126,000.

Required

Allocate the partnership losses for the year ended 31 March 2023 between Frank and Wendy.

Answer

	Total	Frank	Wendy
	£	£	£
Salary	70,000	45,000	25,000
Interest on capital introduced (8% × £70,000)	11,200	5,600	5,600
	81,200	50,600	30,600
Balance of loss (40%: 60%)	(207,200)	(82,880)	(124,320)
Allocation of loss	(126,000)	(32,280)	(93,720)

Note that the balance of the partnership loss is the adjusted trading loss of the partnership after capital allowances, **plus** the partners' salaries and interest on capital. This balancing loss is shared between the partners in their profit-sharing ratio.

3.2 The loss relief options available to each partner

Each partner can choose to use their share of the trading loss in the most beneficial way. There is no requirement for all partners to utilise their losses in the same way.

The options available are the same as those available to a sole trader, and depend on whether the partner is joining the firm, leaving the firm or is an ongoing partner.

In summary, the options are as follows:

Opening years	Ongoing years	Closing years
= When the partner joins the firm, the first four tax years	The partner is in at least their fifth tax year and continues to be a partner	= When the partner leaves the firm
- claim against general income - extension claim against capital gains - carry forward against future trading profits	- claim against general income - extension claim against capital gains - carry forward against future trading profits	- claim against general income - extension claim against capital gains
- early years' claim		- terminal loss relief claim

As far as the TX-UK examination is concerned, the £50,000 cap that applies where the loss is set off against non-trading income only applies to claims against general income.

Taxation – United Kingdom
(TX-UK) FA2022

CHAPTER 10

Simpler Income Tax for Small Businesses

Contents
1   Fixed rate adjustments
2   The cash basis

> **Fixed rate adjustments**
>
> - What is the purpose of fixed rate adjustments?
> - Who can claim fixed rate adjustments?
> - Motor expenses
> - Business premises used as home

1 Fixed rate adjustments

1.1 What is the purpose of fixed rate adjustments?

As you have seen in earlier chapters, in order for a business to claim an expense for trading income purposes it must be incurred 'wholly and exclusively for the purposes of the trade'. Expenditure which is partly for business and partly for private purposes must normally be apportioned in order to determine the amount that is deductible.

A business must therefore keep full records of the expenditure that it has incurred and must be able to identify how much of the expenditure is for business purposes.

As an alternative, a business can use the fixed rate adjustments specified in the tax legislation. These are an optional way of calculating allowable expenditure and enable a business to simplify its record keeping.

1.2 Who can claim fixed rate adjustments?

Fixed rate adjustments may be claimed by unincorporated businesses of any size, i.e. sole traders and partnerships. However, for the purpose of the TX-UK examination, fixed rate adjustments will only be tested in the context of a question on the cash basis. The cash basis is covered in the next section.

1.3 Motor expenses

Businesses are generally required to keep records of all of their expenditure on motor vehicles, e.g. fuel, insurance, servicing, repairs, etc. They must also keep mileage records that allow them to identify how much of the proprietor's mileage is for business purposes. All of the proprietor's motor expenses (and any capital allowances due) are then apportioned on the basis of business mileage/total mileage in order to determine the amount deductible for tax purposes.

As an alternative, a sole trader or partner can calculate the amount deductible for tax purposes using the approved mileage allowances. These allowances were covered in the chapter on employment income.

Under the approved mileage allowances for cars, a business can claim 45p per mile for the first 10,000 business miles, with a rate of 25p per mile thereafter. The actual running costs of the vehicle are then ignored. It is also not possible to claim capital allowances for a vehicle if the approved mileage allowances are being claimed.

When an unincorporated business first acquires a vehicle, which will be used privately by the proprietor it must therefore decide whether to:

- claim the approved mileage allowances in respect of its business mileage, or
- claim the business element of the actual running costs incurred, together with capital allowances.

Once the choice has been made, it is not possible to swap to the other method.

There are different rates of approved mileage allowances for vans, motor cycles and bicycles. The approved mileage allowances for cars are given in the table of tax rates and allowances. If required in the examination, the approved mileage rates for other vehicles will be given in the question.

Example

Desmond is self-employed. He purchased a car on 6 April 2022 for £4,600. The car has a CO_2 emission rate of 70 g/km. During the year ended 5 April 2023, Desmond incurred motor expenses totalling £1,700. He drove 8,000 miles, of which 85% were for business purposes.

Required

Calculate the motor expenses and capital allowances deductible by Desmond for the year ended 5 April 2023 assuming:

(a) He uses the normal basis of calculating his motor expenses.

(b) He claims fixed rate allowances for the business use of his vehicle.

Answer

(a) Using the normal method Desmond will be able to claim motor expenses of £1,700 x 85% = £1,445.

He will also be able to claim capital allowances of £4,600 x 6% x 85% = £235.

This gives a total of £1,445 + £235 = £1,680.

(b) If he uses fixed rate allowances instead, Desmond will be able to claim 8,000 x 85% x 45p = £3,060. He will not be permitted to claim capital allowances as well.

Claiming fixed rate allowances is therefore beneficial for Desmond as it allows him to deduct an additional £3,060 - £1,680 = £1,380.

1.4 Business premises used as home

A trader who uses their business premises as their home will usually be required to add back a proportion of the expenditure incurred on the premises in order to reflect their private use. This applies, for example, to small hotels or guest houses, or where a proprietor lives in a flat above their shop.

Alternatively, the private use of food and light and heat can be calculated using a fixed rate adjustment according to the number of occupants (including children) using the premises as a private home.

Number of occupants	Annual fixed rate adjustment
1	£4,200
2	£6,000
3 or more	£7,800

Note that these figures represent the amount disallowed, i.e. they are deducted from the actual expenditure incurred.

If required, the relevant figure will be provided as part of an examination question.

There is no fixed rate adjustment for other property expenses such as rent, rates, council tax or mortgage interest. For these types of expenditure, the amount to be added back is calculated in the normal way.

Example

Chris and Clive are in partnership running a guest house. They live on the premises. For the year ended 5 April 2023 their trading profit is £30,000, but this is before adding back any adjustment in respect of the private use of the property.

The total cost of food was £28,000, and the total light and heat cost was £9,200. These figures have been deducted in calculating the trading profit of £30,000.

Chris and Clive estimate that they use 25% of the property for private purposes and consume a total of £60 of food a week. The annual fixed rate adjustment for a property with two occupants is £6,000.

Required

Calculate the trading profit for the year ended 5 April 2023 assuming Chris and Clive use:

(a) The normal basis of calculating their private expenditure.

(b) The fixed rate adjustment for the use of their business premises as a home.

Answer

(a) Using the normal method, the adjusted trading profit is as follows:

	£
Trading profit	30,000
Addback	
Food (£60 x 52)	3,120
Heat and light (£9,200 x 25%)	2,300
Trading profit	35,420

(b) Rather than calculating the actual private use for food and light and heat, Chris and Clive can simply use the fixed rate private use adjustment of £6,000, so their trading profit is £36,000 (30,000 + 6,000).

In the above example, Chris and Clive were actually worse off using the fixed rate adjustment. However, the position will differ from business to business and possibly from year to year. The time saved by using the fixed rate adjustment should also be considered, although this is probably hard to quantify.

Although the use of fixed rate adjustments is optional, in any examination question involving the cash basis it should be assumed that, where relevant, expenses are claimed on this basis.

> **The cash basis**
>
> - What is the purpose of the cash basis?
> - Who can use the cash basis?
> - How does the cash basis work?
> - The treatment of losses

2 The cash basis

2.1 What is the purpose of the cash basis?

Businesses are normally required to compute their accounting profits using the accruals basis. This involves:

- Recording income according to when it is earned, rather than when it is received.
- Deducting expenses which relate to the period, irrespective of when they are paid.

As the accruals basis may be difficult for non-accountants to understand, it is possible for small businesses to calculate their trading income using their cash receipts and payments. This is a much simpler method of accounting that can be easily understood by most business people.

2.2 Who can use the cash basis?

The cash basis is only available to unincorporated businesses, i.e. sole traders and partnerships where all of the partners are individuals.

It can be used where the business's total receipts for the tax year do not exceed £150,000. This limit is time-apportioned if the basis period is less than 12 months.

An election to use the scheme is made by ticking the relevant box in the self-assessment tax return. The election applies for both income tax and Class 4 national insurance purposes.

Once a business has started to use the cash basis, it may continue to do so until:

- it elects to calculate its profits using the normal method because a change in circumstances means that it is no longer appropriate to use the scheme, or
- receipts for the previous year exceeded £300,000 (unless receipts for the current year will not exceed £150,000).

However, in any examination question involving an unincorporated business, it should be assumed that the cash basis is **not relevant** unless it is specifically mentioned. If the question states that the cash basis is to be used, it should be assumed that fixed rate adjustments are used.

2.3 How does the cash basis work?

With the cash basis, receivables, payables and inventory are ignored, and tax-deductible capital and revenue expenditure will be treated the same:

- purchases of equipment (other than cars) are deducted as an expense
- the proceeds from any capital disposals are included with receipts.

The trading profit (or loss) under the cash basis is therefore calculated as follows:

	£
Receipts (including the sale of equipment)	X
Expense payments (including the purchase of equipment)	(X)
Trading profit (or loss)	X

Traders can make up their accounts to any date in the same way as other traders and the basis of assessment rules apply as normal.

Example

Shanta commenced self-employment as an engineering consultant on 6 April 2022. The following information is available for the year ended 5 April 2023:

Revenue was £54,600, of which £4,200 was owed as receivables at 5 April 2023.

On 16 May 2022 she purchased office equipment for £2,700.

On 10 June 2022 a motor car with CO_2 emissions of 45 grams per kilometre was purchased for £12,600. The motor car is used by Shanta, and 50% of the mileage is for private journeys. Motor expenses were £3,800. During the year ended 5 April 2023 Shanta drove 7,000 business miles.

Other expenses (all allowable) were £6,300, of which £1,200 was owed as payables at 5 April 2023.

Required

Calculate the trading profit for the year ended 5 April 2023 assuming Shanta uses:

(a) The normal basis of calculating trading profits.
(b) The cash basis.

Answer

(a) If Shanta uses the normal basis, her trading profit for the year ended 5 April 2023 will be calculated as follows:

	£	£
Revenue		54,600
Expenses		
Motor expenses (3,800 x 50%)	1,900	
Other expenses	6,300	
Capital allowances (2,700 + 1,134)	3,834	(12,034)
Trading profit		42,566

The office equipment purchased for £2,700 qualifies for the annual investment allowance.

The motor car has CO_2 emissions between 1 and 50 grams per kilometre, and therefore qualifies for writing down allowances at the rate of 18%. The allowance for the year ended 5 April 2023 is £1,134 (12,600 x 18% = 2,268 x 50%).

(b) However, if Shanta uses the cash basis, her trading profit will be calculated as follows:

	£	£
Revenue		
(54,600 – 4,200)		50,400
Expenses		
Office equipment	2,700	
Motor expenses (7,000 miles at 45p)	3,150	
Other expenses (6,300 – 1,200)	5,100	(10,950)
Trading profit		39,450

Note that the cost of the car is not deductible as the approved mileage allowances have been claimed.

In the above example, Shanta is better off using the cash basis. However, the position will differ from business to business and possibly from year to year. The time saved by using the cash basis should also be considered, although this is probably hard to quantify.

2.4 The treatment of losses

Where the use of the cash basis results in a trading loss, the only relief available is to carry the loss forward against future trading profits. There is no relief against total income.

Taxation – United Kingdom
(TX-UK) FA2022

CHAPTER 11

Tax relief for pension contributions

Contents

1. Overview of pension schemes
2. Relief for pension contributions
3. Limits on the amount of relief available

> **Overview of pension schemes**
>
> - The choices available for providing a pension for retirement
> - Overview of the options available for pension contributions

1 Overview of pension schemes

1.1 The choices available for providing a pension for retirement

A pension scheme is a fund of assets set up with the intention of providing a lump sum and an income (pension) for the members of the scheme on their retirement and/or benefits for dependants after their death.

An individual usually starts to contribute into a pension scheme early in their working life, with the intention of accumulating sufficient funds to pay for their retirement years.

The Government wishes to encourage individuals to make provision for their retirement, therefore generous tax relief is given for pension contributions.

In addition to tax relief for the pension contributions, any income or profits earned by the pension fund itself are exempt from income tax and capital gains tax. Investments held in a pension fund will therefore grow in value more rapidly than investments held by an individual personally.

From the age of 55, an individual can withdraw up to 25% of the pension fund as a tax-free lump sum. The balance of the fund can be withdrawn as income. These income withdrawals can be made whenever the individual chooses. They are added to any other taxable income that the individual has and taxed at the normal non-savings rates of income tax.

Rules on pension contributions

The choices for providing a pension and the tax relief available for the pension contributions depend on whether the individual is:

- employed, or
- self-employed, or
- not working.

There are two types of pension scheme that may be **available to employees**:

- an employer's occupational pension scheme (sometimes known as a workplace pension scheme), or
- their own personal pension plan (PPP).

Occupational pension schemes

An occupational pension scheme is a scheme established by an employer solely for the benefit of the employees of that business. Therefore, an occupational pension scheme only relates to that employment. If an individual leaves that employment they will need to set up new pension arrangements for any future contributions.

There are two types of occupational pension scheme:

- **Defined benefit schemes** (also known as final salary schemes). With this type of scheme, the eventual pension depends on the individual's length of service and salary at the time of retirement.

- **Defined contribution schemes** (also known as money purchase schemes). With this type of scheme, the eventual pension depends on the performance of the investments in the pension fund.

Most occupational schemes are now defined contribution schemes.

Personal pension plans

A PPP is a separate fund, usually established by way of a contract between the individual and an approved pension provider (e.g. a bank or life assurance company).

PPPs do not relate to a particular job, trade or profession. They are personal to that individual taxpayer and are set up for the duration of their life, regardless of their employment status. All PPPs are money purchase schemes.

Unlike an employed individual who has a choice of an occupational pension scheme and/or a PPP, a self-employed individual and those who are not working can only set up a PPP.

1.2 Overview of the options available for pension contributions

The options available for pension contributions depend on the status of the individual as follows:

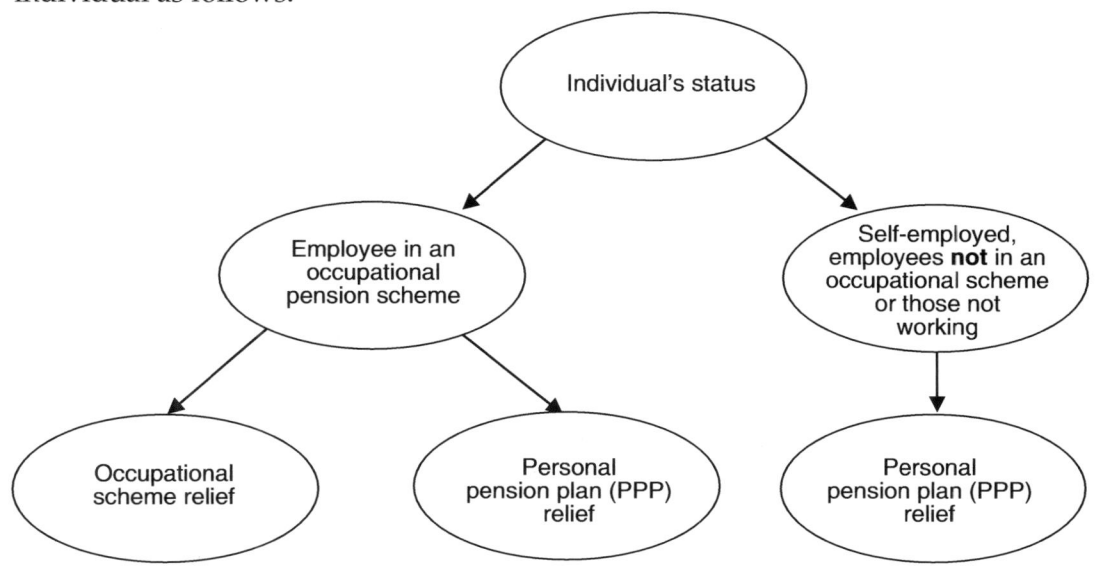

```
                    ┌─────────────────┐
                    │ Individual's    │
                    │ status          │
                    └────────┬────────┘
                   ┌─────────┴─────────┐
                   ▼                   ▼
        ┌──────────────────┐   ┌──────────────────┐
        │ Employee in an   │   │ Self-employed,   │
        │ occupational     │   │ employees not in │
        │ pension scheme   │   │ an occupational  │
        │                  │   │ scheme or those  │
        │                  │   │ not working      │
        └────────┬─────────┘   └────────┬─────────┘
          ┌─────┴─────┐                 │
          ▼           ▼                 ▼
    ┌──────────┐ ┌──────────┐     ┌──────────┐
    │Occupat'l │ │Personal  │     │Personal  │
    │scheme    │ │pension   │     │pension   │
    │relief    │ │plan (PPP)│     │plan (PPP)│
    │          │ │relief    │     │relief    │
    └──────────┘ └──────────┘     └──────────┘
```

> **Relief for pension contributions**
>
> - Relief for contributions into an occupational pension scheme
> - Relief for contributions into a personal pension plan

2 Relief for pension contibutions

2.1 Relief for contributions into an occupational pension scheme

Tax relief for contributions made into an occupational pension scheme is given as follows:

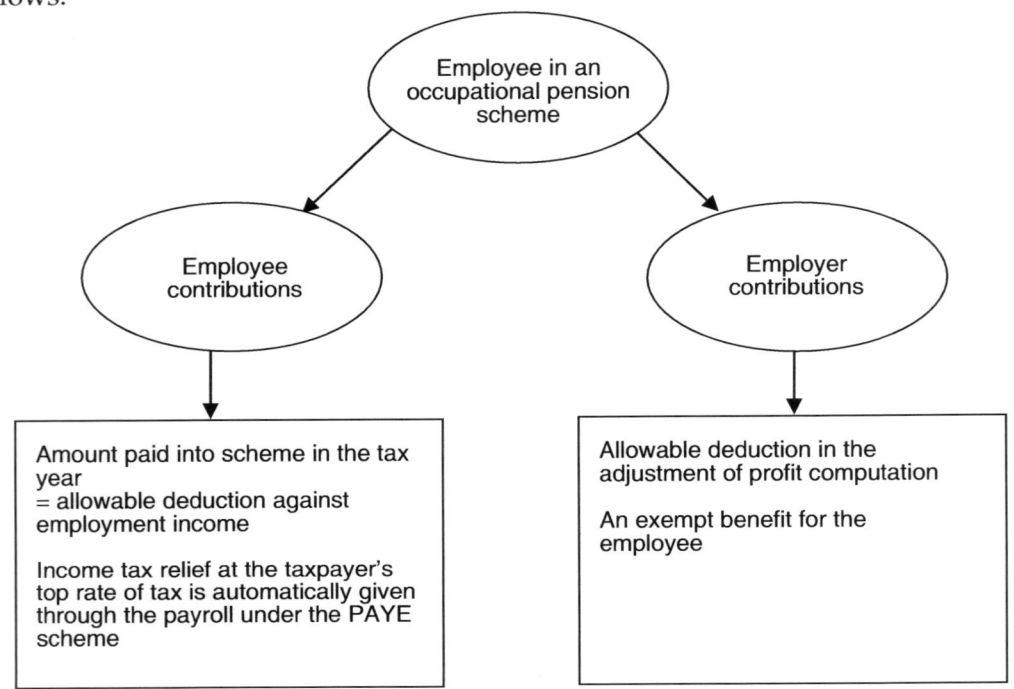

```
                    Employee in an
                 occupational pension
                        scheme
                   /              \
        Employee                    Employer
       contributions              contributions
            |                          |
            v                          v
┌────────────────────────────┐  ┌────────────────────────────┐
│ Amount paid into scheme    │  │ Allowable deduction in the │
│ in the tax year            │  │ adjustment of profit       │
│ = allowable deduction      │  │ computation                │
│ against employment income  │  │                            │
│                            │  │ An exempt benefit for the  │
│ Income tax relief at the   │  │ employee                   │
│ taxpayer's top rate of tax │  │                            │
│ is automatically given     │  │                            │
│ through the payroll under  │  │                            │
│ the PAYE scheme            │  │                            │
└────────────────────────────┘  └────────────────────────────┘
```

2.2 Relief for contributions into a personal pension plan

Basic rate taxpayers

Basic rate relief (20%) is **automatically** given at source as pension contributions are paid **net** of 20% tax therefore pension contributions are ignored in the individual's income tax computation. (For example, if an individual chooses to contribute £200 each month gross into their pension scheme, they will actually pay only £160. This is the £200 less tax relief at 20%.)

Higher and additional rate taxpayers

As basic rate relief (20%) is **automatically** given at source, the additional relief needed for higher rate and additional rate taxpayers is obtained by extending the basic rate band (and higher rate band) in the same way as for gift aid contributions.

The basic rate band is extended by adding the **gross** amount of the pension contributions to the £37,700 threshold. Similarly, the higher rate band is extended by adding the **gross** amount of the pension contributions to the £150,000 threshold.

Example

Zinan is aged 49 and is a self-employed electrician who has been trading for many years. His trading profits have been steadily increasing and his results for the last two years are as follows:

Year ended	Adjusted profit after capital allowances
	£
31 January 2022	53,400
31 January 2023	71,470

Zinan has non-trading income of £6,000 each year.

Required

Assuming Zinan decides to make a gross pension contribution of £20,000 for 2022/23, explain how the relief will be obtained.

Answer

Pension contributions are paid net of 20% tax therefore, to make a gross contribution of £20,000, Zinan must pay £16,000 (= £20,000 × 80%) into the scheme.

Zinan is clearly a higher rate taxpayer as shown below:

	£
Trading income	71,470
Non-trading income	6,000
Total income	77,470
Minus PA	(12,570)
Taxable income	64,900

Relief at 20% is given at source for his payments into the pension scheme.

Higher rate relief is obtained by extending his basic rate band to £57,700, i.e. by adding the gross pension contribution of £20,000 to the basic rate band limit of £37,700. This means that less of Zinan's income will be subject to tax at the higher rate.

> **Limits on the amount of relief available**
>
> - The amount of relief available
> - Individuals who are not working
> - Relevant earnings of working individuals
> - The annual allowance
> - Contributions in excess of the annual allowance
> - The lifetime allowance

3 Limits on the amount of relief available

3.1 The amount of relief available

Individuals under the age of 75 are entitled to tax relief for their contributions to registered pension schemes.

Any amount can be contributed into a pension scheme. However, tax relief is only available on contributions up to the higher of:

(1) £3,600, and

(2) 100% of relevant earnings.

3.2 Individuals who are not working

Individuals who are not working will have no relevant earnings and therefore their maximum (gross) contribution is £3,600. This figure is given in the tax rates and allowances table in the examination.

As contributions are made into a pension scheme **net** of 20% tax, the maximum amount of contributions payable into a scheme by a non-working individual is £2,880 (= £3,600 × 80%).

3.3 Relevant earnings of working individuals

Relevant earnings are trading profits, employment income and income from furnished holiday lettings. Therefore, if a working individual puts all of their earned income into a pension scheme, they can obtain tax relief for the full amount.

3.4 The annual allowance

Although individuals can receive tax relief on contributions of up to 100% of their earnings, there is effectively an upper limit of £40,000 on the amount of contribution which can qualify for relief. The figure of £40,000 is known as the annual allowance.

Tapering the annual allowance

The annual allowance is reduced by £1 for every £2 by which an individual's adjusted income exceeds £240,000. However, the minimum tapered annual allowance is £4,000.

The definition of adjusted income depends on whether the individual is employed or self-employed.

For employees, adjusted income is:

	£
Net income (i.e. total income less deductible interest)	X
Plus any employee contributions to occupational pension schemes	X
Plus any employer contributions to either occupational or personal pension schemes.	X
Adjusted income	X

For the self-employed, adjusted income will simply be net income.

Tapering applies on a tax year basis, so a taxpayer with variable income might find themselves entitled to the full £40,000 annual allowance for some years and a tapered annual allowance in other years.

Example

(a) Mario is an employee. For 2022/23 his net income is £270,000. He makes contributions of £12,000 into his employer's occupational pension scheme and his employer contributes a further £10,000.

(b) Mavis is self-employed. For 2022/23 her net income is £270,000. She makes contributions of £12,000 (gross) into her personal pension plan.

(c) Martin is self-employed. For 2022/23 his net income is £320,000. He makes contributions of £15,000 (gross) into his personal pension plan.

Required

Calculate the tapered annual allowance available to all three taxpayers for 2022/23.

Answer

(a) Mario's tapered annual allowance is:

	£
Annual allowance	40,000
Less: (292,000 – 240,000) x ½	(26,000)
Tapered annual allowance	14,000

Working	£
Net income (i.e. total income less deductible interest)	270,000
Plus any employee contributions to occupational pension schemes	12,000
Plus any employer contributions to either occupational or personal pension schemes.	10,000
Adjusted income	292,000

(b) Mavis's tapered annual allowance is:

	£
Annual allowance	40,000
Less: (270,000 – 240,000) x ½	(15,000)
Tapered annual allowance	25,000

(c) Martin is entitled to the minimum tapered annual allowance of £4,000:

	£
Annual allowance	40,000
Less: (320,000 – 240,000) x ½ = £40,000 (restricted)	(36,000)
Tapered annual allowance	4,000

Note

The contributions to the occupational pension scheme are added back because they will have been deducted when calculating net income. By contrast, the personal pension plan contributions are not added back because they are not deducted when calculating net income; instead, relief is given by extending the basic rate band.

Carrying forward unused annual allowances

If the annual allowance (or tapered annual allowance) is not fully used in any tax year, the unused amount can be carried forward on a first-in-first-out (FIFO) basis for up to three years. However, the current year's annual allowance must always be used first.

The unused allowance is lost for any year in which a person is not a member of a pension scheme.

The figure of annual allowance is given in the table of tax rates and allowances provided in the examination.

Example

Li and Nina made the following gross personal pension contributions during 2019/20, 2020/21 and 2021/22:

	Li	Nina
	£	£
2019/20	22,000	66,000
2020/21	Nil	29,000
2021/22	38,000	Nil

Li was not a member of a pension scheme during 2020/21. Nina was a member of a pension scheme for all three tax years.

Required

Calculate the maximum amount of contribution Li and Nina can obtain tax relief for during 2022/23.

Answer

Li

Li has unused allowances of £18,000 (40,000 – 22,000) from 2019/20 and £2,000 (40,000 – 38,000) from 2021/22, so a total of £60,000 (40,000 + 18,000 + 2,000) is available for 2022/23. She was not a member of a pension scheme for 2020/21 so the annual allowance for that year is lost.

Nina

Nina has unused allowances of £11,000 (40,000 – 29,000) from 2020/21 and £40,000 from 2021/22, so a total of £91,000 (40,000 + 11,000 + 40,000) is available for 2022/23. The annual allowance for 2019/20 was fully utilised, but Nina was a member of a pension scheme for 2021/22 so the annual allowance for that year is available in full.

Remember that the annual allowance for the current year is utilised first, and then any unused allowances from earlier years with those from the earliest year used first.

3.5 Contributions in excess of the annual allowance

Contributions in excess of the annual allowance (including any brought forward unused allowances) are taxed at the individual's marginal rate of tax. This is known as an annual allowance charge. The purpose of this charge is to cancel out the tax relief that will have been given in respect of the contribution, therefore there is no charge where contributions have not qualified for relief.

Note that all contributions to an individual's pension scheme(s) during a particular tax year count towards this annual allowance. This means that you need to take account of any contributions paid by the individual's employer in deciding whether the annual limit has been exceeded.

Example

Flora has a trading profit of £340,000 for 2022/23. She made gross personal pension contributions of £80,000. She does not have any brought forward unused annual allowances.

Required

Calculate Flora's income tax liability for 2022/23.

Answer

As Flora has earnings of £340,000 for 2022/23, all of the pension contributions qualify for tax relief. Flora's income tax liability is therefore as follows:

		£
Trading profit		340,000
Personal allowance	(W1)	Nil
Taxable income		340,000
Income tax:		
£117,700 at 20%	(W2)	23,540
£112,300 at 40%	(W2)	44,920
£110,000 at 45%		49,500
Annual allowance charge		
£76,000 at 45%	(W3)	34,200
Tax liability		152,160

Workings

1. Flora's adjusted net income exceeds £125,140, so no personal allowance is available.

2. Higher and additional rate tax relief is given by extending the basic and higher rate tax bands by the full amount of her pension contribution to £117,700 (37,700 + 80,000) and £230,000 (150,000 + 80,000) respectively.

3. Flora is entitled to the minimum annual allowance of £4,000 as her adjusted income exceeds £312,000. The annual allowance charge is £76,000 (80,000 – 4,000) being the excess of the pension contributions over the annual allowance for 2022/23.

3.6 The lifetime allowance

The total funds that can be built up within a person's pension schemes is £1,073,100. This figure is known as the lifetime allowance. Where it is exceeded, there will be an additional tax charge when the funds are eventually withdrawn.

Taxation – United Kingdom
(TX-UK) FA2022

CHAPTER 12

Residence

Contents
1 Liability to UK tax
2 The statutory residence test

> **Liability to UK tax**
>
> - Liability to UK income tax
> - Liability to UK capital gains tax
> - Liability to UK inheritance tax

1 Liability to UK tax

1.1 Liability to UK income tax

Individuals are liable to pay income tax on their taxable income for a tax year.

As far as the TX-UK examination is concerned, the scope of income tax for individuals is as follows:

Taxable person:	Liable on:
UK resident individual	Worldwide taxable income
Non-UK resident individual	UK income only

1.2 Liability to UK capital gains tax

Individuals are liable to pay capital gains tax on their taxable gains for a tax year.

As far as the TX-UK examination is concerned, the scope of capital gains tax for individuals is as follows:

Taxable person:	Liable on:
UK resident individual	Worldwide capital gains
Non-UK resident individual	No liability to UK capital gains tax (apart from on disposals of UK assets used in a trade and UK land and buildings)

1.3 Liability to UK inheritance tax

Liability to UK inheritance tax is determined by domicile rather than residence.

The term 'domicile' is a legal term that means the permanent home of an individual. An individual can only have one domicile at any point in time.

A UK domiciled individual is liable to pay UK inheritance tax on their worldwide assets.

The TX-UK examination will only cover the position of individuals who are domiciled in the UK.

Chapter 12: Residence

> **The statutory residence test**
> - Overview of the residence rules
> - Automatic overseas tests
> - Automatic residence tests
> - The UK ties test

2 The statutory residence test

2.1 Overview of the residence rules

The UK has a statutory test to determine whether a person is resident in the UK for tax purposes. Under these rules, an individual is either UK resident or non-UK resident for the whole of the tax year.

The rules for determining residence are rather complicated and it is therefore important to work through them in the following order:

- Consider whether an individual meets the **automatic overseas tests**. If one of these is met, the individual is classed as not UK resident and there is no need to consider the other tests.

- If none of the automatic overseas tests is met, consider whether an individual meets the **automatic residence tests**. If one of these is met, the individual is classed as UK resident and there is no need to consider the next test.

- If none of the automatic tests apply, look at how many **ties** an individual has with the UK and how many days they stay in the UK during a tax year.

2.2 Automatic overseas tests

This is the starting point for determining an individual's residence status.

The following individuals will automatically be treated as **not resident** in the UK:

- A person who is in the UK for **less than 16 days** during a tax year.
- A person who is in the UK for **less than 46 days** during a tax year, and who has not been UK resident during any of the three previous tax years.
- A person who **works full-time overseas**, subject to them not being in the UK for more than 90 days during a tax year. Full time for this purpose is an average of 35 hours per week.

Example

Mihaela is in the UK for 30 days during the tax year 2022/23. She has not previously been resident in the UK. Her home is in Romania.

Required

Explain Mihaela's residence status for 2022/23.

Answer

Mihaela will automatically be treated as not resident in the UK for 2022/23 as she is in the UK for less than 46 days during the tax year and has not been UK resident during the three previous tax years.

Example

Maurice was born in the UK but now works full-time in the USA. He is in the UK for 30 days during the tax year 2022/23 visiting his old school friends.

Required

Explain Maurice's residence status for 2022/23.

Answer

Maurice will automatically be treated as **not resident** in the UK for 2022/23 as he works overseas on a full-time basis and is in the UK for less than 90 days during the tax year.

2.3 Automatic residence tests

The following individuals will automatically be treated as **resident** in the UK, provided they do not meet any of the automatic overseas tests:

- A person who is in the UK for **183 days or more** during a tax year.
- A person whose **only home** is in the UK.
- A person who carries out **full time work in the UK**.

Example

Max is a student. He is in the UK for 70 days during the tax year 2022/23. He spent the remainder of the tax year travelling in Asia. He shares a flat in London with his girlfriend. This flat is his only home.

Required

Explain Max's residence status for 2022/23.

Answer

Max cannot be treated as automatically not resident in the UK for 2022/23 as he is in the UK for more than 45 days during the tax year.

He is treated as **automatically resident** in the UK for 2022/23 as his only home is in the UK.

Example

Miu is a student. She is in the UK for 210 days during the tax year 2022/23 attending a course at Oxford University. She has not previously been resident in the UK. Her family lives in China.

Required

Explain Miu's residence status for 2022/23.

Answer

Miu cannot be treated as automatically not resident in the UK for 2022/23 as she is in the UK for more than 45 days during the tax year.

She is treated as automatically **resident in the UK** for 2022/23 as she is in the UK for at least 183 days.

2.4 The UK ties test

Where a person's residence status cannot be determined according to any of the automatic tests, then their status will be based on:

- how many ties they have with the UK, and
- how many days they stay in the UK during a tax year.

As a general rule, the longer someone spends in the UK the fewer ties are needed for them to be classed as UK resident.

There are five UK ties as follows:

- Having **close family** (i.e. a spouse/civil partner or minor child) in the UK.
- Having a **house in the UK** which is made use of during the tax year. This does not necessarily have to be a house that the individual owns. It could, for example, be a room in their parent's house that they use when they are in the UK.
- Doing substantive **work in the UK**. Substantive means working at least three hours a day for a period of 40 days or more.
- Being in the UK for more than **90 days** during either of the **two previous tax years**.
- Spending **more time in the UK** than in any other country in the tax year (but see below).

How the UK ties test is applied depends on whether a person has been resident in the UK for any of the previous three tax years:

- A person who has been resident during any of the previous three tax years will typically be someone who is leaving the UK, and for them all five UK ties are relevant.
- A person who has not been resident during any of the previous three tax years will typically be someone who is arriving in the UK, and for them the final 'country' tie is ignored.

Days in UK	Previously resident	Not previously resident
Less than 16	Automatically not resident	Automatically not resident
16 to 45	Resident if 4 UK ties (or more)	Automatically not resident
46 to 90	Resident if 3 UK ties (or more)	Resident if 4 UK ties
91 to 120	Resident if 2 UK ties (or more)	Resident if 3 UK ties (or more)
121 to 182	Resident if 1 UK tie (or more)	Resident if 2 UK ties (or more)
183 or more	Automatically resident	Automatically resident

A day in the UK is any day in which a person is present in the UK at midnight.

The above table will be given in the tax rates and allowances section of the examination paper.

Example

Mark has retired from work. He has always been resident in the UK and has spent at least 320 days in the UK each year. On 6 April 2022 Mark purchased an overseas apartment where he lived for most of the tax year 2022/23. He also has a home in the UK where his wife and children live. During the tax year 2022/23 Mark visited the UK for a total of 80 days, staying in his UK home each time.

Required

Explain Mark's residence status for 2022/23.

Answer

For 2022/23 Mark spent 80 days in the UK. This exceeds 45 days and so he cannot automatically be treated as non-UK resident.

He will not automatically be treated as UK resident because he does not meet the only home test. We must therefore consider the sufficient ties test.

Mark has been resident in the UK during the three previous tax years. The 'previously resident' column is therefore relevant for him.

He was in the UK between 46 and 90 days during 2022/23. This means that he needs three or more UK ties to be classed as UK resident.

Mark's UK ties are as follows:

- He has close family in the UK.
- He has a house in the UK which he made use of.
- He was in the UK for more than 90 days during the previous two tax years.

He is therefore **resident** in the UK for 2022/23.

You can see from the above table that it is more difficult for a person leaving the UK to become non-resident than it is for a person arriving in the UK to become UK resident.

Example

Mary has not previously been resident in the UK, being in the UK for less than 15 days each tax year. On 6 April 2022 she purchased a house in the UK, and during the tax year 2022/23 stayed in the UK for a total of 160 days. Mary also has an overseas house which was where she stayed for the remainder of the tax year 2022/23.

Required

Explain Mary's residence status for 2022/23.

Answer

For 2022/23 Mary spent 160 days in the UK. This exceeds 45 days and so she cannot be automatically treated as non-resident. She will not automatically be treated as resident because she does not meet the only home test.

Mary has not been resident in the UK during the three previous tax years. The 'not previously resident' column is therefore relevant for her.

She was in the UK between 121 and 182 days, therefore she needs two UK ties in order to be classed as UK resident.

Her only UK tie is the house in the UK which she uses. She is therefore not resident in the UK for 2022/23.

Taxation – United Kingdom (TX-UK) FA2022

CHAPTER 13

National insurance contributions

Contents
1   Class 1 NICs
2   Class 1A NICs
3   Class 2 and Class 4 NICs

> **Class 1 NICs**
> - The scope of Class 1 NICs
> - The calculation of primary and secondary Class 1 NICs
> - Employment for part of a year
> - The employment allowance

1 Class 1 NICs

1.1 The scope of Class 1 NICs

Employees are personally liable to Class 1 primary NI contributions. In addition, employers (whether a sole trader, a partnership or a company) are liable to Class 1 secondary contributions in respect of salaries paid and Class 1A contributions in respect of benefits provided to their employees.

These are commonly referred to as employee's NICs and employer's NICs.

Both Class 1 primary and Class 1 secondary contributions are paid to HMRC under the PAYE system. The employer acts as a collector of taxes on behalf of HMRC and deducts the primary contributions from the employee's salary/wages before payment.

The due date of payment for Class 1 primary and secondary NICs is the 19th of every month (i.e. 14 days after the end of each tax month, which is defined as the 6th of one month to the 5th of the following month). If payment is made electronically the payment date is extended by three days to the 22nd of the month. (Employers with more than 250 employees must pay electronically.)

Class 1 secondary contributions paid by the employer are part of the total cost of employing staff and are charged against profit in the financial accounts. The contributions are incurred wholly and exclusively for the purposes of the trade and are therefore allowable deductions in the employer's adjustment of profit computation.

Employees and employers are assessed to Class 1 primary and secondary contributions:

- on a cash receipts basis
- for an earnings period
- based on the employee's cash earnings.

Cash receipts basis

Taxing an employee on a cash receipts basis means that the employee and employer are assessed to NICs in the week or month in which the cash is paid to the employee.

Earnings period

Employees who are paid weekly have their NICs calculated on a weekly basis using weekly limits and rates. If they are paid monthly, their NICs are calculated on a monthly basis using monthly limits and rates.

However, in the examination, questions will usually require calculations to be made using the annual limits and rates. The appropriate limits and rates required for the examination questions will be given in the tax rates and allowances sheet.

Cash earnings

An employee's cash earnings are calculated as follows:

Cash earnings for Class 1 NICs	£
Salary/wages	X
Bonuses/commissions	X
Any other cash receipts and cash benefits (e.g. excess mileage allowance)	X
Cash **and** non-cash vouchers **excluding** vouchers exempted under the benefit rules	X
Receipts of marketable assets that can be converted into cash (e.g. gold bars, fine wines, shares, diamonds)	X
Cash earnings for Class 1 NICs	X

Note that cash earnings are not the same as the employment income assessment, as they are calculated before any allowable deductions (e.g. occupational pension scheme contributions, subscriptions).

Cash earnings also exclude the following:

- exempt benefits per employment income rules
- non-cash benefits (e.g. company car, fuel, living accommodation)
- business expenses reimbursed by the employer
- tips from third parties.

1.2 The calculation of primary and secondary Class 1 NICs

The annual limits and rates for Class 1 NICs to be used in the examination are as follows:

		%
Class 1 Employee	£1 – £12,570 per year	Nil
	£12,571 – £50,270 per year	13.25
	£50,271 and above per year	3.25
Class 1 Employer	£1 – £9,100 per year	Nil
	£9,101 and above per year	15.05

Note that the lower threshold of £12,570 has only been in force since 6 July 2022. However, for the purpose of the examination, it will be assumed that the threshold applies throughout the tax year 2022/23.

Similarly, the rates above include an increase of 1.25% that was only in force for part of the tax year; however, for simplicity, the examination will assume that this additional 1.25% applies throughout the tax year 2022/23.

You do not need to learn these rates. The appropriate limits and rates required for any examination question will be given in the tax rates and allowances sheet.

Example

Peter and Paula are both employed by Quality Games Ltd. Their remuneration for 2022/23 is as follows:

	Peter	Paula
	£	£
Salary	60,000	24,000
Bonus	8,000	Nil
Car benefit	3,450	Nil
Employer's pension scheme contribution	3,600	1,440
Employee's pension scheme contribution	2,400	960

Required

Calculate all of the Class 1 NICs payable by the employer to HMRC in respect of Peter and Paula for the tax year 2022/23 using the annual limits and rates.

Answer

(1) Calculate cash earnings

	Peter	Paula
	£	£
Salary	60,000	24,000
Bonuses	8,000	0
Cash earnings for Class 1 NICs	68,000	24,000

The **car benefit** is excluded as it is a non-cash benefit. The **employer's pension contributions** are excluded as they are an exempt benefit. The **employees' pension contributions** are ignored as they are not allowable deductions for NIC purposes.

(2) Calculate the NICs for the employee and the employer

The requirement of the question is to calculate all the Class 1 NICs that the employer has to pay to HMRC. In addition to paying the employer's Class 1 secondary contributions, the employer also pays the employees' Class 1 primary contributions to HMRC on behalf of the employees, under the PAYE system.

	Peter	Paula	Total Class 1 NICs payable by Quality Games Ltd
	£	£	£
Class 1 primary contributions			
(£50,270 - £12,570) × 13.25%	4,995		
(£68,000 - £50,270) × 3.25%	576		
(£24,000 - £12,570) × 13.25%		1,514	1,514
	5,571		5,571
Class 1 secondary contributions			
(£68,000 - £9,100) × 15.05%	8,864		8,864
(£24,000 - £9,100) × 15.05%		2,242	2,242
	14,435 +	3,756	= 18,191

1.3 Employment for part of a year

If an individual is only employed for part of a year, the relevant annual thresholds must be time-apportioned.

Example

On 1 January 2023, Elliott started his first job after leaving university. He is employed at a monthly salary of £2,000.

Required

Calculate the Class 1 NICs payable by both Elliott and his employer for the tax year 2022/23.

Answer

As Elliott is only employed for three months during 2022/23, the lower limits must be time-apportioned:

Employee: £12,570 / 12 months = £1,048 a month
Employer: £9,100 / 12 months = £758 a month

Elliott's Class 1 NIC for 2022/23 will therefore be:

(£2,000 - £1,048) x 13.25% x 3 months = £378

His employer's Class 1 NIC for 2022/23 will be:

(£2,000 - £758) x 15.05% x 3 months = £561

If Elliott's annual salary had been in excess of £50,270, the upper limit would also have had to be time-apportioned: £50,270 / 12 months = £4,189 a month. Elliott would have paid NIC at the 13.25% rate on a maximum of £3,141 (£4,189 - £1,048) a month, with any monthly salary in excess of £4,189 liable at the 3.25% rate.

1.4 The employment allowance

An annual employment allowance of up to £5,000 a year may enable a business to reduce the amount of **employer's** class 1 NIC that it pays to HMRC. The allowance does not affect the amount of class 1A or employee class 1 NIC that is payable.

If the total employer's class 1 NIC is £5,000 or less, then the liability will be nil.

Note, however, that the employment allowance is not available to:

- companies where a director is the sole employee. (This point is especially relevant when a sole director is making a decision whether to extract profits from their company as remuneration or as dividends.)
- businesses where employers' contributions were £100,000 or more for the previous tax year.

Example

Following on from the earlier example involving Peter and Paula.

Required

Explain how the annual employment allowance will affect the amount of national insurance payable for the tax year 2022/23.

Answer

The class 1 secondary contributions calculated above total £11,106 (8,864 + 2,242). The employment allowance will reduce the amount payable to £6,106 (11,106 – 5,000).

Chapter 13: National insurance contributions

> **Class 1A NICs**
>
> - The nature of Class 1A NICs
> - The basis of calculating Class 1A NICs

2 Class 1A NICs

2.1 The nature of Class 1A NICs

Class 1A NICs are payable by **employers only**, not employees.

They are charged on the non-cash benefits provided by the employer to their employees (e.g. company cars, private fuel, living accommodation).

Note that non-cash benefits **exclude:**

- exempt benefits (as defined for the employment income rules)
- non-cash vouchers (as these are either specifically exempt or, if not exempt, liable to Class 1 primary and secondary NICs, not Class 1A NICs).

2.2 The basis of calculating Class 1A NICs

For the purpose of the examination, Class 1A NICs are charged at 15.05% on the amount of the benefit measured using the employment income rules.

The due date of payment of Class 1A NICs is 19 July following the end of the tax year, i.e. 19 July 2023 for 2022/23. If payment is made electronically the payment date is extended by three days to the 22nd of the month.

Class 1A contributions paid by the employer are part of the total cost of employing staff and are charged against profit in the financial accounts. The contributions are incurred wholly and exclusively for the purposes of the trade and are therefore allowable deductions in the employer's adjustment of profit computation.

Example

Robert is employed by Swain Products Ltd. In 2022/23 he received the following benefits from his employment:

(a) A new petrol car costing £16,500 with a list price of £17,600 and CO_2 emissions of 143 g/km. Robert contributed £40 per month for the use of the car.

(b) All fuel, which cost the company £4,440 for the year 2022/23.

(c) A car parking place at the work premises.

(d) Private medical insurance which cost the company £1,100.

(e) Private use of a video camera with a market value of £350 when first made available.

Required

Calculate the Class 1A NIC payable by Swain Products Ltd for 2022/23.

Answer

(1) Calculate the assessable benefits under the employment income rules

	g/km		Petrol %
CO_2 emissions (rounded down to nearest 5 g/km)	140		
Base level of CO_2 emissions	(55)		
	85	÷ 5	17
Minimum percentage			16
Appropriate percentage			33

	£		£
Manufacturer's list price	17,600	at 33%	5,808
Minus: Contribution for the use of the car (£40 × 12)			(480)
Car benefit			5,328
Private fuel benefit (£25,300 × 33%)			8,349
Parking space at workplace = exempt benefit			Nil
Private medical insurance (cost to employer)			1,100
Private use of video camera (£350 × 20%)			70
Total benefits liable to Class 1A NICs			14,847

(2) Calculate the Class 1A NICs at 15.05%

Class 1A NICs = £14,847 × 15.05% = £2,234

> **Class 2 and Class 4 NICs**
>
> - Class 2 NICs
> - Class 4 NICs
> - The calculation of Class 4 NICs

3 Class 2 and Class 4 NICs

3.1 Class 2 NICs

Class 2 NICs are paid by self-employed individuals (i.e. sole traders and each partner in a partnership).

For 2022/23, Class 2 NICs are payable at a flat rate of £3.15 per week. This rate is given in the tax rates and allowances section in the examination paper.

The maximum Class 2 NICs payable for 2022/23 are therefore £164 (£3.15 × 52).

However, they are only payable if the self-employed individual has taxable profits in excess of £12,570.

Payment dates

Class 2 NIC is payable via the self assessment system. The full amount is due, together with the balancing payment of income tax and Class 4 NIC, on 31 January following the end of the tax year (see Chapter 17). The amount due is based on the number of weeks of self-employment during the tax year.

Tax treatment

Class 2 NICs are a personal tax on the self-employed individual, not the unincorporated business. If the Class 2 NICs are paid for by the business, they are not allowable as they are a personal expense of the owner and treated as an appropriation of profit. They must be added to profit in the adjustment of profit computation if they have been accounted for as an expense in the business accounts.

3.2 Class 4 NICs

Class 4 NICs are paid by self-employed individuals (i.e. sole traders and each partner in a partnership), **in addition to Class 2 NICs.**

Class 4 NICs are paid together with the individual's income tax liability under the self-assessment system.

Self-employed individuals are assessed to Class 4 NICs based on their taxable trading profits for a tax year.

Tax treatment

As is the case for Class 2 NICs, Class 4 NICs are a personal tax on the self-employed individual, not the unincorporated business. If the Class 4 NICs are paid for by the business, they are not allowable as they are a personal expense of the owner and treated as an appropriation of profit. They must be added to profit in the adjustment of profit computation if they have been accounted for as an expense in the business accounts.

3.3 The calculation of Class 4 NICs

For the purpose of the examination, the annual limits and rates for Class 4 NICs for 2022/23 are as follows:

Profits	Rate for Class 4 NICs
	%
First £12,570	Nil
£12,571 - £50,270	10.25
£50,271 and above	3.25

Note that the amount of Class 4 contributions depends solely on the level of taxable profits for the year. Class 4 contributions are unaffected by the number of weeks or months of self-employment.

Example

Sarah is self-employed, aged 39, and has been trading for many years. Her results for the last two years are as follows:

Year ended	Adjusted profit after capital allowances
	£
31 May 2022	60,000
31 May 2023	46,000

Sarah has property income of £600 each year.

Required

Calculate the Class 4 NICs Sarah is liable to pay for the tax year 2022/23.

Answer

Sarah is only liable to pay class 4 on her trading income. The amount due is:

Class 4 contributions	£
(£50,270 - £12,570) × 10.25%	3,864
(£60,000 - £50,270) × 3.25%	316
	4,180

Taxation – United Kingdom
(TX-UK) FA2022

CHAPTER 14

Capital gains tax

Contents

1. Overview of the taxation of chargeable gains of an individual
2. Computing gains and losses
3. Transfers between spouses
4. Part disposals
5. Wasting assets and chattels
6. Insurance and compensation

> **Overview of the taxation of chargeable gains of an individual**
>
> - The basic charging rules
> - The basis of assessment for capital gains tax
> - Calculating the capital gains tax liability of an individual
> - Proforma: capital gains tax computation
> - Calculating the capital gains tax liability
> - The due date of payment
> - CGT on death

1 Overview of the taxation of chargeable gains of an individual

1.1 The basic charging rules

Individuals are liable to:

- income tax on their taxable income, and
- capital gains tax (CGT) on their chargeable gains.

A chargeable gain arises if:

- a chargeable person
- makes a chargeable disposal
- of a chargeable asset.

A chargeable person is someone who is resident in the UK in the tax year in which the chargeable disposal is made.

A chargeable disposal is the **sale or gift** of the whole or part of an asset.

CGT is only charged on the disposal of capital assets during lifetime. No CGT is payable on the transfer of assets **due to the death of an individual**. Legacies on death are therefore exempt disposals for the purpose of CGT.

Exempt assets

The following list shows the most common examples of exempt assets:

- cars (including vintage cars and veteran cars)
- gilts (i.e. government securities)
- National Savings certificates
- current assets (trade receivables, inventory, cash).

If assets are exempt, they are ignored in the gain/loss computations:

- Any gain on the disposal of an exempt asset is not taxable.
- Any loss on the disposal of an exempt asset is not allowable.

1.2 The basis of assessment for capital gains tax

Individuals are taxed on their taxable gains in respect of chargeable disposals made in the **tax year** (i.e. 6 April to 5 April).

The date of disposal is the date on which the asset legally changes hands (i.e. when the contract of sale is legally binding), which is not necessarily the same as the payment date or delivery date.

1.3 Calculating the capital gains tax liability of an individual

The calculation of the capital gains tax liability of an individual is as follows:

- **Step 1: Calculate the gains or losses arising on the chargeable disposals.** A separate gain or loss calculation is needed for each chargeable asset that is disposed of in the tax year.

- **Step 2: Calculate and deduct any specific reliefs, if applicable.** Relief is available to reduce or defer the tax on some gains if certain conditions are satisfied.

- **Step 3: Aggregate the net chargeable gains arising in the tax year and deduct allowable capital losses (if any).**

- **Step 4: Deduct the annual exempt amount available to individuals.** Every individual can realise some gains tax-free each tax year. The 2022/23 annual exempt amount is £12,300. If the individual's total net chargeable gains do not exceed £12,300, the unused annual exempt amount is lost.

- **Step 5: Calculate the capital gains tax liability of the individual.** Apply the appropriate rate(s) of tax to calculate the liability to capital gains tax. The rate of capital gains tax depends on the individual's taxable income and the type of asset being disposed of.

1.4 Proforma: capital gains tax computation

Where several assets are disposed of, steps (1) and (2) above are usually shown as workings to an answer. These steps are explained in more detail later.

Steps (3) to (5) are shown in a summary capital gains tax liability computation as follows:

Name of individual	
Capital gains tax computation – 2022/23	£
Asset 1 - Gain after specific reliefs	X
Asset 2 - Gain after specific reliefs	X
Minus current year capital losses	(X)
Total net **chargeable gains**	X
Minus annual exempt amount *(note)*	(12,300)
	X
Minus capital losses brought forward	(X)
Taxable gains	X
Tax due at appropriate rate(s)	X

1.5 Calculating the capital gains tax liability

The rate of capital gains tax depends on the individual's taxable income and the type of asset being disposed of:

- As a general rule, the rate of 10% applies to gains falling within the basic rate band. Gains in excess of the basic rate band are taxed at the rate of 20%.

- However, gains on the disposal of residential property are charged at the rates of 18% and 28% instead of the normal rates of 10% and 20%.

- Gains qualifying for business asset disposal relief or investors' relief are chargeable at the rate of 10% irrespective of the level of the individual's taxable income.

Note that, as for income tax purposes, the basic rate band is extended if the individual makes a personal pension contribution or a gift aid donation.

Example

Terry realised taxable gains of £21,780 in the tax year 2022/23 in respect of the disposal of shares.

Required

Calculate Terry's capital gains tax liability assuming he has the following alternative levels of taxable income:

(a) £25,000

(b) £40,000

(c) £40,000 but he also made a personal pension contribution of £4,000.

Answer

	Taxable income (a) £25,000 £	(b) £40,000 £
Basic rate band remaining (£37,700 – £25,000)	12,700	Nil
Higher rate band	9,080	21,780
	21,780	21,780
Capital gains tax		
£12,700 × 10%	1,270	Nil
£9,080 / £21,780 × 20%	1,816	4,356
	3,086	4,356

(c) **Assuming that Terry makes a personal pension contribution of £4,000:**

	Taxable income
	£40,000
	£
Extended basic rate band: £37,700 + (£4,000 × 100/80) = £42,700	
Basic rate band remaining (£42,700 - £40,000)	2,700
Gain falling into higher rate band (£21,780 - £2,700)	19,080
	21,780
Capital gains tax	
£2,700 × 10%	270
£19,080 × 20%	3,816
	4,086

1.6 The due date of payment

CGT is payable under the self-assessment system. The normal due date is 31 January following the end of the tax year. For disposals in the tax year 2022/23, the due date will therefore be 31 January 2024.

Payments on account for disposals of residential property

Where CGT is payable in respect of the disposal of a residential property, a payment on account of the tax must be made within 60 days of the date of disposal. A return must be submitted to HMRC at the same time.

The calculation of the payment of account takes into account:

- the annual exempt amount
- any brought forward capital losses
- any capital losses incurred in the same tax year up to the date of disposal of the property.

The calculation of the payment on account ignores:

- any other chargeable gains
- any capital losses incurred after the disposal of the property.

In order to calculate the amount payable, the individual needs to estimate the amount of basic rate band, if any, that will be available to set against the gain.

Following the end of the tax year, the gain will have to be included in the taxpayer's self-assessment tax return as normal (see Chapter 17). The payment on account will be deducted from the finalised figure of capital gains tax. Any additional CGT is payable on 31 January following the end of the tax year. If the payment on account exceeds the CGT due, the excess will be repaid.

Example

Xin, a higher rate taxpayer, had the following chargeable gains and capital losses during the tax year 2022/23:

1 May 2022	Chargeable gain of £20,000 from the disposal of a painting
1 June 2022	Capital loss of £14,000 from the disposal of shares
1 September 2022	Chargeable gain of £70,000 from the disposal of residential property
1 December 2022	Capital loss of £9,000 from the disposal of land

Required

Calculate the payment on account required by Xin in respect of the disposal of the residential property.

Answer

Payment on account

	£
Gain on residential property	70,000
Minus capital loss on 1 June 2022	(14,000)
	56,000
Minus Annual exempt amount	(12,300)
Taxable gain	43,700
CGT at 28%	12,236

This CGT is payable on 31 October 2022, i.e. within 60 days of the disposal of the residential property.

Note that the other chargeable gain and the capital loss incurred on 1 December 2022 are ignored when calculating the payment on account. They will, however, be included when calculating the total CGT payable for the year.

The allocation of the annual exempt amount and capital losses where there is more than one type of gain is covered in the following section.

1.7 CGT on death

CGT is a **lifetime tax.** The transfer of assets due to the death of an individual is not a chargeable disposal.

The beneficiaries of a will are deemed to receive the assets at full market value on the date of the individual's death (known as probate value).

CGT is therefore not payable on the increase in value of the asset from the date the deceased purchased it to the date of their death. On the death of an individual there is therefore a tax-free uplift on all of the deceased's assets to market value.

Computing gains and losses

- Overview of the computation
- Treatment of capital losses
- Tax planning
- Relief for trading losses against capital gains

2 Computing gains and losses

2.1 Overview of the computation

The first step in calculating the capital gains tax liability of an individual is the calculation of separate gains and allowable losses on every chargeable asset disposed of in the tax year, **after** taking account of specific reliefs (e.g. rollover relief and gift holdover relief).

The proforma computation is as follows:

	£
Gross sale proceeds	X
Minus Incidental costs of sale	(X)
Net sale proceeds	X
Minus Allowable costs	
Acquisition cost (including incidental costs)	(X)
Enhancement expenditure	(X)
Gain/(loss) before specific reliefs	X/(X)
Minus Reliefs (if applicable)	(X)
Gain after specific reliefs/(allowable loss)	X/(X)

Gross sale proceeds or full market value

The gross sale proceeds are used as the starting point of the computation where the asset is sold in a commercial arm's length transaction.

However, **the gross sale proceeds are replaced with the full market value** of the asset at the date of disposal if the asset is:

- gifted, or
- sold to a **connected person** or
- disposed of otherwise than by way of a bargain at arm's length.

An individual is **connected** to the following persons:

- spouse or civil partner (i.e. same-sex partner recognised by a civil ceremony under the Civil Partnership Act)

- direct relatives and their spouses (brothers, sisters, ancestors and lineal descendants)
- spouse's direct relatives and their spouses
- business partners and their spouses and direct relatives.

The **net sale proceeds** from the disposal of a chargeable asset is the amount of the consideration received on the sale of the asset, after deducting any incidental selling costs.

Allowable costs consist of:

- the original purchase cost of the asset
- any incidental acquisition costs (see below)
- any enhancement expenditure (costs incurred in improving or enhancing the value of the capital asset).

Incidental selling costs and **incidental acquisition costs** both include estate agent fees, legal fees, commissions, auctioneer's fees, valuation fees, advertising costs, and stamp duty.

Enhancement expenditure is only allowable if it:

- is capital expenditure (and not revenue expenditure, such as repairs)
- improves the value of the asset (for example, extensions and additions), and
- is reflected in the state of the asset sold.

    (For example, if an extension to a property is built but later demolished, the cost of the extension is not allowable when the property is disposed of, because the proceeds from the sale relate to the property without the extension).

2.2 Treatment of capital losses

The treatment of capital losses depends on the type of loss. A summary of the rules for capital losses are as follows:

Type of capital loss:	Explanation:
Current year losses	▪ Must be set off against current year gains first.
	▪ An individual cannot restrict the set off to preserve the annual exempt amount.
	▪ If current year losses reduce the chargeable gains below the annual exempt amount, the unused annual exempt amount is lost.
	▪ If current year losses exceed current year gains, the net losses are carried forward and set off against future gains.
Losses brought forward	▪ These are set off **after the deduction of** current year losses and the annual exempt amount.
	▪ Must be set off against the **first available** gains. (It is not possible for an individual to skip a year.)

Type of capital loss:	Explanation:
Losses on disposals to connected persons	• These can only be set against gains from disposals in the current or future years to the **same connected person**.
Relief of trading losses against capital gains	• Trading losses can sometimes be treated **as if they are current year capital losses.** • This relief is explained later.

Example

Victoria made a chargeable gain of £18,700 in respect of the disposal of an asset in 2022/23.

Required

Calculate Victoria's taxable gains for 2022/23 assuming the following alternative losses arise:

(a) current year loss of £14,500

(b) current year loss of £4,500 and brought forward losses of £10,000

Answer

Situation (a): Victoria

Capital gains tax computation – 2022/23

	£
Gain	18,700
Minus capital loss	(14,500)
Net chargeable gain	4,200
Minus Annual exempt amount *(see note)*	(4,200)
Taxable gains	Nil

Note

Current year losses must be off set even if they result in the wastage of the annual exempt amount.

Situation (b): Victoria

Capital gains tax computation – 2022/23

	£
Gain	18,700
Minus current year capital loss	(4,500)
	14,200
Minus Annual exempt amount	(12,300)
	1,900
Minus brought forward capital loss (restricted)	(1,900)
Taxable gains	Nil

Note

Brought forward capital losses must be set off against the first available gains, but **after** the deduction of the annual exempt amount. Only £1,900 of the loss brought forward is set off. Victoria still has £8,100 of capital loss remaining to carry forward to the following tax year.

2.3 Tax planning

As explained earlier, gains on residential property are chargeable at the rates of 18% and 28% depending on the level of the individual's taxable income.

Individuals who make gains on both residential property and other assets in the same tax year can choose how to allocate their annual exempt amount and any capital losses.

In order to minimise the amount of CGT payable, the annual exempt amount and any capital losses should be relieved against gains on residential property first as these are chargeable at higher rates of tax than gains on other assets.

To help calculate the CGT in such cases, you should keep the gains on the two types of assets separate.

Example

In 2022/23, Riley made a chargeable gain of £28,000 on the disposal of a flat in Birmingham and a chargeable gain of £15,000 on the disposal of a painting.

Riley has taxable income of £25,000.

Required

Calculate Riley's capital gains tax for 2022/23.

Answer

Riley's annual exempt amount should be set against the gain on the flat as this will save CGT at the rates of 18% and 28%. If this approach is followed, the amount of CGT due will be:

	£	£
Gain on residential property	28,000	
Gain on painting		15,000
Less Annual exempt amount	(12,300)	
Taxable gains	15,700	15,000
Basic rate band £12,700 (37,700 – 25,000)		
£12,700 at 18%	2,286	
£3,000 at 28%	840	
£15,000 at 20%		3,000
	3,126	3,000

Total CGT £6,126 (£3,126 + £3,000)

Note that Riley would have made a payment on account in respect of the gain on the flat and this would be deducted from the total CGT due.

If the annual exempt amount had been allocated to the chargeable gain on the painting instead, the amount of CGT due would have been as follows:

	£	£
Gain on residential property	28,000	
Gain on painting		15,000
Less Annual exempt amount		(12,300)
Taxable gains	28,000	2,700
Basic rate band £12,700 (37,700 – 25,000)		
£12,700 at 18%	2,286	
£15,300 at 28%	4,284	
£2,700 at 20%		540
	6,570	540

Total CGT £7,110 (£6,570 + £540)

The increased tax of £984 (£7,110 - £6,126) is due to the differential between the two higher rates of CGT, i.e. £12,300 x (28% - 20%).

Note that although the annual exempt amount and capital losses should be deducted from the residential gains first in order to minimise the amount of CGT payable, the CGT is unaffected by the order in which the remaining basic rate band is allocated.

2.4 Relief for trading losses against capital gains

The relief for trading losses of an unincorporated business against income is the subject of an earlier chapter. Several options for relief are available, and the choices depend on whether the business is in its opening, closing or ongoing years.

However, regardless of whether an individual is in the opening, closing or ongoing years of an unincorporated business, trading losses can always be set against total income in the tax year of the loss and/or the preceding year.

In addition, after a claim against general income has been made in a particular tax year, an individual can make a claim to extend the relief and to set off some of the trading loss against gains of the same year.

The rules for relieving trading losses against capital gains

An individual can make a claim to set off trading losses against capital gains:

- in the tax year of the loss, **and/or**
- in the preceding tax year,
- **but only if** a claim against total income has been made in the **same** year first.

When setting off the trading loss against capital gains in the current or preceding tax year, the following rules apply:

Rule:	Explanation:
Set off against gains	- Treat the trading loss as if it is a **current year capital loss**: i.e. it must be set off against current year gains.
Must set off as much as possible in the tax year	- It is an all or nothing relief. - The claim is optional. However, if the claim is made, the maximum amount must be deducted from the current year's gains. - An individual cannot restrict the set off to preserve the annual exempt amount. - Loss relief may reduce the chargeable gains so that the relief for the annual exempt amount is lost.

The maximum amount of claim for a particular year is calculated as follows:

		£
Lower of (1) The unrelieved trading loss **after** the claim has been made against general income		X
(2) Total gains for the year		X
Minus: Total capital losses for the year		(X)
All capital losses brought forward		(X)
Maximum amount		X

In this calculation, ignore the annual exempt amount, and deduct **all** capital losses in full.

A claim must be made for relief against capital gains within the same timescale as a claim against general income. This is within one year of the 31 January following the end of the tax year of the loss (i.e. the 31 January immediately prior to the second anniversary of the end of the tax year of the loss).

If an individual claims a loss against both general income and capital gains, any trading loss left unrelieved is **automatically** carried forward and set off against future trading profits.

Example

Ethan prepares accounts to 31 March each year. In the year ended 31 March 2023 he incurred a trading loss of £32,000. He has provided the following information relating to the tax year 2022/23:

	£
UK rental income	17,150
Gains	22,800

Ethan also has capital losses of £13,200 brought forward.

Required

Calculate Ethan's taxable gains assuming that current year claims are made against both general income and capital gains. State the amount of any losses remaining unrelieved, if any.

Answer

The maximum amount of claim against capital gains is the lower of:

		£
(1)	The unrelieved trading loss **after** the claim against general income has been made (£32,000 - £17,150)	14,850
(2)	Total gains for the year	22,800
	All capital losses (current year and brought forward)	(13,200)
	Maximum amount	9,600

Ethan
Capital gains tax computation – 2022/23

	£
Total net chargeable gains	22,800
Minus: loss relief claim	(9,600)
	13,200
Minus: Annual exempt amount	(12,300)
	900
Minus: Capital loss brought forward (restricted)	(900)
Taxable gains	Nil

Notes

(1) The claim against capital gains is an all or nothing claim, therefore the maximum amount must be deducted from the current year's gains.

(2) Brought forward capital losses are set off after the deduction of the annual exempt amount.

Losses remaining unrelieved

Trading losses	£
Trading loss in tax year	32,000
Current year claim against general income	(17,150)
Current year claim against capital gains	(9,600)
Trading loss c/f	5,250

Capital losses	£
Capital loss brought forward	13,200
Current year set off	(900)
Capital loss c/f	12,300

Transfers between spouses

- Transfers between spouses

3 Transfers between spouses

3.1 Transfers between spouses

The computation for a disposal to an individual's spouse (or civil partner) is fixed so that at the time of the transfer no gain arises on the disposal and there is no allowable loss.

Inter-spouse transfers are therefore referred to as 'no gain/no loss' transfers.

| Disposal consideration = Allowable Cost (AC) |

On the subsequent disposal of the asset by the spouse, a normal computation is required using a deemed acquisition cost equal to the deemed disposal consideration at the time of the inter-spouse transfer.

Tax planning tip – Making a no gain no loss transfer prior to a disposal to a third party enables a couple to ensure that an asset is sold by whichever spouse has an unused annual exempt amount and pays CGT at the lowest possible rate.

Example

Michelle bought some land in September 2016 for £30,000 as an investment. She gave the land to Andy, her husband, in December 2020 when it was worth £78,000.

In January 2023 Andy sold the land to an unconnected person for £125,000.

Required

Calculate the chargeable gains arising on the transfer to Andy and on the sale by Andy.

Answer

Gain on disposal to Andy in December 2020

	£
Deemed disposal consideration (Cost)	30,000
Less: Cost of asset (September 2016)	(30,000)
Gain / (loss)	Nil

Subsequent disposal by Andy in January 2023

	£
Sale proceeds	125,000
Less: Deemed acquisition cost	(30,000)
Gain	95,000

Part disposals

- The problem with part disposals
- The part disposal formula

4 Part disposals

4.1 The problem with part disposals

Where only part of an asset is disposed of, it is necessary to allocate the allowable cost (AC) of the whole asset between:

- the part of the asset that is being disposed of, and
- the part of the asset that is being retained.

It is only the allowable costs incurred prior to the sale that need to be allocated. Costs relating wholly to the part that is sold (for example, incidental selling expenses) are allowable in full on the part disposal.

4.2 The part disposal formula

When calculating the allowable cost:

- Any allowable costs that **relate to the whole asset** are allocated between the two parts on the basis of market values at the date of the part disposal as follows:

$$AC \text{ re part disposal} = AC \times \frac{\text{MV of part disposed of}}{\text{MV of part disposed of} + \text{MV of part retained}}$$

$$AC \text{ re part retained} = (AC \text{ less } AC \text{ re part disposed of})$$

The market value of the part disposed of is usually the gross sale proceeds received. The market value of the part retained will be given in the examination question and is usually referred to as the market value of the remainder.

- Any allowable costs that **relate only to the part disposed of** can be deducted **in full** in the **part disposal** computation.

- Any allowable costs that **relate only to the part retained** can be deducted **in full** in the **subsequent disposal** computation.

Chapter 14: Capital gains tax

Example

Penelope acquired a non-business asset in July 2007 for £29,600. Incidental costs of acquisition totalled £530. The asset was enhanced in July 2009 at a cost of £14,200.

On 11 September 2022 Penelope sold a one-third interest in the asset to an unconnected person for £48,000. Incidental selling expenses amounted to £900. At that time the value of the remaining two-thirds was £105,000.

On 31 March 2023 Penelope sold the remaining two-thirds interest for £147,500. Incidental selling expenses amounted to £2,300.

Required

Calculate the chargeable gains arising in 2022/23.

Answer

Part disposal	Sept 2022
	£
Gross sale proceeds	48,000
Less Incidental selling expenses	(900)
Net sale proceeds	47,100
Less Allowable cost	
$(£29,600 + £530 + 14,200) \times \dfrac{48,000}{48,000 + 105,000}$	(13,907)
Gain	33,193

Subsequent disposal	Mar 2023
	£
Gross sale proceeds	147,500
Less Incidental selling expenses	(2,300)
Net sale proceeds	145,200
Less Allowable cost	
$((£29,600 + £530 + 14,200) - £13,907)$	(30,423)
Gain	114,777

Tax planning tip – Delaying the subsequent disposal until 6 April 2023 would have enabled Penelope to make use of the annual exempt amount for 2023/24 and would have delayed payment of the tax on that disposal for a further year.

> **Wasting assets and chattels**
>
> - The definition of wasting assets and chattels
> - A summary of the consequences of the disposal of chattels
> - Gains on the disposal of chattels
> - Losses on the disposal of chattels
> - The disposal of plant and machinery
> - A summary of the consequences of the disposal of wasting assets

5 Wasting assets and chattels

5.1 The definition of wasting assets and chattels

A **wasting asset** is an asset with an expected useful life of 50 years or less.

A **chattel** is tangible moveable property (for example, most things you would put into a removal van if you were to move house).

A **wasting chattel** is therefore tangible moveable property with an expected life of 50 years or less. Examples include a caravan, boat, dishwasher, cooker, greyhound, horse.

A **non-wasting chattel** is tangible moveable property with an expected life of more than 50 years. Examples include antiques, jewellery, paintings.

5.2 A summary of the consequences of the disposal of chattels

Chattels are treated as follows:

- **Wasting chattels** are **exempt** from capital gains tax.
- **Non-wasting chattels** are chargeable but the treatment depends on the amount of gross disposal consideration (i.e. sale proceeds or market value) and the allowable cost.

		Gross Disposal Consideration	
		£6,000 or less	More than £6,000
Cost	£6,000 or less	Exempt	5/3 rule applies
	More than £6,000	Deemed disposal for £6,000	Normal gain computation

5.3 Gains on the disposal of chattels

Where a chattel is sold for more than £6,000 but the item cost £6,000 or less, the gain is restricted to the lower of:

(i) the gain calculated applying the normal rules, and

(ii) (Gross sale proceeds − £6,000) × 5/3

Example

Teresa purchased an antique for £2,200 on 23 March 2005. She sold it for £7,600 on 16 October 2022.

Required

Calculate the chargeable gain arising in 2022/23.

Answer

Gain calculated applying the normal rules:

	£
Sale proceeds	7,600
Less Acquisition cost	(2,200)
Gain	5,400

Marginal gain calculation:

(£7,600 − £6,000) × 5/3	2,667

Decision:
The lower gain of £2,667 is taken.

5.4 Losses on the disposal of chattels

Where a chattel is sold for less than £6,000 but the item cost more than £6,000, the actual sale proceeds received are ignored and the allowable loss is calculated assuming the gross sale proceeds are £6,000.

Example

John purchased an antique for £7,200 on 23 March 2005. He sold it for £4,600 on 16 October 2022 and incurred £540 of incidental selling expenses.

Required

Calculate the allowable loss arising in 2022/23.

Answer

	£
Deemed gross sale proceeds	6,000
Less Incidental selling expenses	(540)
Net sale proceeds	5,460
Less Allowable cost	(7,200)
Allowable loss	(1,740)

5.5 The disposal of plant and machinery

Items of plant and machinery are always deemed to have a life of less than 50 years and are therefore wasting assets.

As most items of plant and machinery are tangible and moveable, they are classed as wasting chattels and, following the rules above, would therefore be exempt from capital gains tax.

However, not all plant and machinery is exempt. Special rules apply as follows:

- If the plant and machinery is **used in a trade** and **capital allowances have been or could have been claimed**:
  - they are chargeable assets and the 5/3 rule applies if sold at a gain
  - no allowable loss arises if sold at a loss.
- If there are **no capital allowances** available on the plant and machinery:
  - they are **exempt** if they are **chattels** (i.e. tangible and moveable), and
  - the rules for **wasting assets** are followed if they are not chattels.

5.6 A summary of the consequences of the disposal of wasting assets

Wasting assets which are chattels (i.e. tangible, moveable property) are exempt assets as explained above.

Wasting assets which are not chattels are chargeable assets, but special rules apply in the calculation of the gain.

As wasting assets usually decline in value over time, they are often referred to as depreciating assets. Wasting assets are deemed to depreciate on a straight-line basis.

When calculating the allowable cost, the net cost of the asset must be depreciated on a straight-line basis as follows:

$$\text{Net cost} \times \frac{\text{Length of ownership by the seller (months)}}{\text{Expected life of the asset (months)}}$$

The net cost of the asset is the original cost of the asset less any anticipated scrap value at the end of the life of the asset.

> **Insurance and compensation**
>
> - The receipt of a capital sum due to the ownership of an asset
> - Assets totally destroyed or lost
> - Damaged assets

6 Insurance and compensation

6.1 The receipt of a capital sum due to the ownership of an asset

The receipt of a capital sum due to the ownership of an asset is a chargeable disposal for capital gains tax purposes. The receipt of compensation or insurance on making a claim due to the loss, destruction or damage to a capital asset is therefore a chargeable event. The date of disposal is deemed to be the date on which the capital sum for the loss is received (not the date on which the asset was lost or damaged).

The treatment of the receipt depends on whether the asset is:

- totally destroyed/lost – i.e. a disposal of the whole asset, or
- damaged but not totally destroyed – i.e. a part disposal of the asset.

6.2 Assets totally destroyed or lost

Where an asset is totally destroyed or lost, the treatment for capital gains tax can be summarised as follows:

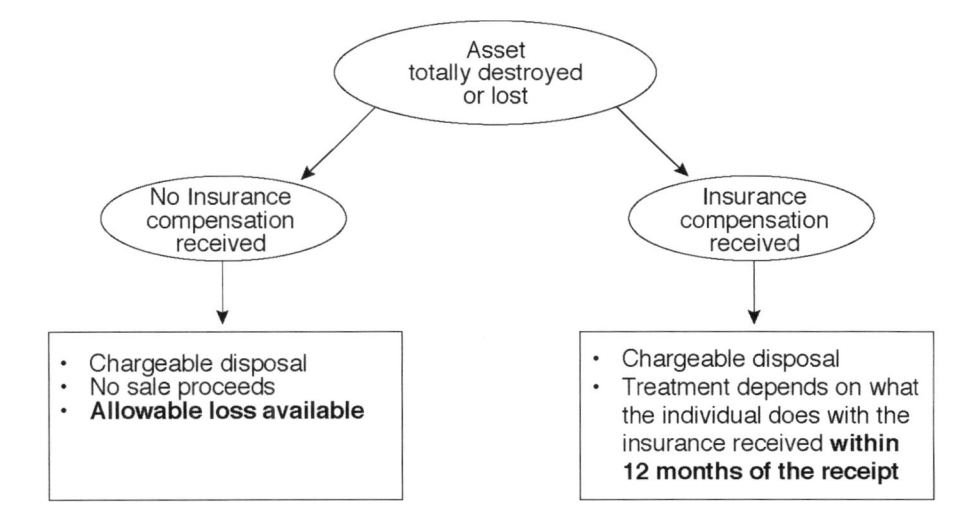

```
                    Asset
              totally destroyed
                   or lost
                 /         \
    No Insurance           Insurance
    compensation          compensation
      received              received
         |                     |
         v                     v
```

- Chargeable disposal
- No sale proceeds
- **Allowable loss available**

- Chargeable disposal
- Treatment depends on what the individual does with the insurance received **within 12 months of the receipt**

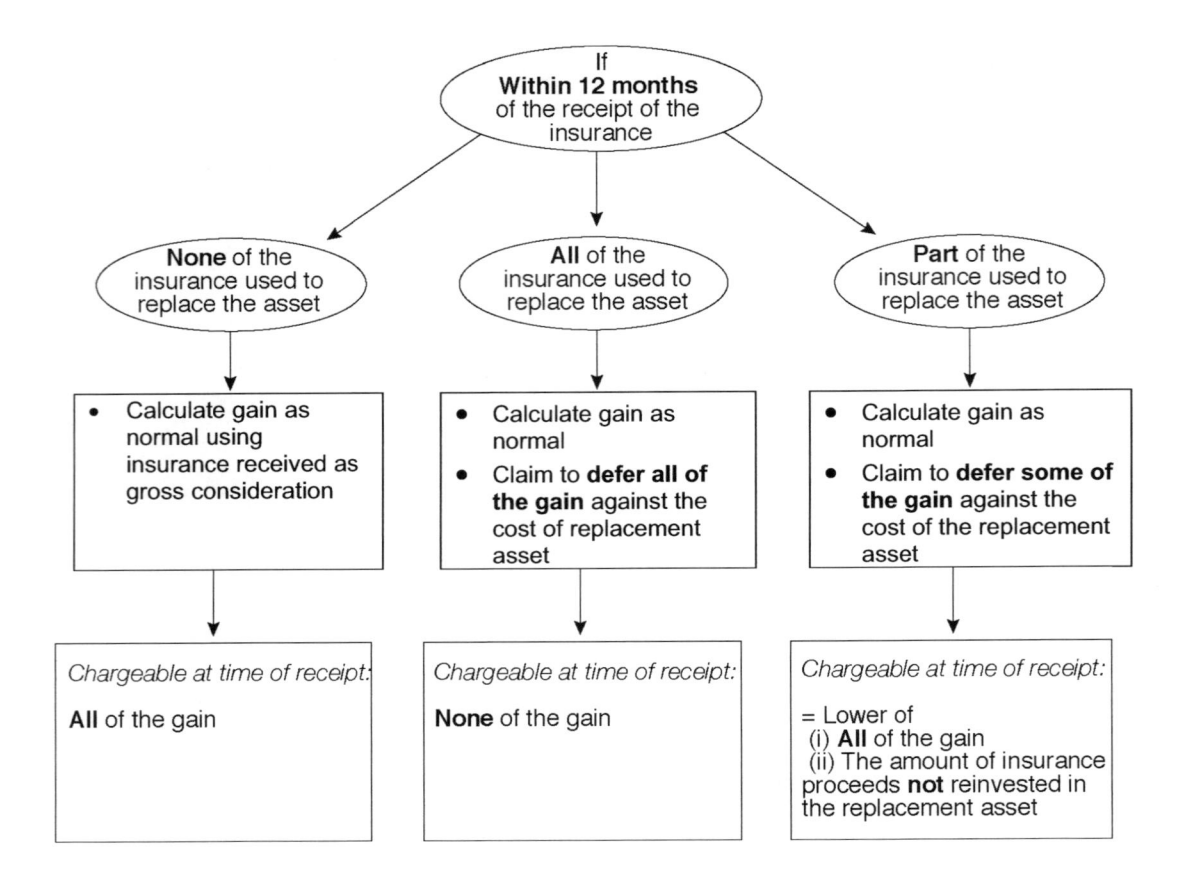

```
                          ┌─────────────────┐
                          │       If        │
                          │ Within 12 months│
                          │ of the receipt of the │
                          │    insurance    │
                          └─────────────────┘
         ┌───────────────────┼───────────────────┐
         ▼                   ▼                   ▼
┌─────────────────┐ ┌─────────────────┐ ┌─────────────────┐
│   None of the   │ │    All of the   │ │   Part of the   │
│ insurance used to│ │ insurance used to│ │ insurance used to│
│ replace the asset│ │ replace the asset│ │ replace the asset│
└─────────────────┘ └─────────────────┘ └─────────────────┘
```

- **None of the insurance used to replace the asset**
  - Calculate gain as normal using insurance received as gross consideration

  Chargeable at time of receipt:
  All of the gain

- **All of the insurance used to replace the asset**
  - Calculate gain as normal
  - Claim to **defer all of the gain** against the cost of replacement asset

  Chargeable at time of receipt:
  None of the gain

- **Part of the insurance used to replace the asset**
  - Calculate gain as normal
  - Claim to **defer some of the gain** against the cost of the replacement asset

  Chargeable at time of receipt:
  = Lower of
  (i) **All** of the gain
  (ii) The amount of insurance proceeds **not** reinvested in the replacement asset

Example

Diane bought a painting for £280,000 in August 2005. In November 2022 the painting was destroyed in a fire. The insurance company settled a claim for £600,000 in January 2023. In May 2023 Diane replaced the painting.

Required

Calculate the chargeable gain arising in 2022/23 and the base cost of the replacement painting assuming the replacement painting cost:

(a) £650,000

(b) £480,000

Answer

	£
Insurance proceeds (January 2023)	600,000
Less Allowable cost (August 2005)	(280,000)
Gain	320,000

(a) If replacement cost £650,000

Gain in 2022/23   £Nil

As all of the insurance proceeds are reinvested in a replacement painting, the whole gain can be deferred until the later disposal of the replacement painting

(b) If replacement cost £480,000

Gain in 2022/23

= Lower of
all of the gain	£320,000
insurance not reinvested	£120,000

Note:
The chargeable gain is assessed in 2022/23 (the tax year of the receipt of the insurance, not the date of the destruction of the asset)

Base cost of replacement painting:

	£		£
Cost	650,000	Cost	480,000
Less Deferred gain	(320,000)	Less Deferred gain (£320,000 – £120,000)	(200,000)
Base cost	330,000	Base cost	280,000

6.3 Damaged assets

Where an asset is damaged but not totally destroyed, the treatment for capital gains tax can be summarised as follows:

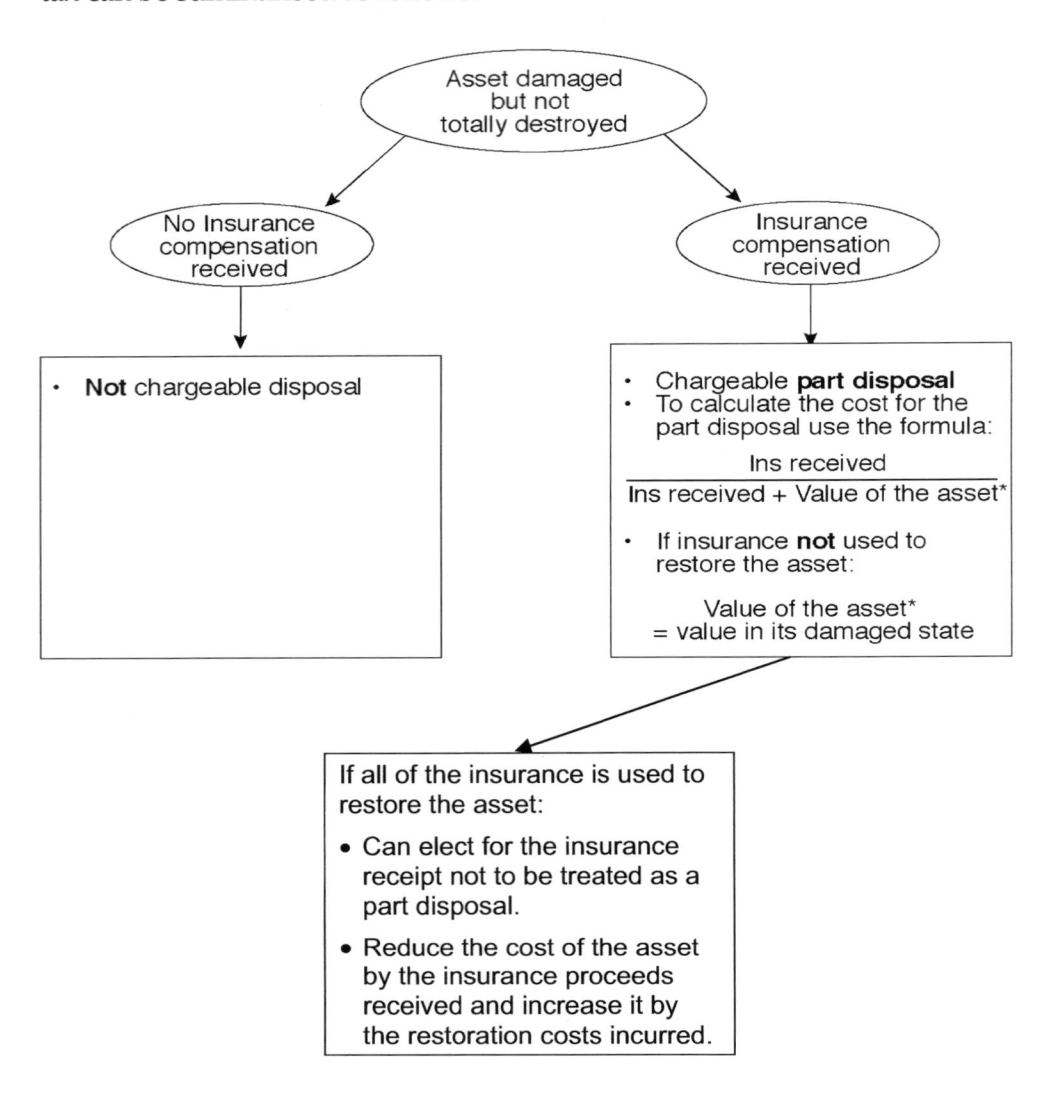

```
                    Asset damaged
                      but not
                   totally destroyed
                   /              \
        No Insurance          Insurance
        compensation         compensation
          received             received
              |                    |
   • Not chargeable disposal    • Chargeable part disposal
                                • To calculate the cost for the
                                  part disposal use the formula:

                                        Ins received
                                ─────────────────────────────
                                Ins received + Value of the asset*

                                • If insurance not used to
                                  restore the asset:

                                  Value of the asset*
                                  = value in its damaged state
```

If all of the insurance is used to restore the asset:

- Can elect for the insurance receipt not to be treated as a part disposal.
- Reduce the cost of the asset by the insurance proceeds received and increase it by the restoration costs incurred.

Example

Ian bought an antique vase in August 2005 for £79,200. In August 2022 the vase was damaged and in December 2022 Ian received £40,000 compensation from his insurance company. The value of the vase in its damaged state is £105,600.

Required

(a) Calculate the chargeable gain arising in the tax year 2022/23 and the base cost of the vase assuming none of the compensation is used to restore the asset.

(b) Explain the capital gains consequences of Ian spending £45,000 on restoring the asset.

Answer

(a) **Part disposal at the time of the receipt of the compensation**

	£
Insurance proceeds (December 2022)	40,000
Less Allowable cost $£79,200 \times \dfrac{40,000}{40,000 + 105,600}$	(21,758)
Gain	18,242
Base cost of the vase:	
Original cost	79,200
Used in the part disposal computation	(21,758)
	57,442
Restoration costs	Nil
Base cost	57,442

(b) **Consequences of restoring the vase**

Receipt of the compensation will be treated as a part disposal as shown above. However, as Ian has used all of the compensation to restore the asset, an election can be made to defer the charge to CGT as follows:

The base cost of the vase is:

- reduced by the insurance proceeds received, and
- increased by the restoration costs which are treated as enhancement expenditure.

The revised base cost of the vase is therefore £84,200 (79,200 − 40,000 + 45,000).

Taxation – United Kingdom
(TX-UK) FA2022

CHAPTER 15

CGT on shares and securities

Contents

1. The disposal of shares and securities by an individual
2. The valuation rules for shares
3. The share identification rules for individuals
4. Bonus issues, rights issues, takeovers and reorganisations

> **The disposal of shares and securities by an individual**
>
> - Shares and securities that are chargeable to CGT

1 The disposal of shares and securities by an individual

1.1 Shares and securities that are chargeable to CGT

All quoted and unquoted shares and securities are chargeable assets for CGT purposes with the exception of the following securities:

- Qualifying Corporate Bonds (QCBs), and
- Gilt-edged securities (gilts).

Disposals of QCBs and gilts by an individual are exempt from CGT. However, they are not exempt assets for company disposals and corporation tax purposes.

QCBs are defined as corporate securities issued after 13 March 1984 which represent a normal commercial loan that is expressed in sterling and cannot be converted into any other currency.

In the examination, company loan notes are assumed to satisfy these conditions and are therefore treated as QCBs, unless it is clearly stated otherwise.

Gilts are government securities, quoted on the Stock Exchange. They are usually called Treasury stock or Exchequer stock.

The valuation rules for shares

- The valuation rules for shares

2 The valuation rules for shares

2.1 The valuation rules for shares

When quoted shares and securities are gifted, or sold to a connected person for less than their market value, it is necessary to place a value on the disposal for CGT purposes.

Quoted shares are quoted by stock market dealers at two prices: a lower price at which they will buy the shares and a higher price at which they will sell them.

For CGT purposes, **quoted shares** are valued at the mid-point between the two quoted prices, as follows:

	Pence
½ × (Higher quoted price + Lower quoted price)	X

Example

Angus gifts his 2,000 ordinary shares in X plc to a friend. At the date of the gift the shares are quoted at 365p - 377p.

Required

Calculate the value of the shares gifted to Angus's friend for capital gains tax purposes.

Answer

The X plc shares are valued at:	pence
The mid-point of the higher and lower quoted prices of that day ½ × (365 + 377)	371

	£
Value of 2,000 shares = 2,000 × £3.71p	7,420

> **The share identification rules for individuals**
>
> - The share identification rules for individuals
> - Acquisitions in the next 30 days
> - The share pool

3 The share identification rules for individuals

3.1 The share identification rules for individuals

When purchasing shares, an individual must keep separate records for each different type and class of company shares purchased. For example, X Ltd ordinary share purchase records are kept separate from Y Ltd ordinary share purchase records, which are kept separate from Y Ltd preference share purchase records, and so on.

To identify which shares have been disposed of, the share identification rules are applied. For the purpose of your examination, shares are disposed of by an individual in the following order:

(1) Acquisitions on the same day as the disposal

(2) Acquisitions in the next 30 days on a first-in-first-out basis

(3) Shares in the share pool

3.2 Acquisitions in the next 30 days

The future 30-day rule exists as an anti-tax avoidance measure. It prevents a practice known as bed and breakfasting.

Without this rule, individuals could deliberately sell shares one day and repurchase them the next day (or shortly afterwards) in order to:

- realise a gain, but pay no tax as the gain was covered by the annual exempt amount, and
- establish a higher base cost for the shares for the purpose of calculating the gain on future disposals.

3.3 The share pool

An individual with many investments in companies will need to construct a share pool **for each company and each class of share**.

The share pool is treated as a single asset, with shares disposed of at their average cost.

The working for the share pool is shown as follows:

	Number of shares	Original cost
		£
Acquisition 1	X	X
Acquisition 2	X	X
	X	X
Sale (at average cost)	(X)	(X)
Pool balance c/f	X	X

The appropriate proportion of cost to deduct when shares are sold is calculated as follows:

$$\text{Total cost to date} \times \frac{\text{Number of shares disposed of}}{\text{Number of shares held (before the disposal)}}$$

Example

Beth purchased shares in Y Ltd as follows:

		Cost
		£
16 May 2013	5,000 shares	34,500
27 March 2023	6,500 shares	37,700

On 13 March 2023 she sold 10,000 shares in Y Ltd for £96,000.

Required

Calculate the chargeable gains arising on the disposal of Beth's shares.

Answer

Matching rules	Number of shares held	Disposal 13 March 2023	Remaining shares
1. Acquisitions in the next 30 days			
27 March 2023	6,500	(6,500)	Nil
2. Pool shares	5,000	(3,500)	1,500
	11,500	(10,000)	1,500

The disposal value of each share was £96,000/10,000 shares = £9.60 per share.

(1) Chargeable gain on the disposal of shares acquired on 27 March 2023

	£
Gross sale proceeds (£96,000 ÷ 10,000) × 6,500	62,400
Minus Cost	(37,700)
Gain	24,700

(2) Chargeable gain on the disposal of shares in the share pool

Working:

	Number of shares	Original cost
		£
Purchase on 16 May 2013	5,000	34,500
Sale on 13 March 2023 (note)	(3,500)	(24,150)
Pool balance c/f	1,500	10,350

Note

Shares sold from the pool are removed at average cost. In this example, 3,500 shares out of 5,000 shares in the pool were sold.

Cost: £34,500 × 3,500/5,000 = £24,150

	£
Gross sale proceeds (£96,000 ÷ 10,000) × 3,500	33,600
Minus Cost (from pool, see working)	(24,150)
Gain	9,450

The total chargeable gains on the share disposal are therefore (1) £24,700 + (2) £9,450 = £34,150.

Bonus issues, rights issues, takeovers and reorganisations
■ Bonus issues
■ Rights issues
■ Takeovers
■ Reorganisations

4 Bonus issues, rights issues, takeovers and reorganisations

4.1 Bonus issues

Bonus issue shares are free shares issued to existing shareholders in proportion to the number of shares already held.

For example, a 1 for 3 bonus issue means that for every 3 existing shares held, 1 free share will be issued to each shareholder.

Bonus shares are treated as if they are acquired on the same day as the original shares to which they relate.

Example

On 23 August 2006 Carl purchased 3,000 ordinary shares in M plc for £45,000. On 6 April 2010 M plc made a 1 for 6 bonus issue.

On 31 December 2022 Carl disposed of 3,000 of his shares in M plc for £60,000.

Required

Calculate the chargeable gain arising on the disposal of the shares.

Answer

Chargeable gain on the disposal of shares in the share pool

Working

	Number of shares	Original cost
		£
Purchase on 23 August 2006	3,000	45,000
Bonus issue	500	Nil
	3,500	45,000
Sale on 31 December 2022 (note)	(3,000)	(38,571)
Pool balance c/f	500	6,429

Note

Shares sold from the pool are removed at average cost:

£45,000 × 3,000/3,500 = £38,571

	£
Gross sale proceeds	60,000
Minus Cost (from pool, see working)	(38,571)
Gain	21,429

4.2 Rights issues

A rights issue takes place when a company makes an offer of new shares to its existing shareholders, giving them the opportunity to purchase shares in the company in proportion to the number of shares they already hold. Shares in a rights issue are sold at an attractive price (i.e. for less than the current market value) to persuade shareholders to buy them.

For example, a 1 for 5 rights issue means that for every 5 existing shares they hold, the shareholders have the right to purchase 1 additional share at the attractive offer price.

Rights shares are treated as if they are acquired on the same day as the original shares to which they relate.

Example

The facts are the same as in the previous example involving Carl. However, it is a rights issue rather than a bonus issue that takes place on 6 April 2010. The rights issue is 1 for 6 at £10 per share and Carl bought all the shares that were offered to him in the issue.

Required

Calculate the chargeable gain arising on the disposal of the shares.

Answer

Chargeable gain on the disposal of shares in the pool

Working

	Number of shares	Original cost
		£
Purchase on 23 August 2006	3,000	45,000
Rights issue	500	5,000
	3,500	50,000
Sale on 31 December 2022 (note)	(3,000)	(42,857)
Pool balance c/f	500	7,143

Note

Shares sold from the pool are removed at average cost:

£50,000 × 3,000/3,500 = £42,857

	£
Gross sale proceeds	60,000
Minus Cost (from pool, see working)	(42,857)
Gain	17,143

4.3 Takeovers

An examination question involving a takeover will only involve a paper-for-paper exchange, such as an exchange of shares in the acquired company for shares in the company making the acquisition. As a result, the treatment for capital gains tax purposes is as follows:

- No chargeable gain or allowable loss arises at the time of the takeover.
- The new shares and securities received are deemed to be:
    - acquired on the same day as the original shares
    - for the same cost as the original shares.
- The original cost of the old shares is allocated to the new shares and securities received, in proportion to the market values of the consideration received.
- Pools for the new shares and securities are set up.

Example

Tareq owns 3,000 ordinary shares in Z Ltd, which he bought for £16,600 on 23 June 2015.

On 15 March 2023 Z Ltd accepted a takeover bid from A plc. The takeover offer consisted of 1 ordinary share and 2 preference shares in A plc for every 3 shares held in Z Ltd.

At the date of the takeover, the market value of A plc shares was as follows:

Ordinary shares	£9 each
Preference shares	£6 each

Required

State the chargeable gain arising at the time of the takeover, and calculate the cost to be entered in the new pools for the A plc shares.

Answer

There is no chargeable gain at the time of the takeover as no cash consideration is received.

Takeover consideration received by Tareq:

	Market value
	£
1,000 Ordinary shares in A plc (1,000 × £9)	9,000
2,000 Preference shares in A plc (2,000 × £6)	12,000
	21,000

Z Ltd: pool	Number of shares	Cost
		£
Balance at time of takeover	3,000	16,600

Allocation of the original cost of the Z Ltd shares	Cost
	£
1,000 Ordinary shares in A plc: 9,000/21,000 × £16,600	7,114
2,000 Preference shares in A plc: 12,000/21,000 × £16,600	9,486
	16,600

Electing to disapply the share for share exchange rules

Although the above share for share rules apply automatically, it is possible for the taxpayer to make an election to disapply them. The election must be made within 1 year of 31 January following the year in which the takeover takes place.

The usual reason for electing to disapply the rules would be in order to generate a gain so that the taxpayer could then claim their annual exempt amount and/or business asset disposal relief, assuming the relevant conditions were satisfied.

4.4 Reorganisations

A reorganisation is where a company reorganises its equity and debt capital by exchanging existing shares and securities for another class of share or security in the same company.

As with takeovers:

- No chargeable gain arises unless cash consideration is received by the shareholders.
- If the new shares and securities are quoted, the cost of the original shares must be allocated in proportion to the market values of the new shares and securities on the first day of quotation after the reorganisation.

Taxation – United Kingdom
(TX-UK) FA2022

CHAPTER 16

Capital gains tax reliefs

Contents
1   Business asset disposal relief and investors' relief
2   Rollover relief
3   Gift holdover relief
4   Private residence relief and letting relief

> **Business asset disposal relief and investors' relief**
> - Overview of business asset disposal relief
> - Conditions
> - Investors' relief

1 Business asset disposal relief and investors' relief

1.1 Overview of business asset disposal relief

Business asset disposal relief (BADR) is a relief that is available to an individual who disposes of a business or part of a business.

The relief covers the first £1 million of qualifying gains that an individual makes **during their lifetime**. Qualifying gains are taxed at a rate of only 10%, irrespective of the level of the taxpayer's income.

Gains in excess of the £1 million lifetime limit are taxed at the normal CGT rates of 10% and/or 20%.

Example
Jan has qualifying gains of £1.2 million from the disposal of her business. She has made no previous qualifying disposals.

Required

Calculate the amount of capital gains tax payable by Jan, assuming she is a higher rate taxpayer and this is her only disposal in the tax year 2022/23.

Answer

	£
Total qualifying gains	1,200,000
Less Annual exempt amount	(12,300)
Taxable gain	1,187,700
CGT £1,000,000 at 10%	100,000
CGT £187,700 at 20%	37,540
CGT payable	137,540

Where an individual has a mixture of qualifying and non-qualifying gains, in order to minimise the amount of CGT payable, the annual exempt amount and any capital losses should be set off in the following order:

- Gains on residential property
- Other gains not qualifying for business asset disposal relief
- Gains qualifying for business asset disposal relief or investors' relief (see later).

Although gains qualifying for BADR are always taxed at the rate of 10%, they must still be taken into account in determining the amount of basic rate band available to set against other non-qualifying gains. This makes it likely that non-qualifying gains will be taxed at the maximum rate of 20% (or 28% if residential property).

1.2 Conditions

In order to claim BADR, the individual must dispose of a qualifying asset which they have held for a qualifying period of time.

Qualifying assets

Business asset disposal relief is available for disposals of the following:

- The whole or part of a business run by a sole trader or a partnership. However, the relief only applies to gains arising from the disposal of assets used in the business; it does not apply to gains arising from the disposal of investments. (Note that a mere disposal of assets used in a business is insufficient to qualify for BADR; the relief requires the disposal of all or part of a business **as a going concern**.)

- The disposal of shares in a trading company, provided the individual:
    - holds at least 5% of the ordinary share capital and voting rights in the company, **and**
    - is an employee of the company.

    The company itself may hold investments without it affecting the availability of the relief.

Qualifying period

In order to qualify for relief, the **business** (or qualifying shares) must have been owned throughout the **two years** leading up to the date of disposal. Note that in the case of a business, it is the length of ownership of the **business** rather than the length of ownership of the assets used in the business that must have been over two years.

The relief is not given automatically. It must be claimed within one year of the 31 January following the end of tax year in which the disposal takes place (i.e. the 31 January immediately prior to the second anniversary of the end of the tax year).

Example

On 1 August 2022, Agnes sold a business that she had operated as a sole trader for ten years.

The disposal resulted in the following gains:

	£
Goodwill	100,000
Freehold office premises (used by the business)	500,000
Freehold office premises (held as an investment)	200,000

Required

Calculate the capital gains tax payable by Agnes on the disposal of her business assuming she has taxable income of £17,400.

Answer

	£	£
Gains qualifying for BADR	600,000	
Gains not qualifying for BADR		200,000
Less Annual exempt amount		(12,300)
Taxable gains	600,000	187,700
CGT at 10%	60,000	
CGT at 20%		37,540

Total CGT £97,540 (60,000 + 37,540).

Notes

1. The gain on the investment property does not qualify for BADR. The annual exempt amount has therefore been set against this gain.

2. The qualifying gains of £600,000 use up the remainder of Agnes's basic rate band meaning that all of her non-qualifying gains must be taxed at the rate of 20%.

3. The remaining £400,000 of BADR (£1,000,000 – 600,000) is available to set against any future qualifying gains.

1.3 Investors' relief

When an individual disposes of shares in a trading company, BADR is only available where the individual has a minimum 5% shareholding and is also an officer or employee of the company. As a result of these restrictions, investors' relief has been introduced.

Investors' relief works in a similar way to BADR but it is available to external investors in **unquoted trading companies**. The individual cannot be an officer or employee of the company concerned (but could be an unremunerated director).

Investors' relief has its own separate £10 million lifetime limit and qualifying gains are taxed at a rate of 10%, irrespective of the level of the taxpayer's income.

To qualify for investors' relief, the shares must be:

- Newly issued shares acquired by subscription.
- Owned for at least **three years** after 6 April 2016.

There is no minimum shareholding.

Example

On 1 October 2022, Saira sold 10,000 £1 ordinary shares in Kannoh Ltd for £80,000.

Kannoh Ltd is an unquoted trading company. It has 500,000 £1 ordinary shares in issue.

Saira had subscribed for the shares on 1 May 2019 at their par value. She has never been a director or employee of the company.

Required

(a) Explain why Saira's disposal qualifies for investors' relief rather than business asset disposal relief.

(b) Calculate the capital gains tax payable by Saira assuming she is a higher rate taxpayer and made no other disposals during the tax year 2022/23.

Answer

(a) Saira's disposal qualifies for investors' relief as:
- Kannoh Ltd is an unquoted trading company
- Saira subscribed for the shares
- There is no minimum shareholding requirement
- The shares have been held for more than three years
- Saira has never been a director or employee of the company.

Saira's disposal does not qualify for business asset disposal relief as she only has a 2% shareholding in Kannoh Ltd. In addition, she does not meet the requirement to be a director or employee of the company.

(b) Saira's CGT liability in respect of this disposal is:

	£
Disposal proceeds	80,000
Less allowable cost	(10,000)
	70,000
Less Annual exempt amount	(12,300)
Taxable gains	57,700
CGT at 10%	5,770

> **Rollover relief**
>
> - Overview of rollover relief
> - Qualifying business assets
> - How much gain can be deferred?
> - What happens to the deferred gain?
> - Non-business use

2 Rollover relief

2.1 Overview of rollover relief

A chargeable gain is usually taxed in the year of disposal. However, if a rollover relief claim is made, the gain is deferred to a later tax year.

Rollover relief (technically known as replacement of business assets relief) is a tax relief to encourage businesses to reinvest in capital assets and continue in business.

The relief is available if the sale proceeds received from the disposal are used to purchase a replacement asset and **all** the following conditions are satisfied:

- The asset being sold is a **qualifying business asset**.
- The replacement asset is a **qualifying business asset** (but it does not need to be the same type of asset as the asset being sold).
- Both assets are used for the purposes of the trade.
- The replacement purchase takes place in the **four-year period** running from 12 months before, to three years after, the date of disposal.
- The new asset is brought into business use at the time that it is acquired.
- A claim for relief is made within four years of the end of the tax year in which the disposal takes place (or four years from the end of the tax year in which the new asset is acquired, if later).

2.2 Qualifying business assets

The main examinable assets eligible for rollover relief are:

- Land and buildings used for the purposes of the trade
- Fixed plant and machinery (but not moveable plant and machinery such as fork lift trucks).
- Goodwill. (Note, however, that goodwill is not a qualifying asset if disposed of by a company.)

It is important to note that:

- rollover relief is never available on a gain arising from the disposal of shares, and
- the purchase of shares is not a qualifying replacement asset for rollover relief purposes.

2.3 How much gain can be deferred?

If **all** the sale proceeds are reinvested, it is presumed that the taxpayer will not have cash available to pay any tax on the gain. **All** the gain arising on the disposal can therefore be deferred and none of the gain is taxed immediately.

If some of the sale proceeds have been retained, it is presumed that the taxpayer does have some cash available to pay some tax on the gain. The amount of relief available is therefore restricted and some of the gain is taxed immediately. The amount that is taxed immediately is the lower of:

- all the gain, or
- the sale proceeds **not** reinvested in QBAs.

2.4 What happens to the deferred gain?

The treatment of the deferred gain depends on whether the **replacement** asset is a depreciating asset or a non-depreciating asset:

Type of QBAs purchased:	Non-depreciating QBAs	Depreciating QBAs
Expected life	More than 60 years.	60 years or less.
Examples	Freehold land and buildings. Leasehold land and buildings with more than 60 years left on lease.	Fixed plant and machinery. Leasehold land and buildings with up to 60 years left on lease.
Mechanics of the deferral	• The gain to be deferred is deducted from the cost of the new asset to calculate the revised base cost of the replacement asset (i.e. the cost minus rollover relief). • On the subsequent disposal of the replacement asset, the revised base cost is deducted in the gain computation instead of the original cost – thus increasing the gain chargeable on this disposal. • The original gain has therefore been rolled over (i.e. deferred) until the disposal of the replacement asset.	• The gain to be deferred is **not** deducted from the cost of the replacement asset. • A separate record of the deferred gain is kept. • The deferred gain is taxed 10 years after the date the replacement asset was acquired *unless*, within the 10 year period, the replacement asset is either sold or ceases to be used in the trade. • If sold, a normal computation of the chargeable gain on the replacement asset is made, using the original cost. • In this situation, the deferred gain is sometimes referred to as a held-over gain, rather than a rolled over gain.

Rollover relief is an all or nothing relief. It is optional but, if claimed, the taxpayer must defer (roll over) the maximum amount of gain allowed by the legislation.

On the disposal of the replacement asset, the deferred gain becomes taxable, unless a further rollover relief claim can be made.

With good tax planning, gains on QBAs can be deferred potentially indefinitely, provided the conditions are satisfied at each disposal date.

Example

Ellen is self-employed. She prepares her accounts to 31 March each year. On 30 November 2022 she sold a freehold warehouse for £230,000, which was purchased in August 2007 and gave rise to a gain (before considering reliefs) of £65,000.

On 24 January 2023 Ellen purchased a 70-year lease on a new warehouse for £218,000. She expects to sell the warehouse on 31 December 2024 for £550,000.

Required

(a) Calculate Ellen's chargeable gains arising in 2022/23 and 2024/25.

(b) Explain the difference in treatment if the replacement warehouse had been a 40-year leasehold interest.

Answer
(a)

Is the asset a QBA for rollover relief purposes?	Yes
Has it been replaced with a QBA?	Yes
Has it been replaced in the four-year qualifying period?	
(30 November 2021 – 30 November 2025)	Yes
Have all the sale proceeds been reinvested in a QBA?	No

Gain arising in 2022/23

Lower of
(1) The gain £65,000, and
(2) The sale proceeds **not** reinvested in QBAs (£230,000 - £218,000) =   £12,000

Rollover relief = The rest of the gain (£65,000 - £12,000)   53,000

Base cost of replacement 70-year leasehold interest	£
Cost	218,000
Minus: Rollover relief	(53,000)
Base cost	165,000

Chargeable gain arising in 2024/25	£
Sale proceeds	550,000
Base cost	(165,000)
Gain	385,000

(b) **If the replacement had been a 40-year leasehold interest**

A 40-year leasehold interest is a QBA, but is a depreciating asset.

The calculation of the amount of rollover relief and the chargeable gain arising in 2022/23 would be the same as above. However, the amount relieved with a rollover relief claim is not deducted from the cost of the replacement asset.

- A record of the amount of rollover relief is kept and that amount is deferred for 10 years from the date of acquisition of the replacement warehouse. However, as the replacement asset is disposed of before 10 years have elapsed, **the deferred gain of £53,000 in respect of the original asset becomes chargeable** in 2024/25 on the disposal of the replacement asset.

- **In addition**, a chargeable gain arises on the disposal of the replacement asset itself. The gain is calculated as normal, using the actual cost of the leasehold interest with no rollover relief deduction.

Chargeable gain arising in 2024/25	£
Sale proceeds	550,000
Base cost	(218,000)
Gain	332,000

2.5 Non-business use

If part of a building is not used for trade purposes (for example, if part of a building is let to another business), rollover relief is only available in relation to the business proportion of the gain.

The non-business proportion of the gain is chargeable immediately in the tax year in which the disposal occurs.

The rollover relief available on the business proportion of the gain is calculated in the normal way. However, consideration is only given to business usage. To calculate the amount of relief, the amount of sale proceeds received relating to the business use of the asset is compared to the amount reinvested in QBAs.

Example

Hamza owned a three-storey building. He purchased it in January 2007 for £65,070 and sold it on 24 November 2022 for £200,000.

Hamza used two floors for the purposes of his trade, but never occupied the ground floor. This was let out to another business which operated as a shoe shop.

In November 2022, Hamza relocated. He purchased a new building for £128,000 on 1 October 2022 and plans to use it exclusively for the purposes of his trade.

Required

Calculate the chargeable gain arising in 2022/23 and the base cost of the new building.

Answer

	£
Gross sale proceeds	200,000
Cost	(65,070)
Chargeable gain before rollover relief	134,930

Is the asset a QBA for rollover relief purposes?	Yes
Has it been replaced with a QBA?	Yes
Has it been replaced in the four-year qualifying period? (24 November 2021 – 24 November 2025)	Yes
Have all the sale proceeds been reinvested in a QBA?	No

Split of chargeable gain before rollover relief		Business	Non-business
	£	£	£
Chargeable gain before rollover relief (2/3:1/3)		89,953	44,977
Chargeable gain for the business element = Lower of:			
(1) the business proportion of the gain	89,953		
(2) the sale proceeds for the business proportion (= £200,000 × 2/3)	133,333		
Minus amount reinvested in QBAs for the business (= £128,000 × 100%)	(128,000)		
	5,333		
Lower =		(5,333)	
Rollover relief = the rest of the business gain (£89,953 – £5,333)		84,620	
Chargeable gains in 2022/23 =		5,333	+ 44,977
Total chargeable gains in 2022/23 =		£50,310	

Base cost of replacement building

	£
Cost	128,000
Minus: Rollover relief	(84,620)
Base cost	43,380

When the replacement building is eventually disposed of, the chargeable gain will be calculated using this base cost, not its original cost.

(Note that although one-third of the building was used by another business, as far as Hamza is concerned this part of the property is being used for investment purposes.)

> **Gift holdover relief**
> - Overview of gift holdover relief
> - Qualifying assets for gift holdover relief
> - The mechanics of gift holdover relief
> - Sales below market value
> - Assets not used wholly for the purposes of the trade

3 Gift holdover relief

3.1 Overview of gift holdover relief

The lifetime gift of an asset is a chargeable disposal at full market value for capital gains tax purposes. However, if defined conditions are satisfied, the gain arising on the gift may be deferred if a gift holdover relief claim is made.

Gift holdover relief is available where:

- an individual makes a disposal of a qualifying asset
- by way of an outright gift or sale for less than its full market valuation
- to a recipient who is **UK resident**.

If the recipient becomes non-UK resident within the following six tax years, the held over gain becomes chargeable immediately before they become non-UK resident.

Note that gift holdover relief is available to individuals, but not to companies. (Rollover relief is the only capital gains relief available to companies.)

The relief is an optional relief, and if required, it must be claimed. It is not given automatically. A joint claim is required, and this must be signed by both the **donor** (i.e. the person making the gift) and the **donee** (i.e. the recipient of the gift).

A joint claim must be made within four years of the end of tax year in which the disposal takes place.

3.2 Qualifying assets for gift holdover relief

Qualifying assets for gift holdover relief purposes are as follows:

- assets used in a business carried on by the donor or by the donor's personal company
- unquoted trading company shares or securities
- quoted shares or securities, but only if they are shares or securities in the donor's personal trading company.

A personal company in this context means a company in which the individual has at least 5% of the voting rights.

Note that this definition of QBA is **not** the same as the definition used for rollover relief purposes.

3.3 The mechanics of gift holdover relief

Where there is an outright gift of a qualifying business asset and gift holdover relief is claimed:

- the whole gain arising on the gift is deferred (i.e. no gain arises and therefore no tax is payable by the donor at the time of the gift)
- the gain is deferred by deduction from the deemed acquisition cost of the asset acquired by the donee (see below)
- on the subsequent disposal of the asset by the donee, the deferred gain becomes chargeable: the lower deemed acquisition cost is used in the computation rather than the full market value of the asset at the date of the gift.

The deemed acquisition cost of the asset acquired by way of an outright gift is calculated as follows:

	£
Full market value of the asset at the date of the gift	X
Minus Gift holdover relief = gain deferred (sometimes referred to as the gain held over)	(X)
Deemed acquisition cost (also referred to as the base cost)	X

Gift holdover relief is an all or nothing relief. It is optional, but if claimed, the maximum amount of gain allowed by the legislation must be deferred.

On the subsequent disposal of the asset by the donee, the gain is calculated using the base cost of the asset as calculated above.

Example

On 4 October 2022 Alan gave a business asset to his daughter which was worth £224,000. He had bought the asset in July 2001 for £11,200. His daughter sold the asset in May 2023 for £245,000. The asset qualifies as a business asset for gift holdover relief.

Required

Calculate the chargeable gains arising on the disposals, both with and without a gift holdover relief claim. State whether a gift holdover relief claim is advisable.

Answer

	No claim	With claim
	£	£
October 2022 - gift to daughter		
Market value at date of gift	224,000	224,000
Minus: Cost	(11,200)	(11,200)
Gain	212,800	212,800
Minus: Gift holdover relief	(Nil)	(212,800)
Gain after relief	212,800	Nil

Chapter 16: Capital gains tax reliefs

	No claim	With claim
	£	£
Deemed acquisition cost for the daughter		
Market value at date of gift	224,000	224,000
Minus: Gift holdover relief	(Nil)	(212,800)
Base cost of the asset	224,000	11,200
May 2023 - sale of asset by the daughter		
Sale proceeds	245,000	245,000
Minus: Market value at date of gift / Base cost	(224,000)	(11,200)
Gain	21,000	233,800
Summary of chargeable gains		
October 2022	212,800	Nil
May 2023	21,000	233,800
Total chargeable gains	233,800	233,800

The total chargeable gains remain the same whether or not a gift holdover relief claim is made. However, the claim results in the payment of the tax being deferred until the date the donee disposes of the asset. The claim is therefore advisable from a cash flow point of view.

Before making a claim, however, it is advisable to look at the full circumstances surrounding the disposal. For example:

- Is business asset disposal relief available to either the donor or the donee?
- Does either party have any capital losses available to offset against the gain?
- Is the annual exempt amount available to one party but not the other?
- What rate of CGT is payable by each party (i.e. does one party have some basic rate band available)?

3.4 Sales below market value

Where a qualifying business asset is sold for less than its full market value, the gain must be calculated using the full market value of the asset. Gift holdover relief is available, but may be restricted, depending on the amount of sale proceeds received.

If the sale proceeds received are:	Treatment:
Less than the original cost of the asset	▪ Full gift holdover relief is available, i.e. all the gain can be deferred as if an outright gift.
More than the original cost of the asset	▪ The excess sale proceeds received are treated as the gain for the donor, arising at the time of the disposal.
	▪ The rest of the gain can be deferred with a gift holdover relief claim.

Example

Assume that the facts are the same as the previous example, except that Alan sold the asset to his daughter for £50,000 and a gift holdover relief claim was made.

Required

Calculate the chargeable gains arising on the disposals.

Answer

With a gift holdover relief claim

October 2022 - sale at undervaluation to daughter	£
Gain (as in the previous example)	212,800
Note: Ignore the actual sale proceeds received. Full market value must be used as the consideration in the gain computation	
Minus: Gift holdover relief (see working)	(174,000)
Gain after relief (see working)	38,800

Working:

Sale for less than full market value but more than the original cost

Gain at the time of the sale:	£
Actual sale proceeds received	50,000
Original cost	(11,200)
Gain at the time of the sale	38,800
Gain calculated using normal rules	212,800
Gain at the time of the sale	38,800
Gift holdover relief =	174,000

Deemed acquisition cost for the daughter	£
Market value at date of gift	224,000
Minus: Gift holdover relief	(174,000)
Base cost of the asset	50,000

May 2023: Sale of asset by the daughter	
Sale proceeds	245,000
Minus: Base cost	(50,000)
Gain	195,000

3.5 Assets not used wholly for the purposes of the trade

The calculation of gift holdover relief has been explained where there is an outright gift and where there is a sale below market value. However, the amount of relief available is restricted if the asset has not been used wholly for the purposes of the trade.

Where an individual qualifying business asset:	
(1) has been used partly for business and partly for non-business use (e.g. 75% of a building used by the business and 25% not)	• Only the business proportion of the gain is eligible for gift holdover relief.
(2) has been used wholly for business use, but only for some of the period of ownership (e.g. for 10 out of 12 years)	• The gain eligible for gift holdover relief is time-apportioned.
(3) is a shareholding in the donor's personal company (i.e. the donor has more than a 5% interest in the company) and the company has investment assets	• The gain eligible for gift holdover relief is the business proportion of the chargeable assets held by the personal company, as calculated below.

The gain eligible for gift holdover relief relating to shares in a personal trading company is calculated as follows:

$$\text{Gain} \times \frac{\text{Market value of the chargeable business assets (CBAs) in the company}}{\text{Market value of the chargeable assets (CAs) in the company}}$$

CAs are the capital assets owned by the company that are chargeable assets for capital gains purposes (e.g. land and buildings, shares held in other companies, investment properties, but not exempt assets such as goodwill, motor cars, inventory, receivables etc).

CBAs are those CAs that are used for the purposes of the trade (e.g. land and buildings, but not investment assets such as shares held in other companies and investment properties).

The restriction is calculated using the market values of these assets at the date of the gift of the shares by the donor.

Example

Herbert gave his son 1,000 shares in an unquoted trading company. The gift gave rise to a chargeable gain of £28,000. At the date of the gift the company had chargeable assets worth £280,000 which included £35,000 worth of investments.

Required

Calculate the gain eligible for gift holdover relief.

Answer

Gain eligible for gift holdover relief = £28,000 × £245,000 (CBA) = £24,500
                                                    £280,000 (CA)

> **Private residence relief and letting relief**
>
> - An overview of private residence relief
> - Choice of main residence
> - Actual and deemed occupation
> - The mechanics of private residence relief
> - Restriction of relief for business use
> - Letting relief

4 Private residence relief and letting relief

4.1 An overview of private residence relief

Where an individual disposes of their only or main residence and grounds of up to half a hectare, the gain is completely exempt from CGT provided the individual:

- occupied the property as their main residence throughout the whole period of ownership, or
- was prevented from living in the house because they were required to live in 'job-related accommodation' (as defined for employment income purposes).

If these conditions are not met, a chargeable gain may arise on the disposal of the property. However, part of the gain may be exempt under the private residence relief (PRR) rules.

In addition to PRR, letting relief may be available if:

- the property has been the individual's only or main residence, and
- after PRR there is a gain remaining in charge to tax, and
- during the period of ownership part or all of the house was let to tenants.

4.2 Choice of main residence

Where an individual owns and lives in more than one residence, it is necessary to determine which property is to be treated as their main residence for CGT purposes. This is because an individual may only have one main residence at any one time. Note also that a married couple (or civil partners) can similarly only have one main residence between them at any one time.

The main residence is usually the property the individual lives in the most. However, as long as the individual lives in the property at some time, they may choose the property they wish to be treated as their main residence. It therefore is advantageous to choose the property likely to have the highest chargeable gain arising on its disposal, so that the highest gain is exempted.

The election to choose the main residence must be:

- made within two years of the acquisition of the second property, and
- signed by all parties, if the property is jointly owned.

If an election is not made, HMRC will choose the property to be treated as the main residence based on the facts of actual occupation (i.e. the property most used as the main residence).

4.3 Actual and deemed occupation

Private residence relief (PRR) is given for periods of actual and deemed occupation and is calculated as follows:

$$\text{Gain} \times \frac{\text{Period of actual and deemed occupation}}{\text{Period of ownership}}$$

Calculations are made to the nearest month in the examination.

Deemed occupation

In addition to periods of actual occupation, HMRC will exempt the following periods of deemed occupation:

Provided the property has been the individual's main residence at some time	Provided additional conditions are satisfied (see below)
The last nine months of ownership	Any period(s) of absence while working overseas
	Maximum total of four years absence while working elsewhere in the UK
	Maximum total of three years for any other reason

The two additional conditions, both of which must normally be satisfied, are as follows:

- During the period of absence this property must be elected as the **individual's main residence at that time**, and
- **at some time both before and after the period of absence** there is a period of actual occupation by the owner.

However, periods of absence while the individual is working elsewhere (either overseas or in the UK) can be counted as deemed periods of occupation even if the property is not reoccupied by the owner after the period of absence, provided the reason the individual does not reoccupy the property is because the terms of their employment prevent them from being able to reoccupy it.

4.4 The mechanics of private residence relief

If the property has not been occupied as an individual's main residence throughout the period of ownership and the individual was not required to live in 'job-related accommodation', a chargeable gain arises as follows:

- The gain on the disposal of the property is calculated in the normal way.

- Periods of actual and deemed occupation are determined and PRR is deducted from the gain.
- If the property has been let, letting relief may be calculated and deducted from the remaining gain.

Example

Barbara sold her house on 1 March 2023 for £850,000. She had purchased the house on 1 April 2010 for £231,240.

She had occupied the property as her home from the date of purchase until 1 April 2014 when she went to live with her disabled mother for two years. She then reoccupied the house from 1 April 2016 until 1 October 2018 when she moved into her boyfriend's house and put her house up for sale.

The property remained empty and was not let during her periods of absence.

Required

Calculate the capital gains tax payable on the sale of Barbara's home, assuming Barbara is a higher rate taxpayer and this was her only disposal during 2022/23.

Answer

	£
Gross sale proceeds	850,000
Less Cost	(231,240)
Gain before PRR	618,760
Less PRR (W)	
£618,760 × (111/155)	(443,112)
Gain after PRR	175,648
Annual exempt amount	(12,300)
Taxable gain	163,348
Tax due at 28%	45,737

Working: PRR

		Notes	Total (mths)	Exempt (mths)	Chargeable (mths)
1.04.2010 to 1.04.2014	Owner occupied		48	48	
1.04.2014 to 1.04.2016	Empty	(1)	24	24	
1.04.2016 to 1.10.2018	Owner occupied		30	30	
1.10.2018 to 1.03.2023	Empty	(2)	53	9	44
			155	111	44

Notes

(1) As the property was Barbara's main residence and she actually occupied it both before and after the period of absence, these 24 months are exempt under the 'three years for any other reason' rule.

(2) The last nine months of ownership are always exempt, provided the property has been Barbara's main residence at some time.

The remaining 12 months of the 'three years for any reason' is not allowed as Barbara did not reoccupy the property after this period of absence. (The exception to the need for reoccupation does not apply as this was not a period of work-related absence.)

4.5 Restriction of relief for business use

PRR is not available to exempt the portion of the gain relating to exclusive business use. The portion of the gain relating to exclusive business use is calculated as follows:

	Situation	Apportionment
(1)	Where the whole of the house is used for business purposes for part of the period of ownership.	Time apportionment
(2)	Where part of the house is used for business purposes for the whole period of ownership. The individual lives in the remaining part.	Usually based on percentage of floor space
(3)	Where part of the house is used for business purposes for part of the period of ownership. The individual lives in the whole house for part of the period of ownership and in the non-business part only for the remaining period of ownership.	Usually based on time apportionment and percentage of floor space

Note that the periods of deemed occupation are not allowed against the business portion of the gain. However, the exemption for the last nine months of ownership will apply to the whole property if the business part of the property was at some time used as the individual's main residence (i.e. situations (1) and (3) above).

Example

Imena purchased a three-storey house on 1 August 2012 to use as her main residence. She sold it on 31 October 2022, giving rise to a gain of £295,000 before PRR.

Required

Calculate the business portion of the gain which becomes chargeable assuming:

(a) Imena used the top floor for business purposes throughout the entire period of ownership

(b) Imena used the top floor for business purposes from 1 August 2016 to the date of sale.

Answer

(a) Top floor used for business purposes throughout the entire period of ownership

Business use of a third of the building for the whole period, therefore the last nine months are not exempt.

Business portion of the gain = (£295,000 × 1/3) = £98,333

(b) Top floor used for business purposes for part of the period of ownership

Length of ownership (01.08.2012 – 31.10.2022) = 123 months

Business use (01.08.2016 – 31.10.2022) = 75 months

As the top floor was used as Imena's main residence at some time, the last nine months are exempt.

Chargeable business use = (75 – 9) = 66 months

Business portion of the gain = (£295,000 × 1/3) × (66/123) = £52,764.

4.6 Letting relief

Letting relief may be available if the property:

- has been let to tenants as residential accommodation **whilst the owner is in shared occupation** with the tenant, and
- qualifies for PRR, but not all of the gain is exempted under the PRR rules.

Note that letting relief is not available for any period during which the **whole** dwelling house was let out.

The amount of letting relief available is the lowest of:

(i) An amount equivalent to the PRR

(ii) That part of the gain which relates to the period of letting

(iii) Maximum of £40,000.

Example

Olivia purchased a house for £90,000 on 1 August 2005.

Olivia occupied the property as her main residence throughout her ownership, but two of the property's eight rooms (i.e. 25% of the property) were always let out exclusively to tenants.

Olivia sold the property on 31 May 2022 for £390,000.

Required

Calculate the chargeable gain arising on the disposal of Olivia's house.

Answer

		£
Gross sale proceeds		390,000
Less Cost		(90,000)
Gain before PRR		300,000
Less PRR		
£300,000 × 75%		(225,000)
Gain after PRR		75,000
Less Letting relief (W)		(40,000)
Chargeable gain		35,000

Working

Letting relief is the lowest of:

			£
(i)	PRR		225,000
(ii)	That part of the gain which relates to the period of letting £300,000 × 25%		75,000
(iii)	Maximum		40,000

Taxation – United Kingdom
(TX-UK) FA2022

CHAPTER 17

Self-assessment for individuals

Contents	
1	Returns and penalties
2	Amendments, compliance checks and appeals
3	Payment of tax
4	The PAYE system

> **Returns and penalties**
>
> - Notification of chargeability
> - Penalties for failure to notify chargeability
> - Reasonable excuse
> - Filing an income tax return
> - Penalties for late filing of an income tax return
> - Determination assessments
> - Penalties for incorrect returns

1 Returns and penalties

1.1 Notification of chargeability

An individual who first comes within the scope of income tax or capital gains tax, or acquires a new source of income, must notify HMRC of their chargeability to tax by 5 October following the end of the tax year in which the new source of income or gain arose. For example, for 2022/23, HMRC must be notified by 5 October 2023.

Notification is not needed if all of the individual's income has had tax deducted at source or is covered by the savings and/or dividend nil rate bands, provided they have no chargeable gains and are not liable to higher rate tax.

1.2 Penalties for failure to notify chargeability

Failure to notify chargeability can result in a penalty. This is determined according to the single penalty regime that applies to income tax, class 2 and class 4 national insurance, capital gains tax, corporation tax and VAT.

The amount of penalty is based on the '**potential lost revenue**'. For individuals, this is the amount of tax due but unpaid by 31 January following the tax year as a result of the late notification.

The taxpayer's behaviour also affects the amount of penalty payable:

Type of behaviour	Maximum penalty	Minimum penalty
Deliberate and concealed	100%	30%
Deliberate but not concealed	70%	20%
Careless	30%	Nil

The penalty percentages will be given to you in the tax rates and allowances sheet in the examination.

An action is **deliberate** if the taxpayer knowingly and intentionally fails to notify HMRC of their liability. If active steps are taken to hide the failure, it is regarded as **concealed**.

Chapter 17: Self-assessment for individuals

The minimum penalties apply only where the taxpayer makes an unprompted disclosure to HMRC. A **disclosure** takes place where the taxpayer tells HMRC about the failure. A disclosure is **unprompted** if the taxpayer has no reason to believe that HMRC has discovered or is about to discover the failure at the time they make the disclosure.

To avoid a penalty entirely the unprompted disclosure must be made within 12 months of the date notification was due.

1.3 Reasonable excuse

If HMRC are entitled to charge a penalty, the taxpayer's only remedy is to satisfy HMRC that they had a reasonable excuse for their actions.

The legislation does not define the term reasonable excuse. Instead, it gives examples of what would **not** be considered a reasonable excuse. These examples include:

- Insufficiency of funds with which to pay any tax liability, and
- Reliance on a third party to submit a return or notify chargeability.

1.4 Filing an income tax return

The self-assessment system for individuals covers income tax, class 2 and 4 NICs, and capital gains tax.

Individuals whose liability to income tax is not settled in full by deduction of tax at source (for example, through the PAYE system) are required to submit a self-assessment return to HMRC.

Individuals who are likely to need to submit a tax return usually receive a blank return automatically from HMRC around the end of the tax year (i.e. March/April). If the individual has filed their return on-line in previous years, a notification that a return is due will be issued instead of a blank return.

An individual must complete the relevant sections of the tax return and submit it to HMRC.

The full income tax return consists of a summary form, supplementary pages and a tax calculation section.

The individual is required to complete the summary form and the appropriate supplementary pages in full. As regards the completion of the tax calculation section:

- If the return is filed on-line, the tax calculation section is automatically completed as part of the filing process.
- If a paper return is filed, HMRC will do the tax calculation if required, provided the return is filed on time.

If the taxpayer wishes to submit their return on-line, the normal due date for filing the return is the later of:

- 31 January following the end of the tax year (i.e. for 2022/23, by 31 January 2024), or

- 3 months after the issue of the return.

If the taxpayer wishes to submit a traditional paper return, they must do so by the later of:

- 31 October following the end of the tax year (i.e. for 2022/23, by 31 October 2023), or
- 3 months after the issue of the return.

1.5 Penalties for late filing of an income tax return

The following penalties apply to the late filing of self-assessment income tax returns.

Filed	Penalty
After the due date	£100 fixed penalty, even where there is no tax outstanding
More than 3 months late	Additional daily penalty of £10 for a maximum of 90 days
More than 6 months late	Additional 5% of the tax due, subject to a minimum of £300
More than 12 months late	A further penalty of 5% of the tax due, subject to a minimum of £300, although a higher percentage will be charged if the failure to submit is deliberate

Example

Gillian was required to file her 2021/22 tax return by 31 January 2023.

Required

Calculate the penalties payable by Gillian assuming she files her 2021/22 tax return on-line on 14 August 2023.

Answer

As Gillian's return is late, she will be subject to a fixed penalty of £100.

HMRC could decide to impose a penalty of £10 a day for a maximum of 90 days as the return is more than 3 months late. This is in addition to the fixed penalty of £100.

As the return is more than 6 months late, HMRC could also impose a penalty of 5% of the tax due. This is subject to a minimum penalty of £300. This penalty is in addition to the £100 fixed penalty and the £10 daily penalty.

1.6 Determination assessments

When a taxpayer does not file their return by the filing date, HMRC may estimate the amount of tax due. A determination assessment may be made at any time within four years of the end of the tax year concerned.

There is no right of appeal against a determination. However, the determination notice will be set aside and replaced with the taxpayer's own self-assessment when it is submitted.

1.7 Penalties for incorrect returns

A single penalty regime for incorrect returns applies:

- to incorrect income tax returns
- to incorrect corporation tax returns and
- where a misdeclaration has been made on a VAT return.

The penalty will be based on the potential lost revenue (i.e. the amount of tax understated) and the taxpayer's behaviour.

The maximum and minimum amounts of penalty are:

Type of behaviour	Maximum penalty	Minimum penalty
Deliberate and concealed	100%	30%
Deliberate but not concealed	70%	20%
Careless	30%	Nil

The penalty percentages will be given to you in the tax rates and allowances sheet in the examination.

Any penalty will be substantially reduced where a taxpayer makes disclosure, especially when this is unprompted by HMRC. For example, if a taxpayer makes an unprompted disclosure of an incorrect return following a failure to take reasonable care, the penalty could be reduced to nil. Penalties can also be reduced by assisting HMRC in quantifying the error and allowing them access to records.

No penalty will be imposed where a taxpayer has taken reasonable care. This can be demonstrated by, for example, keeping accurate records and checking the correct position where something has not been understood.

A penalty can be suspended for two years provided:

- it was charged due to failure to take reasonable care (rather than for deliberate conduct)
- the suspension conditions agreed with HMRC are kept, and
- no further penalties are incurred in the suspension period.

The suspension is intended to help taxpayers learn to meet their obligations by giving them time to improve their systems.

> **Amendments, compliance checks and appeals**
>
> - Deadlines for amendments
> - Compliance checks
> - Appeals
> - Discovery assessments
> - Record keeping

2 Amendments, compliance checks and appeals

2.1 Deadlines for amendments

HMRC's right to repair

HMRC have the right to repair (i.e. correct) a taxpayer's return within nine months of the date of receipt, if there are obvious errors or omissions (such as arithmetical errors and missing pages).

The taxpayer's right to amend

The taxpayer has the right to amend their return within 12 months of the due filing date.

For example, for 2022/23, an individual has the right to amend until 31 January 2025, regardless of whether the return is paper-based or filed on-line.

Claims for recovery of overpaid tax

Taxpayers who believe they have overpaid tax may make a claim for repayment after the amendment deadline but within four years of the end of the tax year. However, a mistake is ineligible for relief if the return was made in accordance with the generally prevailing practice at the time.

2.2 Compliance checks

HMRC have the right to make a compliance check into a return to check for completeness and accuracy.

A return may be investigated:

- because information is received by HMRC that does not tie up with the return, or
- as a result of HMRC's random selection process, whereby it selects a small percentage of returns to check.

HMRC are not obliged to disclose the reason for the compliance check. However, they must normally give written notice before commencing a compliance check, within 12 months of the date of receipt of the return. If the return was filed late, the deadline for opening a compliance check is extended to the quarter date following the first anniversary of the actual filing date. Quarter dates are 31 January, 30 April, 31 July and 31 October.

Example

Gordon filed his 2021/22 tax return on 14 August 2023.

Required

State the date by which HMRC must give notice if they wish to carry out a compliance check into his return.

Answer

Gordon's 2021/22 return should have been submitted by 31 January 2023.

As it was submitted late, the notice period runs to the first quarter date after the anniversary of the actual filing, i.e. 31 October 2024.

If a taxpayer amends their return after the filing date, the deadline for opening a compliance check is extended to the quarter date following the first anniversary of the amendment date. However, if it is opened beyond the normal date for opening a compliance check, the check is confined to matters contained in the amendment.

On the completion of a compliance check, HMRC must issue a written notice stating:

- that the compliance check has been completed, and
- the outcome of the compliance check.

The taxpayer can appeal against HMRC's amendment, in writing, within 30 days of the amendment.

2.3 Appeals

The taxpayer has the right to appeal against:

- an amendment to a return
- the imposition of a penalty
- a discovery assessment (see below).

An appeal should be in writing, and must be made within 30 days of the relevant event. It must also state the grounds for the appeal.

Appeals may initially be made to HMRC. An officer unconnected with the case will undertake a review. This review must normally be carried out within 45 days. The taxpayer then has 30 days in which to appeal to the Tribunal.

The tribunal system consists of a First-tier Tribunal and an Upper Tribunal. The First-tier Tribunal deals with all but the most complex cases. The Upper Tribunal deals with the more complex cases and appeals against decisions of the First-tier Tribunal.

If the decision of the First-tier Tribunal is based on:

- a matter of fact, the decision is binding and final

- a point of law, the case can be referred to the Upper Tribunal, but only with the permission of either the First-tier or Upper Tribunal.

A decision of the Upper Tribunal can be referred to the Court of Appeal.

2.4 Discovery assessments

Where a taxpayer filed their return on time but HMRC did not make a compliance check into the return within the permitted 12 months, HMRC can raise a discovery assessment where they suspect that full disclosure has not been made.

The time limits for making a discovery assessment depend on the circumstances of the case:

Situation	Time limit
Ordinary time limit	4 years from the end of the tax year
Careless omission	6 years from the end of the tax year
Deliberate omission	20 years from the end of the tax year

2.5 Record keeping

An individual must keep adequate records to support their tax return:

- personal records must be retained for at least 1 year after the annual filing date (i.e. for a 2022/23 return personal records must be kept until 31 January 2025), and
- business records must be retained for at least 5 years after the annual filing date (i.e. for a 2022/23 return business records must be kept until 31 January 2029).

The above dates are replaced by:

- the date on which HMRC have completed any compliance check, or
- the date on which HMRC no longer have the power to make a compliance check into a return, if later.

A penalty of up to £3,000 per tax year can be levied for failure to keep records.

The obligation to preserve records may be satisfied by preserving the information contained in the records, rather than the actual records themselves. It is therefore permissible to preserve the information in electronic form.

Chapter 17: Self-assessment for individuals

> **Payment of tax**
>
> - Payment dates for income tax, NIC and capital gains tax
> - Penalties for failure to pay on time
> - Interest on underpaid and overpaid tax

3 Payment of tax

3.1 Payment dates for income tax, NIC and capital gains tax

Income tax and class 4 NIC

Income tax that is not collected under PAYE **and** class 4 NICs (if applicable) are usually paid in three instalments, as follows:

Payment	Due date	For 2022/23
1st payment on account	31 January in the tax year	31 January 2023
2nd payment on account	31 July following the end of the tax year	31 July 2023
Balancing payment	31 January following the end of the tax year	31 January 2024

The amount of each payment on account (POA) is calculated as follows:

POA = ½ × Tax paid by self-assessment in the preceding tax year

The tax paid by self-assessment for the preceding year is calculated as follows:

	£
Income tax liability	X
Plus Class 4 NICs	X
Total tax liability	X
Minus: PAYE	(X)
Tax paid by self-assessment	X

POAs are not required if the tax paid by self-assessment in the preceding tax year is either:

- less than £1,000, or
- less than 20% of the total tax liability.

Capital gains tax

Capital gains tax is collected under self-assessment and is normally due in one single payment by 31 January following the end of the tax year (i.e. for 2022/23, by 31 January 2024).

However, a payment on account in respect of CGT due on disposals of residential property is payable within 60 days of the date of disposal (see Chapter 14). Any balancing payment is due on the normal due date of 31 January.

Class 2 NIC

Class 2 NICs are payable by 31 January following the end of the tax year (i.e. for 2022/23, by 31 January 2024).

Example

Graham has provided the following information:

	2021/22	2022/23
	£	£
Income tax liability	21,450	31,200
Class 2 NICs	159	164
Class 4 NICs	2,430	2,560
Capital gains tax liability	5,600	3,200
PAYE	15,800	22,670

Required

Calculate the tax payable under self-assessment for 2022/23 and state the due dates of payment.

Answer

2021/22 (= preceding tax year)	£
Income tax liability	21,450
Plus Class 4 NICs	2,430
Total tax liability	23,880
Minus: PAYE	(15,800)
Amount payable	8,080

This amount of £8,080 is more than £1,000 and more than 20% of the total tax liability (= 20% × £23,880 = £4,776). Therefore, payments on account are required in 2022/23.

2022/23:	£
Income tax liability	31,200
Plus: Class 4 NICs	2,560
Total tax liability	33,760
Minus: PAYE	(22,670)
Amount payable	11,090

Due dates of payment and amounts of each payment:

	Due date		Amount
			£
Payments on account	31 January 2023	½ × £8,080	4,040
	31 July 2023	½ × £8,080	4,040
			8,080
Balancing payment	31 January 2024	£11,090 – £8,080	3,010
Income tax and Class 4 NICs			11,090
Capital gains tax	31 January 2024		3,200
Class 2 NICs	31 January 2024		164

Note

On 31 January 2024, the first POA of £5,545 (½ × £11,090) for 2023/24 is also due.

Reduction of POAs

If an individual believes that their total tax liability will be less than the previous year, they can claim to reduce their payments on account. The claim must be made by 31 January following the tax year and must state the grounds for the reduction. HMRC cannot dispute the claim.

If at the end of the year it is found that the POAs were incorrectly reduced, but it was as a result of an innocent error, interest will be payable on the instalments but no further consequences arise. However, if the individual deliberately reduced the payments fraudulently or negligently, penalties will be levied in addition to interest payments.

3.2 Penalties for failure to pay on time

If all or any part of the **balancing payment** is unpaid more than one month after the due date, an individual is liable to a penalty of 5% of the overdue tax.

A further 5% penalty is levied if the tax is still unpaid more than 6 months after the due date, and again after 12 months.

Penalties are not levied on POAs that are paid late (although interest is charged).

Example

Isabel made the following self-assessment payments in relation to 2021/22:

	Amount paid	Paid on
1st POA	£1,750	31.1.2022
2nd POA	£1,750	30.9.2022

The balancing payment was £1,500.

Required

Calculate the penalties arising if Isabel paid the balancing payment on the following alternative dates:

(a) 16 February 2023

(b) 31 March 2023

(c) 9 September 2023.

Answer

The second POA is paid late (on 30.9.22 instead of 31.7.22). However, penalties are not levied on POAs.

The due date for the balancing payment is 31 January 2023.

Penalties due:

Date paid	How late?	Penalty
(a) 16 February 2023	Less than one month	Nil
(b) 31 March 2023	More than one month	5% × £1,500 = £75
(c) 9 September 2023	More than 6 months	10% × £1,500 = £150

3.3 Interest on underpaid and overpaid tax

Late payment interest

HMRC charges late payment interest on any underpaid tax. This interest runs:

- **from** the date the tax should have been paid
- **to** the date the tax is actually paid to HMRC.

Interest may also be payable on penalties and where a self-assessment is amended or a discovery assessment is raised.

In the examination, the annual rate of late payment interest is given in the tax rates and allowances table (as 3.25%) and interest should be calculated to the nearest month.

Chapter 17: Self-assessment for individuals

Example

Helen made the following self-assessment payments in relation to 2021/22:

	Amount paid	Paid on
1st POA	£6,500	31 March 2022
2nd POA	£6,500	30 September 2022
Balancing payment	£5,000	28 February 2023

Required

Calculate the interest due on any tax paid late.

Answer

Interest will be calculated as follows:

		Due date	Payment date
1st POA	£6,500 × 3.25% × 2/12 = £35	from 31.1.2022	to 31.3.2022
2nd POA	£6,500 × 3.25% × 2/12 = £35	from 31.7.2022	to 30.9.2022
Balancing payment	£5,000 × 3.25% × 1/12 = £14	from 31.1.2023	to 28.2.2023

Repayment interest

Repayment interest on overpaid income tax runs **to** the date the tax is repaid by HMRC. Interest runs:

- **from** 31 January following the end of the tax year for PAYE and
- **from** the date of payment for POAs and other tax payments
- **to** the date the tax is repaid by HMRC.

In the examination, the annual rate of repayment interest is given in the tax rates and allowances sheet (as 0.5%).

> **The PAYE system**
>
> - Overview of the PAYE system
> - Notice of coding
> - Reporting information to HMRC

4 The PAYE system

4.1 Overview of the PAYE system

The Pay-as-you-earn (PAYE) system deals with payments for employed individuals of:

- income tax and
- Class 1 primary NI contributions

by deduction from the employee's earnings at source.

It also deals with Class 1 secondary contributions and Class 1A contributions paid by the employer.

Payment at source means that the employer deducts the payments from the employee's wages or salary, and makes the payments to HMRC.

PAYE income tax and Class 1 primary and secondary NICs are paid to HMRC on a monthly basis. The income tax and Class 1 NICs in relation to a tax month are paid to HMRC 14 days following the end of the month (i.e. the liabilities for the tax month of 6 March to 5 April 2023 are paid to HMRC on 19 April 2023).

- Employers with more than 250 employees must make the monthly payments electronically and must do so by the 22nd of each month.
- If the average monthly total of PAYE tax and NICs is not in excess of £1,500, payments can be made quarterly on 19 January, 19 April, 19 July and 19 October.

Interest is charged on late payments. Penalties may also be charged.

The first late payment does not attract a penalty, unless it is over six months late. The penalties for subsequent late payments depend on how late the payment is and how many times payments have been made late in that tax year.

PAYE is applied to the following payments:

- Salary/wages
- Bonuses/commissions
- Any other cash receipts and cash benefits (e.g. mileage allowances that exceed the approved mileage allowance rates)
- Cash and non-cash vouchers, excluding vouchers exempted under the benefit rules
- Receipts of marketable assets that can be converted into cash (e.g. gold bars, fine wines, shares, diamonds).

In order to calculate the correct amount of tax, the employer must use the individual's tax code.

4.2 Notice of coding

HMRC produce a notice of coding (a form P2) for every employee each tax year and send a copy to the employee.

The P2 details the allowances and deductions available to that employee in that tax year and gives the individual a tax code. The employer is also sent a copy of the tax code, on form P6, but this does not give any detail as to how the code has been calculated.

A tax code is usually a number followed by a suffix.

- The number shows the tax-free allowance the individual employee is entitled to.
- The suffix shows the main personal circumstances of the employee.

The most common suffix for a tax code is L. This shows that the taxpayer is entitled to the basic personal allowance.

Occasionally a tax code will have the prefix K rather than a suffix. This shows that the deductions exceed the allowances. K codes are negative allowances; they are added to the taxpayer's pay for tax purposes, thereby increasing their PAYE. However, to ensure that an employee's entire salary is not wiped out by PAYE deductions, the maximum amount of tax that can be deducted through PAYE is 50% of the employee's salary for that pay period.

Some tax codes consist solely of letters. For example:

- Code BR indicates that basic rate tax must be deducted from the full payment.
- Code D0 indicates that higher rate tax must be deducted from the full payment.

These codes would be used where, for example, an individual had two employments and all of their allowances were set against just one of them.

The tax code is calculated as follows:

Calculation of an individual's tax code	£
Allowances	
The personal allowance	12,570
Allowable expenses	X
	X
Deductions	
Assessable benefits of employment	(X)
Adjustment for underpaid tax	
(Underpaid tax × 100/20 or 100/40 or 100/45) (see below)	(X)
Net allowances	X
Tax code = 1/10 × Net allowances, rounded down to a whole number	

For example, a tax code of 523 indicates net allowances of £5,230 (up to £5,239).

If an employee has underpaid tax of less than £3,000, HMRC will automatically collect it via PAYE by reducing the employee's tax code unless the employee asks them not to do so. (Unpaid Class 2 National Insurance can also be collected in this way.) A paper return must be filed by 31 October or an on-line return by 30 December for the underpayment to be collected in this way. Otherwise, the underpayment will be collected through the self-assessment system in the usual way.

The adjustment for underpaid tax is calculated as the amount of underpayment grossed up at:

- 100/20 if the individual is a basic rate taxpayer
- 100/40 if a higher rate taxpayer and
- 100/45 if an additional rate taxpayer.

Example

Jack earns £63,200 a year. He is provided with a company car with a benefit of £3,965. He pays professional subscriptions of £360. He has an underpayment of tax of £450 which he has requested to be collected via PAYE. Jack is single and has no other source of income.

Required

Calculate Jack's tax code for 2022/23.

Answer

Allowances	£
The personal allowance	12,570
Allowable expenses	360
	12,930
Deductions	
Assessable benefits of employment	(3,965)
Adjustment for underpaid tax (£450 × 100/40)	(1,125)
Net allowances	7,840

Tax code = 1/10 × 7,840 = **784L**

Note that benefits will not be included in an employee's tax code if their employer has chosen to report and pay benefits through the payroll. Payrolling of benefits is voluntary and employers can choose which benefits they want to payroll. The employer must register these benefits with HMRC before the start of the tax year.

4.3 Reporting information to HMRC

The payments of income tax and national insurance due under the PAYE system must be reported using a system called 'real time information'. Under this system, employers are required to report information electronically each month **on or before the time an employee is paid**, rather than waiting until the end of the tax year and reporting annually. This notification is done by making a Full Payment Submission (FPS).

If an employer does not pay any employees during a particular tax month, they must make an Employer Payment Summary (EPS) rather than an FPS. This tells HMRC that there are no payments to report.

Penalties are imposed on a monthly basis if these submissions are made late:

- There is no penalty for the first month in a tax year for which submissions are late.

- Thereafter a monthly late filing penalty of between £100 and £400 is charged depending on the number of employees.

- An additional penalty of 5% of the tax and NIC due can be charged where a submission is more than three months late.

The other PAYE forms that an employer is required to complete are as follows:

Form number	Purpose	Due date, if applicable
P45	Given to an employee when they leave.	
	The form records their tax code, pay and income tax to the date of leaving that employment.	
	There is no need to send this form to HMRC as this information is provided through the real time information system.	
P60	Given to employees who were in employment at the end of the tax year.	31 May
	Shows the total pay, tax and national insurance deducted in the year.	
	The form must also give details of any taxable benefits that have been payrolled.	
P11D	Submitted to HMRC, with a copy provided to the employee.	6 July
	Provides details of taxable benefits that have not been payrolled.	

Taxation – United Kingdom
(TX-UK) FA2022

CHAPTER 18

Inheritance tax on lifetime gifts

Contents
1 An overview of inheritance tax
2 Lifetime gifts
3 The calculation of lifetime tax on chargeable lifetime transfers (CLTs)
4 The calculation of death tax on lifetime gifts

> **An overview of inheritance tax**
> - Introduction
> - Chargeable persons
> - A transfer of value
> - The occasions of charge

1 An overview of inheritance tax

1.1 Introduction

Individuals are taxed on the value of the net assets they leave in their estate when they die. However, in addition, **some lifetime gifts attract an immediate IHT charge**, and a **further tax charge** may be due on certain lifetime gifts **on the event of death**.

IHT is essentially **a donor-based tax**. This means that for all charges to IHT:

- the calculations of the amounts of tax payable are based on the circumstances of the individual making the gift (the donor), and
- the donor is primarily responsible for paying any IHT due.

The person receiving the transfer (i.e. gift) is known as the donee.

IHT is imposed on **chargeable transfers of value.** An IHT liability therefore arises if:

- a **chargeable person**
- makes a **transfer of value**
- of capital assets.

1.2 Chargeable persons

Individuals who are domiciled in the UK are chargeable to IHT on their worldwide assets, whether or not they are resident in the UK. (The TX-UK examination will only cover the position of individuals who are domiciled in the UK.)

1.3 A transfer of value

A **transfer of value** means any gratuitous disposition of wealth. A transfer of value occurs where an individual transfers a capital asset and their estate decreases in value as a result of the transfer.

Transfers of value can occur during an individual's lifetime or on death (via a will or under the rules of intestacy).

For the transfer to be caught by the IHT regime, there must be gratuitous intent (i.e. it must be a gift). A genuine commercial transaction or bad bargain (i.e. the unintentional sale of an asset for less than it is worth) would not be a transfer of value for IHT purposes. Similarly, expenditure on family maintenance is not considered to be a transfer of value.

The concept of the fall in value as a result of a gift, or the **diminution in value concept**, is the fundamental starting point of all IHT calculations.

The diminution in the value of the estate is usually the open market value of the capital asset that is gifted. However, where unquoted shares are concerned, it may be necessary to compare the value of the donor's estate before the transfer with the value after the transfer. This is because shares forming part of a controlling shareholding are normally valued higher than shares forming part of a minority holding.

Example

Larry gifted 2,000 of his shares in XYZ Ltd to his daughter, Sally.

XYZ Ltd is an unquoted investment company with an issued share capital of 18,000 £1 ordinary shares. Larry owned 9,500 of the shares before the transfer.

At the date of the transfer, XYZ Ltd shares were valued as follows:

	Price per share
	£
0 – 50% holding	18
51 – 100% holding	30

Required

Calculate the value of the transfer to Sally.

Answer

Before the gift	After the gift
No. of shares = 9,500	No. of shares = 7,500
Controlling shareholding (53%)	Minority shareholding (42%)

	£
Value of estate before the gift (9,500 × £30)	285,000
Value of estate after the gift (7,500 × £18)	(135,000)
Transfer of value	150,000

Note that the diminution in value method of calculating the amount transferred applies only to inheritance tax. For capital gains tax purposes, the shares would simply be valued at the price applicable to an 11% shareholding, i.e. 2,000 × £18 = £36,000.

1.4 The occasions of charge

There are three key occasions of charge to IHT as follows:

Timing of the event:		IHT charged on:
During the individual donor's lifetime	(1)	Chargeable lifetime transfers (CLTs), **at the time the gift is made**
On the death of the individual	(2)	Chargeable Lifetime Transfers (CLTs), and Potentially Exempt Transfers (PETs) **if the gift is within seven years of death**
	(3)	The value of the individual's estate on the date of death

The two IHT charges on lifetime gifts are covered in this chapter. The next chapter covers the third IHT charge on the value of an individual's estate.

Lifetime gifts

- The three types of lifetime gifts
- Exempt gifts
- Potentially exempt transfers (PETs)
- Chargeable lifetime transfers (CLTs)
- Advantages of making lifetime transfers

2 Lifetime gifts

2.1 The three types of lifetime gifts

For IHT purposes an individual may make the following three types of gifts during their lifetime:

(1) Exempt gifts

(2) Potentially exempt transfers (PETs), and

(3) Chargeable lifetime transfers (CLTs).

2.2 Exempt gifts

The following lifetime gifts are exempt from IHT:

- **Gifts to a spouse or civil partner**

    Gifts to a spouse or civil partner are exempt regardless of the amount of the gift. (This exemption also applies to gifts made on death.)

- **Gifts which represent normal expenditure out of income**

    To prove that a gift is an item of normal expenditure, HMRC would expect the expenditure to be regular payments out of income (not capital) and the payments not to affect the standard of living of the individual donor (for example, Christmas and birthday presents).

- **Small gifts**

    Gifts **to individuals of £250 or less** per recipient per tax year are exempt. If a gift exceeds £250, or the total gifts to the same person in a tax year exceed £250, the full amount of the gift is chargeable.

- **Gifts in consideration of marriage (or civil partnership)**

    Wedding presents are exempt, subject to monetary limits as follows:

Relationship of the donor to one of the couple:	Limit
	£
Parent	5,000
Grandparent	2,500
One of the couple to the other	2,500
Anyone else	1,000

If the gift exceeds the limit, only the excess is chargeable. (Note that these limits are not given in the examination.)

- **Gifts covered by the annual exemption**

    In each tax year an individual has an annual exemption (AE) of £3,000.

    The AE is allocated in strict chronological date order irrespective of whether a gift is a PET or a CLT. It is deducted after other specific exemptions, such as the marriage exemption.

    Any unused AE may be carried forward and set off in the following year. However, the carry forward of unused AE is for one year only and can only be utilised after the current year AE has been set off.

The IHT consequences of exempt gifts

There is no IHT to pay at any time on exempt gifts.

2.3 Potentially exempt transfers (PETs)

A **potentially exempt transfer** (PET) is a gift **by** an individual (the donor) **to** another individual (the donee).

The IHT consequences of PETs

- There is **no IHT** to pay on PETs **at the time of the gift**.
- A PET is potentially exempt. Therefore, it may never become chargeable.
- A PET will only become chargeable if the donor dies within seven years of making the gift. It is then taxed using the rates and allowances applicable in the year of death.

The gross chargeable value of a PET

Despite the fact that a PET does not become chargeable unless the donor dies within the following seven years, the value of a PET is fixed at the time of the gift and is calculated as follows:

	£
Value of the estate before the gift	X
Value of the estate after the gift	(X)
Transfer of value (or diminution in value)	X
Less: Exemptions (e.g.)	
Marriage exemption	(X)
Annual exemption – current tax year	(X)
– preceding tax year (if unused)	(X)
Gross chargeable amount	X

2.4 Chargeable lifetime transfers (CLTs)

A **chargeable lifetime transfer** (CLT) is a gift which is not a PET and is not exempt.

The main example of a CLT is a gift into a trust.

A trust is an arrangement laid down in a formal legal trust deed whereby:

- a group of persons (known as the **trustees**)
- are given the duty and responsibility
- to hold and administer **assets** put into a fund
- by a person (known as the **settlor**)
- for the benefit of other persons (known as the **beneficiaries**).

A trust enables the benefits arising out of owning property to be enjoyed by someone other than the legal owner. For example, parents might put assets into a trust for their children. The trustees will control the trust assets until the children are old enough to own them directly.

The IHT consequences of CLTs

- A CLT is taxed **at the time of the gift**. CLTs are the only lifetime gifts by a donor which are immediately chargeable to IHT.
- There is a choice of who pays the lifetime tax, the donor or donee.
- A CLT becomes chargeable again if the donor dies within seven years of making the transfer.

The gross chargeable value of a CLT

The gross chargeable value of a CLT is calculated in the same way as the gross value of a PET, if the donee agrees to pay the lifetime tax. However, it is slightly different if the donor agrees to pay the lifetime tax.

The detailed computations of lifetime IHT on CLTs is covered in the next section of this chapter.

Example

Lucy made the following lifetime cash gifts:

		£
10 July 2021	To her son	55,000
8 April 2022	To her husband	43,000
25 May 2022	To a friend	245
12 June 2022	To her grandson on the occasion of his marriage	4,500
30 September 2022	To a trust (the trustees are to pay any lifetime IHT)	100,000

Required

(a) State whether each gift is an exempt gift, a PET or CLT.

(b) Calculate the gross chargeable value of each gift.

Answer

Date:	Gift to:			£
10.7.2021	Son	PET	Transfer of value = cash	55,000
			Less AE for 2021/22	(3,000)
			AE for 2020/21	(3,000)
			Value of PET	49,000
8.4.2022	Spouse		Exempt – unlimited amount	Nil
25.5.2022	Friend	PET	Transfer of value = cash	245
			Less Small gift exemption	(245)
			Value of PET	Nil
12.6.2022	Grandson	PET	Transfer of value = cash	4,500
			Less Marriage exemption	(2,500)
			AE for 2022/23	(2,000)
			Value of PET	Nil
30.9.2022	Trust	CLT	Transfer of value = cash	100,000
			Less AEs	
			– 2022/23 - balance	(1,000)
			– 2021/22 - already used	(Nil)
			Value of CLT	99,000

2.5 Advantages of making lifetime transfers

The easiest way for an individual to reduce their potential IHT liability is by making lifetime transfers. This is for a number of reasons:

- Some lifetime transfers are exempt from IHT (e.g. small gifts, wedding gifts, gifts covered by the annual exemption).

- A PET is completely exempt from IHT if the donor survives for seven years.

- There will be no additional liability on a CLT if the donor survives for seven years.

- Even if the donor dies within seven years of making the PET or CLT, the value of the transfer is fixed at the time it is made. This means that any increase in value between the date of transfer and the date of death escapes IHT.

- Taper relief is available to reduce the amount of IHT payable if the donor survives for at least three years after making the transfer. This is covered later.

Chapter 18: Inheritance tax and lifetime gifts

> **The calculation of lifetime tax on chargeable lifetime transfers (CLTs)**
>
> - The procedure for calculating lifetime IHT
> - The chargeable amount
> - The nil rate band
> - The seven year cumulation period
> - The lifetime rate of tax
> - The proforma computation for lifetime IHT

3 The calculation of lifetime tax on chargeable lifetime transfers (CLTs)

3.1 The procedure for calculating lifetime IHT

Lifetime IHT is payable on CLTs at the time of the gift.

The procedure to adopt for calculating lifetime IHT is as follows:

Step 1: Deal with gifts in strict chronological date order and calculate **the chargeable amount** of any CLTs **and** PETs

Although there is no lifetime tax payable on PETs, the gross chargeable amount of the PETs needs to be calculated in order to decide whether the annual exemptions have been utilised

Step 2: Calculate the lifetime tax on each CLT separately starting with the earliest (ignore the PETs at this stage) and take into account:

- the **available nil rate band**, and
- **who has agreed to pay the tax**

Step 3: If required, state the **due date for payment** of the lifetime tax.

3.2 The chargeable amount

The IHT payable on CLTs can be paid by either:

- the donor of the gift, or
- the donee (i.e. the recipient of the gift).

As the main example of a CLT is a gift into a trust, the donee will be the trustee(s) of the trust fund.

As mentioned earlier, the gross chargeable value of a CLT is calculated in the same way as the gross value of a PET if the donee (i.e. trustee) agrees to pay the lifetime tax. However, it is slightly different if the donor agrees to pay the lifetime tax.

If the trustee (the **donee**) agrees to pay the tax:

- The gift is known as a **gross gift**.
- This means that the value of the gift is the total (gross) amount that the donor is gifting out of their estate.

However, if the **donor** agrees to pay the tax:

- The gift is known as a **net gift.**
- This means that the donor is not only gifting the value of the asset but is paying the associated tax bill. Therefore, the value of the gift **plus** the associated lifetime IHT payable is the total (gross) amount that the donor is gifting out of their estate.

IHT is principally a donor-based tax. Therefore, if an examination question does not state who has agreed to pay the lifetime tax, always assume that it is a net gift and the donor will pay the tax.

3.3 The nil rate band

There is a nil rate band available for IHT transfers.

To calculate the lifetime IHT due on a CLT, the nil rate band applicable at the time of the transfer should be used. The nil rate band for 2022/23 is £325,000. The nil rate band for 2022/23 will be provided in the tax rates and allowances section of the examination paper. The nil rate bands for earlier years will be given to you within the examination question, if required.

3.4 The seven year cumulation period

The nil rate band covers a 'cumulation period' of seven years.

Lifetime IHT is only payable if the CLT **plus** any other gross chargeable transfers in the preceding seven years exceed the nil rate band.

This means that when calculating the IHT payable on a CLT, it is necessary to look back seven years **before the gift** and to work out the total value of any other gross **chargeable** transfers in that period. This step is important to find out whether or not there is any nil rate band left available to match against the latest CLT.

Note that **only CLTs are cumulated** in lifetime IHT calculations. Exempt gifts are ignored as they never become chargeable and all PETs are ignored as they do not become chargeable until the donor dies.

3.5 The lifetime rate of tax

The rate of lifetime IHT payable on the excess over the available nil rate band is calculated as follows:

Type of gift:	The payer of the lifetime IHT:	Rate:
Gross CLT	The trustees	20%
Net CLT	The donor	20/80 or 25%

3.6 The proforma computation for lifetime IHT

Step 1: The chargeable amount of a CLT or PET is calculated as follows

	£
Value of the estate before the gift	X
Value of the estate after the gift	(X)
Transfer of value (or diminution in value)	X
Less: Exemptions (e.g.)	
Marriage exemption	(X)
Annual exemption – current tax year	(X)
– preceding tax year (if unused)	(X)
Chargeable amount	X

= gross chargeable amount if a PET or a CLT where the trustees agree to pay the IHT

= net chargeable amount if a CLT and the donor agrees to pay the IHT

Step 2: The lifetime IHT is calculated as follows

	£	£
Chargeable amount		X
Nil rate band (NRB)	X	
Gross CLTs in the seven years before this gift	(X)	
Nil rate band available		(X)
Taxable amount		X
Lifetime IHT at 20% (if gross gift) or 25% (if net gift)		X

If the CLT is a net gift, the lifetime IHT must be added to the net chargeable amount to calculate the correct figure of gross chargeable transfer to use when calculating the IHT on the next gift.

	£
Net chargeable amount	X
Add: Lifetime IHT	X
Gross chargeable amount to carry forward for future calculations	X

If there are only a few gifts, adopting a columnar form layout with two columns for each gift (as in the example below) will save time in the examination.

Step 3: State the due date of payment of the IHT and who has agreed to pay the tax

- The donor and the donee can choose who is to pay the lifetime IHT. (If the question does not say who is to pay the tax, assume it is the donor as they are the person with the primary liability.)
- The date of payment depends on when the CLT occurs in the tax year as follows:

Date of CLT:	Due date:
6 April to 30 September	30 April in the following year
1 October to 5 April	Six months after the end of the month in which the CLT is made

Example

Michael made the following lifetime gifts:

Date of gift	Recipient of the gift	£
13 February 2015	Daughter's trust	200,000
24 May 2017	Nephew	140,000
29 September 2018	Son's trust	175,000
9 December 2022	Daughter's trust	171,000

The nil rate band for all of the earlier tax years is £325,000.

The trustees of the daughter's trust agreed to pay the lifetime IHT in respect of the gifts into that trust. Otherwise, Michael paid any tax due.

Required

Calculate the lifetime IHT due on these gifts and state the due date for payment.

Chapter 18: Inheritance tax and lifetime gifts

a) Answer

The gift on 24 May 2017 to the nephew is a PET. There is no lifetime IHT payable on PETs.

This gift is ignored when calculating the lifetime tax on the CLTs, except that the annual exemptions for 2017/18 and 2016/17 will be matched against this PET. Therefore the 2017/18 annual exemption is not available to match against CLT 2 as shown below:

	CLT 1 13.2.2015		PET 24.5.2017		CLT 2 29.9.2018		CLT 3 9.12.2022
	£	£	£	£	£	£	£
Transfer of value		200,000	140,000		175,000		171,000
Less AE							
2014/15		(3,000)					
2013/14 b/f		(3,000)					
2017/18			(3,000)				
2016/17 b/f			(3,000)				
2018/19					(3,000)		
2022/23							(3,000)
2021/22 b/f							(3,000)
Chargeable amount		194,000	134,000		172,000		165,000
NRB	325,000			325,000		325,000	
Gross CLTs in 7 yrs before the gift							
13.2.08 – 13.2.15	(Nil)						
29.9.11 – 29.9.18 (*ignore the PET*)				(194,000)			
9.12.15 – 9.12.22 (*first gift drops out, ignore PET, bring in gross amount of CLT2*)						(182,250)	
NRB available		(325,000)			(131,000)		(142,750)
Taxable amount		Nil			41,000		22,250
		Gross gift			**Net gift**		**Gross gift**
Lifetime IHT							
Covered by NRB		Nil					
No IHT = PET			Nil				
41,000 × 25%					10,250		
22,250 × 20%							4,450
Paid by					Michael		Trustees
Due date					30.4.19		30.6.23
Gross CLT c/f to next gift calculation:							
Gross CLT		194,000					
Net CLT + tax (172,000 + 10,250)					182,250		
Gross CLT							165,000

The calculation of death tax on lifetime gifts

- The procedure for calculating death tax on lifetime gifts
- The gross chargeable amount on death
- The nil rate band available
- The seven year cumulation period
- The death rate of tax
- Taper relief
- Lifetime IHT paid
- The proforma computation for death tax on lifetime gifts

4 The calculation of death tax on lifetime gifts

4.1 The procedure for calculating death tax on lifetime gifts

On the death of an individual, IHT is payable on both CLTs and PETs at the death rates of tax, but only if the gifts are within seven years of the date of death.

The procedure to adopt for calculating IHT payable on death is as follows:

Step 1: Deal with the gifts in strict chronological date order and calculate the **gross chargeable amount** of any **CLTs** and **PETs**

Step 2: Calculate the death tax on each gift if it is within seven years of the date of death starting with the earliest and taking into account:

- the **available nil rate band**,
- **the death rates of tax**,
- **taper relief**, and
- **lifetime IHT paid** (if any)

Step 3: If required, state the **due date for payment** of the death tax.

4.2 The gross chargeable amount on death

The amount chargeable on death is the **gross chargeable amount** calculated when computing the lifetime IHT calculations.

Therefore, in the previous example, if Michael were to die on 31 December 2022, the gross chargeable amounts that would become taxable on death would be:

			Gross chargeable amount on death
			£
13.2.15	CLT 1	More than seven years before death	Nil
24.5.17	PET	Becomes chargeable for the first time	134,000
29.9.18	CLT 2	Becomes chargeable again on death	182,250
9.12.22	CLT 3	Becomes chargeable again on death	165,000

4.3 The nil rate band available

The additional tax payable on lifetime gifts as a result of the donor's death is computed using the nil rate band available in the year of death.

The nil rate band is matched against lifetime gifts first, before computing the IHT on the value of the individual's estate at the date of death. Therefore, the death tax on lifetime gifts must be calculated before the death tax due on the estate.

4.4 The seven year accumulation period

As in the lifetime calculations, in death calculations the nil rate band covers a cumulation period of seven years **before the date of the gift**.

Death IHT is payable on a lifetime gift if:

- the gross chargeable amount **plus**
- the total gross chargeable amount of gifts in the preceding seven years

exceed the nil rate band.

This means that when calculating the IHT payable on a CLT or PET which has become chargeable on death, it is necessary to look back seven years **before the gift** and to work out the value of any other **gross chargeable transfers** in that period.

However, when looking back seven years from the date of the gift in death calculations:

- **all** CLTs must be totalled together with
- any PETs which are **within seven years of death**.

In the death calculations the only gifts that can be ignored are exempt gifts and PETs which are more than seven years before the date of death.

4.5 The death rate of tax

The death rate of IHT is 40% on the excess over the nil rate band. The death tax due on lifetime gifts can be reduced by:

- taper relief, and
- any lifetime IHT paid in respect of that gift.

4.6 Taper relief

Taper relief is available if the lifetime gift was made more than three years before the date of death.

The rate of taper relief is as follows:

Years before death	Percentage reduction %
Over 3 but less than 4 years	20
Over 4 but less than 5 years	40
Over 5 but less than 6 years	60
Over 6 but less than 7 years	80

4.7 Lifetime IHT paid

If the gift is a CLT some lifetime IHT may have been paid. If so, it can be deducted from any IHT due as a result of the donor's death. Credit is given for the lifetime tax paid irrespective of whether it was paid by the donor or donee.

If the lifetime IHT paid exceeds the death tax due, there is **no repayment** of lifetime IHT.

4.8 The proforma computation for death tax on lifetime gifts

Step 1: Start with the gross chargeable amount of any CLTs and PETs per the lifetime tax calculations.

Step 2: The death IHT is calculated for each gift as follows

	£	£
Gross CLT or PET per lifetime calculations		X
Nil rate band (NRB) at date of death	X	
Gross chargeable transfers in the seven years before this gift	(X)	
Nil rate band available		(X)
Taxable amount		X
Death IHT at 40%		X
Less Taper relief		(X)
Lifetime IHT paid (if any)		(X)
IHT payable on death		X

Step 3: State the due date of payment of the IHT and who pays the tax

- Death tax on lifetime gifts is **always** paid by the recipient of the gift.
- Death tax is due six months after the end of the month of death.

Example

Assume that Michael in the previous example died on 31 December 2022.

Required

Calculate the death tax arising on the lifetime gifts as a result of Michael's death. State the due date for payment and who will pay the tax.

Answer

Date of death: 31 December 2022

Seven years before: 31 December 2015

There is no further tax due in respect of CLT 1 on 13 February 2015 as it is more than seven years before the date of death. However, it must be taken into account in determining how much of the nil rate band remains available for the subsequent transfers.

There is death tax to calculate in respect of the PET and the other two CLTs.

	PET 24.5.2017		CLT 2 29.9.2018		CLT 3 9.12.2022	
	£	£	£	£	£	£
Gross chargeable amount per lifetime		134,000		182,250		165,000
NRB	325,000		325,000		325,000	
Gross CLTs in 7 yrs before the gift						
24.5.2010 – 24.5.2017 *(include CLT 1)*	(194,000)					
29.9.2011 – 29.9.2018 *(include CLT1 and the PET)* (194,000 + 134,000)			(328,000)			
9.12.2015 – 9.12.2022 *(first gift drops out, include PET and gross amount of CLT 2)* (134,000 + 182,250)					(316,250)	
NRB available		(131,000)		(Nil)		(8,750)
Taxable amount		3,000		182,250		156,250

			PET	**CLT 2**	**CLT 3**
			24.5.2017	29.9.2018	9.12.2022
			£	£	£
IHT at death rates at 40%			1,200	72,900	62,500
Less	Taper relief				
	24.5.17 – 31.12.22 = 5-6 yrs	60%	(720)		
	29.9.18 – 31.12.22 = 4-5 yrs	40%		(29,160)	
	9.12.22 – 31.12.22 = less than 3 years				(Nil)
			480	43,740	62,500
Less	Lifetime IHT paid		(Nil)	(10,250)	(4,450)
IHT payable on death			480	33,490	58,050
Paid by			Nephew	Trustees	Trustees
Due date			30.6.23	30.6.23	30.6.23

Taxation – United Kingdom
(TX-UK) FA2022

CHAPTER 19

Inheritance tax on the value of an estate

Contents
1   Inheritance tax on the death of an individual
2   The valuation of a deceased individual's estate
3   The calculation of IHT on a deceased individual's estate
4   The residence nil rate band

> **Inheritance tax on the death of an individual**
> - The charges to inheritance tax on death
> - The calculation of IHT on a deceased individual's estate

1 Inheritance tax on the death of an individual

1.1 The charges to inheritance tax on death

On the death of an individual there are two key charges to IHT:

(1) the IHT arising on lifetime gifts (PETs and CLTs) as a result of the death of the donor

(2) the IHT payable on the value of the individual's estate on the date of death.

The IHT arising on lifetime gifts must be calculated first. This is because an individual's nil rate band must be utilised against lifetime gifts before considering the death estate.

This chapter covers the last IHT charge to be calculated, i.e. the IHT arising on a deceased individual's estate.

1.2 The calculation of IHT on a deceased individual's estate

The procedure to adopt for calculating IHT on a death estate is as follows:

Step 1 Calculate the **gross chargeable value** of the deceased individual's estate at the date of death.

Step 2 Calculate the death tax payable taking into account:
- the **available nil rate band and residence nil rate band**
- the **death rates of tax**
- the **terms of the will** (e.g. whether any of the estate is left to an exempt person).

Step 3 If required in an examination question:
- state the **due date for payment** of the death tax
- identify how much each beneficiary will inherit.

The valuation of a deceased individual's estate

- An overview of an estate computation
- A proforma estate computation

2 The valuation of a deceased individual's estate

2.1 An overview of an estate computation

The chargeable value of an estate is:

	£
Value of assets legally owned by the deceased at the date of death	X
Assets acquired on death (e.g. lump sums payable on death)	X
Less: Value of liabilities due at the date of death	(X)
	X
Less: Allowable expenditure	(X)
	X
Less: Exempt legacies (= gifts in the will to exempt persons)	(X)
Chargeable estate	X

Assets are usually brought into the estate computation at their **probate value**. This means the **open market value** of the asset at the date of death. The open market value will be given in an examination question.

2.2 A proforma estate computation

	Notes	£
Freehold property		X
Less: Repayment mortgage or interest-only mortgage	1	(X)
		X
Leasehold property		X
Unincorporated business		X
Shares and securities		X
Motor cars	2	X
Personal chattels		X
Debts due to the deceased		X
Insurance policy proceeds	3	X
ISAs, cash at bank and on deposit	2	X
		X
Less: Allowable deductions:	4	(X)
		X
Less: Exempt legacies (e.g. to spouse or civil partner)		(X)
Chargeable estate		X

Notes

(1) Mortgages

The estate value must include assets owned by the individual **net of any outstanding liabilities.**

Any outstanding repayment mortgage or interest-only mortgage at the date of death must be deducted in the estate valuation as the mortgage will have to be repaid from the estate funds on death.

(2) Exempt assets for CGT

Motor cars, ISAs and cash balances are exempt assets for CGT purposes. However, they are not exempt for IHT and must be brought into the estate computation.

(3) Insurance policy proceeds

Proceeds from life insurance policies must be brought into the estate value. It is the amount of the proceeds received that is taxable (not the open market/surrender value).

(4) Allowable expenses

Reasonable funeral expenses and legally enforceable debts are allowable deductions in the estate computation. Outstanding tax bills are also allowable deductions. However, debts which are not legally enforceable are not allowable deductions. Gambling debts are only allowable if owed to licensed businesses, such as a casino or betting shop. Debts arising from gambling between friends or illegal gambling are not allowable.

Example

Rachel owned the following assets when she died:

(1) A flat which was valued at £390,000. She bought the flat with the help of a £180,000 repayment mortgage, which is still outstanding.

(2) Personal chattels in the flat and a motor car worth £45,000.

(3) 3,000 £1 ordinary shares in DEF plc valued at £12,000.

(4) An ISA worth £14,500 and a bank account with a balance of £560.

Rachel was owed £250 by a friend. Rachel owed £2,300 income tax to HMRC and £1,650 to a credit card company.

Rachael held a life insurance policy. At the date of her death the policy had an open market value of £22,000. The executors received proceeds of £25,000 following Rachael's death and spent £3,500 on her funeral.

Under the terms of her will, Rachel left £35,000 to her spouse and the residue of her estate to her daughter.

Required

Calculate the chargeable value of Rachel's estate.

Answer

	£
Flat (£390,000 - £180,000 mortgage)	210,000
Personal chattels and motor car	45,000
Shares in DEF plc	12,000
ISA	14,500
Bank account	560
Debt owed by friend	250
Life insurance policy proceeds	25,000
	307,310
Less: Funeral expenses	(3,500)
Credit card outstanding	(1,650)
Income tax	(2,300)
	299,860
Less: Exempt legacies to spouse	(35,000)
Chargeable estate	264,860

> **The calculation of IHT on a deceased individual's estate**
>
> - The nil rate band available
> - The proforma computation for death tax on the death estate
> - The due date of payment and who pays the tax

3 The calculation of IHT on a deceased individual's estate

3.1 The nil rate band available

On the death of an individual, IHT is payable on the gross chargeable value of the estate at the death rates of tax. The nil rate band at the date of death is available, but must be matched against lifetime gifts before computing the IHT on the estate.

As in the lifetime calculations, the nil rate band covers a cumulation period of seven years. For the death estate it is necessary to look back seven years **before the date of death** and to work out the value of any lifetime **gross chargeable transfers** (both CLTs and PETs) in that period.

Transfer of a spouse's unused nil rate band

Every individual has their own nil rate band for IHT purposes. However, any unused nil rate band on a person's death can be transferred to their surviving spouse (or civil partner).

A claim for the transfer of the unused nil rate band is made by the personal representatives of the second spouse. The amount that can be claimed is based on the **proportion** of the nil rate band that was unused at the time the first spouse died. An amount equivalent to this proportion is added to the second spouse's nil rate band. (Note that the date the first spouse died is irrelevant).

Example

Brian and Haruka were married for 30 years. Brian died in August 2006. Half of his nil rate band was unused.

Required

Calculate the nil rate band available to Haruka.

Answer

Haruka will be entitled to her own nil rate band of £325,000 plus an additional £162,500 (£325,000 x ½) as this proportion was unused at the date of Brian's death.

An individual may have survived more than one spouse or civil partner and so it is possible for them to claim unused nil rate bands from more than one estate. However, the maximum nil rate band a person can have is two times the nil rate band for the year of death (i.e. £650,000 for 2022/23).

3.2 The proforma computation for death tax on death estate

The death IHT is calculated as follows:

	£	£
Chargeable estate		X
Nil rate band (NRB)	X	
Gross chargeable transfers in the seven years before death	(X)	
Nil rate band available		(X)
Taxable amount		X
IHT on the taxable amount at 40%		X

3.3 The due date of payment and who pays the tax

- All death tax is due six months after the end of the month of death. However, the IHT must be paid when the account of the estate assets is delivered to HMRC, which may be earlier than the due date.

- The personal representatives (executors) are responsible for paying the IHT due on the death estate.

- Note that specific legatees of UK assets from a will do not suffer any IHT on the gift to them. The tax on their gift is suffered by the residual legatee. Therefore, if an individual is left £200,000 in a will, they will receive exactly £200,000. The associated tax on that gift is suffered by the person who is bequeathed the rest of the estate.

Example

Grace died on 12 January 2023 leaving the following estate:

	£
House in Nottingham	454,500
Flat in London	79,000
Shares in XYZ plc	16,000
Personal chattels, motor car and bank accounts	36,700
	586,200
Less: Allowable deductions	(34,700)
Chargeable estate	551,500

In her will Grace left the shares in XYZ plc to her nephew and the rest of her estate to her sister.

Grace's only lifetime gift was a gross chargeable transfer of £258,000 into a trust in June 2019. No lifetime IHT was payable.

Required

Calculate the IHT payable on Grace's death estate. State who is liable to pay the tax, who will suffer the tax and the due date of payment.

Answer

The CLT is within seven years of death but is covered by the nil rate band of £325,000; therefore, no death tax is due on this gift.

IHT on the death estate

	£	£
Chargeable estate		551,500
Nil rate band (NRB)	325,000	
Gross chargeable transfers in the seven years before death	(258,000)	
Nil rate band available		(67,000)
Taxable amount		484,500
IHT payable on estate at 40%		193,800

The personal representatives are responsible for paying all of the IHT by the due date of 31 July 2023.

Although the shares are left in the will to the nephew, he does not bear the tax on the gift; the tax is suffered by the sister (i.e. the residual legatee). She will inherit the residue of £341,700 (£551,500 − £16,000 − £193,800).

> **The residence nil rate band**
> - The residence nil rate band
> - Transferring the RNRB
> - Additional points

4 The residence nil rate band

4.1 The residence nil rate band

An additional nil rate band, known as the residence nil rate band, applies where a main residence is inherited on death by direct descendants of the deceased person.

The residence nil rate band (RNRB) for the tax year 2022/23 is £175,000.

The RNRB applies where:

- an individual dies on or after 6 April 2017
- their estate exceeds the normal nil rate band of £325,000
- their estate includes a main residence
- the main residence is inherited on death by direct descendants (children and/or grandchildren).

The RNRB does not apply to other types of property, such as rental properties or holiday homes.

In the examination, if there is no mention of a main residence, you should assume that the RNRB is not available.

Example

Mohammed died on 21 February 2023 leaving an estate valued at £600,000. The estate included Mohammed's main residence, which was valued at £250,000 at the time of his death. Mohammed made no chargeable transfers during his lifetime.

Required

Calculate the IHT payable on Mohammed's estate assuming:

(a) Mohammed's main residence is left to his son.

(b) Mohammed's main residence is left to his brother.

Answer

(a) The RNRB is available as the main residence is left to Mohammed's direct descendant. The IHT liability is therefore:

	£
Chargeable estate	600,000
Residence nil rate band (RNRB)	(175,000)
Nil rate band (NRB)	(325,000)
Taxable amount	100,000
IHT payable on estate at 40%	40,000

(b) The RNRB is not available as Mohammed's brother is not a direct descendant. The IHT liability is therefore:

	£
Chargeable estate	600,000
Nil rate band (NRB)	(325,000)
Taxable amount	275,000
IHT payable on estate at 40%	110,000

As you can see from the above example, if the RNRB is available Mohammed's IHT is reduced by £70,000. It is therefore worth an individual taking the time to review their will to ensure that their main residence is left to a qualifying beneficiary. (It is unnecessary for the beneficiary to retain the residence for any length of time.)

4.2 Transferring the RNRB

Any unused RNRB is transferrable to a surviving spouse (or civil partner) in the same way as the normal nil rate band. The date on which the first spouse died is irrelevant.

Example

Ken died on 1 October 2016 leaving his entire chargeable estate of £600,000 to his wife, Puja. The estate included a main residence that was owned jointly by Ken and Puja.

Puja died on 12 December 2022 leaving her entire estate of £1,200,000 to her daughter, Sophie. The estate included the main residence, which was valued at £400,000 at the time of Puja's death.

Required

Calculate the IHT payable on Puja's estate, assuming that neither she nor Ken made any lifetime transfers.

Answer

Ken left the whole of his estate to Puja, therefore his whole nil rate band of £325,000 was unused. This can be transferred to Puja.

Ken will not have used his RNRB as he died before the RNRB was introduced. However, because Puja has died after 5 April 2017, her personal representatives are able to claim Ken's RNRB.

The IHT payable on Puja's estate is therefore:

	£
Chargeable estate	1,200,000
Residence nil rate band (RNRB) – Puja's own	(175,000)
RNRB – transferred from Ken	(175,000)
Nil rate band (NRB) – Puja's own	(325,000)
Nil rate band (NRB) – transferred from Ken	(325,000)
Taxable amount	200,000
IHT payable on estate at 40%	80,000

4.3 Additional points

Mortgages

If the main residence is valued at less than the RNRB, the RNRB is restricted to the value of the residence. Note that the value of the residence is after the deduction of any repayment mortgage or interest-only mortgage secured on the property.

Example

Naima died on 1 November 2022 leaving her entire chargeable estate of £600,000 to her grandson, Vlad. Naima's estate included a main residence valued at £150,000 on which there was an outstanding repayment mortgage of £60,000.

Required

Calculate the IHT payable on Naima's estate, assuming she made no lifetime transfers.

Answer

The repayment mortgage is deducted from the value of the property, reducing it to £90,000 (150,000 – 60,000). Therefore, the RNRB is restricted to £90,000.

The IHT payable on Naima's estate is therefore:

	£
Chargeable estate	600,000
Residence nil rate band (RNRB)	(90,000)
Nil rate band (NRB)	(325,000)
Taxable amount	185,000
IHT payable on estate at 40%	74,000

Non-examinable aspects

There are a number of further complications, but these are not examinable on TX-UK:

- The tapered withdrawal of the RNRB where the net value of the estate exceeds £2,000,000.
- The implications of an individual downsizing to a less expensive property.
- Nominating which property qualifies for relief where an individual has more than one residence.

Taxation – United Kingdom (TX-UK) FA2022

CHAPTER 20

Introduction to corporation tax

Contents
1   The scope of corporation tax
2   Overview of a corporation tax computation
3   The statement of taxable total profits (TTP)
4   The corporation tax liability
5   Self-assessment for companies

> **The scope of corporation tax**
>
> - The basic charging rules
> - Determining the residence status of a company

1 The scope of corporation tax

1.1 The basic charging rules

A company is liable to pay UK corporation tax on its taxable total profits (TTP) for a chargeable accounting period (CAP). Both public limited companies and private limited companies are liable to corporation tax on their profits.

To calculate the corporation tax liability, it is first of all necessary to calculate the amount of taxable total profits. To determine a company's TTP, it is important to establish whether or not the company is resident in the UK. The residence status of a company is important because:

- A UK resident company is liable to UK corporation tax on all of its profits, generated anywhere in the world (worldwide TTP).

- A non-UK resident company is only liable to UK corporation tax on profits that have been generated in the UK through a permanent establishment situated in the UK (for example, profits earned by a branch or an agency). Its foreign income (profit earned in other countries) is not taxable in the UK.

1.2 Determining the residence status of a company

A company is UK resident, and therefore liable to UK corporation tax on its worldwide TTP, if one of the following conditions applies:

- it is incorporated in the UK, or
- its centre of management and control is situated in the UK.

To determine where the centre of management and control for a company is situated, HMRC look at where the directors hold their regular board meetings.

> **Overview of a corporation tax computation**
>
> - Taxable total profits
> - The chargeable accounting period

2 Overview of a corporation tax computation

2.1 Taxable total profits

A company is liable to pay corporation tax on its taxable total profits (TTP) for a chargeable accounting period (CAP).

The figure of taxable total profits (TTP) consists of:

- taxable income generated from all sources, **plus**
- capital gains from the disposal of chargeable capital assets, **minus**
- qualifying charitable donations.

Taxable income is listed in a statement of TTP according to its nature and source. The rules for the preparation of this statement are explained later in this chapter.

2.2 The chargeable accounting period

A chargeable accounting period (CAP) for corporation tax purposes is usually the same as the period of account, i.e. the period for which the company prepares its financial accounts.

- A CAP commences on:
  - the commencement of trade
  - the date the profits of the company first become liable to corporation tax (i.e. it acquires a source of income, such as a bank account that pays interest)
  - the day following the end of the previous CAP.
- A CAP ends on the earliest of:
  - 12 months after the beginning of the CAP
  - the end of the company's period of account
  - the date the company ceases to trade
  - the commencement of winding up or entering administration.

It is important to note that **a CAP cannot exceed 12 months in length.** The treatment of a long period of account is covered later.

> **The statement of taxable total profits (TTP)**
>
> - Overview of the TTP statement
> - Dividends

3 The statement of taxable total profits (TTP)

3.1 Overview of the TTP statement

The first step in preparing a corporation tax computation (a statement of TTP) is to produce a list of the sources of income and chargeable gains which are taxable.

The list should be presented as follows.

Name of company Corporation tax computation – year ended dd.mm.yy	£
Income	
Trading income (adjusted profits less capital allowances)	X
Interest income	X
UK property income	X
Capital gains	
Net chargeable gains (chargeable gains less allowable losses)	X
Total profits	X
Qualifying charitable donations	(X)
Taxable total profits (TTP)	X

It is important to list each source of income separately. This is because the rules for determining the amount of income that is chargeable to corporation tax are different for each source of income. The detailed rules are explained later.

3.2 Dividends

It is important to note the following points when preparing a TTP statement:

Dividends received

For the purpose of the TX-UK examination, dividends from both UK and overseas companies are ignored in computing TTP. However, dividends from non-group companies are taken into account in determining the recipient company's 'augmented profits'. These determine whether the company has to pay its corporation tax liability in instalments. These rules are covered later.

Dividends paid

Dividends paid by the company to its own shareholders are excluded from the TTP statement.

Example

A Ltd is preparing its accounts for the year ended 31 December 2022. It has received income from various sources and made some payments, as listed below. All income is shown gross.

	£
Rental income from letting a warehouse in London	12,000
Dividends from an overseas company	3,600
Profits from the trade	460,000
Chargeable gain on the disposal of a showroom	23,500
Bank deposit interest	2,800
Dividends from a UK company	6,200
Loan note interest from a UK company	21,000
Qualifying charitable donation paid	4,000
Dividends paid to shareholders	5,500

Required

Prepare a TTP statement for A Ltd for the year ended 31 December 2022.

Answer

A Ltd: Corporation tax computation – year ended 31 December 2022

	£
Trading income	460,000
Interest income (£2,800 + £21,000)	23,800
UK property income	12,000
Net chargeable gains	23,500
Total profits	519,300
Qualifying charitable donation	(4,000)
Taxable total profits	515,300

Notes

(1) Both the overseas and the UK dividends are exempt from corporation tax and are therefore not included in the computation of TTP.

(2) The dividends paid by A Ltd are not deductible in calculating TTP.

> **The corporation tax liability**
> - The Financial Year
> - Payment dates

4 The corporation tax liability

4.1 The Financial Year

A company pays corporation tax on its TTP for a CAP.

The government fixes the corporation tax rate for each Financial Year. A Financial Year (FY) runs from 1 April in one year to the following 31 March.

Financial Years are stated using the calendar year in which they start. For example, FY2021 means the period from 1 April 2021 to 31 March 2022. FY2022 runs from 1 April 2022 to 31 March 2023.

The rate of corporation tax for FY21 and FY22 is 19%.

Example

For the year ended 31 March 2023 B Ltd had trading income of £200,000 and property income of £6,000. It received dividends of £7,200.

Required

Calculate the corporation tax payable by B Ltd for the year ended 31 March 2023.

Answer

B Ltd - Corporation tax computation – year ended 31 March 2023

	£
Trading income	200,000
UK property income	6,000
TTP	206,000

Corporation tax liability: £206,000 × 19% = £39,140.

Note

The dividends are ignored in calculating TTP as they are not taxable.

4.2 Payment dates

All companies must pay their corporation tax electronically.

Unless a company is large, it is liable to pay its corporation tax liability nine months and one day after the end of its chargeable accounting period (CAP). Therefore, a company with a CAP ending on 31 March 2023 will be required to pay its corporation tax liability on 1 January 2024.

A large company must pay its corporation tax liability in four quarterly instalments. A large company in this context is a company that has augmented profits exceeding £1,500,000.

The £1,500,000 profit threshold is time-apportioned where the company's CAP is less than 12 months. It is also divided equally by the number of related 51% group companies at the end of the **preceding** accounting period. (Related 51% group companies are covered in chapter 24.)

Augmented profits

Augmented profits are defined as follows:

	£
TTP	X
Dividends received from non-group companies	X
Augmented profits	X

Dividends from group companies

Dividends received from group companies are excluded when calculating augmented profits. A company is regarded as a group member for this purpose if the parent company owns, directly or indirectly, more than 50% of the ordinary share capital.

Therefore, where a company receives dividends from a 51% subsidiary, these dividends are simply ignored. (The group implications of corporation tax are considered in more detail in a later chapter.)

Due dates for instalment payments

If a large company has a 12-month accounting period, the following procedure is adopted:

- First instalment - 14 days after the end of the 6th month from the **start** of the accounting period.
- Second instalment - 14 days after the end of the 9th month.
- Third instalment - 14 days after the end of the 12th month.
- Fourth (i.e. final) instalment - 14 days after the end of the 15th month.

The instalments are based on the **estimated** corporation tax liability for the **current** accounting period. The company should revise its estimates, if necessary, throughout the year and pay any shortfall in respect of the previous quarterly payments.

A large company with a 12-month accounting period ending 31 March 2023 will therefore pay its corporation tax liability on 14 October 2022, 14 January 2023, 14 April 2023 and 14 July 2023.

(Very large companies, defined as those with profits in excess of £20 million, have different payment dates; however, these are not examinable.)

Accounting periods of less than 12 months

When a large company has an accounting period of less than 12 months, the amount of the instalments is calculated as follows:

Estimated corporation tax liability $\times \dfrac{3 \text{ months}}{\text{Number of months in the accounting period}}$

- The first instalment is payable six months and 14 days after the **start** of the accounting period.
- The last payment can never be later than three months and 14 days after the **end** of the accounting period.
- The company will pay as many three-monthly instalments as possible in between the earliest and latest payment dates, and will pay on the 14th day of the appropriate month.

Therefore, if a company prepares nine-month accounts to 30 September 2022 (i.e. 1 January 2022 to 30 September 2022). Tax payments are due as follows:

- First instalment: 14 July 2022. This is six months and 14 days after the start of the accounting period.
- Second instalment: 14 October 2022. This is three months later.
- Third instalment: 14 January 2023. This is three months later, and it is the last instalment.

Exceptions to paying in instalments

A large company does not have to pay by instalments if:

- it has a corporation tax liability of less than £10,000, or
- it was not large in the preceding 12 months and does not have TTP in excess of £10 million in the current accounting period.

The £10 million limit is divided equally by the number of related 51% group companies at the end of the **preceding** accounting period.

Example

T Ltd has TTP of £1,400,000 for the year ended 31 March 2023. It also received dividends of £120,000 from non-group companies. T Ltd has no 51% subsidiaries.

Required

Calculate T Ltd's corporation tax liability for the year ended 31 March 2023 and state the due date.

Answer

T Ltd – corporation tax liability – year ended 31 March 2023

	£
TTP	1,400,000
Dividend income	120,000
Augmented profits	1,520,000

Corporation tax liability: £1,400,000 x 19% = £266,000

If T Ltd was a large company in the previous year (i.e. the year ended 31 March 2022) it will pay its corporation tax liability in four instalments of £66,500 each on 14 October 2022, 14 January 2023, 14 April 2023 and 14 July 2023.

If T Ltd was not a large company in the year ended 31 March 2022 it will pay its corporation tax liability on 1 January 2024.

Interest

HMRC charges late payment interest of 3.25% a year on any underpaid tax. Repayment interest of 0.5% a year on overpaid corporation tax runs:

- **from** the later of the date the tax was due to be paid and the date the tax was actually paid
- **to** the date the tax is repaid by HMRC.

> **Self-assessment for companies**
> - Introduction
> - Notification of chargeability
> - Filing a corporation tax return
> - iXBRL tagging
> - Penalties for late filing of a corporation tax return
> - Record keeping

5.1 Introduction

Unless otherwise stated, the self-assessment rules for companies are the same as those applying to individuals (see Chapter 17). However, time limits generally run from the end of the company's accounting period rather than the end of the tax year or filing date.

5.2 Notification of chargeability

When a company first comes within the scope of corporation tax (i.e. when it first has profits that are chargeable to corporation tax), it must notify HMRC of its chargeability to tax within three months after the start of its first accounting period. Failure to do so can result in a penalty of £300, plus £60 for each day the information is outstanding.

Companies that have been trading for a while usually receive a notice (reminder), a few weeks before the end of their regular accounting end date, of their self-assessment obligation to file a corporation tax return. If a company with taxable profits does not receive a notice, it must notify HMRC within 12 months of the end of its accounting period.

Failure to notify chargeability for an accounting period can result in a penalty. This is determined according to the same behaviour-based penalty regime that applies to individuals. However, for companies, the potential lost revenue is the amount of tax due but unpaid 12 months following the end of the accounting period.

5.3 Filing a corporation tax return

All companies must file their corporation tax returns on-line.

A company must complete a corporation tax return and submit it to HMRC within 12 months of the end of its **period of account**, or three months from the date on which the notice to complete a return was issued, if later.

The return contains all the information required to calculate the company's TTP for the accounting period. It also enables the company to claim reliefs and allowances (e.g. loss reliefs and capital allowances).

The company must also calculate its own corporation tax liability, although this is done automatically as part of the filing process if the company uses the software provided by HMRC.

5.4 iXBRL tagging

Companies must submit supporting tax computations and a copy of their accounts with their tax returns. These must be submitted on-line using inline eXtensible Business Reporting Language (iXBRL).

iXBRL is a standard for reporting business information in an electronic format using tags that can be read by computers. Small companies using the software provided by HMRC will have their accounts and tax computation automatically produced in the correct format.

Other companies have a number of options. They can use:

- Other software that automatically produces iXBRL accounts and computations.
- A tagging service which will apply the appropriate tags to accounts and computations.
- Software that enables the appropriate tags to be added to accounts and computations.

The tags used are contained in dictionaries known as taxonomies, with different taxonomies for different purposes. The tagging of tax computations is based on the corporation tax computational taxonomy, which includes over 1,200 relevant tags.

5.5 Penalties for late filing of a corporation tax return

Penalties are levied if the corporation tax return is filed late, as follows:

Filed within	Maximum penalty
3 months of filing date	£100 fixed penalty.
	Increased to £500 if the company becomes liable to the fixed penalty for three consecutive years.
3 to 6 months of the filing date	£200 fixed penalty.
	Increased to £1,000 if the company becomes liable to the fixed penalty for three consecutive years.
18 to 24 months after the end of the accounting period	£200 fixed penalty
	plus 10% of the tax outstanding 18 months after the end of the accounting period
More than 24 months after the end of the accounting period	£200 fixed penalty
	plus 20% of the tax outstanding 18 months after the end of the accounting period

When a company does not file its return by the filing date, HMRC may estimate the amount of tax due. A determination assessment may be made at any time within four years of the end of the accounting period concerned.

5.6 Record keeping

A company must keep its records until the latest of the following dates:

- six years from the end of the relevant accounting period
- the date on which HMRC have completed any compliance check, or
- the date on which HMRC no longer have the power to make a compliance check into a return.

The records to be retained by companies include records of:

- All receipts and expenses
- All sales and purchases
- Supporting documents including accounts, books, deeds, contracts, vouchers and receipts.

A penalty of up to £3,000 per accounting period can be levied for failure to keep records.

Taxation – United Kingdom
(TX-UK) FA2022

CHAPTER 21

Taxable total profits

	Contents
1	Trading income
2	Interest income
3	UK property income
4	Chargeable gains
5	Qualifying charitable donations
6	Long periods of account

> **Trading income**
>
> - Overview of the taxable total profits statement
> - Trading income: overview
> - Detailed proforma adjustment of profit computation
> - Enhanced capital allowances

1 Trading income

1.1 Overview of the taxable total profits statement

The proforma TTP statement, shown in the previous chapter, starts by listing taxable income from all sources. Each source of income has different rules for determining the amount that is chargeable to corporation tax.

This chapter begins by explaining the rules for each source of income and the workings that are usually required for each to prepare a corporation tax computation.

1.2 Trading income: overview

Trading income is usually the primary source of income for a company. It is computed in the same way as for income tax purposes. However, the following differences should be noted:

(1) There is no adjustment for private expenditure. Thus, if the company provides a car for the use of a director or employee all of the expenditure, including that relating to private mileage, is deductible.

(2) Costs of share issues are classed as capital expenditure and are therefore not allowable. Any such costs, if deducted in arriving at the figure for profit before tax, must be added back as an adjustment of profit.

(3) Any incidental costs incurred in raising long-term finance such as loan notes are **specifically allowable** for trading purposes in the tax legislation. No adjustment for this expenditure is therefore required. These costs are allowable even if the long-term finance is not actually raised.

(4) Although the write off of **non-trade** debts such as a loan to a customer, supplier or an employee, must be adjusted for by adding back to the figure of profit before taxation, relief is given for any loss in respect of the write off of non-trade loans against **interest income** under the loan relationship rules.

(5) When calculating capital allowances, the full WDA/AIA is available for a company even if there is an element of private use of an asset by a director or employee (for example, a company car used for both business and private mileage). The benefit of private use will be assessed on the individual as a benefit of employment; but this is irrelevant for calculating the corporation tax of the company.

Chapter 21: Taxable total profits

(6) Companies can benefit from enhanced capital allowances when they purchase new plant and machinery. These are covered later.

1.3 Detailed proforma adjustment of profit computation

To calculate the adjusted profit before capital allowances figure in a trading income assessment, it is often necessary to produce a separate working. The proforma below sets out some of the more common adjustments that may be required.

(W1) Proforma computation: Adjustment of profit	£
Profit before taxation	X
Add Items of expenditure charged in the accounts that are not allowable for tax under the trading income rules	
Capital expenditure (may be eligible for capital allowances)	X
Legal or professional fees relating to capital expenditure (including leases, except fees relating to the renewal of a short lease)	X
Depreciation/amortisation charges for non-current assets	X
Loss on the disposal of a non-current asset	X
Non-trade debt written off	X
Political donations and subscriptions	X
Charitable donations	X
Interest on overdue tax	X
Interest on loans to purchase shares or property	X
Professional fees in relation to tax advice	X
Disallowable portion of lease rental on a car with CO_2 emissions over 50 g/km	X
Gifts to customers (if > £50 and no advertisement, or if a gift of alcohol, food or tobacco)	X
Fines and penalties	X
Entertaining expenses (except entertainment of employees)	X
	X
Minus Amounts credited in the accounts that are not taxable as trading income	
Income taxed under other assessment rules (e.g. income taxed as property income, interest income)	(X)
Exempt income (e.g. dividends)	(X)
Capital profits (may be assessed as a chargeable gain instead) (e.g. profit on the disposal of a non-current asset, profit on the sale of shares etc)	(X)
Minus Amounts not credited in the accounts that are allowable for trading income purposes	
Allowable deduction for short leases	(X)
Adjusted profits before capital allowances	X

1.4 Enhanced capital allowances

From 1 April 2021 to 31 March 2023, companies can benefit from enhanced capital allowances when they purchase **new** plant and machinery, excluding cars. (Note that these allowances are not available to sole traders and partnerships.)

- Main pool expenditure qualifies for a 130% super deduction. (This should be given instead of the annual investment allowance.)

- Special rate pool expenditure qualifies for a 50% first year allowance. (This is not as generous as the 100% annual investment allowance and so should only be given where the AIA is not available.)

A question will not be set involving the disposal of plant and machinery on which these enhanced capital allowances have been claimed.

Example

During the year ended 31 March 2023, J Ltd purchased new equipment for £1,750,000, of which £250,000 is main pool expenditure and £1,500,000 is special rate pool expenditure.

Required

Calculate the capital allowances due in respect of the new expenditure for the year ended 31 March 2023.

Answer

As J Ltd is a company, it can claim enhanced capital allowances in respect of this expenditure.

The main pool expenditure qualifies for a super-deduction of £325,000 (250,000 × 130%).

J Ltd should claim the maximum annual investment allowance of £1,000,000 in respect of the expenditure qualifying for the special rate pool as this gives 100% relief. The 50% first year allowance should be claimed in respect of the balance of the expenditure, i.e. (£1,500,000 - £1,000,000) × 50% = £250,000.

J Ltd is therefore entitled to total allowances of £1,575,000 (325,000 + 1,000,000 + 250,000) for the year ended 31 March 2023.

Interest income

- Loan relationships
- Interest receivable
- Interest payable
- Proforma interest income computation

2 Interest income

2.1 Loan relationships

A loan relationship occurs where the company is either:

- lending money

    (for example, purchases a debt instrument such as loan notes in another company, or purchases gilt-edged securities from the Government such as Treasury stock or Exchequer stock), or

- borrowing money

    (for example, borrows from a bank or building society, or issues its own corporate debt instruments such as loan notes).

Lending and borrowing money can be undertaken either:

- for the purposes of the trade, for example to provide working capital for the business or to buy plant and machinery, or

- for non-trading purposes, for example investing surplus cash in a bank deposit account.

2.2 Interest receivable

In the examination, all interest **receivable** should be treated as **non-trading income**. It is therefore taxed as interest income, rather than as a part of trading income.

All interest received by companies, such as bank interest, building society interest, loan note interest and interest received from HMRC on overpaid tax, is received gross. This means that no tax has been deducted at source.

Interest income is taxed on an accruals basis. This means that the gross amounts of interest income credited in the financial accounts for the CAP (i.e. amounts received and receivable) must be brought into the TTP statement.

2.3 Interest payable

Non-trading interest payable and trading interest payable are both allowable expenses, but they are treated differently.

Non-trading interest payable includes items such as interest payable in respect of a loan to purchase an investment property or an investment in shares in another company, and interest payable to HMRC on underpaid tax. Non-trading interest payable is an allowable deduction against **interest income**.

Trading interest payable is treated as an allowable trading expense against **trading income** and is not deducted against interest income.

In the examination, interest payable on the company's loan notes, hire purchase interest payable and interest payable on a loan to purchase plant and machinery, are all deemed to be interest payable for a trading purpose. These items of interest are therefore allowable against trading income for the TTP statement, and are not deducted from interest income.

2.4 Proforma interest income computation

To calculate the interest income assessment for a TTP statement, it is often necessary to prepare a separate working, as follows:

Interest income	£
Interest receivable	X
Minus: Interest payable to purchase investment property	(X)
Interest payable to purchase shares	(X)
Interest on underpaid corporation tax	(X)
Non-trade loan written off	(X)
Interest income	X

Notes

(1) Loan note interest **payable** is usually treated as allowable trading interest and is therefore not deducted in this working.

(2) If this working produces a negative figure, the interest income assessment in the TTP statement is £0. Knowledge of how to utilise any such loss is not required for the examination.

Example

K plc has given you the following information in respect of the year ended 31 December 2022:

	Received/paid	Credited/charged in the accounts
	£	£
Bank interest received / receivable	4,800	5,500
Interest received / receivable on £100,000 10% loan stock purchased in X Ltd	12,000	10,000
Interest paid / payable on £50,000 12% loan notes K plc issued last year	6,600	6,000
Interest paid / payable on a loan taken out to buy shares in a Z Inc, a foreign company	2,300	2,300

Required

Calculate the interest income to be included in K plc's TTP statement for the year ended 31 December 2022.

Answer

K plc – Interest income	£
Bank interest receivable	5,500
Loan stock interest receivable	10,000
	15,500
Minus: Interest payable to purchase shares	(2,300)
Interest income	13,200

Note: The loan note interest **payable** of £6,000 is treated as an allowable deduction against trading income and is therefore not deducted from interest income. (There is no evidence to suggest that the loan notes were issued for non-trading purposes.)

> **UK property income**
> - Rental income
> - Premiums received on the granting of a short lease
> - UK property income losses

3 UK property income

3.1 Rental income

Rental income is assessed on an **accruals basis** for the company's CAP as follows:

- All **income accrued** (i.e. earned in the CAP) from any rental property is pooled, and
- All **allowable revenue expenditure** incurred in relation to the rental properties is deducted.

The actual dates of receipt of rent and the payment of expenses are not relevant.

Interest **payable** on any loan taken out to purchase or improve the property is **not** an allowable deduction in calculating property income. Instead, it is treated as non-trading loan interest payable under the loan relationship rules and is deducted from interest income.

Example

L Ltd rented out two residential properties during its accounting year ended 31 March 2023: Nos. 3 and 4 Belgravia Avenue.

No. 3 was let all year at a rent of £1,500 per month. However, the rent for March 2023 was not received until 10 April 2023.

No. 4 was purchased on 1 January 2023. It was immediately let on a six-month agreement as unfurnished property at a rent of £800 per month. In order to purchase the property, L Ltd took out a £100,000 loan with a bank on 1 January 2023, with a fixed mortgage interest rate of 6%.

The following additional expenses were incurred during the year ended 31 March 2023:

	No. 3	No. 4
	£	£
Advertising for new tenants	Nil	420
Estate agent management fees	1,440	240
Council tax	1,360	1,050
Insurance (see below)	900	1,440
Repairs	3,200	Nil
New double garage	5,000	Nil
Replacement cooker	500	-

The insurance paid in respect of property number 4 covers the period 1 January to 31 December 2023.

Required

Calculate L Ltd's property income for the year ended 31 March 2023.

Answer

Property income – year ended 31 March 2023

	£	£
Rents accrued in y/e 31 March 2023		
(£1,500 × 12) + (£800 × 3)		20,400
Minus Allowable expenses		
Advertising	420	
Agents' management fees (£1,440 + £240)	1,680	
Council tax (£1,360 + £1,050)	2,410	
Insurance (£900 + (£1,440 × 3/12))	1,260	
Repairs	3,200	
Replacement furniture relief	500	
		(9,470)
Property income assessment		10,930

Notes

(1) The rent due for March 2023 is assessable in the year ended 31 March 2023 as property income for companies is assessed using the accruals basis.

(2) Only 3/12 of the insurance paid in respect of No. 4 is deductible as the property was only let for three months of the year.

(3) Interest payable on the bank loan to purchase No. 4 is not an allowable expense for property income purposes. It is treated as non-trading interest payable and is an allowable deduction from interest income.

(4) The cost of the new garage is capital expenditure and therefore not an allowable expense for property income purposes.

(5) As property No. 3 is furnished, the cost of a replacement cooker which is substantially the same as the old cooker is a deductible expense.

3.2 Premiums received on the granting of a short lease

The treatment of a premium is the same as for income tax purposes (see chapter 3).

Example

M plc owns a warehouse which is surplus to its requirements. Rather than selling the warehouse, M plc granted a 40-year short lease on the property to Q Ltd on 1 November 2022 for a premium of £75,000. It charges rent of £6,000 a year payable in advance on a quarterly basis starting on 1 November 2022.

Required

Calculate the property income of M plc for the year ended 31 March 2023.

Answer

	£
Premium received	75,000
Minus 2% × £75,000 × 39	(58,500)
Assessable as property income	16,500
Rental income accrued in CAP (£6,000 × 5/12)	2,500
Total UK property income	19,000

3.3 UK property income losses

If several properties are let, income and expenses are pooled.

- Therefore, any losses arising on a property are automatically set off against the profits of the other properties in this single pooled computation.

- If this computation produces an overall negative result (i.e. there is an overall net loss arising on all of the property lettings), the property income in the TTP statement is technically £0 and a property business loss arises.

    However, the tax rules state that a property business loss must, if possible, be set against the other total profits (i.e. income and chargeable gains) of the company in that CAP.

    The inclusion of the negative property income figure in the TTP statement will automatically set off the property business loss against the company's other profits. This is an acceptable method in the examination.

Any excess property business loss (= any property income loss exceeding the total profits of the company in that CAP) can be:

- group relieved to 75% subsidiaries (this is explained in a later chapter), and/or

- carried forward and set off against the first available total profits (i.e. income and chargeable gains) in a future CAP.

> **Chargeable gains**
>
> - Overview

4 Chargeable gains

4.1 Overview

A company pays corporation tax not only on its income but also on capital gains arising from the disposal of certain capital assets (i.e. capital assets which are not exempt).

The TTP statement includes the net chargeable gains of a company. These consist of:

- chargeable gains arising in the CAP, minus
- allowable capital losses arising in the CAP, and minus
- any capital losses brought forward from an earlier CAP.

A separate chargeable gain or allowable loss computation is required for each capital disposal. As a result, additional workings are required to obtain the net chargeable gains for the TTP statement.

The detailed computation of net chargeable gains is described in a later chapter.

> **Qualifying charitable donations**
>
> - Qualifying charitable donations
> - Comprehensive examples

5 Qualifying charitable donations

5.1 Qualifying charitable donations

Companies are allowed to deduct the amount of any qualifying charitable donations paid in the CAP from their total profits.

Note that the amount charged in the financial accounts in respect of qualifying charitable donations is calculated on an accruals basis (i.e. amounts paid and payable in the CAP) but only the gross amount actually paid is an allowable deduction for tax purposes.

5.2 Comprehensive examples

Example

O Ltd provides you with the following information in respect of the year ended 31 March 2023:

	£
Income	
Rental income from letting an empty factory in Manchester	12,000
Adjusted trading profit	1,304,800
Bank deposit interest	7,800
Dividends from a UK company	32,400
Loan note interest from a UK company	151,000
Expenditure	
Estate agent management fees	1,200
Repairs to factory in Manchester	17,500
Interest payable on a loan taken out to purchase shares	33,750
Qualifying charitable donation	24,000
Dividends paid to shareholders	105,500

O Ltd disposed of one capital asset which gave rise to a chargeable gain of £100,000 and another capital asset which gave rise to an allowable loss of £24,000. It has capital losses of £10,000 brought forward from previous years.

Required

Prepare the TTP statement for O Ltd and calculate its corporation tax liability for the year ended 31 March 2023.

Chapter 21: Taxable total profits

Answer

O Ltd: Corporation tax computation – year ended 31 March 2023

	£
Trading income	1,304,800
Interest income (W1)	125,050
UK property income (W2) (see note below)	(6,700)
Net chargeable gains (W3)	66,000
Total profits	1,489,150
Qualifying charitable donation	(24,000)
TTP	1,465,150
Corporation tax liability (= £1,465,150 × 19%)	**£278,378**

Workings

(W1) Interest income

	£
Bank interest receivable	7,800
Loan note interest receivable	151,000
	158,800
Minus Interest payable to purchase shares	(33,750)
Interest income	125,050

(W2) UK property income

	£
Rents accrued in CAP	12,000
Minus Agents' management fees	(1,200)
Repairs	(17,500)
Property income	(6,700)

Note

Property income losses are first set against other income in the CAP. The inclusion of a negative figure will ensure relief is given in this way, and is an acceptable method in the examination.

(W3) Net chargeable gains

	£
Chargeable gains in the CAP	100,000
Minus Allowable losses in the CAP	(24,000)
Allowable losses brought forward	(10,000)
Net chargeable gain	66,000

Example

T Ltd has prepared its accounts for the year ended 31 March 2023 and has recorded a profit before taxation of £357,600 after taking account of the following income and expenditure:

	Notes	£
Income		
Sales revenue		760,000
Bank deposit interest receivable	1	38,000
Rental income from let property		25,200
Dividends received from a UK company		68,400
Profit on the disposal of a warehouse	2	80,000
Expenditure		
Cost of sales		328,250
Wages and salaries		128,000
Depreciation		57,000
Motor expenses	3	16,800
Repair and maintenance	4	30,400
Donations and gifts	5	2,700
Interest on loan to purchase the property which is let		9,600
Loss on the sale of plant and machinery	2	2,500
Patent royalty paid		4,000
Non-trade debt written off		400
Legal and professional fees	6	22,800
Entertaining customers		550
Sundry allowable expenses		11,000

Notes

(1) The bank deposit interest actually received in the CAP was £30,000.

(2) The warehouse was sold for £375,000 and cost £295,000 some years ago. The disposal gave rise to a chargeable gain of £66,150. There is no allowable loss arising on the disposal of the plant and machinery.

(3) The motor expenses relate to company vehicles and include £4,500 in relation to the managing director's car which was used 70% for business purposes.

(4) Repairs and maintenance include £19,000 relating to the installation of a new canteen kitchen and £6,000 relating to the redecoration of the sales office.

(5) Donations consist of a qualifying charitable donation of £1,000 and a donation to the Labour party of £900. The gifts cost £800 and were Christmas hampers given to 40 customers. Each hamper carried an advert for T Ltd on the lid.

(6) The legal and professional fees consist of the following:

	£
Audit and accountancy fees	9,120
Legal fees re-the issue of loan notes in the CAP	5,320
Legal fees re-the granting of a new 10 year lease on office space	8,360

(7) The capital allowances available for the CAP total £49,400.

Required

(a) Calculate T Ltd's tax-adjusted trading income for the year ended 31 March 2023. (Your answer should start with the figure of profit before taxation of £357,600 and you should indicate by the use of zero (0) any items that do not require adjustment.)

(b) Calculate T Ltd's TTP for the year ended 31 March 2023.

Answer

(a) T Ltd: Trading income – year ended 31 March 2023

		£
Profit before taxation		357,600
Add	Depreciation	57,000
	Motor expenses	0
	Installation of new canteen kitchen	19,000
	Redecoration	0
	Qualifying charitable donation	1,000
	Political donation	900
	Gifts of food	800
	Interest on loan to purchase the property which is let	9,600
	Loss on the sale of plant and machinery	2,500
	Patent royalties	0
	Non-trade debt written off	400
	Audit and accountancy fees	0
	Legal fees re issue of loan notes	0
	Legal fees relating to the new lease	8,360
	Entertaining customers	550
		457,710
Minus	Bank deposit interest receivable	(38,000)
	Rental income from let property	(25,200)
	Dividends received from a UK company	(68,400)
	Profit on the disposal of a warehouse	(80,000)
Adjusted profits before capital allowances		246,110
Minus	Capital allowances	(49,400)
Trading income		196,710

Tutorial notes

These notes are provided in order to help you to understand the above answer. They are not part of the answer. If a question simply asks for a calculation, explanations such as these are not required.

(1) The motor expenses are allowable in full. Private use by an employee is irrelevant for the calculation of trading income.

(2) Redecoration costs are allowable. However, it has been assumed that the installation of the new kitchen is capital expenditure and not allowable.

(3) The qualifying charitable donation is not an allowable expense for trading income purposes. It is, however, allowed as a deduction in calculating TTP.

(4) The interest on the loan to purchase the property which is let and the non-trade debt written off are not allowable expenses for trading income purposes. They are allowable in calculating interest income instead.

(5) Patent royalties payable are allowable deductions for trading income purposes, so no adjustment is required.

(6) Legal fees relating to the issue of long-term finance are specifically allowable.

(7) Fees relating to leases are capital-related and therefore not allowable, unless they are incurred in relation to the **renewal** of a short lease.

(b) T Ltd: TTP statement – year ended 31 March 2023

	£
Trading income	196,710
Interest income (W1)	28,000
UK property income	25,200
Net chargeable gains	66,150
Total profits	316,060
Qualifying charitable donation	(1,000)
TTP	315,060

Working: Interest income

	£
Bank interest receivable	38,000
Minus Interest on loan to purchase the property which is let	(9,600)
Non-trade debt written off	(400)
Interest income	28,000

> **Long periods of account**
>
> - The treatment of a long period of account
> - The allocation of income, gains and payments between CAPs

6 Long periods of account

6.1 The treatment of a long period of account

As explained in the previous chapter, a CAP cannot exceed 12 months. Therefore, if a company draws up a long period of account it must be split into two CAPs using the following rules:

- CAP 1: The first 12 months of the long period of account
- CAP 2: The balance period.

Example

A company prepares a 17-month set of accounts from 1 June 2021 to 31 October 2022.

Required

State how the 17-month set of accounts will be assessed to corporation tax.

Answer

For corporation tax purposes, the 17-month financial accounting period would be split into two CAPs as follows:

- CAP 1: 12-month period ended 31 May 2022
- CAP 2: 5-month period ended 31 October 2022

For each CAP the following must then be produced:

- A separate TTP statement allocating the income, gains and qualifying charitable donations made in the long period of account.
- Separate corporation tax liability computations, as each CAP has a different due date of payment.

6.2 The allocation of income, gains and payments between CAPs

The tax legislation requires income, gains and qualifying charitable donations in a long period of account to be allocated to the separate CAPs as follows:

Item	Allocation method
Adjusted profit **before** capital allowances	Produce one adjustment of profit computation for the long period, ignoring capital allowances. Then time-apportion between the two CAPs.
Capital allowances	Produce a separate computation for each CAP, bringing in the appropriate additions and disposals according to the dates of acquisition and disposal.
Interest income	Allocate on an accruals basis to each CAP.
Property income	Produce one property income assessment for the long period, then time-apportion.
Net chargeable gains	Allocate gains and losses according to the date of disposal of the capital asset.
Qualifying charitable donations	Allocate between CAPs according to the dates of payment of donations.

Example

P Ltd prepared a 17-month set of accounts to 31 August 2022. The following information relates to the 17-month period:

	£
Income	
Adjusted profit before capital allowances	1,530,000
Interest received on £200,000 12% loan notes on 31 March 2022	24,000
Dividends received from a non-group company on 31 January 2022	56,700
Rental income	51,000
Expenditure	
Qualifying charitable donation paid on 30 June each year	16,000
Dividends paid to shareholders on 30 April 2021	96,000

P Ltd disposed of one capital asset which gave rise to an allowable loss of £34,000 on 30 September 2021 and another capital asset which gave rise to a chargeable gain of £125,000 on 30 June 2022. It has capital losses of £18,000 brought forward from previous years.

Capital allowances are calculated as £35,000 for the first CAP and £23,000 for the second CAP.

Required

Calculate the corporation tax liabilities of P Ltd for the 17 months ended 31 August 2022 and state the due dates for payment.

Answer

P Ltd: Corporation tax computations	12 months ending 31 March 2022	5 months ending 31 August 2022
	£	£
Adjusted profit before capital allowances (£1,530,000 × 12/17 : £1,530,000 × 5/17)	1,080,000	450,000
Capital allowances	(35,000)	(23,000)
Trading income	1,045,000	427,000
Interest income (£200,000 × 12% : £200,000 × 12% × 5/12)	24,000	10,000
UK property income (£51,000 × 12/17 : £51,000 × 5/17)	36,000	15,000
Net chargeable gains (no gain in first CAP : £125,000 - £52,000 b/f losses)	Nil	73,000
Total profits	1,105,000	525,000
Qualifying charitable donation	(16,000)	(16,000)
TTP	1,089,000	509,000
Dividend income	56,700	0
Augmented profits	1,145,700	509,000
Corporation tax liabilities		
£1,089,000 × 19%	£206,910	
£509,000 × 19%		£96,710
Due dates for payment	1 Jan 2023	1 June 2023

Tutorial notes

(1) The due date for payment is 9 months and 1 day after the end of the CAP as P Ltd is not a large company.

(2) P Ltd's corporation tax returns for **both** periods must be filed within 12 months of the end of its **period of account**. Therefore, both returns must be submitted by 31 August 2023.

Taxation – United Kingdom
(TX-UK) FA2022

CHAPTER 22

Chargeable gains of a company

	Contents
1	Overview of the taxation of chargeable gains of a company
2	Disposal of chargeable assets other than shares and securities
3	Rollover relief
4	Disposal of shares and securities

> **Overview of the taxation of chargeable gains of a company**
> - The basic charging rules
> - Calculating the net chargeable gains of a company

1 Overview of the taxation of chargeable gains of a company

1.1 The basic charging rules

A chargeable gain arises if a chargeable person (for example, a company) makes a chargeable disposal of a chargeable asset.

- A **chargeable disposal** is the sale or gift of the whole or part of an asset.
- A **chargeable asset** is any **capital asset** (tangible or intangible) except those specifically exempted from tax.

Exempt assets

Exempt assets for companies are the same as for individuals, but with one exception. Goodwill **is** an exempt asset in the hands of a company as it is dealt with under the intangible asset rules.

Liability to corporation tax for net chargeable gains

A company is liable to **corporation tax** on its total net chargeable gains in the CAP. A chargeable gain or allowable loss is brought into a CAP according to the date of disposal (i.e. the date of sale of the asset). In other words, chargeable gains or allowable losses apply to the CAP in which the disposal occurs.

Note that, unlike individuals, companies do not receive an annual exempt amount.

1.2 Calculating net chargeable gains of a company

There are three steps in the calculation of the net chargeable gains of a company:

Step 1: Calculate the gains or losses arising on the chargeable disposals

A separate gain or loss calculation is needed for each individual chargeable asset that is disposed of in the CAP.

Step 2: Calculate and deduct any rollover relief, if applicable

Relief is available to defer the tax on some gains if certain conditions are satisfied. Rollover relief is explained later.

Step 3: Calculate the net chargeable gain to include in the TTP statement

Net chargeable gains are included in the TTP statement. The net chargeable gain is calculated as follows:

	£
Total chargeable gains arising on individual disposals in the CAP	X
Minus Allowable losses arising on disposals in the CAP	(X)
Allowable losses brought forward from previous CAPs	(X)
Net chargeable gains	X

If allowable losses exceed chargeable gains

Where allowable losses exceed the chargeable gains in the CAP, the following rules apply:

- The net chargeable gain in the TTP statement is £0.

    (It is not permitted to have a negative chargeable gain in a corporation tax computation. Capital losses cannot be set off against the company's other income in the CAP.)

- Excess allowable losses can be **carried forward** to future CAPs, but cannot be carried back to previous CAPs.

- Excess allowable losses **must** be set off against the **first available** net chargeable gains in future CAPs.

There is no choice in treatment. If a current period set off is possible, a company cannot choose to skip a CAP and wait to set off losses against a future period.

Example

A company had allowable losses in excess of its chargeable gains for its CAP to 31 December 2022.

- It cannot set these losses against any other taxable income for the year.

- It must carry the excess allowable loss forward to set off against chargeable gains in future CAPs. It cannot carry the losses back and set them against chargeable gains for the year to 31 December 2021.

- It must set off the excess allowable loss against the first available chargeable gains in future CAPs. For example, if there are sufficient chargeable gains for the year to 31 December 2023, it must set off the excess allowable loss against these gains, and cannot carry the loss forward to set off against the chargeable gains for the year to 31 December 2024 (or a later year).

Capital losses can only be set off against future net chargeable gains. They can not be set off against the company's other income in future CAPs.

> **Disposal of chargeable assets other than shares and securities**
> - Overview of a chargeable gain computation
> - Incidental costs
> - The indexation allowance

2 Disposal of chargeable assets other than shares and securities

2.1 Overview of a chargeable gain computation

The first step in calculating the net chargeable gain of a company is the calculation of separate chargeable gains and allowable losses on every chargeable asset disposed of in the CAP.

The computation for a company differs slightly from the computation for an individual as it includes an allowance for inflation, known as the indexation allowance.

The chargeable gain computation is as follows:

	£
Gross sale proceeds	X
Minus Incidental costs of sale	(X)
Net sale proceeds	X
Minus Allowable costs	
Acquisition cost (including incidental costs)	(X)
Enhancement expenditure	(X)
Unindexed gain/(loss)	X/(X)
Minus Indexation allowance (IA) (see 2.3 below)	
Cost x indexation factor	(X)
Chargeable gain/(allowable loss) before rollover relief	X/(X)
Minus Rollover relief (if applicable)	(X)
Chargeable gain/(allowable loss)	X/(X)

2.2 Incidental costs

When calculating the chargeable gain for a company, it is important to keep incidental selling costs separate from acquisition costs because indexation allowance:

- is available on incidental acquisition costs, but
- is not available on incidental selling costs.

2.3 The indexation allowance

The indexation allowance (IA) eliminates any inflationary gains. As a result, a company is only taxed on the real growth in value of any capital assets it disposes of. However, the indexation allowance is frozen at December 2017. This means that:

- Expenditure incurred prior to December 2017 will only receive indexation allowance up to December 2017.
- Expenditure incurred after December 2017 will not receive any indexation allowance.

The IA is **calculated separately for each element of allowable expenditure** as follows:

$$IA = Cost \times \text{Indexation factor}$$

The indexation factor is based on the movement in the retail prices index (RPI). The appropriate indexation factors (if required) will be given in the question. However, some past examination questions have provided the relevant information in other ways:

- by giving the indexation allowance as a monetary amount, or
- by stating that the cost given in the question is the indexed cost (i.e. it already includes indexation allowance).

If there is **enhancement expenditure**, a separate IA calculation is needed, based on the indexation factor from the month of enhancement to the month of disposal (or to December 2017 if sooner).

The IA cannot create nor increase an allowable loss. At best, the IA brings the gain down to £Nil.

Example

G Ltd purchased an investment property in June 2002 for £42,000. Estate agents' and solicitors' fees totalled £2,500. In August 2005 an extension costing £36,000 was added, and the whole property was redecorated at a cost of £5,500.

G Ltd sold the property on 25 June 2022. The estate agents' and solicitors' fees were arranged at a fixed price and totalled £4,800.

Required

Calculate the chargeable gain/(allowable loss) assuming the property is sold for each of the following alternative amounts:

(a) £150,000

(b) £120,000

(c) £70,000

Assume the relevant indexation factors are as follows:

June 2002 to December 2017: 0.659

August 2005 to December 2017: 0.407

Answer

	(a)	(b)	(c)
	£	£	£
Gross sale proceeds (June 2022)	150,000	120,000	70,000
Minus Incidental selling expenses	(4,800)	(4,800)	(4,800)
Net sale proceeds	145,200	115,200	65,200
Original cost (June 2002) (including incidental acquisition costs)	(44,500)	(44,500)	(44,500)
Cost of extension (August 2005)	(36,000)	(36,000)	(36,000)
Unindexed gain / (loss)	64,700	34,700	(15,300)
IA on original cost From June 2002 to December 2017			
£44,500 x 0.659	(29,326)	(29,326)	0
IA on extension From August 2005 to December 2017			
£36,000 x 0.407	(14,652)	(5,374)	0
Chargeable gain / (Allowable loss)	20,722	0	(15,300)

Notes

(1) Redecoration costs are not capital expenditure and are therefore not allowable in the capital gain computation.

(2) Indexation allowance can not create or increase a loss. In scenario (b) the IA is restricted to the amount where the net chargeable gain is £0. In scenario (c) no IA is available as a loss arises before the application of indexation.

(3) Indexation allowance stops at December 2017.

Chapter 22: Chargeable gains of a company

> **Rollover relief**
>
> - Overview of rollover relief
> - Qualifying business assets

3 Rollover relief

3.1 Overview of rollover relief

Rollover relief is the only capital gains relief available to companies. It allows the deferral of the **indexed** gains arising on the disposal of qualifying business assets (QBAs).

Relief must be claimed within four years of the end of the chargeable accounting period in which the disposal is made (or four years after the end of the period in which the new asset is acquired, if later).

3.2 Qualifying business assets

The definition of a qualifying business asset is the same as discussed earlier in relation to individuals, but with one exception. Goodwill is not a qualifying asset if disposed of by a company

Example

H Ltd prepares its accounts to 31 March each year. On 31 December 2022 it sold a freehold warehouse for £450,000, which gave rise to a chargeable gain (after indexation, but before considering reliefs) of £123,350.

On 24 February 2023 H Ltd purchased a 99-year lease on a new warehouse. It is anticipated that the leasehold warehouse will be sold in September 2026 for £750,000.

Required

(a) Calculate the chargeable gain arising in the year ended 31 March 2023, assuming the lease was purchased for each of the following alternative amounts:

  (i) £480,000

  (ii) £418,000

  (iii) £320,000

  For each scenario, calculate the gain that is anticipated to arise in the year ending 31 March 2027.

(b) Explain the difference in treatment if the replacement warehouse were a 55-year leasehold interest.

Answer

Part (a)

Is the asset a QBA for rollover relief purposes?	Yes
Has it been replaced with a QBA?	Yes
Has it been replaced in the four-year qualifying period? (31 December 2021 – 31 December 2025)	Yes

	(i)	(ii)	(iii)
	£	£	£
Sale proceeds received	450,000	450,000	450,000
Cost of replacement	480,000	418,000	320,000
Sales proceeds not reinvested	-	32,000	130,000
Have all the sale proceeds been reinvested in a QBA?	Yes	No	No

	(i)	(ii)	(iii)
Chargeable gain arising in y/e 31 March 2023			
Lower of			
(1) All the gain			123,350
(2) The sale proceeds not reinvested in QBAs	0	32,000	
Rollover relief = the rest of the gain			
£123,350 / (£123,350 – £32,000) / £0	123,350	91,350	Nil
Base cost of replacement 99-year leasehold interest			
Cost	480,000	418,000	320,000
Minus: Rollover relief	(123,350)	(91,350)	(Nil)
Base cost	356,650	326,650	320,000
Unindexed gain arising in y/e 31 March 2027			
Sale proceeds	750,000	750,000	750,000
Base cost	(356,650)	(326,650)	(320,000)
Gain	393,350	423,350	430,000

Part (b): If the replacement had been in a 55-year leasehold interest

- A 55-year leasehold interest is a QBA, but is a depreciating asset.

- The calculation of the amount of rollover relief and the chargeable gain arising in the year ended 31 March 2023 would be the same as above for each scenario.

- However, the amount relieved with a rollover relief claim is not deducted from the cost of the replacement asset.

- A record of the amount of rollover relief is kept and that amount is deferred for a maximum of 10 years from the date of acquisition of the replacement warehouse. However, as the replacement asset is disposed of before 10 years have elapsed, the deferred gain becomes chargeable in y/e 31 March 2027 on the disposal of the replacement asset.

- In addition to the deferred gain on the original asset becoming chargeable, a gain of £430,000 arises on the disposal of the replacement asset itself. This is calculated in the normal way, using the actual cost of the leasehold interest with no rollover relief deduction (i.e. as in scenario (iii) above).

Chapter 22: Chargeable gains of a company

> **Disposal of shares and securities**
>
> - Overview of the gain computation for shares and securities
> - The share identification rules
> - The share pool
> - Proforma: share pool for companies
> - The chargeable gain on the disposal of shares from the pool
> - Bonus issues
> - Rights issues
> - Takeovers

4 Disposal of shares and securities

4.1 Overview of the gain computation for shares and securities

If a company buys shares in another company and then **sells them all** at a later date:

- the chargeable gain computation is the same as for assets other than shares, and
- rollover relief is not available.

However, if a company buys shares in another company over a period of time in a series of transactions, and then **disposes of some, but not all the shares**, the calculations of chargeable gains are more complex. In this situation:

- it is necessary first of all to **identify** which shares have been sold, before
- the appropriate gain can be calculated.

4.2 The share identification rules

When purchasing shares, a company must keep separate records for each different type and class of shares that it has purchased. For example, records for purchases of X Ltd ordinary shares are kept separate from the purchase records for Y Ltd ordinary shares, which are kept separate from Y Ltd preference share purchase records.

Share identification rules are applied to identify which of the shares have been disposed of. (These are also known as matching rules). **These rules are different to the identification rules that apply to disposals made by individuals.**

In the examination, shares are deemed to be disposed of in the following order:

(1) Acquisitions on the same day as the disposal
(2) Acquisitions in the previous nine days on a last-in-first-out basis
(3) Shares in the pool.

Shares in the first two categories never enter the pool and no indexation allowance is available on their disposal.

4.3 The share pool

A company with many investments in other companies will need to construct a share pool **for each company and each class of share.**

Shares in the pool are treated as a single source of shares, disposed of at their average cost.

A proforma share pool is shown on the next page.

Purchasing shares to increase the pool

When the company purchases shares:

- the number of shares acquired is entered in the number of shares column, and
- the cost of the shares acquired is entered in both the cost and indexed cost columns.

However, **before** recording any change in the pool cost, the indexation allowance (IA) available up to that purchase date (or December 2017, if sooner) has to be calculated for the shares already in the pool. This IA is added to the indexed cost column.

Selling shares from the pool

When the company sells some shares, the appropriate proportion of cost and indexed cost is deducted from the appropriate columns in the pool.

However, **before** recording a sale, the IA available up to the date of the sale (or December 2017, if sooner) has to be calculated and added to the indexed cost column.

Summary: the working for the share pool

The IA available on shares is calculated on a piecemeal basis, **before** recording each operative event (for example, before recording a purchase of shares or a sale of shares).

The IA is based on the indexed cost to date and is calculated in the normal way.

4.4 Proforma: share pool for companies

The share pool is constructed in chronological date order. The working for a share pool should be presented as shown in the proforma below.

	Number of shares	Original cost	Indexed cost
		£	£
First operative event (a purchase that creates the pool). Original cost = indexed cost.	X	X	X
Second operative event (for example, a purchase)			
(i) Indexation allowance from the previous operative event to this operative event: Balance in the Indexed cost column × Indexation factor			X
(ii) Purchase of shares	X	X	X
	X	X	X
Third operative event (for example, a sale)			
(i) Indexation allowance from the previous operative event to this operative event: Balance in the Indexed cost column × Indexation factor			X
			X
(ii) Sale of shares (see note)	(X)	(X)	(X)
Pool balance carried forward	X	X	X

Notes

The appropriate proportion of cost and indexed cost to deduct from each column when shares are sold is calculated as follows:

Total cost to date, or Total indexed cost to date × $\dfrac{\text{Number of shares disposed of}}{\text{Number of shares held (before the disposal)}}$

Example

J plc purchased shares in K Ltd as follows:

		Cost
		£
16 May 2002	5,000 shares	34,500
27 September 2008	6,500 shares	37,700

On 13 April 2022, J plc sold 10,000 of the shares in K Ltd for £98,000.

Required

Construct the pool for shares in K Ltd to record these events, assuming that the relevant indexation factors are as follows:

May 2002 to September 2008	0.240
May 2002 to December 2017	0.424
September 2008 to December 2017	0.263

Answer

Share Pool

	Number of shares	Original cost	Indexed cost
		£	£
16 May 2002: Initial purchase	5,000	34,500	34,500
27 September 2008: subsequent purchase			
(i) IA: from May 2002 to September 2008 £34,500 x 0.240			8,280
(ii) Purchase of shares	6,500	37,700	37,700
	11,500	72,200	80,480
13 April 2022: sale of shares			
(i) IA: from September 2008 to December 2017 £80,480 x 0.263			21,166
			101,646
(ii) Sale of shares (see note below)	(10,000)	(62,783)	(88,388)
Pool balance c/f	1,500	9,417	13,258

Note

Shares sold from the pool are removed at average cost. This applies to both the original cost and the indexed cost column in the pool calculation.

Original cost: £72,200 × 10,000/11,500 = £62,783

Indexed cost: £101,646 × 10,000/11,500 = £88,388

4.5 The chargeable gain on the disposal of shares from the pool

The gain on the disposal of pool shares is calculated as follows:

	£
Gross sale proceeds	X
Minus Incidental costs of sale (e.g. stockbrokers' commission)	(X)
Net sale proceeds	X
Minus Allowable costs	
i.e. The cost deducted from the cost column in the pool	(X)
Unindexed gain/(loss)	X/(X)
Minus Indexation allowance (IA)	
(indexed cost minus cost) see notes (1) and (2) below	(X)
Chargeable gain/(allowable loss)	X/(X)

Notes

(1) These are the figures obtained from the workings for the pool that are calculated in relation to the sale.

(2) The IA must be shown separately because the IA deduction cannot create nor increase an allowable loss.

(3) Rollover relief is not available on the disposal of shares.

Example

Using the data in the previous example for shares held by J plc, we would calculate the chargeable gain arising on the disposal of shares as follows.

	£
Gross sale proceeds	98,000
Minus Cost (from the working for the pool)	(62,783)
Unindexed gain	35,217
Minus IA (from the pool working) (£88,388 - £62,783)	(25,605)
Chargeable gain	9,612

4.6 Bonus issues

The treatment of a bonus issue for tax purposes is as follows:

For identification purposes	Treatment in the pool
Bonus shares are treated **as if** they are acquired on the same day as the original shares to which they relate.	• Bonus issues are not an operative event. • Therefore do not calculate an IA before recording a bonus issue. • Simply add the number of shares into the number of shares column. • No entries are needed in the cost and indexed cost columns.

Example

On 23 August 2009, L Ltd purchased 3,000 ordinary shares in M plc for £45,000. On 6 April 2012 M plc made a 1 for 6 bonus issue. On 30 April 2022 L Ltd disposed of 2,000 of its shares in M plc for £40,000.

Required

Calculate the chargeable gain arising on the disposal of shares, assuming that the relevant indexation factors are as follows:

August 2009 to April 2012	0.214
August 2009 to December 2017	0.287
April 2012 to December 2017	0.192

Answer

	£
Gross sale proceeds	40,000
Minus Cost (from the pool working below)	(25,714)
Unindexed gain	14,286
Minus IA (from the pool, working shown below) (£33,094 - £25,714)	(7,380)
Chargeable gain	6,906

Pool working	Number of shares	Original cost	Indexed cost
		£	£
23 August 2009: Initial purchase	3,000	45,000	45,000
6 April 2012 : Bonus issue	500	-	-
	3,500	45,000	45,000
30 April 2022: Sale of shares			
(i) IA: from August 2009 to December 2017			
£45,000 x 0.287			12,915
			57,915
(ii) Sale of shares:			
(2,000/3,500) × £45,000	(2,000)	(25,714)	
(2,000/3,500) × £57,915			(33,094)
Pool balance c/f	1,500	19,286	24,821

4.7 Rights issues

The treatment of a rights issue for tax purposes is as follows:

For identification purposes	Treatment in the pool
Rights shares are treated as if they are acquired on the same day as the original shares to which they relate (i.e. the same as the treatment of a bonus issue).	- A rights issue is an operative event. - An IA must therefore be calculated before recording the rights issue. - Treat the event in exactly the same way as a normal purchase.

Example

On 10 May 2006, N Ltd purchased 8,000 shares in O plc for £16,000. On 25 July 2011 O plc made a 1 for 4 rights issue at £5 per share. N Ltd decided to take up the offer and purchased the shares to which it was entitled. On 30 April 2022 N Ltd disposed of 4,000 of its shares in O plc for £55,000.

Required

Calculate the chargeable gain arising on the disposal of shares, assuming that the relevant indexation factors are as follows:

May 2006 to July 2011	0.133
May 2006 to December 2017	0.245
July 2011 to December 2017	0.237

Answer

	£
Gross sale proceeds	55,000
Minus Cost (from pool working, shown below)	(10,400)
Unindexed gain	44,600
Minus IA (from pool working, shown below) (£13,918 - £10,400)	(3,518)
Chargeable gain	41,082

Pool working	Number of shares	Original Cost	Indexed cost
		£	£
10 May 2006: Initial purchase	8,000	16,000	16,000
25 July 2011: Purchase in rights issue			
(i) IA: from May 2006 to July 2011			
£16,000 x 0.133			2,128
(ii) Rights issue (1 for 4) at £5 per share	2,000	10,000	10,000
	10,000	26,000	28,128

Pool working	Number of shares	Original Cost £	Indexed cost £
30 April 2022: Sale of shares			
(i) IA: from July 2011 to December 2017			
£28,128 × 0.237			6,666
			34,794
(ii) Sale of shares:	(4,000)	(10,400)	
(4,000/10,000) × £26,000			
(4,000/10,000) × £34,794			(13,918)
Pool balance c/f	6,000	15,600	20,876

4.8 Takeovers

Where shares are held in a company that is subsequently taken over by another company, the treatment of this event for tax purposes depends on the consideration received in exchange for the old shares.

For example, suppose that X Ltd owns shares in Y plc, and Y plc is taken over by Z plc. X Ltd will receive consideration from Z plc for the sale of its shares in Y plc to Z plc. If the purchase consideration is 100% cash, the chargeable gain is calculated in the normal way for a sale from the pool. However, the purchase consideration might not include cash, or might include some cash and some shares in Z plc.

In summary, the appropriate treatment is as follows:

Consideration: Does not include cash	Includes cash
For example, the consideration consists of shares or other securities, but *no* cash.	For example, the consideration consists of a mixture of shares (and/or other securities) and some cash.
This is not a chargeable disposal. (It is a paper-for-paper exchange) The new shares and securities received are deemed to be: • acquired on the same day as the original shares • for the same cost and indexed cost as the original shares. Therefore, at the time of the take-over, no chargeable gain or allowable loss arises. The original cost and the indexed cost of the old shares are allocated to the new shares and securities received in proportion to the market values of the consideration received. New pools for the new shares and securities are set up (one pool for each class of shares or securities received as consideration).	A chargeable gain may arise, but only in respect of the cash consideration received. The amount of cash consideration received is treated as the sale proceeds. The 'cost' of the cash is calculated by applying the part disposal formula to the cost (and indexed cost) of the original shareholding.

Example

P plc owns 3,000 ordinary shares in Q Ltd, which it bought for £6,600 on 13 June 2000.

On 5 April 2022 Q Ltd accepted a takeover bid from R plc. The takeover offer consisted of 1 ordinary share and 2 preference shares in R plc for every 3 shares held in Q Ltd.

At the date of the takeover, the market values of R plc shares were as follows:

Ordinary shares   £20 each

Preferences shares   £15 each.

Required

(a) Explain whether a chargeable gain arises at the time of the takeover.

(b) Calculate the cost and indexed cost to be entered in the new pools for the R plc shares, assuming that the indexation factor from June 2000 to December 2017 is 0.613.

Answer

(a) There is no chargeable gain at the time of the takeover as no cash consideration is received.

(b) Takeover consideration received by P plc:

	Market value
	£
1,000 Ordinary shares in R plc	20,000
2,000 Preference shares in R plc	30,000
	50,000

Q Ltd – Pool	No of shares	Original cost	Indexed cost
		£	£
13 June 2000 Purchase	3,000	6,600	6,600
5 April 2022 IA: from June 2000 to December 2017 £6,600 x 0.613			4,046
Balance at time of takeover	3,000	6,600	10,646

Allocation of the original cost and indexed cost of the Q Ltd shares	Original cost	Indexed cost
	£	£
1,000 Ordinary shares in R plc	2,640	4,258
20,000/50,000 × £6,600/£10,646		
2,000 Preference shares in R plc	3,960	6,388
30,000/50,000 × £6,600/£10,646		
	6,600	10,646

Two new pools should be set up, one for the ordinary shares in R plc and one for the preference shares in R plc, with an original cost and indexed cost for each pool as shown above.

Taxation – United Kingdom
(TX-UK) FA2022

CHAPTER 23

Company trading losses

Contents
1   Introduction
2   Loss relief options
3   Tax planning

> **Introduction**
>
> - Calculation of trading losses
> - Changes to loss relief rules
> - Proforma corporation tax loss relief computation

1 Introduction

1.1 Calculation of trading losses

A trading loss occurs when a company has:

- an adjusted trading loss before capital allowances which is increased by the addition of capital allowances, or
- an adjusted trading profit before capital allowances which becomes a loss when capital allowances are deducted.

If a trading loss occurs, the trading income in the TTP statement for the CAP:

- is £0, and
- is not the amount of the loss.

This is shown in the table below:

	£
Adjusted profit / (loss) before capital allowances	X/(X)
Capital allowances on plant and machinery	(X)
Trading loss (= negative figure)	(X)
Trading income in the TTP statement	£Nil

Although the trading income for the CAP is £Nil, the company is able to obtain relief for the trading loss. As several options are available, the company needs to consider the options and choose the one that gives it the optimum use of its trading loss.

1.2 Changes to loss relief rules

The treatment of trading losses (and property business losses) carried forward to future periods was changed in respect of losses arising on or after 1 April 2017. This chapter covers only the rules applicable from that date. Carried forward losses incurred prior to that date will not be examinable.

In addition, there was a temporary change to the relief available for losses incurred within the period 1 April 2020 and 31 March 2022. This change is not examinable and so is not mentioned in this chapter.

1.3 Proforma corporation tax loss relief computation

The following proforma should be used to set out computations to calculate trading loss relief. In this proforma, it is assumed that a trading loss occurs in CAP 2.

Name of company:
Corporation tax computations

	CAP 1	CAP 2	CAP 3
	£	£	£
Trading income	X	Nil	X
Other income	X	X	X
Net chargeable gains	X	X	X
Total profits	X	X	X
Minus: Loss relief	(X)	(X)	(X)
	Nil	Nil	X
Minus: Qualifying charitable donations	lost	lost	(X)
Total taxable profits	Nil	Nil	X

Working
Record of trading losses

Trading loss in CAP 2	X
Loss relief:	
- in current year (CAP 2)	(X)
- carried back to CAP 1	(X)
- carried forward to CAP 3	(X)
Unrelieved trading loss c/f	X

> **Loss relief options**
>
> - Current year and carry back relief
> - Carrying forward trading losses
> - The effect of a short CAP in the carry back period
> - Terminal loss relief

2 Loss relief options

2.1 Current year and carry back relief

A company may choose to claim relief for its trading losses against total profits:

- in the loss-making CAP only (i.e. make a claim for the current period), or
- in the loss-making CAP first, and then carry back the unrelieved loss to the previous 12 months (i.e. make a current year **and** carry back claim).

A carry back claim cannot be made unless the current loss-making period is relieved first.

When setting off the trading loss, the following rules apply:

- A claim for loss relief is optional.
- If relief is claimed, the trading loss is set off against total profits in the current CAP as much as possible. Any loss that cannot be relieved against total profits in the current CAP may be carried back 12 months.
- **Any trading losses left unrelieved are automatically carried forward.**
- The claim must be made within two years of the end of the loss-making CAP.

These rules are explained in some further detail in the table below.

Rule:	Explanation
• Set off against total profits	• Total profits are all other income plus net chargeable gains, **but before deducting qualifying charitable donations.**
• Must set off as much as possible in the CAP	• The claim is optional. However if the claim is made, the maximum amount of trading loss must be deducted from total profits of the CAP.
	• The loss relief may reduce the total profits to nil, so that relief for qualifying charitable donations is lost. (The donations cannot be carried forward, or carried back; they are wasted/lost.)

2.2 Carrying forward trading losses

Trading losses can also be carried forward and set off against total profits. There is no time limit for carrying losses forward provided the company continues to trade.

In contrast to a current year or carry back claim, with a carry forward claim the company can choose how much loss it wishes to relieve. This will allow the company to restrict the set off in order to preserve relief for qualifying charitable donations.

A claim for relief must be made within two years of the end of the accounting period **in which the loss is relieved**.

Example

S Ltd commenced trading on 1 April 2021. Its accounting reference date is 31 March. It has supplied the following information:

Year ended 31 March	2022	2023
	£	£
Trading profit / (loss)	(125,000)	28,000
Interest income	20,000	20,000
Net chargeable gains	Nil	135,000
Qualifying charitable donations	(3,000)	(3,000)

Required

Calculate the TTP for each year, assuming:

(a) the whole of the loss is carried forward

(b) the loss is relieved in the current year before being carried forward.

(a) **S Ltd: Corporation tax computations**

Year ended 31 March	2022	2023
	£	£
Trading income	0	28,000
Interest income	20,000	20,000
Net chargeable gains	0	135,000
	20,000	183,000
Loss relief	0	(125,000)
	20,000	58,000
Qualifying charirable donations	(3,000)	(3,000)
TTP	17,000	55,000

Record of trading losses

	£
Trading loss b/f	125,000
Loss relieved in 2023	(125,000)
Trading loss c/f	0

(b) S Ltd: Corporation tax computations

Year ended 31 March	2022	2023
	£	£
Trading income	0	28,000
Interest income	20,000	20,000
Net chargeable gains	0	135,000
	20,000	183,000
Loss relief	(20,000)	(105,000)
	0	78,000
Qualifying charitable donations	lost	(3,000)
TTP	0	75,000

Record of trading losses

	£
Trading loss b/f	125,000
Loss relieved in 2022	(20,000)
Loss relieved in 2023	(105,000)
Trading loss c/f	0

Note

If the whole of the loss is carried forwards, S Ltd will have total TTP of £72,000 (£17,000 + £55,000) compared to £75,000 if the loss is relieved in the current year first. This difference occurs because it is not possible to restrict a current year claim in order to preserve relief for qualifying charitable donations.

Example

T Ltd has an accounting reference date of 31 March. It has supplied the following information:

Year ended 31 March	2021	2022	2023
	£	£	£
Trading profit / (loss)	58,500	(323,000)	164,250
UK property income	14,000	15,000	16,000
Net chargeable gains / (loss)	(5,000)	45,000	0
Qualifying charitable donations	(1,000)	(1,000)	(1,000)

Required

Calculate the TTP for each year assuming losses are relieved as soon as possible.

Answer

T Ltd: Corporation tax computations

Year ended 31 March	2021	2022	2023
	£	£	£
Trading income	58,500	0	164,250
UK property income	14,000	15,000	16,000
Net chargeable gains (see note 1)	0	40,000	0
Total profits	72,500	55,000	180,250
Minus loss relief			
- current loss making CAP		(55,000)	
- carry back to previous 12 months	(72,500)		
- carry forward			(179,250)
	0	0	1,000
Minus Qualifying charitable donations (see note 2)	lost	lost	(1,000)
TTP	0	0	0

Working

Record of trading losses £
Trading loss in CAP 323,000
Loss relief   - in loss-making CAP (55,000)
              - in carry-back CAP (72,500)
              - carried forwards (179,250)
Trading loss c/f 16,250

Notes

(1) **Capital losses** must be carried forward and set against the first available future chargeable gains. They cannot be set against other profits in the CAP. Net chargeable gains in the year to 31 March 2022 are therefore £45,000 - £5,000 loss brought forward = £40,000.

(2) If as a result of current year or carry back loss relief there are no profits against which to set off qualifying charitable donations, the benefit of the donations is lost. It is not possible to restrict a loss in a current year or carry back claim.

2.3 The effect of a short CAP in the carry back period

Trading losses can be carried back against total profits generated in the 12 months before the **start** of the loss-making CAP.

This usually means carrying back the loss into the immediately-preceding CAP. However, if the company changed its accounting reference date in the 12-month carry back period, two CAPs will fall in the 12-month carry back period.

If this is the case, the following rules apply:

- Losses carried back should be set off against total profits on a last-in first-out (LIFO) basis.
- The losses can be carried back against total profits in the previous 12 months.
- The losses must be carried back for the full 12-month period.
- The length of the loss-making CAP does not affect how far it can be carried back.

These rules are explained in further detail in the table below.

Rule:	Explanation
Set off the losses on a LIFO basis	The trading loss is carried back on a last-in-first-out basis, i.e. the loss is set off against total profits in the previous CAP first, and then the CAP before that.
Can only carry back against the profits of the previous 12 months	Trading losses can be carried back exactly 12 months from the **start** of the loss-making CAP, but no more than 12 months.
	Therefore, the total profits of the earliest CAP must be time-apportioned to calculate the total profits eligible for relief.
Must carry back loss for the whole 12 month carry back period	The losses must be set off as much as possible in both CAPs that fall into the 12 month carry back period (on a LIFO basis).
	A company cannot decide to claim relief in only one of the carry back CAPs.
The length of the loss making period does not affect how far the loss can be carried back	Regardless of the length of the loss-making CAP itself, trading losses can be carried back exactly 12 months from the start of the loss-making CAP.
	For example, trading losses incurred in the 7 month CAP to 31 March 2023 can be carried back to 1 September 2021 (i.e. 12 months before the start of the 7-month CAP).

These rules also apply to terminal losses (see next section).

Example

U Ltd prepared its accounts annually until 31 December 2020. It then changed its accounting reference date to 31 March by preparing a three-month set of accounts. U Ltd has supplied the following information:

	y/e 31 December 2020	3 months ended 31 March 2021	y/e 31 March 2022	y/e 31 March 2023
	£	£	£	£
Trading profit / (loss)	321,000	64,500	(457,000)	123,000
Property income	6,000	1,500	6,000	6,000
Net chargeable gains / (loss)	Nil	(14,000)	26,000	48,500
Qualifying charitable donation	(1,500)	(375)	(1,500)	(1,500)

Required

Calculate the TTP for each CAP assuming losses are relieved as soon as possible.

Answer

U Ltd:

Corporation tax	y/e 31.12.20	p/e 31.3.21	y/e 31.3.22	y/e 31.3.23
	£	£	£	£
Trading income	321,000	64,500	Nil	123,000
Property income	6,000	1,500	6,000	6,000
Net chargeable gains (see note)	Nil	Nil	12,000	48,500
Total profits	327,000	66,000	18,000	177,500
Minus loss relief				
Current period claim - y/e 31.3.22			(18,000)	
Carry back 12 months:				
- 3 months to 31.3.21		(66,000)		
- 9 months of y/e 31.12.20				
(£327,000 × 9/12)	(245,250)			
Carry forward to y/e 31.3.23				(127,750)
	81,750	Nil	Nil	49,750
Minus Qualifying charitable donations	(1,500)	lost	lost	(1,500)
TTP	80,250	Nil	Nil	48,250

Working

Record of trading losses	y/e 31.3.22
	£
Trading loss in CAP	457,000
Loss relief	
- in loss making CAP	(18,000)
Carry back 12 months:	
- 3 m/e 31.3.21	(66,000)
- 9 months of y/e 31.12.20 (£327,000 × 9/12)	(245,250)
Trading loss c/f	127,750
Loss relief in y/e 31.3.23	(127,750)
Trading loss c/f	0

Note

Capital losses must be carried forward and set against the first available future chargeable gains. They cannot be set against other profits in the CAP. Net chargeable gains in the year to 31 March 2022 are therefore £12,000 (£26,000 - £14,000 loss brought forward).

2.4 Terminal loss relief

When a company ceases to trade, it will have no future trading profits. If it has trading losses in its final year of trading it can claim terminal loss relief. Terminal loss relief is more generous than normal ongoing trading loss relief.

When a loss-making company ceases to trade, it must first claim relief against total profits in the current loss-making period before considering a carry-back claim.

The carry-back claim is dealt with in the same way as normal ongoing losses except that **trading losses of the last 12 months of trading can be carried back three years** before the start of the CAP in which the loss was incurred.

These rules are explained in further detail in the table below.

Rule:	Explanation
Trading losses of the last 12 months trading may be carried back	All the trading losses incurred in the 12 months before the date of cessation of business may be carried back. The last 12 months of trading may span two CAPs. If so, trading losses eligible for the relief must be calculated in two parts: • the last CAP, and • a part of the previous CAP. The trading losses of the previous (penultimate) CAP must be time-apportioned to calculate the amount falling into the last 12 months of trading.
These trading losses can be carried back three years from the start of the CAP in which the loss was incurred	Trading losses can be carried back exactly 36 months from the **start** of the loss-making CAP, but no more than 36 months, on a LIFO basis. The carry-back could affect more than three CAPs if the company changed its accounting date in the three-year carry-back period. If so, the total profits of the earliest CAP must be time-apportioned to calculate the total profits eligible for relief (i.e. the profits that fall into the 36-month carry-back period).

Example

V plc ceased to trade on 31 December 2022 and in its last 12 months of trading it incurred a trading loss of £278,500. In this last year it had no other income or gains and made no qualifying charitable donations. It has supplied the following information in respect of the preceding CAPs:

	y/e 31 May 2019	7 months ended 31 December 2019	y/e 31 December 2020	y/e 31 December 2021
	£	£	£	£
Trading profit / (loss)	121,000	47,000	67,000	23,000
Interest income	12,000	7,000	12,000	12,000
Chargeable gains	Nil	Nil	12,000	48,500
Qualifying charitable donations	(600)	Nil	(600)	(600)

Required

Calculate the TTP for each CAP, assuming terminal loss relief is claimed.

… Chapter 23: Company trading losses

a Answer

(Note that in this example, the final 12 months of trading coincide with the final 12-month CAP.)

V plc Corporation tax	y/e 31 May 2019	7 m/e 31 December 2019	y/e 31 December 2020	y/e 31 December 2021
	£	£	£	£
Trading income	121,000	47,000	67,000	23,000
Interest income	12,000	7,000	12,000	12,000
Net chargeable gains	0	0	12,000	48,500
	133,000	54,000	91,000	83,500
Minus: loss relief Current period claim: - y/e 31.12.22 = £Nil Carry back 36 months: - y/e 31.12.21 - y/e 31.12.20 - 7 months ended 31.12.19 - 5 months of y/e 31.5.19: maximum (£133,000 × 5/12) = £55,417 - (also see working)	(50,000)	(54,000)	(91,000)	(83,500)
	83,000	Nil	Nil	Nil
Minus: Qualifying charitable donations	(600)	Nil	lost	lost
TTP	82,400	Nil	Nil	Nil

Working Record of trading losses	y/e 31 December 2022
	£
Trading loss in final CAP/12 months of trading	278,500
Loss relief:	
In the loss-making CAP	(0)
Carry back 36 months:	
- y/e 31.12.21	(83,500)
- y/e 31.12.20	(91,000)
- 7 months ended 31.12.19	(54,000)
- 5 months of y/e 31.5.19: Maximum relief = £133,000 × 5/12 = £55,417	(50,000)
Trading loss remaining unrelieved	0

> **Tax planning**
>
> - Choosing the optimum loss relief
> - Dealing with different types of losses

3 Tax planning

3.1 Choosing the optimum loss relief

As all companies pay the same rate of corporation tax irrespective of the level of their profits, cash flow is the key consideration in determining the choice of loss relief, particularly if the company has a cash flow problem.

Claiming loss relief against the current CAP and then making a carry-back claim will result in a repayment of corporation tax that the company has previously paid, and may possibly also carry repayment interest (i.e. a repayment supplement).

Where possible, the loss should be allocated to a year in which the corporation tax is payable in quarterly instalments as these are payable much earlier than a single payment of corporation tax.

The wastage/loss of relief for qualifying charitable donations is not desirable and is another consideration to bear in mind. However, this is unlikely to be the key deciding factor.

3.2 Dealing with different types of losses

Where a company has more than one type of loss in an accounting period, it is usual to relieve the non-trading losses first. This is because, in general, non-trading losses cannot be carried backwards:

- Capital losses must be set against **chargeable gains** arising in the current period. Any remaining capital losses must be carried forward and set against future chargeable gains.
  Capital losses cannot be carried back.
- Property business losses must be set against **total profits** (i.e. before qualifying charitable donations) of the loss making accounting period.

    Any remaining property business losses are carried forward and set against total profits of future periods. However, the set off of losses carried forward can be restricted to preserve relief for qualifying charitable donations.

    Property losses cannot be carried back.

Taxation – United Kingdom
(TX-UK) FA2022

CHAPTER 24

Group corporation tax

Contents
1   Related 51% group companies
2   Group loss relief
3   Group chargeable gain provisions

> **Related 51% group companies**
>
> - Introduction
> - Definition of a related 51% group company
> - Consequences of being a related 51% group company

1 Related 51% group companies

1.1 Introduction

A group of companies is **not** treated as a single entity for the purpose of corporation tax. The consolidated accounts for the group are irrelevant for tax purposes. Instead, for corporation tax purposes, each company within a group is taxed separately in its own right.

However, in calculating the corporation tax of each company, the tax legislation allows the group to deal with certain items on a group wide basis **as if** it were a single entity.

There are several different types of group for corporation tax purposes. Each has its own definition and consequences:

- **Related 51% group companies** are taken into account in determining whether a company needs to pay its corporation tax by quarterly instalments
- **75% group relief groups** enable losses to be transferred from one group member to another
- **75% chargeable gains groups** enable capital assets, gains and losses to be transferred from one group member to another.

1.2 Definition of a related 51% group company

Companies are related 51% group companies if:

- one is a 51% subsidiary of the other, or
- both are 51% subsidiaries of the same company.

A 51% subsidiary is a company in which the parent company owns more than 50% of the ordinary share capital.

For example:

```
         H Ltd                              Mr Herbert
       /       \                          /           \
    55%         60%                    65%            51%
     ↓           ↓                      ↓              ↓
   A Ltd       B Ltd                  A Ltd          B Ltd
```

Number of related 51% group companies = 3   Number of related 51% group companies = 0

As shown in the first diagram, where a group relationship exists, the companies are 51% subsidiaries of the holding company and therefore they are related 51% group companies for corporation tax purposes. However, as shown in the second diagram, where the shares in the two companies are held by an individual rather than a company, the companies are not related 51% group companies.

The definition of a related 51% group company also includes overseas companies, but it excludes dormant companies (i.e. non-trading companies).

Where there is a sub-subsidiary, i.e. where the shares in a subsidiary are held via another company, the sub-subsidiary is only classed as a related 51% group company if the holding company has an 'effective interest' of at least 50% in the sub-subsidiary. (This point is covered in the next section.)

1.3 Consequences of being a related 51% group company

The consequences of being a related 51% group company are as follows:

- When calculating augmented profits for each company in the group, any dividends from 51% subsidiaries are ignored entirely.

- For the purpose of establishing the due date for payment of the corporation tax liability, the profit threshold of £1,500,000 must be divided by the number of related 51% group companies **at the end of the preceding accounting period**. (The figure for the previous accounting period is used because the quarterly instalments commence during the current accounting period.)

Example

For the year ended 31 March 2023, I Ltd had TTP of £400,000. It has three wholly owned subsidiaries. All subsidiaries have been owned for many years. It received dividends of £10,000 from its subsidiaries.

Required

(a) Calculate the corporation tax liability of I Ltd for the year ended 31 March 2023 and state the due dates for payment.

(b) Show how your answer would differ if one of the subsidiaries had joined the group on 1 January 2023.

Answer

(a) **I Ltd – corporation tax liability computation – y/e 31 March 2023**

	£
TTP	400,000
Dividend income	Nil
Augmented profits	400,000

Corporation tax liability

£400,000 × 19%   £76,000

I Ltd has three 51% subsidiaries, therefore the profit threshold of £1,500,000 must be divided by four (i.e. I Ltd plus three). This will reduce it to £375,000 (£1,500,000 /4), which makes I Ltd a large company.

Assuming I Ltd was a large company in the previous year, it is liable to pay its corporation tax in four instalments of £19,000 each on 14 October 2022, 14 January 2023, 14 April 2023 and 14 July 2023.

If I Ltd was not a large company in the previous year it will pay its corporation tax liability on 1 January 2024.

(b) The profit threshold of £1,500,000 is divided by the number of related 51% group companies at the end of the preceding accounting period.

At 31 March 2022, I Ltd only had two 51% subsidiaries, therefore the profit threshold of £1,500,000 must be divided by three (i.e. I Ltd plus two). This will reduce it to £500,000 (£1,500,000/3).

This means that I Ltd is not a large company for the year ended 31 March 2023 and it will therefore pay its corporation tax liability on 1 January 2024.

Group loss relief

- Definition of a 75% group for group loss relief purposes
- An outline of how group loss relief works
- The rules for group relief from the surrendering company's point of view
- The rules for group relief from the recipient company's point of view
- Tax planning and group loss relief

2 Group loss relief

2.1 Definition of a 75% group for group loss relief purposes

Where one company owns, directly or indirectly, at least a 75% interest in the ordinary share capital of another company, or both companies are 75% subsidiaries of the same parent company, **group loss relief** (often referred to simply as **group relief**) may be available.

For group relief to be available, the company must **also** be entitled to at least 75% of the rights to the distributable profits **and** 75% of the net assets on a winding up of the company. However, for the examination, the ownership of the shares is the key deciding factor.

Directly-owned 75% subsidiaries will be part of a loss relief group. For example:

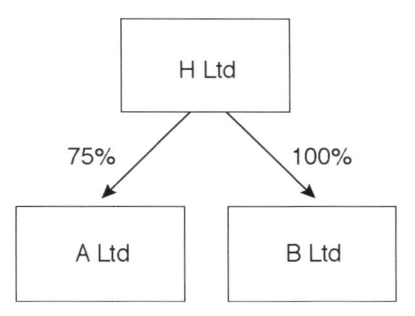

```
         H Ltd
        /     \
      75%    100%
      /         \
    A Ltd      B Ltd
```

Both A Ltd and B Ltd are directly owned 75% subsidiaries of H Ltd for group loss purposes.

Indirect subsidiaries (sub-subsidiaries)

An **indirect subsidiary** is the term used to refer to the situation where the holding company of a group owns shares in a subsidiary via another company (often referred to as a **sub-subsidiary**).

Example

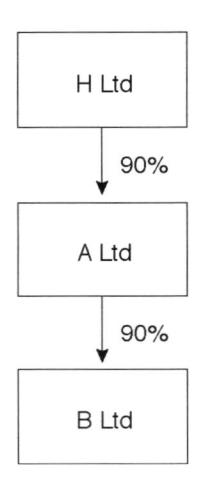

```
    H Ltd
      │ 90%
      ▼
    A Ltd
      │ 90%
      ▼
    B Ltd
```

In this situation, the sub-subsidiary (B Ltd) can only be part of the holding company's loss relief group if the holding company (H Ltd) has an effective interest of at least 75% in the sub-subsidiary (B Ltd).

The **size of the effective interest** is calculated by multiplying together:

- the percentage of the subsidiary owned by the holding company, and
- the percentage of the sub-subsidiary owned by the subsidiary.

In the above example, the effective interest of H Ltd in the sub-subsidiary B Ltd is 81% (= 90% × 90%). Both A Ltd and B Ltd are therefore 75% subsidiaries of H Ltd for group loss relief purposes.

The composition of a loss relief group

To determine the **composition** of a loss relief group, both UK and overseas companies in the group are considered. For example, an overseas holding company with two UK 75% subsidiaries would form a loss relief group. However, it is only possible to move losses between the UK companies in the group.

A company can be a member of more than one loss relief group.

Example

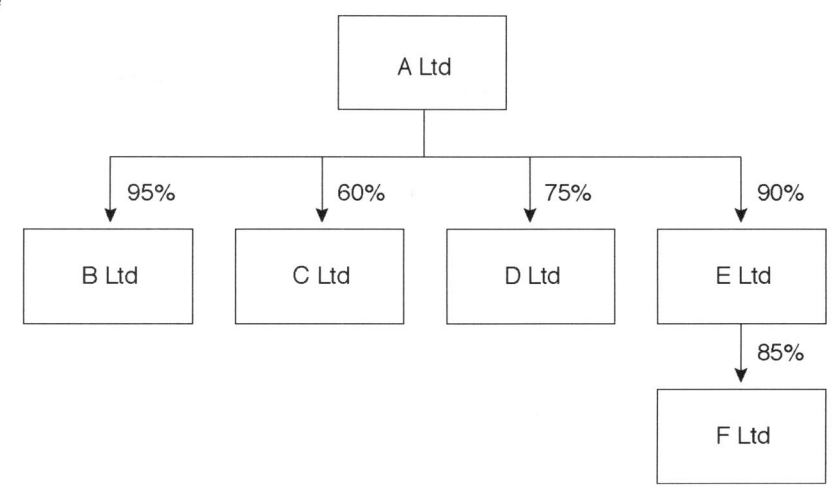

```
                        A Ltd
          ┌───────┬──────┴──────┬───────┐
         95%     60%           75%     90%
          ▼       ▼             ▼       ▼
        B Ltd   C Ltd         D Ltd   E Ltd
                                        │
                                       85%
                                        ▼
                                      F Ltd
```

Required

Calculate the number of related 51% group companies and state which companies form a loss relief group making each of the following alternative assumptions:

(a) All companies are UK companies

(b) A Ltd is an overseas company.

Answer

(a) **Assuming all companies are UK companies**

Number of related 51% group companies = 6

All the companies are related 51% group companies as A Ltd has an interest of more than 50% in each.

Loss relief group = A Ltd, B Ltd, D Ltd, E Ltd and F Ltd

Notes

(1) C Ltd is not included as A Ltd owns less than 75%.

(2) F Ltd is included as A Ltd has an effective interest of at least 75% (90% × 85% = 76.5%).

(b) **Assuming A Ltd is an overseas company:**

The answer is the same as above.

Overseas companies can be classed as related 51% group companies; therefore, there are still six related 51% group companies.

The composition of a **loss relief group** includes overseas companies; the group is therefore defined as above.

However, group losses may only move between the UK-resident companies (i.e. between B Ltd, D Ltd, E Ltd and F Ltd).

2.2 An outline of how group loss relief works

The group relief provisions allow losses to be transferred in any direction between UK companies within a loss relief group.

The loss relief is deducted from the TTP of the recipient company and therefore reduces its corporation tax liability.

Group relief is not automatic. It must be claimed within two years of the end of the CAP of the company receiving the group relief. The claim must be supported by a statement of consent from the surrendering company.

The claimant company can pay the surrendering company in return for the loss. Such a payment is ignored for corporation tax purposes, provided it does not exceed the amount of loss surrendered.

2.3 The rules for group relief from the surrendering company's point of view

The following losses can be surrendered:

- trading losses
- unrelieved UK property business losses (i.e. losses left unrelieved after making a the claim against total profits for the current period)
- unrelieved qualifying charitable donations.

It is important to note that **capital losses cannot be surrendered** using these rules (but see below for the options available under the chargeable gains group provisions).

As a general rule, **only current period losses can be surrendered**. However, carried forward losses created after 1 April 2017 can be group relieved if they cannot be set against the surrendering company's own profits.

As far as trading losses are concerned, the surrendering company can utilise its own losses against its own profits (for example, with a current year claim) before surrender, if it wishes to do so. However, it is **not obliged** to utilise its own current year trading losses first. It can transfer all its current year trading losses to one or more group members, and pay tax itself, if it wishes to do so for tax planning reasons or other commercial reasons.

However, it cannot surrender losses if the recipient company cannot utilise them against its own available profits.

2.4 The rules for group relief from the recipient company's point of view

The recipient company can only accept losses up to the amount of its available profits.

Available profits are defined as **TTP after deducting** the following amounts relating to the recipient company:

- any trading losses brought forward
- a current period loss relief claim (see below), and

- current period qualifying charitable donations.

In calculating the available profits, a current period claim **must** be deducted even if a claim is not actually made. However, there is no requirement to take account of a carry back claim.

Losses can only be matched against profits of a corresponding accounting period (i.e. the period when both the surrendering and recipient company were part of the same group).

If both companies have the same CAPs and are part of the group for the whole CAP the position is straightforward. The maximum group relief claim = Lower of:

- the loss of the surrendering company, or
- the available profits of the recipient company.

Example

G Ltd owns a 100% subsidiary, K Ltd. In the year ended 31 March 2023 the two companies had the following results:

	G Ltd	K Ltd
	£	£
Trading profit / (loss)	(125,000)	28,000
Interest income	20,000	20,000
Net chargeable gain	Nil	135,000
Qualifying charitable donations	(2,000)	(5,000)
Trading loss brought forward	(10,000)	(50,000)

Required

Calculate the maximum group relief surrender for the year ended 31 March 2023.

Answer

K Ltd - Available profit

	£
Trading income	28,000
Interest income	20,000
Net chargeable gains	135,000
	183,000
Minus: Loss brought forward	(50,000)
	133,000
Qualifying charitable donations	(5,000)
Available profits of K Ltd	128,000
G Ltd - Available loss = All the current period trading loss of G Ltd (see notes below)	125,000
Maximum group relief = Lower of available profits (£128,000) and available loss (£125,000)	125,000

Notes

(1) G Ltd cannot surrender the £10,000 trading loss brought forward as it is possible to use it against its own total profits.

(2) G Ltd does not need to use its own current year loss first. It can surrender all the loss for its current period.

(3) G Ltd cannot group relieve its qualifying charitable donations because the payment can be set off against the interest income in the CAP and is not therefore unrelieved.

(4) K Ltd's brought forward trading loss does not have to be claimed (i.e. K Ltd could, if it wishes, carry it forward to the following year), but it must be taken into account in determining the amount of group relief that K Ltd can receive.

Year ends that are not coterminous

Where the two companies have non-coterminous year ends (i.e. they do not have the same year end dates) or where a company joins or leaves a group during the CAP, the maximum group relief available is calculated by **time-apportionment** of:

- the surrendering company's losses, and
- the recipient company's available profits.

In effect, this means that the available profits are matched with the available losses in the common CAPs.

Example

S Ltd and T Ltd are members of the same loss relief group.

S Ltd incurred a trading loss of £12,000 in its year ended 31 March 2023. The company had no chargeable profits in that year and so wishes to surrender its loss to T Ltd.

T Ltd has an accounting reference date of 31 December. It has taxable total profits of £4,000 for the year ended 31 December 2022 and anticipates taxable total profits of £15,000 for the year ended 31 December 2023.

Required

Calculate the maximum group relief available.

Answer

Losses can only be transferred for overlapping periods. These are as follows:

1 April 2022 to 31 December 2022

S Ltd's loss	£12,000 x 9/12 =	£9,000
T Ltd's profits	£4,000 x 9/12 =	£3,000

A maximum of £3,000 can therefore be transferred from S Ltd to T Ltd for this period.

1 January 2023 to 31 March 2023

S Ltd's loss   £12,000 x 3/12 =   £3,000

T Ltd's profits   £15,000 x 3/12 =   £3,750

S Ltd's full loss of £3,000 for this period can be transferred to T Ltd as T Ltd has sufficient profits to absorb it.

As at 1 April 2023 S Ltd has a carried forward loss of £6,000 (12,000 – 3,000 – 3,000).

If S Ltd is unable to use this carried forward loss against its own profits, the loss can be group relieved. It is treated as if it is a loss for the year ended 31 March 2024 and must again be time apportioned and matched to T Ltd's profits:

1 April 2023 to 31 December 2023

S Ltd's c/f loss   £6,000 x 9/12 =   £4,500

T Ltd's profits   £15,000 x 9/12 =   £11,250

£4,500 of the carried forward loss can therefore be used against T Ltd's profits for the year ended 31 December 2023.

1 January 2024 to 31 March 2024

S Ltd's c/f loss   £6,000 x 3/12 =   £1,500

T Ltd's profits   ? x 3/12 =   ?

If T Ltd's profits for the period 1 January 2024 to 31 March 2024 exceed £1,500, it will be able to relieve the loss.

Note that a different method of apportionment can be used in the periods in which a company joins or leaves a group if time-apportionment would give an unreasonable result.

2.5 Tax planning and group loss relief

In utilising the group loss provisions, the aim of the group should be to save the maximum amount of corporation tax for the group as a whole. However, as all companies currently pay corporation tax at the same rate irrespective of the level of their profits, cash flow should be the main consideration in deciding how to relieve a loss.

The cash flow implications of the different loss relief claims are as follows:

- If the loss-making company carries its losses back this will result in a repayment of tax. Remember, however, that a carry back claim can only be made after the loss has been relieved in the current year.

- A group relief claim reduces the group's current tax liabilities. If companies can be kept below the relevant profit threshold, they may be able to avoid paying their corporation tax in quarterly instalments. Quarterly instalments are payable much earlier than a single payment of corporation tax and so should be avoided or minimised, where possible.

- Carrying losses forward delays the benefit of using the losses. However, it may result in a higher tax saving if corporation tax rates rise.

When allocating losses, the following points should be remembered:

- The current year and carry back claims are all or nothing reliefs. If the relief is claimed, the maximum possible amount of loss must be used.
- A carry forward claim allows a company to choose how much loss to relieve. This enables losses to be restricted so as to preserve relief for qualifying charitable donations.
- Group relief is flexible. Any amount can be surrendered to any other group company (or several group companies).

Deciding between several group members

The due dates of payment of the corporation tax liability should be taken into account in deciding which group member should claim a loss. It is necessary to compare each company's profits to the apportioned £1,500,000 profit threshold to decide the date on which the tax liability is payable.

The profit threshold of £1,500,000 is divided by the number of related 51% group companies at the **end of the preceding** CAP. If the current year's CAP is less than 12 months, the amount should also be time-apportioned to match the length of the period.

Dealing with several losses

Where several losses arise in a group, relief should first be given in respect of those losses having the most restricted usage. For example, capital losses can only be set against capital gains.

Example

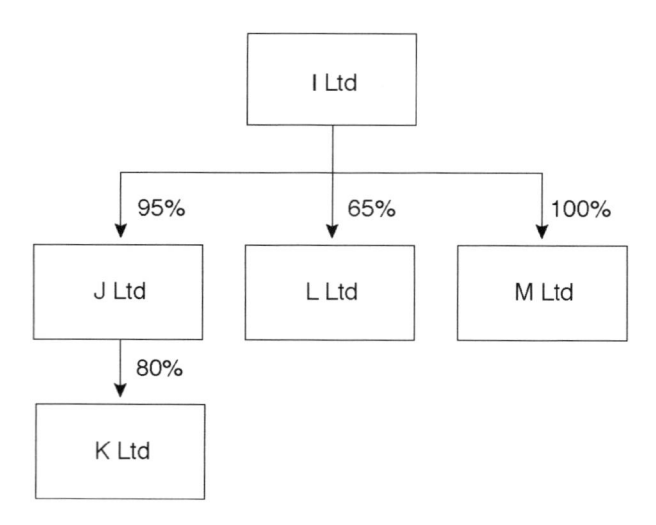

```
                    I Ltd
         ┌────────────┼────────────┐
        95%          65%          100%
         │            │            │
       J Ltd        L Ltd        M Ltd
         │
        80%
         │
       K Ltd
```

The results of these companies for the year ended 31 March 2023 are as follows:

	I Ltd	J Ltd	K Ltd	L Ltd	M Ltd
	£	£	£	£	£
Trading profit/(loss)	340,000	(120,000)	34,000	134,000	75,000
Interest income	50,000	5,000	Nil	9,000	4,500

All companies are UK resident and none of the companies received any dividends. They have all been group members for several years.

Required

Calculate the TTP for each company assuming group relief is claimed in the most tax-efficient manner, and calculate the tax saving achieved.

Answer

Start by identifying the number of related 51% group companies.

Number of related 51% group companies = 5

Next, identify the group or groups which exist for group loss surrender purposes:

Loss relief group = I Ltd, J Ltd, K Ltd, M Ltd

Notes

(1) L Ltd is not included as I Ltd owns less than 75%.

(2) K Ltd is included as I Ltd has an effective interest of at least 75% (95% × 80% = 76%).

Next: Establish the profit threshold for the purpose of identifying the due date for payment of the corporation tax liability:

Profit threshold   1,500,000 ÷ 5   £300,000

Next: Loss relief is then allocated to group companies in such a way as to achieve the best cash flow for the group.

	I Ltd	J Ltd	K Ltd	L Ltd	M Ltd
	£	£	£	£	£
Trading income	340,000	Nil	34,000	134,000	75,000
Interest income	50,000	5,000	Nil	9,000	4,500
TTP before loss relief	390,000	5,000	34,000	143,000	79,500

Best tax planning option

J Ltd cannot surrender losses to L Ltd as this company is not part of the loss group.

As all of the 75% group companies pay the same rate of corporation tax, the decision should be based on cash flow.

J Ltd, K Ltd and M Ltd pay their corporation tax nine months and one day following the end of the CAP. However, I Ltd's profits exceed the threshold and therefore it will pay its corporation tax in quarterly instalments (unless this is the first year in which it is a large company).

To avoid it having to pay its corporation tax in quarterly instalments, £90,000 of the loss should be surrendered to I Ltd. J Ltd should then claim £5,000 of the loss against its own current year profits and carry the remainder back to the previous year (assuming it has profits available to relieve it).

> **Group chargeable gain provisions**
>
> - Definition of a 75% group for the group chargeable gain provisions
> - An outline of the advantages of being in a gains group
> - The treatment of intra-group transfers of capital assets
> - Claiming group rollover relief
> - Electing to make maximum usage of capital losses
> - Tax planning: using capital losses

3 Group chargeable gain provisions

3.1 Definition of a 75% group for the group chargeable gain provisions

Where one company owns, directly or indirectly, at least 75% of the ordinary share capital of another company, the group chargeable gains provisions will apply.

Indirect sub-subsidiaries can also be part of the gains group, provided that the holding company has an effective interest of over 50%.

Unlike group loss relief, a company cannot be a member of two gains groups.

Example

	Workings for answer		
	≥ 75% direct holding test	≥ 75% effective interest test	> 50% effective interest test
H Ltd → 75% → A Ltd	√	√	√
A Ltd → 75% → B Ltd	√	75% × 75% = 56.25% X	√
B Ltd → 75% → C Ltd	√	56.25% × 75% = 42.1875% X	X

Required

(a) State which companies form a loss relief group and which form a gains group.

(b) Would there be a difference to the answer if A Ltd were an overseas company?

Answer

(a)

Group loss relief groups	Gains group
Group 1: H Ltd and A Ltd Group 2: A Ltd and B Ltd Group 3: B Ltd and C Ltd	Group 1 H Ltd, A Ltd and B Ltd
Notes: (1) Neither B Ltd nor C Ltd can be grouped with H Ltd for group loss relief purposes as the 75% effective interest test is not satisfied. (2) A company can be a member of more than one loss group.	**Notes:** (1) C Ltd cannot be grouped with H Ltd for group gains purposes as H Ltd's effective interest is less than 50%. (2) B Ltd and C Ltd cannot form another gains group as a company can not be a member of more than one gains group.

(b) To determine the composition of a group, overseas companies in the group are included. However, the advantages of being in a group only apply to the UK companies in the group.

Therefore, in the example above, if A Ltd was an overseas company there would be no difference in the definitions of the groups. However:

- H Ltd and B Ltd can take advantage of the capital gains provisions, but not with A Ltd (overseas).
- Only B Ltd and C Ltd can transfer losses to each other.

3.2 An outline of the advantages of being in a gains group

There are three key advantages of being in a gains group. These are the ability to:

- transfer capital assets between group companies at no gain / no loss
- claim group rollover relief, and
- transfer capital gains and losses between group companies.

Each of these advantages is now considered in more detail.

3.3 The treatment of intra-group transfers of capital assets

No chargeable gain or loss arises on transfers of capital assets between members of a gains group.

Assets are deemed to be transferred for a price equal to their cost to the transferor plus indexation up to the date of the transfer (or up to December 2017, if earlier). The actual sale proceeds, if any, are ignored for tax purposes.

This treatment is automatic (i.e. a claim is not required).

When the recipient company sells an asset outside the group at a later date, the normal chargeable gain computation applies, using the deemed acquisition cost as allowable expenditure.

Example

N Ltd owns 80% of O Ltd. Both companies prepare accounts to 31 March each year.

On 14 September 2016 N Ltd sold a warehouse to O Ltd for £200,000. Its market value at that date was £250,000. N Ltd had purchased the warehouse on 30 August 2005 for £120,000.

On 25 March 2023 O Ltd sold the warehouse for £300,000 to an unconnected company, P Ltd.

Required

Calculate the gains arising in the year ended 31 March 2017 and year ended 31 March 2023, assuming the relevant indexation factors are as follows:

August 2005 to September 2016	0.165
August 2005 to December 2017	0.601
September 2016 to December 2017	0.233

Answer

Year ended 31 March 2017: Intra-group transfer from N Ltd to O Ltd

	£
Deemed sale proceeds (ignore actual proceeds received. Use cost + IA)	139,800
Cost (August 2005)	(120,000)
Unindexed gain	19,800
IA on cost - from August 2005 to September 2016	
£120,000 x 0.165	(19,800)
Chargeable gain	Nil

Year ended 31 March 2023: Disposal by O Ltd outside the group to P Ltd

	£
Sale proceeds	300,000
Deemed cost	(139,800)
Unindexed gain	160,200
IA on cost - from September 2016 to December 2017	
£139,800 x 0.233	(32,573)
Chargeable gain arising in O Ltd	127,627

Note

Indexation allowance stops at December 2017.

Structures and buildings allowance

If an asset on which structures and buildings allowance has been claimed is transferred within a 75% gains group, the SBA due for the year of transfer is split between the vendor and the purchaser.

However, unlike with a normal SBA disposal, there is no clawback of SBA for the original owner via the capital gains computation. Instead, when the transferee eventually disposes of the SBA asset, all the SBAs claimed to date **by both the transferor and the transferee** are added to the building's disposal proceeds.

3.4 Claiming group rollover relief

For the purposes of rollover relief (replacement of business asset relief), a gains group is treated as a single entity.

Therefore, a gain arising on the disposal of a qualifying business asset (QBA) by one company in the group, can be deferred against the base cost of a replacement QBA acquired by another group company from outside the group.

The computation of rollover relief and the mechanics of deferral are the same as for a single company. (If all the sale proceeds are reinvested, all the gain can be deferred, etc).

Note, however, that both companies must make the rollover relief claim, and no gain / no loss transfers between group members do not count as acquisitions for the purpose of rollover relief.

3.5 Electing to make maximum usage of capital losses

Companies in a chargeable gains group can make an election to transfer the whole or part of any current period chargeable gain or allowable loss to another group member.

The election enables chargeable gains to be matched against capital losses.

The election must be made within two years of the end of the CAP in which the chargeable gain or loss arises. To be effective, both group companies must sign the election.

3.6 Tax planning: using capital losses

The capital gains provisions provide the opportunity to save corporation tax by making effective use of losses. In addition, gains may be deferred using rollover relief claims.

The primary aim of the group is usually to minimise the overall group tax liability.

The election to match gains and losses is flexible. Any amount of a gain or loss can be transferred in any direction to any other group company (or several companies).

Example

Q plc owns 100% of the ordinary share capital of R Ltd. Both companies make up their accounts to 31 March annually.

On 1 July 2022 Q plc sold a building, and this resulted in a capital gain of £120,000. On 2 January 2023 R Ltd sold a factory, and this resulted in a capital loss of £55,000.

As at 31 March 2022 R Ltd had unused capital losses of £50,000.

Required

Explain what the group should do to minimise its corporation tax liability for the year ended 31 March 2023.

Answer

Q plc and R Ltd should make an election to transfer Q plc's gain to R Ltd.

The election must be made by 31 March 2025. It will enable R Ltd to relieve both of its capital losses. The balance of the gain £15,000 (120,000 – 55,000 – 50,000) will then be taxed in the hands of R Ltd.

Alternatively, the election could transfer only £105,000 of the gain to R Ltd. The balance would then be taxed in the hands of Q plc.

Taxation – United Kingdom
(TX-UK) FA2022

CHAPTER 25

Value Added Tax

Contents

1 Overview of Value Added Tax
2 VAT registration
3 Accounting for VAT
4 VAT returns and penalties
5 Schemes for small businesses
6 Imports and exports

> **Overview of Value Added Tax**
>
> - The scope of VAT
> - Taxable person
> - Taxable supplies
> - Rates of VAT
> - The mechanics of VAT

1 Overview of Value Added Tax

1.1 The scope of VAT

Value Added Tax (VAT) is an indirect tax levied on the final consumers (or end consumers) of goods and services in the UK.

VAT is charged on the **taxable supply** of goods and services in the UK by a **taxable person** in the course or furtherance of a business carried on by them.

1.2 Taxable person

A taxable person is a person who is registered for VAT (or who is required to be registered for VAT).

A person in this context is a sole trader, a partnership, a company, a club, association or charity.

1.3 Taxable supplies

A taxable supply is any supply of goods or services made in the UK other than **exempt supplies** or those **outside the scope of VAT**.

The following supplies are the main examples of supplies that are **exempt from VAT**:

- Land and buildings (except for the sale of new buildings, residential buildings and those used for charitable purposes)
- Insurance premiums
- Postal services
- Financial services, such as banking
- Education services provided by state schools, colleges and universities
- Health and welfare services provided by NHS-registered doctors, dentists, hospitals and pharmacies
- Burial/cremation services
- Subscriptions to professional bodies.

The main supplies that are **outside the scope of VAT** are as follows:

- Wages and salaries
- Dividends
- The sale of a business as a going concern.

It is important to appreciate that no VAT is charged on exempt supplies or on supplies outside the scope of VAT. These supplies are ignored in determining whether a person should register for VAT.

By definition, taxable supplies are any other supplies of goods and services that are not exempt or not outside the scope of VAT. However, there are three types of taxable supply, each taxable at a different rate of VAT.

1.4 Rates of VAT

Taxable supplies may be:

- standard-rated
- reduced-rated, or
- zero-rated.

Reduced-rated taxable supplies

The reduced rate of VAT is 5%. The main reduced-rated supplies are as follows:

- Domestic fuel and power
- Installation of energy-saving materials.

Zero-rated taxable supplies

The zero rate generally applies to supplies of goods and services that are considered to be essential requirements. The main zero-rated supplies are:

- Food for human and animal consumption, except for:
    - food supplied in the course of catering (e.g. in restaurants, hotels etc),
    - luxury food (e.g. sweets and chocolate biscuits),
    - pet foods and
    - hot take-away food
- Books and newspapers
- Construction of new residential buildings or those used for charitable purposes
- Prescription drugs and medicines and aids for the disabled
- Children's clothing and footwear
- Exports of goods.

Zero-rated supplies are taxable supplies, but the VAT rate charged is 0%. Therefore, no VAT is charged. However (unlike exempt supplies or supplies outside the scope of VAT) zero-rated supplies are considered in determining whether a person should be registered for VAT.

The standard rate of VAT

The standard rate applies to any other supply of goods and services not listed above.

The standard rate of VAT is calculated as:

- 20% of the VAT exclusive (or net) price, or
- 1/6 (i.e. 20/120) of the VAT inclusive (or gross) price.

1.5 The mechanics of VAT

VAT is a tax on the final consumer of goods and services. It is levied at the point of sale.

HMRC could collect all the tax from the final retailer at the end of the production and distribution process. However, rather than waiting until the final sale of the end product or service, HMRC requires all businesses that are required to be registered for VAT to account for VAT **at each stage** in the production and distribution process.

Every business liable to charge VAT must therefore charge VAT on its supplies, such as its sales. This is known as **output VAT**. It must pay the output VAT to HMRC, usually on a quarterly basis.

However, as the business is not the final consumer of the goods and services, it can recover any VAT that it has paid to its suppliers on its raw material purchases and other expenses. These VAT payments are known as **input VAT**.

A VAT-registered business therefore only pays HMRC the difference between its output and input VAT.

VAT-registered businesses are therefore acting as collectors of tax on behalf of HMRC and only account for the tax on the value that they have added to the product in that stage of the production and distribution process. (This is how the name of the tax was derived.)

> **VAT registration**
>
> - Compulsory registration
> - Exemption from registration
> - Voluntary registration
> - Group registration
> - Deregistration
> - Transfer as a going concern

2 VAT registration

2.1 Compulsory registration

A person is required to register for VAT if they make taxable supplies in excess of the VAT threshold of £85,000. This VAT registration threshold is given in the tax rates and allowances table in the examination.

Failure to register for VAT is an offence. Penalties may be payable and any outstanding VAT that **should have been accounted for** from the compulsory effective registration date will be payable to HMRC.

There are two circumstances where compulsory registration is required. These are where the business exceeds the VAT threshold, based on:

- **historical** taxable supplies (known as the historical test)
- taxable supplies in the **following 30 days** (known as the future test).

Historical test rules

The historical test rules are as follows:

(1) A **person must register for VAT** if, at the end of any month, their turnover of taxable supplies in the 12 months ending on that date has exceeded the threshold of £85,000.

(2) **Exception to this rule.** A person is not required to register for VAT in these circumstances if their taxable turnover in the next 12 months is not expected to exceed the deregistration threshold of £83,000. Deregistration is explained later.

(3) **Taxable supplies** are the total of all standard-rated, zero-rated and reduced-rated supplies, **but excluding** supplies of capital items (for example, sales of non-current assets of the business).

(4) HMRC must be notified within 30 days of the end of the month in which the threshold is exceeded.

(5) The newly-registered person must charge VAT from the first day after the end of the month in which notification to HMRC is required, or an earlier agreed date.

Taxation - United Kingdom (TX-UK) FA2022

Example

Kim commenced trading on 1 January 2022. In the first four months of trading her sales totalled £3,000 per month. All her sales are standard-rated supplies. Thereafter her sales have been as follows:

2022	£	2023	£
May	4,100	January	9,800
June	4,200	February	10,100
July	4,400	March	10,900
August	5,000	April	11,700
September	5,600	May	12,800
October	6,700	June	13,500
November	7,100		
December	8,600		

Required

State:

(a) when it is compulsory for Kim to register for VAT

(b) when she must notify HMRC and

(c) the first date she should start to charge VAT on her invoices.

Answer

12 months ended	Workings	Taxable supplies
		£
31 December 2022	(4 × £3,000) + £4,100 + £4,200 + £4,400 + £5,000 + £5,600 + £6,700 + £7,100 + £8,600	57,700
31 January 2023	£57,700 - £3,000 + £9,800	64,500
28 February 2023	£64,500 - £3,000 + £10,100	71,600
31 March 2023	£71,600 - £3,000 + £10,900	79,500
30 April 2023	£79,500 - £3,000 + £11,700	88,200

Kim exceeded the £85,000 threshold on 30 April 2023. She is therefore required to register for VAT.

She must notify HMRC by 30 May 2023 (i.e. 30 days after the end of the month in which the threshold is exceeded).

She must start to charge VAT from 1 June 2023 (i.e. the first day of the month after notification).

Future test rules

The future test rules are as follows:

(1) A **person must register for VAT** if at any time there are reasonable grounds to believe that their taxable turnover in the next 30 days **in isolation** will exceed £85,000.

(2) HMRC must be notified **within** the 30-day period in which it is thought that the threshold will be exceeded.

(3) The newly-registered person must charge VAT from the **first day** of the 30-day period in which it is thought that the threshold will be exceeded, or an earlier agreed date.

This test is less likely to be satisfied than the historical test. It only applies if the business has on average a taxable turnover of less than £7,000 per month but then receives a large order or signs a large contract in excess of £85,000 to be completed in the next month.

Example

Kelly commenced trading on 1 March 2022 making taxable supplies of £5,000 a month. On 8 September 2022 she signed a contract for £88,000 for work to be completed by the end of the month.

Required

State:

(a) when it is compulsory for Kelly to register for VAT

(b) when she must notify HMRC and

(c) the first date from which she should start to charge VAT on her invoices.

Answer

On 8 September 2022, Kelly believes that she will exceed the threshold in the next 30 days, therefore she must register for VAT.

Kelly must notify HMRC by 8 October 2022 (i.e. by the end of the 30 day period in which it is thought that the threshold will be exceeded).

She must start to charge VAT from 8 September 2022 (i.e. the first day of the 30 day period).

Note: The historical test is checked **at the end of every month**. The future test should be considered **every day**.

Registration certificate and VAT registration number

When a person registers for VAT, HMRC will issue a registration certificate and a VAT registration number. This number must appear on the business invoices and other documentation from the effective date of registration.

2.2 Exemption from registration

When a person makes taxable supplies in excess of the VAT threshold, VAT registration is compulsory. However, where the taxable supplies are **all zero-rated**, HMRC will allow the person exemption from registration.

The advantage of exemption from registration is that the business does not have to incur the administrative burden and costs of accounting for VAT.

Remember, however, that a zero-rated business will not charge any output VAT on its sales, but can recover its input VAT suffered. Therefore, if it claims the exemption and does not register for VAT, it will be unable to recover its input VAT.

A taxable person is therefore only likely to claim the exemption if they do not have significant amounts of input VAT to recover, so that the benefits of recovering the input VAT paid are less than the administrative costs of accounting for VAT.

2.3 Voluntary registration

A person who makes taxable supplies below the VAT threshold is not required to register for VAT. However, they can choose to register voluntarily.

Advantages of voluntary registration

The main advantage of voluntary registration is that input VAT can be recovered from HMRC on purchases and expenses. This will save money for the business by reducing the cost of its purchases by the amount of the input VAT.

It is particularly advantageous to register **if the business is zero-rated**, as it can recover input VAT but does not have to pay output VAT as it is charged at 0%.

In this situation the business will receive regular repayments of VAT from HMRC. These will help the cash flow of the business.

A possible further advantage of voluntary registration is that being VAT-registered may suggest to third parties that the business has a taxable turnover of at least £85,000, giving them a perception of an enduring, sizeable and successful business.

Disadvantages of voluntary registration

Registering for VAT will mean that the business is required to maintain up-to-date accurate accounting records. The administrative burden of accounting for VAT to HMRC will increase the costs of running the business.

The business must charge VAT on sales, adding to the amounts payable by customers. However, this is not a disadvantage if:

- the business is zero-rated (and so does not charge any VAT), or
- all customers are VAT-registered and so can recover the VAT charged (as their input VAT).

However, if customers are not VAT-registered (e.g. members of the general public) they cannot recover the VAT charged and so have to suffer the VAT payable in the prices they pay. In this situation, the business has a choice between two unwelcome options:

- It may keep its total selling prices, by reducing the net-of-VAT sales prices. This means in effect that it absorbs the cost of the VAT itself and reduces its profit margins.
- Alternatively, it may add VAT to its normal selling prices. This will risk losing customers to competitor businesses that are not VAT-registered and so can sell at a lower price.

2.4 Group registration

Two or more companies can elect for group registration provided that:

- each company is either established in the UK or has a fixed place of business in the UK, and
- they are under common control or one of them controls the other. (Control requires the ownership of over 50% of the company's share capital, and the controller may be a company, sole trader or a partnership.)

An application for group registration takes immediate effect, although HMRC have 90 days in which they can refuse the application. They will normally only refuse or cancel group registration where:

- the companies concerned are ineligible for group registration, or
- membership would pose a threat to VAT revenue.

It is not necessary for all eligible companies to be members of a VAT group. It may, for example, be advisable to leave out companies making zero-rated supplies as their refund of VAT would be used to offset any VAT payable by the group.

The effect of group registration

The group appoints a representative member to be responsible for submitting VAT returns and paying VAT on behalf of the group. However, all group members are jointly and severally liable for any VAT due.

Supplies between group members are ignored.

Only one VAT return is submitted for the whole group. This should, in theory, cut down on the amount of administration involved. However, collating the information from the various group members may prove problematic.

One further disadvantage is that the various limits, such as those for the cash and annual accounting schemes (see later), apply to the group as a whole rather than to each individual member.

2.5 Deregistration

Compulsory deregistration

A person is required to deregister for VAT when they **cease to make taxable supplies**.

Notification must be given to HMRC within 30 days of ceasing to make taxable supplies. Deregistration is effective from the date when taxable supplies cease or an agreed later date.

Deregistration is also required when the status of the business changes (for example, from a sole trader to a company).

Voluntary deregistration

Voluntary deregistration is allowed if at any time:

- there are reasonable grounds for a registered person to estimate that their taxable supplies in the **next 12 months** will not exceed the deregistration threshold of £83,000, and
- the fall in value of taxable supplies is not due to a **temporary** reduction.

In this situation, deregistration will be effective from the date on which the request for deregistration is made or an agreed later date.

The deregistration threshold is given in the tax rates and allowances table in the examination.

Consequences of deregistration

On deregistration there is a **deemed supply** of all of the business assets held by the business on the last day of registration. VAT is therefore charged on the non-current assets (except cars) and inventory owned by the business on which input VAT has been recovered in previous VAT returns.

Output VAT is charged on this deemed supply at the standard rate unless the amount of VAT payable is less than £1,000, in which case it is ignored.

2.6 Transfer as a going concern

Where a business is transferred/sold as a going concern, no VAT is charged as long as the following conditions are satisfied:

- The whole business (or a significant part of a business which is capable of independent operation) is transferred as a going concern.
- There is no significant break in the normal trading pattern.
- The assets continue to be used in the same type of trade.
- The transferee business is already VAT-registered or will become registered immediately after the transfer.

Note that it is possible for the new purchaser to take over the same VAT registration number, but this will involve taking over the past VAT history of the business and so it is probably better for the new owner to reregister the business.

Example

HT Ltd has been registered for VAT since 2007, but intends to cease trading on 31 March 2023. On the cessation of trade, HT Ltd can either sell its non-current assets on a piecemeal basis to individual purchasers, or it can sell its entire business as a going concern to a single purchaser.

Required

Outline the VAT consequences of each course of action.

Answer

Sale of assets on a piecemeal basis

- HT Ltd will cease to make taxable supplies so its VAT registration will be cancelled on 31 March 2023 or an agreed later date.

- The company will have to notify HMRC by 30 April 2023 (i.e. 30 days after the date of cessation).

- Output VAT must be charged in respect of the non-current assets sold, unless the VAT amounts to less than £1,000.

Sale of business as a going concern

- A sale of a business as a going concern is not treated as a taxable supply for VAT, and therefore output VAT is not due on the sale of the business assets.

- If the purchaser is already registered for VAT then HT Ltd's VAT registration will be cancelled, as above.

- If the purchaser is not registered for VAT then it can take over the VAT registration of HT Ltd, if it wishes.

> **Accounting for VAT**
>
> - Principles of VAT accounting
> - Output VAT
> - Input VAT
> - Tax point
> - Relief for impairment losses on trade debts
> - Proforma computation: VAT accounting

3 Accounting for VAT

3.1 Principles of VAT accounting

For each return period, every business liable to charge VAT:

- charges output VAT on its taxable supplies
- recovers input VAT on its raw material purchases and other expenses
- completes a VAT return and submits it to HMRC
- accounts to HMRC for any VAT payable if there is excess output VAT (if output VAT exceeds input VAT) for the return period
- claims a repayment of excess input VAT (if input VAT exceeds output VAT) for the return period.

3.2 Output VAT

Output VAT is charged on taxable supplies of goods and services.

The main types of taxable supply of **goods** are as follows:

- Sales of goods (for a consideration, usually a money payment)
- Gifts of business assets (excluding gifts to the same person that total no more than £50 excluding VAT in any 12-month period and gifts of trade samples)
- Goods permanently withdrawn from the business by the owner or an employee
- Import of goods into the UK.

The main types of taxable supply of **services** are as follows:

- Sales of services (for consideration)
- Hiring goods to a customer
- Temporary private use of business assets by the owner or an employee
- Private use of services supplied by the business to the owner or an employee
- Provision of private fuel for the owner or an employee.

Note that the **gift of services** and the **private use of cars** are **not** taxable supplies.

Output VAT is charged at the appropriate rate on the value of the taxable supply.

The value of taxable supplies is straightforward where there is a sale at arm's length for full consideration. VAT is charged at the appropriate rate on the sale price (excluding VAT).

Special rules apply to the following supplies:

- **Gifts of business assets**: The value of the taxable supply is the replacement price (i.e. the price that would be payable by the person making the supply, at the time of the supply, to replace the goods with identical items, taking account of the age and condition of the goods gifted).

- **Private use of business assets**: The value of the taxable supply is the cost to the taxable person providing the service.

- **Private fuel**: Scale rates are set by HMRC (see below).

- **Discounts:** Output VAT is calculated on the full price of the goods or services less any trade discounts.

    If the customer is offered a prompt payment discount and takes advantage of it, the supplier can issue a credit note as evidence of the reduction in consideration.

    Alternatively, if the supplier does not wish to issue credit notes, its invoices must clearly state the terms of the discount and it must retain proof of receipt of the discounted price in order to account for the reduced amount of output tax.

3.3 Input VAT

Input VAT can usually be recovered if:
- the goods or services purchased are used for business purposes, and
- the expenditure is supported by a valid VAT invoice.

Where expenditure is partly for business and partly for private purposes, the input VAT is apportioned and only the business proportion is recoverable according to the rules explained below.

The amount of input VAT that can be recovered depends on the type of taxable supplies made by the business, as follows:

If the business makes	Input VAT recovery
Wholly taxable supplies	All input VAT is recoverable, except for blocked items.
Wholly exempt supplies	Recoverable input VAT = £Nil. A person making wholly exempt supplies is not a taxable person, cannot register for VAT, does not charge VAT on its output and cannot recover any input VAT.
Partly taxable/partly exempt supplies	This person is a partially exempt trader and special rules apply for the recovery of input VAT. These rules are outside the syllabus for this examination.

Blocked items

Blocked items are items of expenditure where the VAT is irrecoverable. The main types of blocked items are as follows:

- the private use apportionment of input VAT on expenditure incurred for both business and private purposes
- the purchase of cars, whether used for private purposes or not, but excluding cars purchased exclusively for business purposes (e.g. pool cars, taxis, self-drive hire cars, and driving school cars)
- entertaining costs (excluding staff entertaining). However, it is possible to recover input tax on the costs of entertaining **overseas customers**.

Motoring expenses

Provided there is some business use of a car, the full amount of input VAT can be recovered on repair and maintenance costs. It can also be recovered on accessories for business use that are fitted after the original purchase of the car.

If private fuel is provided to the owner or an employee, the input VAT is not apportioned. **All** the input VAT on the cost of the fuel paid by the business is recoverable, but output VAT must be charged for the provision of private fuel to the owner or employee.

There are two ways of charging output VAT in respect of private fuel:

- by using the scale charges specified in the legislation. (If required, the appropriate fuel scale rate will be given in an examination question.)
- by charging the employee for the cost of the private fuel provided to them and calculating the output VAT on the amount charged.

Alternatively, the output VAT charge can be avoided if **no claim** is made for any input VAT on fuel or if the business keeps detailed mileage records to enable it to prove that the fuel it has bought has only been used for business purposes.

Example

Holly is a director of her personal company, Holly Ltd. The company owns a car which Holly uses for both business and private mileage. The total cost of fuel used each quarter is £810, of which 40% is for private mileage. The relevant quarterly scale charge is £402. Both figures are inclusive of VAT.

Required

Calculate the input and output VAT that Holly Ltd must account for in respect of fuel.

Answer

If Holly does not reimburse the company for the private fuel, then Holly Ltd will claim input VAT of £135 (810 x 20/120) and will have to account for output VAT of £67 (402 x 20/120) based on the scale charge.

If Holly pays the company £324 (810 x 40%) for the private fuel, then Holly Ltd will claim input VAT of £135 and will have to account for output VAT of £54 (324 x 20/120) based on the charge paid by Holly.

Pre-registration expenditure

Input VAT suffered on business expenditure incurred prior to registration can be recovered if the following conditions are satisfied:

- If goods, they must have been acquired in the four years prior to registration and still be owned by the business on the date of registration
- If services, they must have been supplied no more than six months before the date of registration.

3.4 Tax point

The tax point date (TPD) is important for two reasons:

- Accounting for VAT is based on a return period. Output VAT is accounted for in the return period in which the TPD of the supply falls. Input VAT can be recovered in the return period in which the TPD of the purchase occurs. The definition of the TPD is therefore important in determining in which return the VAT is accounted for.
- VAT is charged at the rate in force on the TPD. The definition of the TPD is therefore important if there is a change in the rate of VAT.

The basic tax point date (BTPD) is as follows:

- for goods: the date the goods are despatched or otherwise made available to the customer
- for services: the date the service is completed.

However, the actual tax point date (ATPD) can be before or after the BTPD as follows:

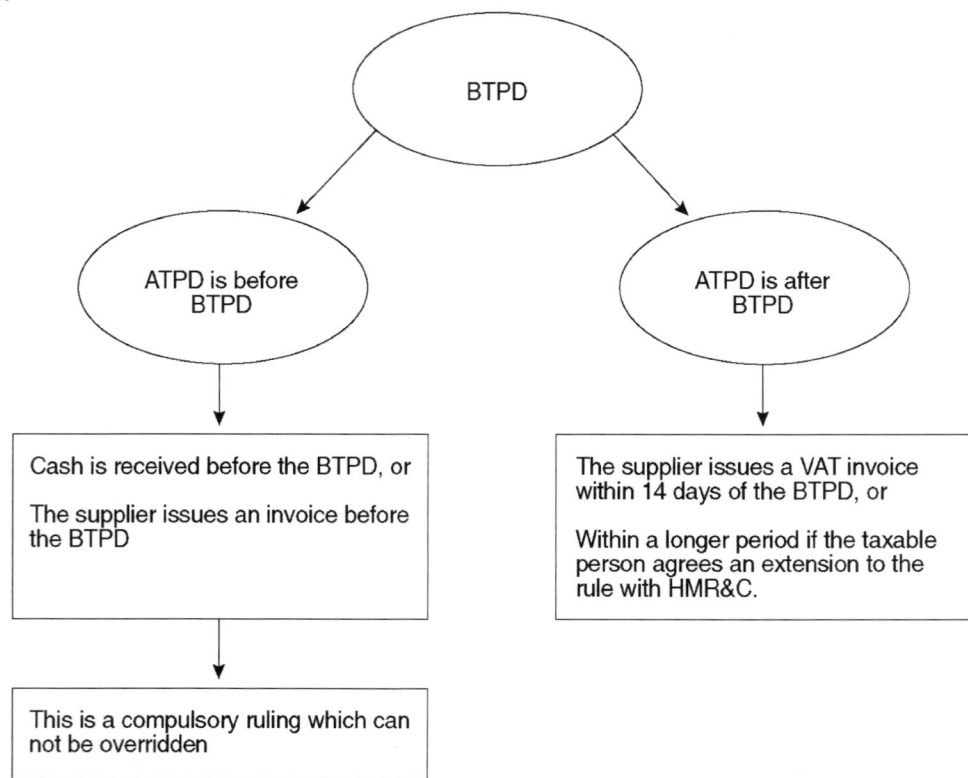

```
                    ┌─────────┐
                    │  BTPD   │
                    └────┬────┘
              ┌──────────┴──────────┐
              ▼                     ▼
      ┌──────────────┐      ┌──────────────┐
      │ ATPD is before│      │ ATPD is after│
      │    BTPD      │      │    BTPD      │
      └──────┬───────┘      └──────┬───────┘
             ▼                     ▼
```

| Cash is received before the BTPD, or

The supplier issues an invoice before the BTPD | The supplier issues a VAT invoice within 14 days of the BTPD, or

Within a longer period if the taxable person agrees an extension to the rule with HMR&C. |

This is a compulsory ruling which can not be overridden

Many businesses agree a **month-end invoicing rule**. This allows the business to invoice all sales at the month end and treat the invoice date as the TPD.

3.5 Relief for impairment losses on trade debts

Output VAT is accounted for on the TPD of the supply. This is usually the invoice date, not the date on which cash is received.

If a customer does not pay for a supply, the business can claim relief for its impairment loss if the following conditions are satisfied:

- The debt is more than six months overdue (measured from the date that the payment was due under the supplier's terms of sale)
- The output VAT has been accounted for and paid to HMRC
- The impairment loss has been written off in the financial accounts
- A claim is made for relief within four years from the date the loss becomes eligible for relief (i.e. four years and six months from the date that payment was due).

Relief is given in the VAT return by claiming input VAT equal to the amount of output VAT charged on the original irrecoverable debt.

Chapter 25: Value Added Tax

3.6 Proforma computation: VAT accounting

The following proforma should be used to calculate the amount of VAT payable or recoverable for a return period.

VAT return for the quarter ended:	£
Output VAT	
Cash and credit sales (including sales of capital assets apart from cars)	X
Withdrawals of inventory by owner or an employee	X
Gifts of business assets if in excess of £50 per recipient	X
Private use of business assets by owner or an employee	X
Private fuel supplied to owner or an employee	X
	X
Input VAT	
Cash and credit purchases of goods	(X)
Cash and credit purchases of capital assets (excluding cars)	(X)
Expenses	(X)
(including repairs and maintenance, car expenses, full cost of fuel)	
(excluding blocked items such as entertaining and items outside of the scope of VAT, such as wages and salaries)	
Relief for impairment losses	(X)
Amount payable to / (repayable by) HMRC	X/(X)
Due date:	
One month and seven days following the end of the return period	

Example

Lena is registered for VAT, and is in the process of completing her VAT return for the quarter ended 31 March 2023.

The following information is available:

- Sales invoices totalling £128,000 were issued in respect of standard-rated sales. Lena offers her customers a 2.5% discount for prompt payment. 50% of her customers take up the discount. Lena's invoices include the wording required by HMRC in respect of discounts and she accounts for VAT on the actual amounts received.

- Standard-rated materials costing £32,400 were purchased, of which £600 were taken by Lena for her personal use.

- Standard-rated expenses amounting to £24,800 were incurred. This includes £1,200 for entertaining UK customers and £2,500 for entertaining overseas customers.

- On 15 March 2023, Lena purchased a car at a cost of £16,450 for use by a sales manager, and machinery at a cost of £21,150. Both of these figures are inclusive of VAT. The car is used for both business and private mileage.

- On 31 March 2023, Lena wrote off £12,000 due from a customer who had gone into liquidation. The debt was in respect of three invoices, each of £4,000, that were due for payment on 15 May, 15 June and 15 November 2022 respectively.

- During the quarter ended 31 March 2023, £600 was spent on mobile telephone calls, of which 40% related to private calls.

Unless stated otherwise, all of the above figures are exclusive of VAT.

Required

Calculate the amount of VAT payable for the quarter ended 31 March 2023 and state the due date of payment.

Answer

VAT return for the quarter ended: 31 March 2023

	Note	£
Output VAT		
Sales (£128,000 × 50% × 20%)		12,800
Sales (£128,000 × 50% x 97.5% × 20%)	1	12,480
Withdrawals of inventory by Lena (£600 × 20%)	2	120
		25,400
Input VAT		
Purchases of goods (£32,400 × 20%)		(6,480)
Purchase of machinery (£21,150 × 20/120)	3	(3,525)
Expenses (£24,800 - £1,200) × 20%	4	(4,720)
Mobile phone calls (£600 × 60% × 20%)	5	(72)
Relief for impairment losses (£8,000 × 20%)	6	(1,600)
Amount payable to HMRC		9,003

Due date: 7 May 2023

Tutorial notes

(1) If Lena had not given details of the prompt payment discount on her invoices, output VAT would have been calculated on the full price. Lena would then have had to issue a credit note to reclaim the VAT on the prompt payment discount.

(2) The withdrawal of inventory by the owner is a deemed supply based on the replacement value, which is assumed in this case to be the cost of £600.

(3) Input VAT on the purchase of the car is irrecoverable.

(4) Input VAT on entertaining UK customers is irrecoverable. However, Lena may recover the input tax incurred on entertaining overseas customers.

(5) An apportionment is made where a service is partly for business and partly for private use, such as mobile phone calls.

(6) Relief for impairment losses is not given until six months have elapsed from the time that payment is due. Therefore, relief can only be claimed in respect of the invoices due for payment on 15 May and 15 June 2022.

Chapter 25: Value Added Tax

> **VAT returns and penalties**
> - VAT returns
> - VAT payments
> - VAT records
> - VAT invoices
> - Default surcharge
> - Default interest
> - Errors in VAT returns

4 VAT returns and penalties

4.1 VAT returns

All businesses, apart from those using the annual accounting scheme, must file their VAT returns on-line within one month and seven days following the end of the return period. For example, a quarterly return to 31 July 2022 must be submitted by 7 September 2022.

Most businesses account for VAT on a quarterly basis. However, monthly accounting is allowed by HMRC on request. Businesses making wholly zero-rated supplies usually prefer monthly accounting as they are in a regular repayment situation and prefer monthly repayments to quarterly repayments.

All VAT-registered businesses must use Making Tax Digital (MTD) compatible software to submit their VAT returns.

4.2 VAT payments

Businesses must normally pay any VAT due electronically within one month and seven days following the end of the return period, i.e. by the filing date for the return.

Any repayment due from HMRC will normally be made within 14 days of the end of the return period. However, HMRC will not refund VAT that was originally paid more than four years earlier.

Very large traders with an annual VAT liability of more than £2.3 million **must pay VAT by instalments** as follows:

Payment date	Nature of the payment
At the end of the second month in a quarter	Payment on account
At the end of the last month in a quarter	Payment on account
At the end of the first month in next quarter	Balancing payment

Each payment on account is 1/24th of the annual VAT liability for the period in which the threshold is exceeded. The amount payable on account is reviewed annually. (There is no seven-day extension to the end of the month rule for the

© Emile Woolf International Limited

payment of the tax.) Alternatively, traders may elect to make monthly VAT payments based on their actual liability for the previous month.

4.3 VAT records

A taxable person is required to keep accurate records and accounts of all transactions to support output and input VAT on the VAT returns (unless it is a member of the flat rate scheme).

Records must be retained for at least six years. The records that must be kept include:

- Sales and purchase invoices
- Sales and purchase day books
- Cash book, bank statements, paying in slips
- VAT accounts and returns
- Annual statements of profit or loss and balance sheets.

The Making Tax Digital rules require traders to keep their VAT records digitally. The software package used can then submit the return directly to HMRC or use bridging software to do so.

4.4 VAT invoices

A VAT invoice must be issued when a taxable person makes a taxable supply to another taxable person, within 30 days of the supply of the goods or services.

A VAT invoice is not required, but may be issued, when the supply is made to a person who is not registered for VAT or the supply is zero-rated. For example, retailers to the general public are only required to issue a VAT invoice if requested to do so by the customer.

To be valid, a **VAT invoice** must normally contain the following information:

(1) invoice date and invoice number
(2) type of supply
(3) quantity and description of the goods supplied
(4) name and address of the supplier
(5) name and address of the customer
(6) details of any prompt payment discounts offered
(7) VAT registration number
(8) tax point date

(9) rate of VAT for each supply

(10) VAT-exclusive amount for each supply

(11) total VAT-exclusive amount

(12) amount of VAT payable.

Less detailed VAT invoices can be issued by all traders if the taxable supply is no more than £250 (including VAT). A simplified VAT invoice must contain the following information:

(1) name and address of the supplier

(2) supplier's VAT registration number

(3) tax point date

(4) description of the goods or services supplied

(5) rate of VAT for each supply

(6) VAT inclusive total.

4.5 Default surcharge

A default surcharge may be levied where a VAT return is submitted late or the payment of VAT is late.

The mechanics of the default surcharge system are as follows:

- A surcharge liability notice is issued when the return or payment is made late. The notice specifies a default notice period which is normally 12 months.

- If a further default occurs within the default notice period (i.e. another return is submitted late or another payment is made late):

    (a) A default surcharge is levied at the following rates:

Number of defaults	Surcharge = appropriate % of tax paid late
1	2%
2	5%
3	10%
4	15%

    (b) The default notice period is extended by another 12 months.

HMRC do not collect the surcharge at the 2% or 5% rate if it is less than £400. However, there is a minimum charge of £30 at the 10% and 15% rates.

Note that the rates of surcharge are not provided in the examination.

Taxation – United Kingdom (TX-UK) FA2022

Example

SQ Ltd has submitted its VAT returns as follows:

Quarter ended	VAT paid £	Date return submitted and VAT paid
30 September 2021	3,100	5 December 2021
31 December 2021	11,300	2 March 2022
31 March 2022	4,300	25 April 2022
30 June 2022	7,600	24 July 2022
30 September 2022	1,900	25 October 2022
31 December 2022	3,200	27 January 2023

Required

Explain whether a default surcharge will be levied on SQ Ltd.

Answer

The 30 September 2021 return is submitted late. A surcharge liability notice will be issued, specifying a default notice period of 12 months to 30 September 2022.

The 31 December 2021 return is also submitted late and therefore:

- a default surcharge of £226 (2% × £11,300) will be levied, but not collected by HMRC as it is below £400, and
- the default notice period will be extended to 31 December 2022.

The next four returns are all submitted on time. Therefore, no default surcharges are levied and the default notice period expires.

Businesses with a turnover below £150,000 are not issued with a surcharge liability notice on their first default. Instead, HMRC issue a letter offering help. It is only if the business makes a further default within the following 12 months that a surcharge liability notice is issued. This modification to the system effectively allows small businesses to make an additional default before they enter the surcharge system.

4.6 Default interest

Default interest may be charged where VAT has been underdeclared or overclaimed. It will not normally be charged where the underpaid VAT could have been immediately reclaimed as input VAT by someone else as in that situation there has been no loss of revenue to the Government.

The interest will run for a maximum of three years from the date the VAT should have been paid to the date HMRC calculate the interest due. It is not deductible in calculating the trader's taxable profits.

4.7 Errors in VAT returns

Because VAT is a self-assessed tax, HMRC can make control visits to VAT registered businesses. The purpose of a control visit is to provide HMRC with an opportunity to check the accuracy of VAT returns.

However, if a taxpayer notices a misdeclaration or error before an investigation by HMRC, and the net effect of the misdeclaration/error does not exceed the higher of:

- £10,000 or
- 1% of the turnover for the VAT period (up to a maximum of £50,000),

the trader is allowed to correct the mistake in the next VAT return. No separate disclosure is required and no interest will be charged.

If the net effect exceeds the above limits, separate disclosure to HMRC is required and interest will be charged.

A penalty may be imposed in both of the above cases. It is determined according to the same penalty regime that applies to incorrect self-assessment income tax and corporation tax returns. (See chapter 17.) Note, however, that correcting the error on a later VAT return does not constitute an unprompted disclosure and so businesses are advised to make a separate full disclosure to HMRC in order to obtain a reduced penalty.

> **Schemes for small businesses**
>
> - Overview of the schemes available for small businesses
> - The cash accounting scheme
> - The annual accounting scheme
> - The flat rate scheme

5 Schemes for small businesses

5.1 Overview of the schemes available for small businesses

There are three schemes available to help small businesses account for VAT: the cash accounting, annual accounting and flat rate schemes.

They all aim to simplify VAT accounting, reduce administration and help cash flow.

All these schemes are optional. A small business is not obliged to join any scheme, but may find it advantageous to do so.

5.2 The cash accounting scheme

Under the cash accounting scheme, small businesses account for VAT when cash is paid and received, rather than on the tax point dates.

As a result, the business does not have to pay VAT until it has received the cash from its customers. It therefore receives automatic relief for its impairment losses if a customer does not pay. The business should, however, be aware that it can only reclaim input tax once it has actually paid the relevant expense. This may delay input tax recovery if goods are purchased on credit.

A business can only join the cash accounting scheme if:

- its taxable supplies in the next 12 months are not expected to exceed £1,350,000
- it is up to date with its VAT returns and has paid all outstanding VAT liabilities
- it has not been convicted of any VAT offences, assessed for penalties for VAT evasion nor denied entry into the scheme in the last 12 months.

Taxable supplies in this context means the value of taxable supplies excluding VAT and capital items.

Once it is a member of the scheme, a business may continue to use the scheme until the value of its taxable supplies in the previous 12 months exceeds £1,600,000.

5.3 The annual accounting scheme

Under the annual accounting scheme, small businesses submit only one VAT return each year and spread their payments of VAT evenly throughout the year. This may help cash flow.

The mechanics of the annual accounting scheme are as follows:

- HMRC estimate the total VAT liability for the year, based on the previous year.
- Nine equal monthly payments on account are made by direct debit.
- Each of these payments on account (POAs) is equal to 1/10th of the total estimated liability. They are paid on the last day of every month starting in the 4th month and finishing on the last day of the 12th month.
- A balancing payment and the annual VAT return are submitted to HMRC within **two months** of the end of the year.

A business can apply to make quarterly POAs of 25% of the total estimated liability at the end of the 4th, 7th and 10th months, rather than making monthly POAs. The balancing payment will be made within two months of the end of the year.

A business can only join the annual accounting scheme if it is up to date with its VAT payments and its taxable supplies in the next 12 months are not expected to exceed £1,350,000.

A business may remain a member of the scheme until the value of its taxable supplies in the previous 12 months exceeds £1,600,000.

Taxable supplies in this context means the value of taxable supplies excluding VAT and capital items.

Example

GF plc has taxable supplies of £392,500 each year and joined the annual accounting scheme in 2009. On 1 September 2021 HMRC estimated its total VAT liability for the year ended 31 August 2022 as £15,950.

Required

Calculate the payments GF plc had to make in respect of the year ended 31 August 2022, stating the due dates for payment assuming the final VAT liability is agreed at £20,250.

Answer

POAs: $1/10^{th} \times £15,950 = £1,595$ per month

Balancing payment = £20,250 – (9 × £1,595) = £5,895

Payments to be made in respect of the year end 31 August 2022:

			£
POA 1	31 December 2021	Last day of 4th month	1,595
POA 2	31 January 2022	Last day of 5th month	1,595
POA 3	28 February 2022	Last day of 6th month	1,595
POA 4	31 March 2022	Last day of 7th month	1,595
POA 5	30 April 2022	Last day of 8th month	1,595
POA 6	31 May 2022	Last day of 9th month	1,595
POA 7	30 June 2022	Last day of 10th month	1,595
POA 8	31 July 2022	Last day of 11th month	1,595
POA 9	31 August 2022	Last day of 12th month	1,595
Total POAs			14,355
Balancing payment 31 October 2022		Last day of 2nd month after year end	5,895
Total agreed VAT liability for the year ended 31 August 2022			20,250

5.4 The flat rate scheme

The flat rate scheme simplifies the preparation of the VAT return by allowing small businesses to account for VAT at a flat rate percentage of VAT-**inclusive** turnover, instead of accounting for VAT on every individual sale and purchase.

The flat rate percentages

The flat rate percentage to apply depends on the trade sector in which the business operates. The flat rates normally range from 4% to 14.5% and have been calculated based on HMRC's past experience of the average level of recovery of VAT for different types of business sectors.

There is a flat rate of 16.5% for those businesses classed as limited cost traders. These are businesses which incur a low amount of expenditure on goods.

If required, the appropriate flat rate percentage will be given in the body of a question in the examination. ACCA have confirmed that questions on TX-UK will not require you to establish whether a business is a limited cost trader.

The operation of the scheme

The mechanics of the flat rate scheme are as follows:

- The business continues to issue VAT invoices to VAT registered customers and to charge all customers for VAT at the normal rates (e.g. standard, reduced or zero-rated)

- However, at the end of the return period, the business pays to HMRC the following amount:

    Appropriate flat rate × VAT inclusive turnover

Notes

1. The business cannot recover any input tax on its purchases and expenses, apart from capital items with a VAT-inclusive cost of £2,000 or more.

2. The appropriate flat rate is reduced by 1% for the first 12 months of VAT registration.

The business does not need to keep records of the individual purchases and input VAT suffered. The scheme therefore **reduces the administrative burden** of keeping detailed records of purchase and expense invoices and recoverable input VAT.

Conditions

A business can only join the flat rate scheme if its taxable supplies (excluding VAT and capital items) in the next 12 months are not expected to exceed £150,000.

It must leave the scheme if its total income (including VAT) in the previous year exceeded £230,000, unless HMRC are satisfied that its expected total income for the next 12 months will not exceed £191,500.

Total income includes the value of exempt supplies and supplies outside of the scope of VAT.

The flat rate scheme can also be used in conjunction with the annual accounting scheme, but not with the cash accounting scheme.

Example

In the quarter ended 31 March 2023, Marcus had the following sales and expenditure:

	£
Credit sales	31,400
Purchases	8,850
Expenses	3,115
Purchase of a car (private use 40%)	17,750

All figures exclude VAT.

Required

Calculate the VAT due to HMRC for the quarter ended 31 March 2023 assuming:

(a) Marcus is registered under the flat rate scheme and the appropriate flat rate percentage for his trade sector is 9%.

(b) Marcus is not registered under the flat rate scheme.

Answer

(a) If registered under the flat rate scheme

	£
VAT inclusive turnover (£31,400 × 120/100)	37,680
VAT due to HMRC (£37,680 × 9%)	3,391

Note that no input tax is recoverable under the flat rate scheme.

(b) If not registered under the flat rate scheme

	£
Output VAT	
Sales (£31,400 × 20%)	6,280
Input VAT	
Purchases of goods (£8,850 × 20%)	(1,770)
Expenses (£3,115 × 20%)	(623)
Purchase of car = blocked	(Nil)
Amount payable to HMRC	3,887

> **Imports and exports**
>
> - Imports
> - Exports
> - International services

6 Imports and exports

6.1 Imports

UK VAT is charged on goods imported into the UK at the same rate as is applicable to goods purchased within the UK.

The UK VAT must be accounted for on the VAT return covering the date the goods come into the UK. The VAT is declared as output VAT. It is reclaimed as input VAT on the **same return** (assuming the business is able to recover its input VAT).

This system of dealing with imports is known as postponed accounting. It prevents goods being held at customs until the VAT is paid. It also ensures that a trader's UK VAT position is the same whether they purchase goods from a UK supplier or an overseas supplier, i.e. in VAT terms there will be no net cost to the business assuming it is able to fully recover its VAT.

For the purpose of the TX-UK exam, it should be assumed that postponed accounting applies to all imports of goods.

6.2 Exports

Exports of goods are zero-rated. The supplier must hold evidence that the goods have been exported, such as a bill of lading or air waybill.

6.3 International services

Supplies of services to business customers are usually treated as taking place where the **customer** is situated.

Therefore, a VAT-registered business within the UK that **purchases services** from overseas must account for UK output tax on those services and reclaim it as input tax in the same return. This is known as the reverse charge procedure.

The **supply of services** by a UK VAT-registered business to an overseas customer will be outside the scope of UK VAT as the place of supply will be outside the UK.

Example

Expo Ltd is situated in the UK and is registered for VAT. It has made the following transactions:

(a) The sale of women's clothing to a VAT-registered customer situated outside the UK.

(b) The purchase of men's clothing from a supplier situated outside the UK.

(c) The receipt of services from a supplier situated outside the UK.

(d) The supply of services to a customer situated outside the UK.

Required

Explain the VAT treatment of the above transactions.

Answer

(a) This is a zero-rated transaction.

(b) Expo Ltd must account for UK output VAT in the return covering the period in which the goods enter the UK. This can then be recovered as input tax on the same VAT return.

(c) UK output VAT must be accounted for. It is reclaimed as input VAT on the same return.

(d) The supply of services to an overseas customer is outside the scope of UK VAT.

Taxation – United Kingdom (TX-UK) FA2022

Q&A

Practice questions

Contents

		Page
Introduction to income tax		
1	Angela	434
2	Andrew	434
3	Briony	434
4	Binta	435
Income from property		
5	Paul	435
Employment income		
6	Flash plc	436
7	Richard	437
Unincorporated businesses		
8	Colin	438
9	Ashley and Cheryl	439
10	Daniel	440
11	Hannah	441
12	Georgina	442
13	Hassan	443
14	Nathan	443

Contents

		Page
15	Oscar	443

Partnerships

16	Eric, Fred and James	444
17	Husna, Kimi and Lesley	444
18	Rajiv and Sumit	445

Simpler income tax for small businesses

19	Zara	445

Pension contributions

20	Philip and Abena	446
21	Stephen	446

Residence

22	Meera, Sanjeev, Gethin and Seema	447

National insurance

23	Vanessa and Wu	448

Capital gains tax

24	Val	449
25	Anthony	449
26	Ahmed	450
27	Melanie	450
28	Judith	452
29	Lisha	452

Self-assessment for individuals

30	Candice	452

Inheritance tax

31	Pat	453
32	Graham	453
33	Craig	454

Contents

Page

Corporation tax

Introduction to corporation tax and TTP

34	ABC Ltd	454
35	DEF Ltd	454
36	GH Ltd	455
37	IJ plc	455
38	KL Ltd	456
39	MN Ltd	458

Capital allowances for companies

| 40 | OPQ Ltd | 459 |
| 41 | RS plc | 461 |

Chargeable gains for companies

42	TUV plc	462
43	WXY Ltd	463
44	Bonus issue	463
45	Rights issue	463
46	Takeover	464

Company trading losses

| 47 | FG Ltd | 464 |
| 48 | HI Ltd | 465 |

Groups

| 49 | UK group | 465 |
| 50 | PQ group | 466 |

Value Added Tax

| 51 | Deborah | 467 |
| 52 | WX Ltd | 467 |

1 Angela

For 2022/23 Angela received a salary of £90,000, building society interest of £3,000, UK dividends of £10,000 and a premium bond prize of £150.

What is Angela's taxable income for 2022/23?

- A £90,430
- B £103,000
- C £92,155
- D £91,930

2 Andrew

For 2022/23 Andrew's taxable income, after the deduction of his personal allowance, consisted of non-savings income of £60,000 and savings income of £3,000.

What is Andrew's income tax liability for 2022/23?

- A £16,797
- B £17,260
- C £17,460
- D £17,660

3 Briony

For 2022/23 Briony's taxable income, after the deduction of her personal allowance, consisted of non-savings income of £60,000 and dividend income of £10,000.

What is Briony's income tax liability for 2022/23?

- A £19,160
- B £19,060
- C £19,835
- D £20,260

Practice questions

4 Binta

Binta has the following income and payments in 2022/23:

		£
Income	Self employment profits	130,000
	Employment income	25,660
	Bank deposit interest	5,125
	Income from an ISA (Individual Savings Account)	260
	Dividends received from UK companies	2,100
	National Lottery winnings	140
Payments	Gift Aid donation	480
	Allowable interest	200

Income tax of £8,287 was deducted from Binta's employment income under the PAYE system.

Calculate the income tax payable by Binta for 2022/23.

5 Paul

Paul owns a furnished house which he rents out.

The annual rent was £8,000, but was increased to £9,000 per year with effect from 6 January 2023. It is payable in advance by equal monthly instalments on the 6th of each month. The tenants paid all the rent on time with the exception of that due for 6 March 2023, which was not received until 2 May 2022.

Paul incurred the following expenditure on the property during 2022/23:

Council tax	£960
Water rates	£380
Agent's fees	£780
Redecoration costs	£1,250
New central heating system	£2,400
Mortgage interest	£2,500

During 2022/23, the washing machine broke. Paul replaced it with a new washer-dryer costing £800. The cost of a washing machine equivalent to the old one would have been £500.

(a) **Calculate the amount of property income assessable on Paul for 2022/23.**

(b) **Outline the conditions that Paul would have to fulfil for the letting to be classed as a furnished holiday letting (FHL) and explain how being classed as an FHL would have affected relief for his mortgage interest.**

6 Flash plc

During 2022/23 Flash plc provided the following benefits to its employees:

(1) Arthur was provided with a new diesel car on 6 August 2022. The car does not meet the RDE2 standard. The car had a list price of £13,500 and an official CO_2 emission rate of 52 g/km. Arthur made no capital contribution towards the car and makes no regular contributions to its use. Arthur was provided with fuel for private use.

(2) Benny was provided with a new petrol car throughout 2022/23. The car had a list price of £20,800 and an official CO_2 emission rate of 144 g/km. Benny contributed £6,000 towards the purchase of the car. Benny was not provided with fuel for private use.

(3) Charlotte was provided with a new petrol car throughout 2022/23. The car had a list price of £25,000 and an official CO_2 emission rate of 184 g/km. Charlotte paid Flash plc £1,200 during 2022/23 for the use of the car. Charlotte was provided with fuel for private use and paid Flash plc £600 towards the cost of private fuel, although the actual cost of her private fuel was £1,000.

(4) Flash plc does not provide Daphne with a company car, but reimburses her with 30p per mile for the use of her own car on business journeys. During 2022/23 Daphne drove 12,000 miles in the performance of her duties. The relevant HMRC approved mileage allowances are 45 pence per mile for the first 10,000 miles, and 25 pence per mile thereafter.

(5) Ernest was provided with a new diesel van on 6 May 2022. The van had a list price of £18,600 and an official CO_2 emission rate of 220 g/km. Ernest is provided with fuel for private use.

(a) **What is the total figure of benefit assessable on Arthur in respect of the car and fuel provided to him in the tax year 2022/23?**

   A   £3,880
   B   £5,173
   C   £7,372
   D   £4,915

(b) **What is the total figure of benefit assessable on Benny in respect of the car and fuel provided to him in the tax year 2022/23?**

   A   £864
   B   £4,884
   C   £5,214
   D   £5,340

(c) **What is the total figure of benefit assessable on Charlotte in respect of the car and fuel provided to her in the tax year 2022/23?**

    A   £16,811

    B   £19,423

    C   £18,167

    D   £17,411

(d) **What effect will the reimbursement of Daphne's business mileage have on her employment income?**

    A   The reimbursement will have no effect on Daphne's income as it is less than the approved mileage allowance.

    B   Daphne will be taxed on the £3,600 received from her employer.

    C   Daphne can deduct £1,400 from her employment income.

    D   Daphne can deduct £5,000 from her employment income.

(e) **What is the total figure of benefit assessable on Ernest in respect of the van and fuel provided to him in the tax year 2022/23?**

    A   £14,889

    B   £3,931

    C   £4,288

    D   £16,243

7 Richard

Richard is the finance director of RS plc. In addition to an annual salary of £56,000 he is entitled to a bonus calculated using a formula applied to the company's annual audited profits. The company prepares accounts to 31 January each year: the bonus is paid to Richard four months later.

Recent bonuses have been:

	£
y/e 31 January 2021	20,000
y/e 31 January 2022	22,000
y/e 31 January 2023	18,500

Richard also received the following benefits.

(1) Overnight expense allowance of £60 for three nights staying away in London on a business trip.

(2) Annual staff party which cost the company £75 a head.

(3) A loan of £30,000 to help him buy a boat. Richard repaid £5,000 of the loan on 6 July 2022. The company charged him £400 interest.

(4) A new hybrid-electric car with a list price of £25,000. The car has CO_2 emissions of 40 grams per kilometre and an electric range of 75 miles. RS plc also provided fuel for Richard's private use.

Richard paid his annual subscription of £270 to ACCA and made a donation of £120 to charity via the company's approved payroll giving scheme.

Calculate Richard's employment income for 2022/23.

8 Colin

Colin started to trade on 1 July 2022. He prepared accounts for the period to 31 January 2023 which show a net profit of £67,750.

Included in expenses are the following items:

	£
Colin's income tax and National Insurance	6,400
Royalties payable	2,000
Legal fees relating to the collection of debts	1,260
Write off of a loan to a customer	2,250
Leasing cost	5,600
Car expenses	3,400

During the period, items of inventory were taken out of the business by Colin for his own private use. The items cost £60 and have a market value of £120. No entry has been made in the accounts in respect of this transaction.

The leasing cost relates to a car with a list price of £20,000 and CO_2 emissions of 65 g/km. The car was used by the sales manager.

Half of the car expenses relate to Colin's car and half to the sales manager's car. Colin uses his car 80% for business purposes. The sales manager's private mileage amounts to 10% of the total mileage.

(a) **Which TWO of the following expenses must be added back when calculating Colin's adjusted trading profits?**

Colin's income tax and National Insurance	£6,400
Royalties payable	£2,000
Legal fees relating to the collection of debts	£1,260
Write off of a loan to a customer	£2,250

(b) **Which TWO of the following items must be added back when calculating Colin's adjusted trading profit?**

Leasing costs	£840
Leasing costs	£4,760
Goods for own use	£60
Goods for own use	£120

(c) How much of the car expenses must be added back when calculating Colin's adjusted trading profit?

A	£340
B	£510
C	£1,360
D	£1,700

9 Ashley and Cheryl

Ashley

Ashley started to trade on 1 October 2022. He prepared accounts for the period to 31 December 2022.

On 1 July 2022 Ashley spent £340,000 on an automated production line with an expected life of 20 years. He also purchased a car on 1 December 2022 for £11,000 for the use of his sales manager. The car has CO_2 emissions of 45 g/km. The manager's private mileage amounts to 20% of the total mileage.

Cheryl

Cheryl prepares accounts to 31 March each year. On 1 April 2022 the tax written down values of plant and machinery were as follows:

	£
Main pool	113,420
Short life asset	3,410

In the year ended 31 March 2023, Cheryl undertook the following transactions:

17 June 2022	Purchased a small car for £11,000
	(The car has CO_2 emissions of 47 g/km and is used wholly for business purposes)
11 August 2022	Sold the short life asset for £500.
25 August 2022	Purchased some IT equipment for £7,370

On 1 July 2022 Cheryl purchased a newly constructed factory from a builder for £470,000 (including land of £110,000). The factory was brought into use on 1 September 2022.

(a) How much capital allowances are available to Ashley in respect of the production line for the period ended 31 December 2022?

A	£250,000
B	£254,050
C	£251,350
D	£340,000

(b) **How much capital allowances are available to Ashley in respect of the car for the period ended 31 December 2022?**

A £495

B £1,980

C £396

D £11,000

(c) **How much capital allowances are available to Cheryl in respect of assets held within the main pool for the year ended 31 March 2023?**

A £22,396

B £27,786

C £29,766

D £38,786

(d) **How much capital allowances are available to Cheryl in respect of her short life asset for the year ended 31 March 2023?**

A Balancing allowance of £2,910

B Balancing charge of £2,910

C Writing down allowance of £524

D Writing down allowance of £175

(e) **How much structures and buildings allowance is available to Cheryl for the year ended 31 March 2023?**

A £6,300

B £8,100

C £10,800

D £14,100

10 Daniel

Daniel prepared accounts for the 15-month period to 30 June 2023 as follows:

	£
Sales revenue	245,000
Cost of sales	(97,500)
Gross profit	147,500
Sundry income	8,000
	155,500
Expenses	(61,000)
Net profit	94,500

Included in expenses are the following:

(1) Depreciation of plant and machinery of £10,000.

(2) Motor expenses relating to Daniel's car of £3,750.

(3) A fine of £5,000 imposed for the breach of environmental health regulations.

(4) Computer software of £2,100 relating to a programme acquired with the new computer system on 3 May 2022. The estimated useful life of the computer and software is three years.

(5) Payment of a premium of £6,000 on 1 April 2023 for a 12-year lease on a workshop granted to Daniel by E Ltd, an unconnected trading company.

(6) Sundry income represents building society interest of £2,000 and rental income of £6,000 from the renting of an office which is surplus to Daniel's requirements.

Daniel also incurred the following capital expenditure:

		£
3 May 2022	New computer system	15,000
16 August 2022	Plant and machinery	28,000

On 11 September 2022 Daniel sold his car for £9,800 and purchased a new car for £16,000. The new car has CO_2 emissions of 83 g/km. Both cars are used 75% for the purposes of the trade.

On 1 April 2022 the tax written down value of Daniel's main pool was £78,000 and Daniel's car was £6,400.

Calculate Daniel's adjusted profit after capital allowances for the period ended 30 June 2023.

11 Hannah

Hannah started trading on 1 May 2018 and ceased trading on 30 April 2022. Her adjusted profits after capital allowances were:

	£
Period to 31 August 2019	60,000
Year to 31 August 2020	84,000
Year to 31 August 2021	90,000
Period to 30 April 2022	70,000

(a) **What is Hannah's trading income assessment for 2018/19?**

    A   Nil

    B   £41,250

    C   £55,000

    D   £60,000

(b) **What is Hannah's trading income assessment for 2019/20?**

　　A　　£45,000

　　B　　£60,000

　　C　　£67,750

　　D　　£74,000

(c) **What is Hannah's trading income assessment for the final tax year of trading?**

　　A　　£8,750

　　B　　£133,750

　　C　　£70,000

　　D　　£43,750

12　Georgina

Georgina has been in business since 1 May 2019 running a small gym. Her adjusted trading profits, before capital allowances, have been as follows:

	£
Year ended 30 April 2020	15,000
Year ended 30 April 2021	12,000
Period to 30 September 2022	19,000

Georgina made the following purchases during the year ended 30 April 2020:

	£
Plant and machinery	3,200
Car (used by Georgina and private use estimated at 75%)	5,600
Car (used by Georgina's assistant and private use estimated at 50%)	4,000

Georgina's car had CO_2 emissions of 45 g/km. Her assistant's car had CO_2 emissions of 50 g/km.

On 1 January 2021 Georgina traded in her car for a new one. She paid £4,800 and was allowed a £3,000 cash allowance on the existing car. Private use remained at 75%.

On 6 April 2021, new gym equipment was purchased for £1,000.

On 6 May 2022 new equipment costing £500 was purchased.

On 30 September 2022 Georgina closed the business and sold all the business assets for the following amounts:

	£
Plant and machinery (all less than cost)	2,000
Georgina's car	6,000
Georgina's assistant's car	2,000

Calculate Georgina's trading income for the tax years 2020/21 to 2022/23 inclusive.

13 Hassan

Hassan has been self-employed for many years. His recent tax adjusted trading profits/(losses) after capital allowances have been as follows:

	£
Year to 31 May 2019	50,200
Year to 31 May 2020	16,600
Year to 31 May 2021	(120,410)
Year to 31 May 2022	36,800

Hassan's other income is as follows:

	2019/20	2020/21	2021/22	2022/23
	£	£	£	£
Employment income	40,000	60,000	60,000	60,000

Calculate the taxable income for each tax year assuming losses are relieved as soon as possible. (Assume the 2022/23 tax rates and allowances apply throughout.)

14 Nathan

Nathan started to trade on 1 July 2020. Agreed results for the first two years were as follows:

		£
Year to 30 June 2021	Loss	(28,800)
Year to 30 June 2022	Profit	6,000

Before starting to trade Nathan had been a full-time employee of a local company. Earnings resulting from this employment in recent years had been:

	£
2019/20	15,000
2018/19	26,000
2017/18	30,000

Nathan had other assessable income of £9,600 a year for all years.

(a) **Calculate Nathan's trading income assessments for the first three tax years.**

(b) **State the amount of loss relief available (i) against total income and (ii) under the early years' loss relief rules, and against which years these claims can be made.**

(c) **Calculate Nathan's taxable income for all relevant years assuming early years' loss relief is claimed.** (Assume tax rates and allowances for 2022/23 apply throughout.)

15 Oscar

Oscar had carried on a trade as a self-employed management consultant for many years. The business had prospered for a time but recently profits started to decline as clients turned to larger, well-known firms of consultants, and losses began to be incurred. As a consequence of this Oscar decided to cease trading and retire on 30 June 2022.

Recent agreed tax-adjusted profits after capital allowances have been as follows:

	£
Year to 31 December 2018	40,000
Year to 31 December 2019	33,000
Year to 31 December 2020	20,000
Year to 31 December 2021	(32,000)
Period to 30 June 2022	(5,000)

Oscar received property income of £5,000 each year. His overlap profits not yet relieved total £6,200.

Calculate Oscar's taxable income for all tax years affected, assuming a terminal loss relief claim is made. (Assume the 2022/23 tax rates and allowances apply for all years.)

16 Eric, Fred and James

Eric, Fred and James have been in partnership for many years, sharing profits and losses in the ratio 3:2:1 respectively. The partnership prepares accounts to 31 December each year.

The agreed trading profits for the year to 31 December 2022 amounted to £60,000. The profit-sharing arrangement was revised with effect from 1 May 2022 by introducing an annual partner salary for Eric of £20,000 and changing the profit-sharing ratio 2:2:1.

What is Eric's trading income assessment for 2022/23?

A	£17,334
B	£20,667
C	£24,000
D	£28,000
E	£30,000
F	£34,000

17 Husna, Kimi and Lesley

Husna, Kimi and Lesley have been in partnership for many years, preparing accounts to 30 June each year and sharing profits and losses equally.

Recent agreed adjusted trading profits after capital allowances have been:

	£
Year to 30 June 2020	24,000
Year to 30 June 2021	32,400
Year to 30 June 2022	43,200

On 1 February 2021 Mike joined and Kimi retired from the partnership. Kimi's overlap profits are £2,000. Profits and losses continue to be shared equally.

Calculate the trading income assessments of each partner for each of the years 2020/21 to 2022/23, and calculate Mike's overlap profits.

18 Rajiv and Sumit

Rajiv and Sumit have been in partnership for many years and have the following partnership agreement:

	Rajiv	Sumit
Salary per annum	£16,000	£28,000
Profit-sharing ratio	65%	35%

On 1 January 2023 Tisha joined the partnership. The new partnership agreement states that no salary will be allocated to any partner and profits and losses are to be shared in the ratio 2:2:1 (Rajiv, Sumit, Tisha respectively).

The adjusted trading loss of the partnership after capital allowances for the year ended 31 March 2023 was £101,600.

(a) **Allocate the partnership loss between the partners.**

(b) **State the loss relief options available to each partner.**

19 Zara

Zara is self-employed and runs a shop. She has provided the following information for the year ended 5 April 2023:

(1) Sales revenue was £120,100, of which £1,100 was owed as receivables at 5 April 2023.

(2) During the year ended 5 April 2023 Zara drove a total of 12,000 miles, of which 4,000 were for private journeys. Zara's car was purchased on 15 April 2022 for £16,000. The car has CO_2 emissions of 45g/km and Zara incurred motor expenses of £6,000 during 2022/23. The approved mileage allowance (AMA) for a car is 45p for the first 10,000 miles and 25p thereafter.

(3) On 15 May 2022 she purchased new equipment for her shop costing £4,800.

(4) Zara lives on her own in a flat that is situated above the shop and one-half of the total property expenses of £9,600 relate to this flat. The relevant flat rate private use adjustment is £4,200.

(5) Zara incurred other allowable expenses of £82,000, of which £18,200 was owed as payables at 5 April 2023.

Calculate the amount by which Zara's trading profit for the year ended 5 April 2023 will change if she elects to use the cash basis rather than the normal accruals basis of calculation.

Taxation - United Kingdom (TX-UK) FA2022

20 Philip and Abena

(a) Philip earns £90,000 a year. He has made the following gross personal pension contributions:

	£
2019/20	32,000
2020/21	21,000
2021/22	29,000
2022/23	68,000

How much unused annual allowance can Philip carry forward to 2023/24?

A   Nil

B   £10,000 from 2019/20

C   £10,000 from 2021/22

D   £10,000 from 2022/23

(b) Abena has net income of £280,000 a year. She makes contributions of £6,000 a year into her employer's occupational pension scheme. Her employer contributes a further £9,000.

How much annual allowance is available to Abena for 2022/23, assuming she has no unused annual allowance brought forward?

A   £12,500

B   £15,500

C   £17,000

D   £20,000

21 Stephen

Stephen is employed by International Megabytes plc at a gross salary of £32,000 before deduction of pension contributions of 5% to the company's occupational pension scheme. International Megabytes plc contributes an additional 7% into the scheme on Stephen's behalf.

In 2021 he transferred to the company's Newcastle office to supervise the installation of a new reporting system. The assignment in Newcastle is expected to last for three years.

During his stay in Newcastle he is living in a company house which cost £72,000 in 2017, the gross annual value being £1,700. The company paid certain household bills, which for 2022/23 were as follows:

	£
Electricity	280
Gas	410
Gardener	240
Redecoration	680

The company furnished the house at a cost of £6,400. Stephen pays the company £70 per month as a contribution toward the cost of accommodation.

The company provides him with a petrol car (CO_2 emissions level 96 g/km), list price £16,400. His mileage in 2022/23 was 24,500, of which 75% represents business mileage. He pays for all petrol and claims reimbursement for the petrol cost relating only to business miles. For the duration of his stay in Newcastle, his wife has also been provided with a diesel car (CO_2 emission level 59 g/km), list price £18,200. His wife pays for all her fuel.

Other benefits provided include:

(1) Medical insurance costing £480 per annum.

(2) Meals in the staff dining room. The dining room is open to all staff. It provides subsidised lunches. The subsidy is estimated to be worth £360 per annum.

(3) The Newcastle office runs a nursery attended by Stephen's daughter. The cost to the company is £2,000 per annum.

In July 2022 Stephen won a family holiday as a prize in the company's productivity incentive scheme. The cost to the company was £1,200.

The company operates a staff loan scheme charging interest of 2% a year. In December 2021 Stephen borrowed £3,000 for personal expenditure. There is to be no repayment of capital in the first two years. The company decided to write off the loan on 31 March 2023.

(a) **Calculate Stephen's employment income for 2022/23.**

(b) **Explain how your calculation would have changed if Stephen had paid his pension contribution into a personal pension scheme.**

22 Meera, Sanjeev, Gethin and Seema

(a) Meera was in the UK for 15 days during the tax year 2022/23. She has not previously been resident in the UK.

(b) Sanjeev worked full-time in the UK during the tax year 2022/23. At weekends and holidays he travelled to France to visit his girlfriend.

(c) Gethin has always been resident in the UK and has spent at least 300 days in the UK each year. On 6 April 2022 he started full-time employment in Germany and rented an apartment on a long lease. His wife and children continued to live in the family home in the UK and Gethin returned to visit them every month. During the tax year 2022/23 Gethin visited the UK for a total of 50 days, staying in his UK home each time.

(d) Seema married an Englishman in March 2022. Her husband lives and works in the UK. During the tax year 2022/23 Seema came to the UK for the first time and stayed for a total of 150 days with her husband in the home owned by him. For the remainder of the time, she lived with her parents in India.

Explain the residence status of Meera, Sanjeev, Gethin and Seema for 2022/23.

23 Vanessa and Wu

Vanessa

Vanessa aged 46 is employed by VX plc. In the tax year 2022/23 she was paid a salary of £60,000 and provided with the following benefits:

	£
Company car	6,450
Private fuel	4,320
Living accommodation	1,800
Employer's pension contribution	1,600

She also made a donation of £200 under the payroll giving scheme.

Wu

Wu has been trading profitably as a self-employed builder for many years. His trading income for 2022/23 was £50,000.

Wu's wife, Yui, is a self-employed consultant. Her trading income for 2022/23 was £60,000. In addition, Yui has savings income of £8,800.

(a) **How much NIC is payable by Vanessa for 2022/23?**

    A   £4,180

    B   £5,720

    C   £6,284

    D   £5,311

(b) **How much Class 1 NIC is payable by VX plc in respect of Vanessa's earnings for 2022/23?**

    A   £5,311

    B   £7,660

    C   £7,138

    D   £9,552

(c) **Which ONE of the following statements is correct?**

    A   Vanessa is liable to pay Class 1A NIC of £1,892 for 2022/23

    B   VX plc is liable to pay Class 1A NIC of £10,922 for 2022/23

    C   VX plc is liable to pay Class 1A NIC of £2,133 for 2022/23

    D   VX plc is liable to pay Class 1A NIC of £1,892 for 2022/23

(d) **When is Wu's class 4 NIC for 2022/23 payable?**

A   31 January 2023, 31 July 2023 and 31 January 2024

B   31 January 2024, 31 July 2024 and 31 January 2025

C   31 July 2023 and 31 January 2024

D   31 January 2024

(e) **How much NIC is payable by Yui for 2022/23?**

A   £4,180

B   £5,311

C   £4,440

D   £7,660

24 Val

In 2022/23 Val disposed of the following assets:

(1) A 30% shareholding in Garnet Ltd, an unquoted trading company. The shares were acquired in June 2006 for £10,000 and sold in July 2022 for £55,000.

(2) A 1% shareholding in Ruby plc, a quoted trading company. The shares were acquired in July 2000 for £6,000 and sold in August 2022 for £66,000.

(3) A holiday cottage which she used as a second home. The cottage was purchased in May 2005 for £17,000 and sold on 1 November 2022 for £128,000.

Val is not an employee of either Garnet Ltd or Ruby plc, and has taxable income of £21,555 for 2022/23.

(a) **Calculate the payment on account due in respect of the disposal of the holiday cottage and state the due date for payment.**

(b) **Calculate Val's capital gains tax liability for 2022/23 and state the due date for payment.**

25 Anthony

Anthony disposed of the following assets in 2022/23:

(1) On 18 July 2022 Anthony gave 40,000 £1 ordinary shares in R plc, a quoted trading company, to his daughter. The shares had a market value of £4.50 per share on 18 July 2022.

Anthony purchased 50,000 shares in the company on 16 October 2006 for £75,000. On 10 August 2008 R plc made a 1 for 10 rights issue for £6 per share. He bought a further 11,000 shares on 22 July 2022 for £36,000. Anthony's shareholding represents a 2% interest in the company.

(2) A plot of investment land. Anthony purchased the land on 20 September 2010 for £14,000. He sold the land on 12 February 2023 for £10,000.

(3) 6,500 shares in S Ltd, an unquoted trading company. Anthony purchased 10,000 shares in S Ltd on 27 September 2022 for £36,600. On 14 March 2023 he sold 6,500 shares for £5 per share.

Anthony has capital losses brought forward of £16,150.

Calculate Anthony's capital gains tax liability for 2022/23, assuming he has taxable income of £29,200.

26 Ahmed

Ahmed made the following disposals in 2022/23:

(1) Sale of 6,000 GH Ltd unquoted trading company shares to his son for £45,000 on 10 July 2022. The shares had a market value of £15 per share on that date. Ahmed purchased the shares for £6,000 on 14 April 2003.

(2) Sale of a painting on 14 July 2022. This gave rise to a gain of £17,650.

Ahmed has capital losses brought forward of £4,610.

Ahmed prepares accounts to 31 March each year. In the year ended 31 March 2023 he incurred a trading loss of £28,500. His total income in 2022/23 is £19,400 and he decides he would like to claim relief against his total income for 2022/23 and extend the claim against his chargeable gains in the same year.

Calculate Ahmed's capital gains tax liability for 2022/23. State the amount of losses, if any, remaining unrelieved.

27 Melanie

Melanie had the following capital transactions in 2022/23:

(1) On 20 May 2022 Melanie gave an antique vase to her sister. The vase was worth £6,800 in May 1996 when she inherited it from her father. In May 2022 it was professionally valued at £15,200.

(2) On 12 July 2022 Melanie gave her daughter 8,500 shares in Match Ltd, an unquoted trading company. She originally purchased 15,000 shares (a 6% interest) in December 2004 at a cost of £16,500. At the date of the gift the shares were worth 180p each. Match Ltd had chargeable assets worth £260,000 which include £40,000 worth of investments.

(3) On 30 November 2022 Melanie sold a workshop for £100,000. The workshop was used in Melanie's business but was too big for her requirements. The workshop was purchased in October 2000 for £35,000. On 31 December 2022 she purchased a smaller workshop which cost £68,000.

(4) On 28 February 2023 Melanie sold a chargeable asset used in her business to her uncle for £18,000. This asset was worth £35,000. Melanie bought the asset in April 2012 for £5,000.

Practice questions

(a) **Which reliefs, if any, can Melanie claim in respect of her disposals?** Make your selection by ticking in the appropriate column for each row. Leave the row blank if no claims may be made.

Disposal	Gift holdover relief	Rollover relief
Antique vase		
Shares in Match Ltd		
Workshop		
Business asset		

(b) **How much gain is chargeable on the disposal of the Match Ltd shares, after giving any reliefs that may be due?**

   A   Nil

   B   £5,950

   C   £5,035

   D   £915

(c) **How much gain is chargeable on the disposal of the warehouse, after giving any reliefs that may be due?**

   A   Nil

   B   £65,000

   C   £33,000

   D   £32,000

(d) **How much gain is chargeable on the disposal of the business asset, after giving any reliefs that may be due?**

   A   Nil

   B   £13,000

   C   £17,000

   D   £30,000

(e) **What are the time limits by which any reliefs in respect of Melanie's 2022/23 disposals must be claimed?** You should select one answer for each column.

Gift holdover relief	Rollover relief
31 January 2025	31 January 2025
5 April 2025	5 April 2025
5 April 2027	5 April 2027
31 January 2029	31 January 2029

28 Judith

Judith purchased a house for £69,379 on 1 April 2006.

She occupied the property as her home until 1 April 2010 when she went to work overseas. During her absence, she let the property to tenants.

On 1 January 2015 she returned to the UK and was required by her employers to work in a different city. On 1 March 2016 she returned to her home town but lived with relatives until 1 July 2016 when she could reoccupy her house on the termination of the tenancy agreement.

On 1 January 2019 Judith purchased another house and elected for it to be her main residence from that date. She moved into her new house and let her original house to tenants until it was sold on 31 March 2023 for £384,000.

(a) **Calculate the chargeable gain arising on the disposal of Judith's house.**

(b) **Explain why Judith's periods of absence do not qualify for letting relief.**

29 Lisha

Lisha sold a house on 1 August 2022, realising a gain of £250,000.

Lisha had purchased the house on 1 August 2014. She had occupied it as her main residence throughout her ownership, but two of the property's ten rooms (i.e. 20% of the property) were always let out exclusively to tenants.

How much chargeable gain arises on the disposal of Lisha's house after giving any reliefs that may be due? (Ignore the annual exempt amount.)

- A Nil
- B £10,000
- C £50,000
- D £250,000

30 Candice

Candice has provided the following information:

	2021/22	2022/23
	£	£
Income tax liability	17,000	20,000
Class 4 NICs	700	880
Capital gains tax liability	Nil	4,600
PAYE deducted	3,500	4,000

(a) **Calculate the tax payable under self-assessment for 2022/23 and state the due dates for payment.**

Practice questions

(b) **Calculate the interest payable assuming Candice made her payments for 2022/23 on the following dates:**

	Paid on
1st POA	28 February 2023
2nd POA	31 August 2023
Balancing payment	31 January 2024

31 Pat

During his lifetime Pat made the following gifts of cash:

Date	Gift to:	£	Occasion:
19 June 2014	Thomas, his son	100,000	On his 18th birthday
14 May 2015	Lin, his wife	60,000	On their silver wedding anniversary
20 February 2018	Trust	373,440	
6 July 2018	Iris, his daughter	200,000	On her wedding day

Pat agreed to pay any lifetime IHT due in respect of these lifetime gifts. The nil rate band for 2017/18 is £325,000.

Pat died on 17 April 2022.

(a) **Calculate the lifetime IHT payable by Pat in respect of the gits made by him and state the due date(s) of payment.**

(b) **Calculate the IHT due in respect of the lifetime gifts as a result of Pat's death. State who is liable to pay the tax and the due dates of payment.**

32 Graham

Graham is a UK domiciled individual who died on 4 July 2022, aged 79. Graham owned the following assets at the date of his death:

(1) A main residence valued at £420,000. The house was purchased in 2004, partly funded by a repayment mortgage of £140,000, which remains outstanding.

(2) Bank accounts with a total value of £180,000.

(3) An ISA with the Nationwide Building Society with a balance of £48,000.

(4) A car worth £20,500 and personal chattels in the UK worth £14,000.

(7) Life assurance policy on his own life with a surrender value on 4 July 2022 of £160,000. The executors received £169,000 on 31 August 2022.

In his will Graham left cash of £60,000 to his wife. The rest of his estate is left to his daughter and son in equal proportions. Graham made no gifts during his lifetime.

Graham had an outstanding income tax liability of £6,300 and credit card bills of £1,280. His executors paid £5,400 for his funeral.

Calculate the inheritance tax due as a result of Graham's death, stating the due date for payment and who is liable to pay the tax.

33 Craig

Craig, a UK domiciled individual, owned the following assets when he died on 14 December 2022:

(1) A main residence which is valued at £446,000. The purchase was partly funded by an interest-only mortgage of £120,000, which is still outstanding.

(2) A flat in London worth £400,000.

(3) Personal chattels and two cars worth a total of £61,000.

(4) Bank and building society accounts with balances totalling £310,000.

(5) Shares worth £48,000.

Craig owed HMRC £7,260 income tax and his funeral cost £7,650.

In his will Craig left the house and the flat to his wife. The rest of his estate was shared between his son and daughter.

During his lifetime, on 16 June 2017 Craig gifted some shares valued at £46,250 to his daughter.

Calculate the IHT payable as a result of Craig's death.

34 ABC Ltd

ABC Ltd prepared accounts for the year ended 31 March 2023 and provided the following information:

	£
Property income from renting a warehouse in the UK	160,000
Dividends received from non-group companies	100,000
Trading income	448,000
Dividends paid	45,000
Interest income	24,000
Qualifying charitable donation	4,000

ABC Ltd disposed of some shares held as an investment on 30 June 2022 and realised a chargeable gain of £242,000.

Calculate the corporation tax liability for ABC Ltd for the year ended 31 March 2023 and state the due date.

35 DEF Ltd

DEF Ltd has been a large company for many years. It has an accounting reference date of 31 May.

On which of the following dates is its corporation tax for the year ended 31 May 2022 payable?

A   14 December 2021, 14 March 2022, 14 June 2022 and 14 September 2022

B   14 December 2022, 14 March 2023, 14 June 2023 and 14 September 2023

C   31 January 2023, 31 July 2023, 31 January 2024

D   1 March 2023

36 GH Ltd

GH Ltd provides the following information for the year ended 31 March 2023:

	Notes	£
Income		
Adjusted trading profits		226,000
Interest receivable on £60,000 12% loan notes	(1)	7,200
Premium received on the granting of a lease	(2)	60,000
Dividends from non-group companies		9,000
Expenditure		
Interest payable on £80,000 8% loan stock	(3)	6,400
Interest on underpaid corporation tax		5,800
Qualifying charitable donation		2,500
Dividends paid to shareholders		50,000

Notes

(1) Loan note interest actually received in the period was £6,000.

(2) GH Ltd granted a 35-year lease to I plc on 30 March 2023.

(3) Loan stock interest actually paid in the period was £5,760. The loan was used to finance the trade.

(4) GH Ltd disposed of a capital asset which gave rise to an allowable capital loss of £16,000.

Calculate the corporation tax liability of GH Ltd for the year ended 31 March 2023.

37 IJ plc

IJ plc decided to change its accounting date and prepared a 15-month set of accounts to 30 June 2022. The following information relates to the 15-month period:

	£
Income	
Adjusted profits before capital allowances	400,000
Bank deposit interest received (see below)	10,000
Rents accrued (see below)	45,000
Dividends received from non-group company on 30 June 2022	5,500
Expenditure	
Qualifying charitable donation paid on 18 March 2022	4,500
Interest payable on £180,000 10% loan notes issued to finance the trade	22,500
Property expenses (see below)	

IJ plc disposed of the following capital assets:

		£
15 April 2021	chargeable gain	15,100
16 May 2022	allowable loss	22,600
20 June 2022	chargeable gain	62,500

There are no capital losses brought forward.

The bank deposit account had a capital balance of £150,000 throughout the period and earned interest at a fixed rate of 6% per annum.

IJ plc accrued rental income of £45,000 from renting a furnished property in London at £3,000 per month. During the 15-month period IJ plc incurred the following expenses in relation to the property:

	£	
Estate agent fees	300	per month
Insurance	100	per month
Repairs to property on 16 January 2022	16,000	
Accountants' fees paid on 30 June 2022	4,200	
A conservatory extension	15,000	
Replacement washing machine	500	

Capital allowances are calculated as £67,640 for the first CAP and £14,910 for the second CAP.

Calculate IJ plc's corporation tax liabilities for the 15 months ended 30 June 2022, and state the due dates of payment.

38 KL Ltd

KL Ltd produced accounts for the year to 31 March 2023 and has supplied the following information:

	Notes	£
Profit before taxation per financial accounts		202,640
This figure is		
– after charging the following items:		
Depreciation		109,880
Gifts and donations	(1)	3,400
Repairs and renewals	(2)	141,000
Professional fees	(3)	13,600
Other expenses	(4)	469,620
– after crediting the following items:		
Profit on the sale of a warehouse	(5)	85,910
Loan interest	(6)	13,560

Notes

(1) Gifts and donations

	£
Qualifying charitable donation	660
Gifts to customers	1,875
Gifts to staff at Christmas	865
	3,400

All the gifts to customers displayed KL Ltd's name. The gifts were 18 bottles of champagne costing £40 each and 21 cut glass decanters costing £55 each.

(2) Repairs and renewals

	£
Maintenance of plant and machinery	62,000
Extension to the workshop	53,100
Rebuilding a chimney damaged in a storm	25,900
	141,000

(3) Professional fees

	£
Accountancy and audit fees	5,950
Legal fees: court case for breaching health and safety legislation	950
Debt collection fees	2,050
Legal fees: renewal of a 60-year lease on a warehouse	1,450
Legal fees: the issue of new loan notes	3,200
	13,600

(4) Other expenses

Other expenses include £100,000 spent on a staff Christmas party, interest on overdue tax of £3,600 and a pollution fine of £16,000. The remaining expenses are all allowable.

(5) Profit on the sale of a warehouse

A chargeable gain of £56,160 arose on the disposal.

(6) Loan interest

The loan interest represents interest receivable in the period and relates to a loan made to another company on 1 January 2023. The loan was made for a non-trading purpose.

(7) Capital allowances

The capital allowances claim for the year ended 31 March 2023 was £45,035.

(a) **Calculate KL Ltd's tax adjusted trading income for the year ended 31 March 2023.** (You should indicate by the use of zero (0) any items that do not require adjustment.)

(b) **Calculate KL Ltd's corporation tax liability for the year ended 31 March 2023.**

39 MN Ltd

MN Ltd prepares accounts to 30 September annually. The profit before taxation for the year to 30 September 2022 was £25,125 after taking account of the following income and expenditure:

	Notes	£
Income		
Sales revenue		510,900
Bank deposit interest		160
Dividend received from non-group company		40
Royalty income		100
Expenditure		
Cost of sales		438,410
Rent and rates		2,740
Lighting and heating		1,120
Office salaries		18,660
Repairs to premises	(1)	2,620
Motor expenses		740
Depreciation – vans		2,800
Depreciation – equipment		750
Amortisation of lease		120
Loss on sale of equipment		40
Professional charges	(2)	1,175
Sundry expenses	(3)	770
Staff salaries		14,000
Directors' salaries		2,130

Notes

(1) **Repairs to premises**

	£
Alteration of floor to install new display stands	1,460
Decoration	475
Re-plastering walls damaged by damp	685
	2,620

(2) **Professional charges**

	£
Accountancy	200
Court action – breach of customs regulations	110
Legal costs – acquiring a new lease	820
Debt collection	45
	1,175

Practice questions

(3) **Sundry expenses**

	£
Fine for breach of customs regulations	250
Trade subscription	50
Donation to police welfare fund	20
Entertaining customers	300
Paperweights bearing firm's name sent to 12 customers	120
Royalties payable	15
Miscellaneous allowable expenses	15
	770

(4) On 25 June 2022 MN Ltd had been granted a 21-year lease by Turin plc on new premises at a premium of £12,600. This has been recognised in the leasehold property account on the balance sheet.

(5) MN Ltd's capital allowances for the year ended 30 September 2022 total £460.

Prepare an adjustment of profit computation and TTP statement for MN Ltd, based on the accounts to 30 September 2022. (You should indicate by the use of zero (0) any items that do not require adjustment.)

40 OPQ Ltd

OPQ Ltd has been trading for many years, preparing accounts to 31 December annually. The tax written down value on the main pool at 1 January 2022 was £22,000. In the year to 31 December 2022 the following transactions took place:

23 April 2022   Sold a van for £16,900. The van had originally cost £18,000.

11 August 2022   Purchased a car costing £12,200. This had CO_2 emissions of 43 g/km. It is used to the extent of 30% by the finance director for private motoring

15 November 2022   Purchased two cars for use by salesmen, one car costing £12,500, the other costing £14,500. The first car has CO_2 emissions of 75 g/km. The second car has zero CO_2 emissions

(a) **How much writing down allowance can be claimed in respect of the main pool for the year to 31 December 2022?**

A   £2,916

B   £918

C   £5,364

D   £3,114

(b) **Identify whether each of the following statements regarding the cars purchased during the year ended 31 December 2022 is true or false.**

	True	False
The car costing £14,500 qualifies for a First Year Allowance of £14,500		
The car costing £12,500 qualifies for a writing down allowance of £750		
The car costing £12,200 must be kept separate from the main pool as there is private use by a director		

(c) In February 2023, OPQ Ltd is planning to purchase some new equipment for £1,800,000. **Complete the following sentences explaining the capital allowances due in respect of the new acquisitions:**

If the expenditure relates to items that can be added to the main pool, OPQ Ltd can claim **an annual investment allowance / a super-deduction** of £...............

If the expenditure relates to items that belong to the special rate pool, OPQ Ltd can claim **an annual investment allowance / a first year allowance** of £............... and a **first year allowance / writing down allowance** of £............ .

Practice questions

41 RS plc

RS plc has traded for many years in Deeside, making up accounts to 31 March annually. Its statement of profit or loss for the year to 31 March 2023 is as follows.

	Notes	£	£
Gross profit			723,884
Interest on Government stock			700
UK dividends			10,800
Gain on sale of shares	(1)		4,700
Royalty income	(2)		2,000
			742,084
Less: Expenses			
Salaries and wages		229,248	
Directors' remuneration		99,819	
Rates, electricity and insurance		2,629	
Travelling expenses		1,791	
General expenses	(3)	18,052	
Repairs	(4)	3,480	
Audit and accountancy		11,210	
Royalties payable	(2)	5,000	
Loan note interest	(5)	5,000	
Depreciation		21,170	
			(397,399)
Profit before tax			344,685

Notes

(1) The chargeable gain arising on the sale of these shares was calculated as £500.

(2) All royalties were received from and paid to other unconnected UK companies.

(3) **Analysis of general expenses**

	£
Stationery, postage and telephone	332
Legal expenses	
Rights issue of shares	3,150
Collection of trade debts	750
Qualifying charitable donations	1,000
Staff Christmas party (200 employees)	3,140
Contribution to Deeside Enterprise Agency	1,000
Director's relocation expenses	4,000
Sundry expenses	4,680
	18,052

(4) Repairs are all allowable.

(5) The loan was used to finance the company's trade.

(6) The written down value of plant at 1 April 2022 was £14,240.

During the year to 31 March 2023 the following transactions in non-current assets took place:

		£
30 June 2022	Sale of plant (cost £750)	780
1 July 2022	New car purchased (CO_2 emissions of 45 g/km)	8,616
1 August 2022	Car purchased for the managing director (zero CO_2 emissions, private use 30%)	27,000

(7) The company paid a dividend of £220,000 on 30 September 2022.

Calculate the corporation tax liability of RS plc for the year to 31 March 2023. (You should indicate by the use of zero (0) any items that do not require adjustment.)

42 TUV plc

In November 2022, a building bought in July 2002 and held for investment purpose was sold by TUV plc for £95,000. Legal fees and estate agent's costs on disposal amounted to £2,450.

The cost of the property was £28,000 plus £1,460 legal fees and estate agent's costs. Immediately on acquisition £2,000 was spent on installing central heating. In August 2006 £1,500 was spent on redecorating the exterior of the property and a new bathroom was added in the same month at a cost of £5,600.

The relevant indexation factors are as follows:

July 2002 to December 2017   0.558

August 2006 to December 2017   0.376

(a) **How much unindexed gain arises on this disposal?**

   A   £53,990

   B   £55,490

   C   £59,590

   D   £61,590

(b) **How much indexation allowance is available in respect of this disposal?**

   A   £21,028

   B   £20,225

   C   £20,679

   D   £19,661

Practice questions

43 WXY Ltd

WXY Ltd sold a freehold office building on 15 August 2022 for £600,000. The building cost £220,000 on 14 July 2004. On 30 June 2022 WXY Ltd purchased a smaller replacement office building for £540,000. WXY Ltd does not expect to sell the replacement building until 2033. WXY Ltd prepares accounts to 31 August each year. Both buildings were used for the purposes of the trade of WXY Ltd.

The indexation factor for the period July 2004 to December 2017 is 0.457.

(a) **Calculate the chargeable gain arising on the disposal of the original office building and the base cost of the new office building, assuming any available relief is claimed.**

(b) **Explain the difference in treatment if WXY Ltd were to purchase fixed plant and machinery instead of the replacement office building.**

44 Bonus issue

On 1 January 2023 ZA plc sold 1,500 shares in Y plc for £7,500. The company's previous transactions in these shares have been as follows:

January 2009	Bought 1,500 shares for £2,000
July 2011	Bonus issue of 1 for 4

Calculate the chargeable gain or allowable loss on the disposal of shares on 1 January 2023. Assume the relevant indexation factors are as follows:

January 2009 to July 2011	0.098
January 2009 to December 2017	0.306
July 2011 to December 2017	0.275

45 Rights issue

BC plc has the following dealings in ordinary shares of X plc:

January 2000	Bought 1,000 shares for £3,000
July 2004	Bought 600 shares for £2,000
February 2008	X plc made a 1 for 2 rights issue for £2 per share
March 2023	Sold 2,200 X plc shares for £14,960

Calculate the chargeable gains arising on the disposal of X plc shares. Assume the relevant indexation factors are as follows:

January 2000 to July 2004	0.121
July 2004 to February 2008	0.132
February 2008 to December 2017	0.303

46 Takeover

DE plc bought 10,000 shares in S plc for £37,000 in August 2008. On 15 March 2013 H plc took over S plc and all shareholders in S plc received:

- ten ordinary shares in H plc; and
- two preference shares in H plc

for every five shares they held in S plc.

Immediately after the takeover the ordinary shares were quoted at £3.80 each, and the preference shares at £2 each.

On 1 March 2023 DE plc sold half its ordinary shares in H plc for £5 per share.

Calculate the chargeable gain or allowable loss arising on the disposal of the H plc shares. Assume the relevant indexation factors are as follows:

August 2008 to March 2013	0.145
August 2008 to December 2017	0.186
March 2013 to December 2017	0.108

47 FG Ltd

FG Ltd's results for recent accounting periods have been as follows:

	Year to 31 December 2021	Period to 31 March 2022	Year to 31 March 2023
	£	£	£
Trading profit/(loss)	88,800	(220,800)	26,400
Interest income	10,000	10,000	10,000
Chargeable gains	30,720	33,600	28,800
Qualifying charitable donations	(2,400)	(2,400)	(2,400)

Calculate the TTP of FG Ltd for each accounting period assuming losses are relieved as soon as possible, and calculate the loss left to carry forward, if any.

48 HI Ltd

HI Ltd prepared its accounts to 30 November each year until 30 November 2020. It then changed its accounting date to 31 March by preparing a four-month set of accounts to 31 March 2021.

HI Ltd has supplied the following information:

	Year ended 30 Nov 2020	Period to 31 Mar 2021	Year ended 31 Mar 2022	Year ended 31 Mar 2023
	£	£	£	£
Trading profit/(loss)	850,380	146,800	(356,460)	85,940
Interest income	10,680	3,560	10,680	10,680
Net chargeable gains/(loss)	48,500	26,000	(14,000)	Nil
Qualifying charitable donations	(1,170)	Nil	(1,170)	(1,170)

(a) Calculate the TTP for each CAP assuming losses are relieved as soon as possible.

(b) Calculate the losses available to carry forward, if any, at 31 March 2023.

49 UK group

The following diagram indicates the percentage holding of ordinary voting shares in the companies shown. All of the shareholdings have been held for many years.

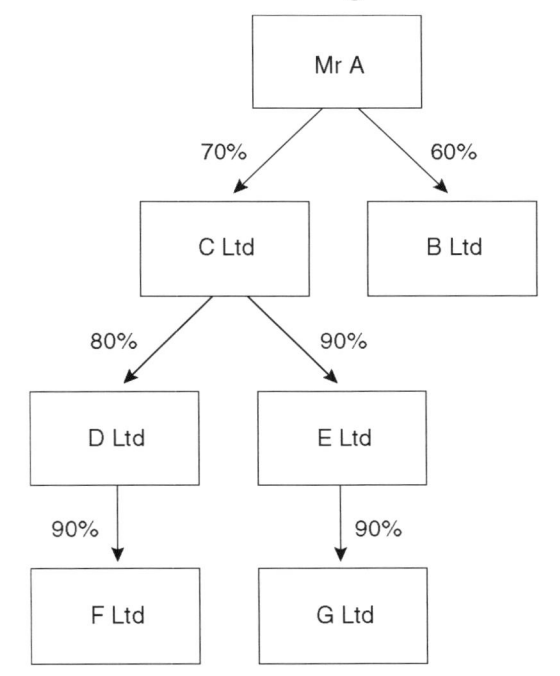

```
                    Mr A
              70% /      \ 60%
               C Ltd      B Ltd
          80% /     \ 90%
           D Ltd    E Ltd
        90% |       | 90%
           F Ltd    G Ltd
```

The income received and qualifying charitable donations paid by each company for the year ended 31 March 2023 were as follows:

	B Ltd	C Ltd	D Ltd	E Ltd	F Ltd	G Ltd
	£	£	£	£	£	£
Trading profit	260,000	80,000	120,000	24,000		10,000
Trading loss					40,000	
Rental income	20,000		8,000	4,000	5,000	6,000
Donations	10,000	6,000	10,000	2,000	4,000	5,000

(a) **Calculate the profit threshold to determine whether the companies in the C Ltd group are classed as large for corporation tax payment purposes.**

(b) **Identify, with explanations, the groups which are present in the above structure for the purposes of surrendering and receiving trading losses.**

(c) **Explain how F Ltd's trading loss should be relieved on the assumption that group relief is claimed in the most efficient manner.**

(d) **Calculate the TTP for each company based on your advice in part (c).**

50 PQ group

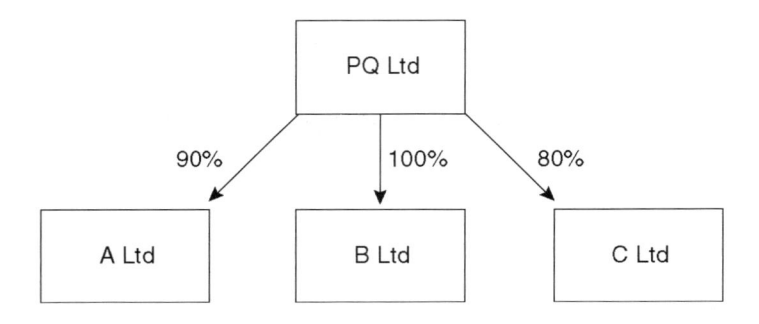

```
              PQ Ltd
        90%   100%   80%
       A Ltd  B Ltd  C Ltd
```

On 24 July 2011 C Ltd sold an office building to A Ltd for £440,000. C Ltd had purchased the building on 26 July 2006 for £260,000.

On 14 June 2022 A Ltd sold the office building for £500,000 to an unconnected company.

PQ Ltd purchased a warehouse on 1 January 2022 for £480,000.

All of the companies have a 31 March year end.

Calculate the chargeable gains arising in the years ended 31 March 2012 and 31 March 2023. Assume all beneficial claims are made and the relevant indexation factors are as follows:

July 2006 to July 2011	0.182
July 2011 to December 2017	0.155

Practice questions

51 Deborah

Deborah started to trade on 1 September 2021.

In her first year of trading, she made sales of £6,000 per month. Her more recent sales are as follows:

2022	£
September	7,300
October	9,600
November	13,000
December	13,500
2023	
January	14,000
February	14,500

(a) **State when it is compulsory for Deborah to register for VAT, when she must notify HMRC and from which date she should charge VAT on her invoices.**

(b) **Explain whether Deborah will be able to recover any pre-registration input tax suffered.**

52 WX Ltd

WX Ltd has prepared the following draft accounts for the quarter to 31 March 2023.

	£	£
Standard rated sales		201,230
Zero rated sales		20,295
Exempt sales		13,750
		235,275
Purchases (standard rated)	41,525	
Distribution expenses (standard rated)	10,000	
Employment costs	47,150	
Impairment loss	1,650	
Entertaining UK customers	715	
Other expenses (standard rated)	16,825	
		(117,865)
Profit		117,410

The impairment loss was written off in February 2023 and relates to a debt which was due for payment on 31 December 2022.

WX Ltd purchased a car for £18,000 on 13 February 2023 and some plant and machinery for £35,000 on 13 March 2023.

All figures include VAT, where applicable.

Calculate the VAT payable for the quarter ended 31 March 2023 and state the due date for payment.

Taxation – United Kingdom
(TX-UK) FA2022

Q&A

Answers to practice questions

Contents		
		Page
Introduction to income tax		
1	Angela	472
2	Andrew	472
3	Briony	472
4	Binta	473
Income from property		
5	Paul	474
Employment income		
6	Flash plc	475
7	Richard	477
Unincorporated businesses		
8	Colin	478
9	Ashley and Cheryl	478
10	Daniel	480
11	Hannah	481
12	Georgina	482
13	Hassan	483
14	Nathan	484

Contents

		Page
15	Oscar	485

Partnerships

16	Eric, Fred and James	486
17	Husna, Kimi and Lesley	487
18	Rajiv and Sumit	488

Simpler income tax for small businesses

19	Zara	489

Pension contributions

20	Philip and Abena	490
21	Stephen	491

Residence

22	Meera, Sanjeev, Gethin and Seema	492

National insurance

23	Vanessa and Wu	493

Capital gains tax

24	Val	494
25	Anthony	495
26	Ahmed	497
27	Melanie	498
28	Judith	500
29	Lisha	501

Self-assessment for individuals

30	Candice	502

Inheritance tax

31	Pat	503
32	Graham	505
33	Craig	506

Contents

		Page
Corporation tax		
Introduction to corporation tax and TTP		
34	ABC Ltd	507
35	DEF Ltd	507
36	GH Ltd	508
37	IJ plc	509
38	KL Ltd	510
39	MN Ltd	511
Capital allowances for companies		
40	OPQ Ltd	512
41	RS plc	513
Chargeable gains for companies		
42	TUV plc	514
43	WXY Ltd	515
44	Bonus issue	516
45	Rights issue	516
46	Takeover	517
Company trading losses		
47	FG Ltd	518
48	HI Ltd	519
Groups		
49	UK group	520
50	PQ group	521
Value Added Tax		
51	Deborah	522
52	WX Ltd	522

1 Angela

D £91,930

Angela's taxable income: 2022/23

	Total income
	£
Employment income	90,000
Building society interest	3,000
UK dividends received	10,000
Premium bond	-
Total income	103,000
PA £12,570 – ½ (103,000 – 100,000)	(11,070)
Taxable income	91,930

2 Andrew

C £17,460

Andrew's income tax liability: 2022/23

Income tax liability		Income	Tax rate	Tax
		£		£
Basic rate band	Non-savings income	37,700	× 20%	7,540
	Non-savings income	22,300	× 40%	8,920
		60,000		
Nil rate band	Savings	500	× 0%	-
Higher rate band	Savings	2,500	× 40%	1,000
		63,000		
Income tax liability				17,460

3 Briony

A £19,160

Briony's income tax liability: 2022/23

Income tax liability		Income	Tax rate	Tax
		£		£
Basic rate band	Non-savings income	37,700	× 20%	7,540
	Non-savings income	22,300	× 40%	8,920
		60,000		
Nil rate band	Dividends	2,000	× 0%	-
Higher rate band	Dividends	8,000	× 33.75%	2,700
		70,000		
Income tax liability				19,160

4   Binta

Binta income tax computation: 2022/23

	Total income	Non-savings income	Savings income	Dividend income
	£	£	£	£
Trading income	130,000	130,000		
Employment income	25,660	25,660		
Bank deposit interest	5,125		5,125	
UK dividends received	2,100			2,100
	162,885	155,660	5,125	2,100
Minus: Allowable interest	(200)	(200)		
Net income	162,685	155,460	5,125	2,100
PA (Nil as income exceeds £125,140)	(Nil)	(Nil)		
Taxable income	162,685	155,460	5,125	2,100

Income tax liability		Income	Tax rate	Tax
		£	£	£
Basic rate band	Non-savings	38,300	× 20%	7,660
Higher rate band	Non-savings	112,300	× 40%	44,920
		150,600		52,580
Additional rate band	Non-savings	4,860	× 45%	2,187
	Savings	5,125	× 45%	2,306
Nil rate band	Dividends	2,000	× 0%	-
Additional rate band	Dividends	100	x 39.35%	39
		162,685		
Income tax liability				57,112
Minus PAYE				(8,287)
Income tax payable				48,825

Notes

(1) Gift Aid donations are paid by an individual net of 20% income tax. The basic rate and higher rate bands are extended by the gross amount.

(2) National lottery winnings and income from ISAs are exempt from income tax.

(3) Additional rate taxpayers do not receive a savings nil rate band.

Working: Extension of basic and higher rate bands	Basic	Higher
	£	£
Original band limit	37,700	150,000
Gift Aid donation: (£480 × 100/80)	600	600
Extended basic/higher rate band	38,300	150,600

5   Paul

(a) **Paul's property income: 2022/23**

	£	£
Rent received:		
April–December – 9/12 × £8,000	6,000	
January–February – 2/12 × £9,000	1,500	7,500
Expenditure:		
Council tax	960	
Water rates	380	
Agent's fees	780	
Redecoration	1,250	
Central heating system	-	
Interest	-	
Replacement furniture relief	500	(3,870)
Assessable amount		3,630

Notes:

(1) The cash basis of assessment applies to rental income received by individuals, therefore the rent for March 2023 will be taxable in 2023/24 as it was paid late.

(2) The new central heating system is capital expenditure and therefore not deductible.

(3) Relief for the mortgage interest is restricted to the basic rate; therefore £500 (£2,500 x 20%) is deducted from Paul's income tax liability.

(4) As the washer-dryer represents an improvement, Paul can only deduct the cost of a replacement washing machine.

(b) To be treated as FHL **all** of the following conditions must be satisfied:

- the property is situated in the European Economic Area, and
- is furnished, and
- is let on a commercial basis with a view to making profits, and
- is available for letting as holiday accommodation for at least 210 days in the tax year, and
- is actually let for at least 105 days in the tax year, and
- is not normally occupied for periods of longer-term occupation (i.e. occupied for more than 31 consecutive days by the same person).

As Paul's property appears to be let on an annual basis to the same tenant, it does not currently qualify as a furnished holiday letting.

If Paul's property had been classed as an FHL, the full £2,500 of mortgage interest would have been deducted in calculating his property income. (Relief for interest on FHL is not restricted to the basic rate of tax.)

Answers to practice questions

6 Flash plc

Benefits assessed in 2022/23

(a) **Arthur**

    D   £4,915

Arthur's car has CO_2 emissions of 52 g/km. This gives a benefit of 15% plus an additional 4% as the car is diesel and does not meet the RDE2 standard. The benefit must be time-apportioned as the car was only available for eight months during 2022/23.

Arthur's benefits

	£		£
Car benefit			
Manufacturer's list price	13,500	× 19% × 8/12	1,710
Fuel benefit	25,300	× 19% × 8/12	3,205
Total assessable benefits for Arthur			4,915

(b) **Benny**

    C   £5,214

		%
CO_2 emissions (rounded down to nearest 5 g/km)	140	
Base level	(55)	
	85 / 5 =	17
Minimum percentage		16
Diesel surcharge		-
		33

Benny's benefits

	£		£
Car benefit			
Manufacturer's list price	20,800		
Minus: Capital contribution (restricted to maximum of £5,000)	(5,000)		
	15,800	× 33%	5,214

(c) **Charlotte**

   D   £17,411

			%
CO_2 emissions (rounded down to nearest 5 g/km)	180		
Base level	(55)		
	125 / 5 =		25
Minimum percentage			16
Diesel surcharge			-
			41
Capped at maximum			37

Charlotte's benefits

	£		£
Car benefit			
Manufacturer's list price	25,000	× 37%	9,250
Minus: Contribution towards use of car			(1,200)
			8,050
Fuel benefit	25,300	× 37%	9,361
Total assessable benefits for Charlotte			17,411

Note

Contributions towards private fuel costs are not an allowable deduction.

(d) **Daphne**

   C   Daphne does not have an assessable benefit. Instead, due to the shortfall of allowance received, Daphne can deduct £1,400 from her employment income.

Daphne's benefits

		£	£
Mileage allowance received	12,000 × 30p		3,600
Approved mileage allowance	10,000 × 45p	4,500	
	2,000 × 25p	500	
			(5,000)
			(1,400)

(e) **Ernest**

   B   £3,931

   Ernest's benefit:

   Company van: £3,600 × 11/12 = £3,300.

   Fuel: £688 × 11/12 = £631.

   Total £3,931 (3,300 + 631)

Answers to practice questions

7 Richard

Richard: Employment income 2022/23	£
Salary	56,000
Bonus (paid 31 May 2022)	22,000
Assessable benefits	
Overnight expense allowance	60
Annual staff party (exempt, because below £150 per head)	Nil
Beneficial loan (see working)	125
Car benefit (see working)	1,250
Car fuel (£25,300 x 5%)	1,265
	80,700
Allowable deductions:	
Subscription to professional body	(270)
Donation under payroll giving scheme	(120)
Employment income	80,310

Note The full amount of the overnight expense allowance is taxable as it exceeds £5 a night.

Workings:

Beneficial loan

(1)	Average method	£
	Average amount = (£30,000 + £25,000)/2 =	27,500
	Interest at the official rate: £27,500 × 2%	550
	Interest paid	(400)
	Assessable benefit, average method	150

(2)	Strict method	£
	Interest at the official rate:	
	From 6 April 2022 to 6 July 2022 (3 months): £30,000 × 2% × 3/12	150
	From 6 July 2022 to 5 April 2023 (9 months): £25,000 × 2% × 9/12	375
		525
Interest paid		(400)
Assessable benefit		125

Note Richard should insist on the strict method being used, because this gives a lower taxable benefit.

Car benefit
With CO_2 emissions between 1 and 50 grams per kilometre, the electric range of the car is relevant. This is between 70 and 129 miles, so the relevant percentage is 5%. The car was available throughout 2022/23, so the benefit is £1,250 (25,000 x 5%).

8 Colin

(a) The following expenses are added back in computaing Colin's adjusted trading profits:

	£
Colin's personal income tax and NICs	6,400
Write off of loan to customer	2,250

Colin's IT and NIC are appropriations of profit. The loan to a customer is not a trading item as Colin's business is not money lending.

(b) Leasing expenses of £840 must be added back in computing Colin's adjusted trading profits.

Lease of car with CO_2 emissions over 50 g/km	£
Disallowable element of hire charge £5,600 × 15%	840

The full market value of goods taken out of the business by the owner (i.e. £120) must be added to profit, as no entry has been made in the accounts of the business.

(c) **A**   £340

Car expenses	£
Colin's car expenses: ½ × £3,400	1,700
Add to profit the private % of these expenses: £1,700 × 20%	340

The sales manager's expenses are fully allowable for the business. Private use by an employee is not relevant. The sales manager will be assessed on the private use of the company car under the employment income rules.

9 Ashley and Cheryl

(a) **B**   £254,050

Ashley: Capital allowances, 3 months ended 31 December 2022

	£	Main pool £	Total allowances £
Additions qualifying for AIA			
Production line	340,000		
AIA (1,000,000 × 3/12)	(250,000)		250,000
		90,000	
WDA: (£90,000 × 18% × 3/12)		(4,050)	4,050
TWDV c/f		85,950	
Total allowances for production line			254,050

The automated production line is not treated as a long-life asset as it has an estimated useful life of less than 25 years. It is treated as if purchased on the first day of trading.

Answers to practice questions

(b) **A** £495

Car for manager
WDA: (£11,000 × 18% × 3/12)   £495

The private use of the car by the sales manager is irrelevant. The sales manager will be assessed on the private use of the company car in their income tax computation. As the car's CO_2 emissions are between 1 and 50 g/km, it is put in the main pool.

(c) **C** £29,766

AIA of £7,370 and WDA of £22,396 are available in respect of the main pool.

(d) **A** £2,910

A balancing allowance arises as Cheryl needs additional allowances to recover the full net cost of the asset. (A balancing charge arises if the disposal proceeds exceed the tax written down value of the asset.)

Workings

Cheryl: Capital allowances computation – y/e 31 March 2023

		Main pool	Short-life asset	Total allowances
	£	£	£	£
TWDV b/f		113,420	3,410	
Additions qualifying for AIAs				
IT equipment	7,370			
AIA	(7,370)	Nil		7,370
Additions not qualifying for AIAs				
Car		11,000		
Disposals –				
Lower of cost or sale proceeds			(500)	
		124,420	2,910	
Balancing allowance			(2,910)	2,910
WDA (18%)		(22,396)		22,396
TWDV c/f		102,024		
Total allowances				32,676

Notes

(1) The IT equipment should not be treated as a short life asset as its cost is covered by the AIA. (Treating it as a short life asset would result in a balancing charge when the asset is eventually sold.)

(2) The car is added to the main pool as it has CO_2 emissions of less than 50g/km.

(e) A £6,300

The qualifying expenditure for SBA is £360,000 (470,000 – 110,000). The factory was brought into use on 1 September 2022, so the SBA for the year ended 31 March 2023 is £6,300 (360,000 at 3% x 7/12).

10 Daniel

Daniel: computation of adjusted profits after capital allowances
15 month period ending 30 June 2023

		£
Net profit		94,500
Add	Depreciation	10,000
	Motor expenses (25% × £3,750)	937
	Fine for breach of health regulations	5,000
	Computer software (capital)	2,100
	Premium for granting of lease (capital)	6,000
		118,537
Minus	Building society interest	(2,000)
	Rental income	(6,000)
	Allowable deduction for short lease (W1)	(98)
Adjusted profit before capital allowances		110,439
Minus	Capital allowances (W2)	(61,000)
Adjusted profit after capital allowances		49,439

Notes

(1) The computer software is disallowable capital expenditure. However, capital allowances are available on the cost of the software with the cost of the new computer system.

(2) The premium paid to purchase the leasehold interest is disallowable capital expenditure. However, an annual allowance is available for part of the cost of the lease if the building is used for the purpose of Daniel's trade.

Workings

W1: Allowable deduction for short lease	£
Premium paid	6,000
Minus: 2% × £6,000 × 11 years	(1,320)
Property income assessment on E Ltd	4,680
Annual allowable deduction for Daniel (£4,680 ÷ 12 years)	£390

Daniel owned the leasehold interest for 3 months in the accounting period. Therefore, the allowable deduction for the period ending 30 June 2023 is:

£390 × 3/12 = **£98**.

Note

The allowable deduction is apportioned by 3/12 because the figure of £390 is the annual (i.e. 12 month) deduction.

Answers to practice questions

W2: Capital allowances		Main pool	P/U car 1	P/U car 2	Total allowances
		£	£	£	£
TWDV b/f		78,000	6,400		
Additions qualifying for AIA					
Computer system	15,000				
Software	2,100				
Plant and machinery	28,000				
	45,100				
AIA	(45,100)	-			45,100
Additions not qualifying for AIA				16,000	
Disposals			(9,800)		
		78,000	(3,400)	16,000	
			× 75%		(2,550)
WDA: 15/12 × 18%		(17,550)			17,550
WDA: 15/12 × 6%				(1,200) × 75%	900
TWDV c/f		60,450		14,800	
Total allowances					61,000

Notes

(1) The computer system and software have an expected useful life of three years. However, it is not beneficial to make a short-life asset election as their cost is fully covered by the AIA.

(2) The accounting period is more than 12 months. The WDA must therefore be adjusted by × 15/12 to allow for the 15-month accounting period.

11 Hannah

(a) **B** £41,250

(b) **A** £45,000

(c) **D** £43,750

Trade starts: 1 May 2018. This is in the tax year 2018/19

Tax year	Basis of assessment	Basis period	Workings	Assessment
				£
2018/19	Actual	1.5.18 – 5.4.2019	11/16 × £60,000	41,250
2019/20	12 months ending in 2nd year	1.9.2018 – 31.8.2019	12/16 × £60,000	45,000
2020/21	12 months ending in 3rd year	Year ended 31.8.2020		84,000
2021/22	CYB	Year ended 31.8.2021		90,000

Tax year	Basis of assessment	Basis period	Workings	Assessment
				£
2022/23	Profits not yet assessed = Period ended 30.4.22			70,000
	Minus: Overlap profits (1.9.2018 – 5.4.2019)		7/16 × £60,000	(26,250)
	Closing year trading income assessment			43,750

12 Georgina

Capital allowances computation

	Main pool £	Georgina's car (1) (business use 25%) £	Georgina's car (2) (business use 25%) £	Total £
Y/e 30.4.20				
Additions	4,000	5,600		
WDA 18%	(720)	(1,008) × 25%		972
Addition	3,200			
AIA	(3,200)			3,200
	3,280	4,592		4,172
Y/e 30.4.21				
Additions	–		7,800	
Sale	–	(3,000)		
	3,280	1,592		
Balancing allowance		(1,592) × 25%		398
WDA 18%	(590)		(1,404) × 25%	941
Addition	1,000			
AIA	(1,000)			1,000
	2,690	–	6,396	2,339
P/e 30.9.22				
Additions	500			
Sales (2,000 + 2,000)	(4,000)		(6,000)	
	(810)		396	
Balancing charge	810			(810)
Balancing allowance			(396) × 25%	99
	–		–	(711)

Adjusted profit

	£
Year ended 30 April 2020 (15,000 – 4,172)	10,828
Year ended 30 April 2021 (12,000 – 2,339)	9,661
Period ended 30 September 2022 (19,000 + 711)	19,711

Trading income assessments

	£	£
2019/20 – First year: Actual (1.5.19 – 5.4.20)		
10,828 × 11/12		9,926
2020/21 (y/e 30.4.20)		10,828
2021/22 (y/e 30.4.21)		9,661
2022/23 (p/e 30.9.22)	19,711	
Less: overlap relief (1.5.19 – 5.4.20)	(9,926)	
		9,785

13 Hassan

Year ended	Basis of assessment	Tax year	Trading income assessment
			£
31 May 2019	CYB	2019/20	50,200
31 May 2020	CYB	2020/21	16,600
31 May 2021	CYB	2021/22	Nil
31 May 2022	CYB	2022/23	36,800

2021/22 is the tax year of the loss.

Hassan: Income tax computations

	2019/20	2020/21	2021/22	2022/23
	£	£	£	£
Trading income	50,200	16,600	Nil	36,800
Minus: loss relief b/f	Nil	Nil	Nil	(3,810)
	50,200	16,600	Nil	32,990
Employment income	40,000	60,000	60,000	60,000
Total income before relief	90,200	76,600	60,000	92,990
Minus: loss relief	-	(66,600)	(50,000)	-
	90,200	10,000	10,000	92,990
PA	(12,570)	(10,000)	(10,000)	(12,570)
Taxable income	77,630	Nil	Nil	80,420

Record of trading losses

	2021/22
	£
Trading loss in tax year	120,410
Loss relief claimed	
- in 2020/21 (W1)	(66,600)
- in 2021/22 (W2)	(50,000)
	3,810
Loss relief claimed in 2022/23	(3,810)
Carried forward	Nil

Workings

(W1) Loss relief for 2020/21

Higher of:
£50,000 and
Non trading income £60,000 x 25% = £15,000

Therefore £50,000

Plus an additional £16,600 as there is no restriction on the amount that can be set off against the trading income.

(W2) Loss relief for 2021/22

Higher of:
£50,000 and
£60,000 x 25% = £15,000

Therefore £50,000

14 Nathan

(a) Trade starts: 1 July 2020. This is in the tax year 2020/21.

Tax year	Basis of assessment	Basis period	Workings (nearest month)		Trading income
				£	£
2020/21	Actual	1.7.2020 – 5.4.2021	9/12 × £28,800 loss	(21,600)	Nil
2021/22	12 months ending in 2nd year	Year ended 30.6.2021	Loss in period	(28,800)	
			Loss already used in calculation	21,600	
				(7,200)	Nil
2022/23	12 months ending in 3rd year	Year ended 30.6.2022		6,000	6,000

(b) **Loss relief available**

Tax year of loss	Amount of loss	Loss relief available	
	£	**Against total income:**	**Early years' rules:**
2020/21	21,600	1. 2020/21 and/or 2. 2019/20 - in either order	1. 2017/18 and then 2. 2018/19 and then 3. 2019/20 - in that strict order
2021/22	7,200	1. 2021/22 and/or 2. 2020/21 - in either order	1. 2018/19 and then 2. 2019/20 and then 3. 2020/21 - in that strict order
	28,800		

(c) **Nathan: income tax computations**

	2017/18 £	2018/19 £	2019/20 £	2020/21 £	2021/22 £	2022/23 £
Trading income				Nil	Nil	6,000
Employment income	30,000	26,000	15,000			
Other income	9,600	9,600	9,600	9,600	9,600	9,600
Total income	39,600	35,600	24,600	9,600	9,600	15,600
Early years' relief						
- 2020/21 loss	(21,600)					
- 2021/22 loss		(7,200)				
Total income after losses	18,000	28,400	24,600	9,600	9,600	15,600
PA	(12,570)	(12,570)	(12,570)	(9,600)	(9,600)	(12,570)
Taxable income	5,430	15,830	12,030	Nil	Nil	3,030

15 Oscar

Oscar: income tax computations

	2018/19 £	2019/20 £	2020/21 £	2021/22 £	2022/23 £
Trading income (W1)	40,000	33,000	20,000	Nil	Nil
Minus: terminal loss	-	(7,200)	(20,000)	(Nil)	(Nil)
	40,000	25,800	Nil	Nil	Nil
Property income	5,000	5,000	5,000	5,000	5,000
	45,000	30,800	5,000	5,000	5,000
PA	(12,570)	(12,570)	(5,000)	(5,000)	(5,000)
Taxable income	32,430	18,230	Nil	Nil	Nil

Workings

(W1) Trading income assessment

Ceased to trade: 30 June 2022. This is in the tax year 2022/23.

	£
Final tax year = 2022/23	
Profits not yet assessed	
Period ending 30 June 2022	(5,000)
Minus: Overlap profits	(6,200)
Net loss	(11,200)
Final tax year assessment	Nil

(W2) Terminal loss

	£	£
Overlap profits not yet relieved		6,200
Last tax year		
Actual loss (6.4.2022 – 30.6.2022): 3/6 × £5,000 loss		2,500
		8,700
12 months before cessation to 5 April before cessation		
1.7.2021 to 5.4.2022 = 9 months		
Actual loss		
Period 1.7.2021 – 31.12.2021: (6/12 × £32,000 loss)	(16,000)	
Period 1.1.2022 – 5.4.2022: (3/6 × £5,000 loss)	(2,500)	
Net loss	(18,500)	18,500
Terminal loss of last 12 months trading		27,200

This loss is carried back against trading income on a LIFO basis.

16 Eric, Fred and James

F £34,000

Note

Although Eric receives a salary from the partnership, this is taxed as trading income.

Partnership allocation: year ending 31 December 2022

	Total	Eric	Fred	James
	£	£	£	£
4 months to 30 April 2022				
Balance of profits (3:2:1)	20,000	10,000	6,667	3,333
(4/12 × £60,000)				
8 months to 31 December 2022				
Salary (£20,000 × 8/12)	13,333	13,333		
Balance of profits (2:2:1)	26,667	10,667	10,667	5,333
	40,000	24,000	10,667	5,333
12 months to 31 December 2022				
Total profit allocation	60,000	34,000	17,334	8,666

Answers to practice questions

17 Husna, Kimi and Lesley

Allocation of partnership profits

	Total	Husna	Kimi	Lesley	Mike
	£	£	£	£	£
Year to 30 June 2020					
Profits shared equally	24,000	8,000	8,000	8,000	-
Year to 30 June 2021					
Profits shared equally					
1.7.2020 – 31.1.2021	18,900	6,300	6,300	6,300	-
(7/12 × £32,400)					
1.2.2021 – 30.6.2021					
(5/12 × £32,400)	13,500	4,500	-	4,500	4,500
	32,400	10,800	6,300	10,800	4,500
Year to 30 June 2022					
Profits shared equally	43,200	14,400	-	14,400	14,400

Trading income assessments of Husna and Lesley (continuing partners)

Tax year	Basis of assessment	Trading income assessment
		£
2020/21	CYB y/e 30.6.2020	8,000
2021/22	CYB y/e 30.6.2021	10,800
2022/23	CYB y/e 30.6.2022	14,400

Trading income assessments of Mike (new partner)

		£
Share of profits:	5 months to 30.6.2021	4,500
	y/e 30.6.2022	14,400

Started to trade: 1 February 2021. This is in the tax year 2020/21.

Tax year	Basis of assessment	Basis period	Workings (nearest month)	Trading income assessment
				£
2020/21	Actual	1.2.2021–5.4.2021	2/5 × £4,500	1,800
2021/22	First 12 months trading	1.2.2021–31.1.2022	£4,500 + (7/12 × £14,400)	12,900
2022/23	12 months ending in 3rd year	Year ended 30.6.2022		14,400

Mike's overlap profits

Opening years		£
1.2.2021 – 5.4.2021	(2/5 × £4,500)	1,800
1.7.2021 – 31.1.2022	(7/12 × £14,400)	8,400
		10,200

Trading income assessments of Kimi (retiring partner)

Ceased to trade: 1 February 2021. This is in the tax year 2020/21.

	£
Penultimate tax year = 2019/20: CYB year ended 30.6.2019	
Final tax year = 2020/21	
Year ending 30.6.2020	8,000
Period ending 31.1.2021	6,300
	14,300
Minus: Overlap profits	(2,000)
Closing year trading income assessment	12,300

18 Rajiv and Sumit

(a) **Allocation of partnership loss: year ending 31 March 2023**

	Total	Rajiv	Sumit	Tisha
	£	£	£	£
9 months 1 April to 31 December 2022				
Salary (£16,000 or £28,000 × 9/12)	33,000	12,000	21,000	-
Balance of the loss (65%:35%)	(109,200)	(70,980)	(38,220)	-
	(76,200)	(58,980)	(17,220)	-
Period 1 January to 31 March 2023				
Balance of the loss (2:2:1)	(25,400)	(10,160)	(10,160)	(5,080)
Allocation of loss	(101,600)	(69,140)	(27,380)	(5,080)

(b) **Loss relief options**

Rajiv and Sumit (continuing partners)

Tax year of the loss = 2022/23

Rajiv and Sumit have the following options with their share of the loss:

- Claim relief against total income in:
  - 2022/23 and/or
  - 2021/22
- Extend the claim against capital gains in the same years.
- Carry forward the loss against future trading profits.

Rajiv and Sumit will make their own decisions independently, according to their own personal circumstances. They are not both obliged to make the same claims. (Note that, in Rajiv's case, the maximum amount of loss that can be set against non-partnership income in any year is the higher of £50,000 or 25% of total income.)

Tisha (new partner)

Opening year loss = 2022/23

Actual loss 1.1.2023 – 31.3.2023 = £5,080.

Tisha has the following options with her share of the loss:

- Claim relief against total income in:
  - 2022/23 and/or
  - 2021/22
- Extend the claim against capital gains in the same years.
- Claim early years' loss relief against total income in:
  - 2019/20 and then
  - 2020/21 and then
  - 2021/22.
- Carry forward the loss against future trading profits.

19 Zara

If Zara uses the cash basis of assessment, her trading profit for the year ended 5 April 2023 will be as follows:

	£	£
Revenue		
(120,100 – 1,100)		119,000
Expenses		
Equipment	4,800	
Motor expenses (8,000 miles at 45p)	3,600	
Property expenses (9,600 – 4,200)	5,400	
Other expenses (82,000 – 18,200)	63,800	(77,600)
Trading profit		41,400

Note that the cost of the car is not deductible as the approved mileage allowances have been claimed.

If Zara uses the normal accruals basis to compute her trading income, her trading profit for the year ended 5 April 2023 will be as follows:

	£	£
Revenue		120,100
Expenses		
Motor expenses (6,000 x 8,000/12,000)	4,000	
Property expenses (9,600 x 50%)	4,800	
Other expenses	82,000	(90,800)
Trading profit before capital allowances		29,300
Capital allowances:		
Equipment (AIA)	4,800	
Car (£16,000 x 18% x 8,000/12,000)	1,920	(6,720)
Trading profit after capital allowances		22,580

It is therefore not beneficial for Zara to use the cash basis of assessment as it will increase her trading profits by £18,820 (41,400 – 22,580).

20 Philip and Abena

(a) **C** £10,000 from 2021/22

The pension contribution of £68,000 for 2022/23 has used all of Philip's annual allowance of £40,000 for 2022/23.

It has also used £8,000 (40,000 – 32,000) of the unused allowance from 2019/20, £19,000 (40,000 – 21,000) of the unused allowance from 2020/21 and £1,000 of the unused allowance from 2021/22.

Philip therefore has an unused allowance of £10,000 (40,000 – 29,000 – 1,000) from 2021/22 available to carry forward to 2023/24.

(b) **A** £12,500

As Abena's adjusted net income exceeds £240,000, her annual allowance must be tapered as follows:

	£
Annual allowance	40,000
Less: (295,000 – 240,000) x ½	(27,500)
Tapered annual allowance	12,500

Working	£
Net income (i.e. total income less deductible interest)	280,000
Plus any employee contributions to occupational pension schemes	6,000
Plus any employer contributions to either occupational or personal pension schemes.	9,000
Adjusted income	295,000

21 Stephen

(a) Stephen: Employment income 2022/23

	£
Salary	32,000
Assessable benefits	
Employer pension contributions (7%) = exempt	Nil
Living accommodation (W1)	3,750
Car benefits (W2)	7,576
Medical insurance – cost to employer	480
Subsidised meals – exempt	Nil
Workplace nursery – exempt	Nil
Holiday prize – cost to employer	1,200
Staff loan scheme	Nil
Write-off of loan	3,000
	48,006
Allowable deductions:	
Employee pension contributions (£32,000 × 5%)	(1,600)
Employment income	46,406

Workings

(W1) Living accommodation	£	£
Annual value		1,700
Expensive accommodation benefit		Nil
(= Not applicable as the property cost less than £75,000)		
Running costs		
Electricity	280	
Gas	410	
Gardener	240	
Redecoration	680	
		1,610
Provision of furniture: (£6,400 × 20%)		1,280
		4,590
Minus: Contribution towards benefit (£70 × 12)		(840)
Total living accommodation benefits		3,750

(W2) Car benefits	Stephen's car	Wife's car		Stephen's car	Wife's car
				petrol %	diesel %
CO_2 emissions (rounded down to nearest 5 g/km)	95	55			
Base level	(55)	(55)			
	40	0	÷ 5	8	0

			16	16
Minimum percentages				
Diesel surcharge			-	4
Appropriate percentages			24	20

	£		£
Stephen's car			
Manufacturer's list price	16,400	× 24%	3,936
Wife's car			
Manufacturer's list price	18,200	× 20%	3,640
			7,576

Notes

1. There is no private fuel benefit as Stephen pays for his petrol and is reimbursed for business travel only. Therefore, the company does not pay for any private fuel. Stephen's wife pays for all her petrol.

2. There is no beneficial loan charge as the sum borrowed does not exceed £10,000.

(b) If Stephen had paid his pension contribution into a personal pension scheme it would not have been deducted in calculating his employment income. Instead, the amount paid would have been grossed up by 100/80. Relief at the higher rate, if applicable, would have been given by extending the basic rate band.

22   Meera, Sanjeev, Gethin and Seema

(a) Meera will automatically be treated as not resident in the UK for 2022/23 as she is in the UK for less than 16 days during the tax year.

(b) Sanjeev cannot be treated as automatically not resident in the UK for 2022/23 as he is in the UK for more than 45 days during the tax year. He is treated as automatically resident in the UK for 2022/23 as carries out full-time work in the UK.

(c) Gethin has spent more than 45 days in the UK during 2022/23 and was UK resident for the three preceding tax years, therefore he cannot automatically be treated as non-resident.

He will not automatically be treated as UK resident because he does not meet the only home test.

Gethin has been resident in the UK during the three previous tax years and was in the UK between 46 and 90 days during 2022/23. He will be classed as UK resident if he has three or more ties. His UK ties are as follows:

- He has close family in the UK.
- He has a house in the UK which he made use of.
- He was in the UK for more than 90 days during each of the two preceding tax years.

He is therefore resident in the UK for 2022/23.

(d) Seema has spent more than 45 days in the UK during 2022/23 and so cannot be automatically treated as non-resident.

She will not automatically be treated as resident because she does not meet the only home test.

Seema has not been resident in the UK during the three previous tax years. She was in the UK between 121 and 182 days, therefore she needs two UK ties in order to be classed as UK resident.

She has a house in the UK which she made use of during the tax year. She also has close family in the UK. She is therefore resident in the UK for 2022/23.

23 Vanessa and Wu

(a) **D** £5,311

Class 1 primary and secondary contributions are based on cash earnings.

Salary = Cash earnings = **£60,000**.

	£
Class 1 primary contributions	
(£50,270 – £12,570) × 13.25%	4,995
(£60,000 – £50,270) × 3.25%	316
	5,311

Notes

Cash earnings exclude all the benefits received by Vanessa. The donation under the payroll giving scheme is ignored as expense deductions are not allowed for NIC purposes.

(b) **B** £7,660

Class 1 secondary contributions	
(£60,000 – £9,100) × 15.05%	7,660

VX plc's total secondary class 1 contributions will be reduced by the employment allowance of £5,000.

(c) **D** £1,892

Class 1A contributions are payable by VX plc. They are based on the benefits received by Vanessa, but excluding the employer's pension contributions as these are exempt.

	£
Car benefit	6,450
Fuel benefit	4,320
Living accommodation	1,800
Total benefits liable to Class 1A NICs	12,570
Class 1A NICs (£12,570 × 15.05%)	1,892

(d) **A**

Class 4 NIC is payable under the self-assessment system together with the taxpayer's income tax. The payment dates for the 2022/23 liability are 31 January 2023, 31 July 2023 and 31 January 2024.

(e) **A** £4,180

	£
Yui's Class 4 NICs	
(£50,270 – £12,570) × 10.25%	3,864
(£60,000 – £50,270) × 3.25%	316
	4,180

24 Val

(a) Val: Payment on account

	£
Holiday cottage (W)	111,000
Minus: Annual exempt amount	(12,300)
Taxable gain	98,700
Capital gains tax	
(37,700 – 21,555) × 18%	2,906
(98,700 – 16,145) × 28%	23,115
Due date for payment: 31 December 2022	26,021

(W)	Holiday cottage	£
	Gross sale proceeds	128,000
	Minus: Cost	(17,000)
	Gain	111,000

Note

The payment on account ignores the other chargeable gains. Val needs to estimate the amount of basic rate band that will be available to set against the gain. The tax is payable 60 days after the date of disposal.

(b) Val: Capital gains tax liability

	Residential gains	Non-residential gains
	£	£
Garnet Ltd shares (W1)		45,000
Ruby plc shares (W2)		60,000
Holiday cottage	111,000	
	111,000	105,000
Minus: Annual exempt amount	(12,300)	-
Taxable gain	98,700	105,000

Capital gains tax
(37,700 – 21,555) x 18%	2,906
(98,700 – 16,145) x 28%	23,115
105,000 x 20%	21,000
	47,021
Less payment on account	(26,021)
Due date for payment: 31 January 2024	21,000

Note

The annual exempt amount has been set against the residential gain as this saves tax at 28% rather than 20%.

The tax could alternatively have been calculated as:

(37,700 – 21,555) x 10%	1,614
(105,000 – 16,145) x 20%	17,771
98,700 x 28%	27,636
	47,021

Workings

(W1)	Garnet Ltd shares	£
	Gross sale proceeds	55,000
	Minus: Cost	(10,000)
	Gain	45,000

(W2)	Ruby plc shares	£
	Gross sale proceeds	66,000
	Minus: Cost	(6,000)
	Gain	60,000

25 Anthony

Anthony: Capital gains tax liability	Gains
	£
Shares purchased 22 July 2022	13,500
Pool shares	75,136
Shares in S Ltd	8,710
Investment land	(4,000)
Net gains for the year	93,346
Minus: Annual exempt amount	(12,300)
	81,046
Minus capital losses b/f	(16,150)
Taxable gain	64,896

Capital gains tax
(37,700 – 29,200) x 10%   850
(64,896 – 8,500) x 20%   11,279
    12,129

Workings

(W1) R plc shares

Matching rules	Number of shares	Disposal	Remaining shares
1: Acquisition in following 30 days			
22 July 2022	11,000	(11,000)	Nil
2: Pool shares	50,000		
Rights issue (1 for 10)	5,000		
	55,000	(29,000)	26,000
		(40,000)	26,000

Chargeable gain on the disposal of shares acquired on 22 July 2022 (11,000 shares)

	£
Market value (11,000 × £4.50)	49,500
Minus: Cost of shares	(36,000)
Gain	13,500

No gift holdover relief is available as the shares are not qualifying assets for gift holdover relief purposes. Gift holdover relief is only available on quoted shares if the taxpayer owns at least a 5% interest in the company.

Chargeable gain on the disposal of shares in the pool (29,000 shares)

	£
Market value (29,000 × £4.50)	130,500
Minus: Cost (from pool)	(55,364)
Gain	75,136

Pool	Number of shares	Original cost
		£
16 October 2006	50,000	75,000
10 August 2008		
Rights issue (5,000 × £6)	5,000	30,000
	55,000	105,000
18 July 2022		
Gift to daughter	(29,000)	(55,364)
Pool balance c/f	26,000	49,636

Shares from the pool are removed at average cost:
£105,000 × 29,000/55,000 = £55,364

(W2) Plot of investment land

	£
Gross sale proceeds	10,000
Minus: Cost	(14,000)
Loss	(4,000)

(W3) S Ltd shares – 6,500 shares

	£
Gross sale proceeds (6,500 × £5)	32,500
Cost (£36,600 × 6,500/10,000)	(23,790)
Gain	8,710

26 Ahmed

Ahmed: Capital gains tax liability	Gains
	£
GH Ltd shares (W1)	39,000
Painting	17,650
Net gains for the year	56,650
Current year loss claim (W2)	(9,100)
Total net gains	47,550
Minus: Annual exempt amount	(12,300)
Taxable gain	35,250
Minus capital losses b/f	(4,610)
Taxable gain	30,640
Capital gains tax	
£30,640 at 10%	3,064

Trading losses

	£
Trading loss in tax year	28,500
Current year claim against income	(19,400)
Current year claim against gains	(9,100)
Trading loss c/f	Nil

Capital losses

	£
Capital loss brought forward	4,610
Current year set off	(4,610)
Capital loss carried forward	Nil

Workings

(W1) Sale at undervaluation – GH Ltd shares

	£
Market value (6,000 × £15)	90,000
Minus: Cost	(6,000)
Gain before specific reliefs	84,000
Gift holdover relief (see below)	(45,000)
Gain after specific reliefs	39,000

Gift holdover relief

	£
Actual sale proceeds received	45,000
Original cost	(6,000)
= Gain	39,000
Gift holdover relief (£84,000 – £39,000)	45,000

(W2) Trading loss relief against capital gains – 2022/23

	£
Amount of relief available – Lower of:	
(1) Unrelieved trading loss after claim against total income (£28,500 – £19,400)	9,100
(2) Total gains for the year (£39,000 + £17,650)	56,650
Minus: Capital losses in year	(Nil)
Capital losses brought forward	(4,610)
Maximum amount	52,040

27 Melanie

(a)

Disposal	Gift holdover relief	Rollover relief
Antique vase		
Shares in Match Ltd	√	
Workshop		√
Business asset	√	

(b) **D** £915

Gift of Match Ltd shares

	£
Market value (£1.80 × 8,500)	15,300
Cost £16,500 × $\frac{8,500}{15,000}$	(9,350)
	5,950

Gift holdover relief is available as unquoted trading company shares are qualifying shares for gift holdover relief purposes. However full gift holdover relief is not available as Match Ltd holds investments.

Gift holdover relief = £5,950 × $\frac{£220,000 \text{ (CBA)}}{£260,000 \text{ (CA)}}$ = £5,035

Gain after gift holdover relief = £5,950 - £5,035 = £915

(c) **D** £32,000

Sale of workshop

	£
Sale proceeds	100,000
Cost	(35,000)
Gain	65,000

The workshop is a qualifying asset for rollover relief. However, full rollover relief is not available as not all of the sale proceeds are reinvested in a qualifying business asset between November 2021 and November 2025.

Gain chargeable in 2022/23 = lower of

(i) full gain £65,000

(ii) sale proceeds not reinvested

(£100,000 - £68,000) = £32,000

A rollover relief claim for £33,000 (£65,000 - £32,000) should therefore be made.

Gain in 2022/23 = £32,000

(d) **B** £13,000

Sale for less than market value

	£
Market value	35,000
(ignore actual sale proceeds)	
Cost	(5,000)
Gain	30,000

Gift holdover relief is available as the asset is a business asset used in Melanie's business. However, full gift holdover relief is not available as the actual sale proceeds received exceed the original cost.

Gain chargeable in 2022/23	£
Sale proceeds received	18,000
Cost	(5,000)
	13,000

Gift holdover relief = (£30,000 - £13,000) = £17,000

(e) The time limit for both reliefs is four years from the end of the tax year of disposal, i.e. 5 April 2027 for disposals in 2022/23.

Gift holdover relief	Rollover relief
31 January 2025	31 January 2025
5 April 2025	5 April 2025
5 April 2027	**5 April 2027**
31 January 2029	31 January 2029

28 Judith

(a) Judith's chargeable gain

	£
Gross sale proceeds	384,000
Less Cost	(69,379)
Gain before PRR	314,621
Less PRR (W1)	
£314,621 × (162/204)	(249,846)
Chargeable gain	64,775

Working

(1) PRR

	Notes	Total (mths)	Exempt (mths)	Chargeable (mths)
01.04.2006 – 31.03.2010	(1)	48	48	
01.04.2010 – 31.12.2014	(2)	57	57	
01.01.2015 – 28.02.2016	(3)	14	14	
01.03.2016 – 30.06.2016	(4)	4	4	
01.07.2016 – 31.12.2018	(5)	30	30	
01.01.2019 – 31.03.2023	(6)	51	9	42
		204	162	42

Notes

(1) Owner occupied – therefore exempt

(2) Working overseas – exempt as she occupied the property as her main residence **at some time before and after** this period of absence.

Answers to practice questions

(3) Working elsewhere in the UK – periods totalling up to four years are exempt as she occupied the property as her main residence **at some time before and after** this period of absence.

(4) In home town but living with relatives – periods totalling up to three years are exempt for 'any reason' as the property is occupied as her PPR both before and after the period of absence.

(5) Owner occupied – therefore exempt.

(6) The property was not Judith's main residence for the 51 months before the sale – but the last nine months are always exempt if the property has been her main residence at some time. The remaining period of 42 months cannot be covered by the 'any reason' rule as the property is not Judith's main residence at that time and she does not reoccupy the property at some time after the period of absence.

(b) Letting relief is not available in periods (2), (3) and (4) as these periods are already exempt under the PRR rules. Letting relief is not available in period (6) as Judith does not share the occupation of the property with the tenant.

29 Lisha

B £10,000

		£
Gain before PRR		250,000
Less PRR		
£250,000 × 80%		(200,000)
Gain after PRR		50,000
Less Letting relief (W)		(40,000)
Chargeable gain		10,000

Letting relief - lowest of:			£
(i)	PRR		200,000
(ii)	That part of the gain which relates to the period of letting £250,000 × 20%		50,000
(iii)	Maximum		40,000

30 Candice

(a) **Candice: Self-assessment payments**

2021/22

	£
Income tax liability	17,000
Class 4 NICs	700
Total tax liability	17,700
Minus: PAYE	(3,500)
Tax payable by self assessment	14,200

This £14,200 is:

(1) more than £1,000

(2) more than (20% × £17,700) = £3,540.

Therefore, payments on account are required in 2022/23.

2022/23

	£
Income tax liability	20,000
Class 4 NICs	880
Total tax liability	20,880
Minus: PAYE	(4,000)
Tax payable by self assessment	16,880

Due dates of payment			£
POAs	31 January 2023	½ × £14,200	7,100
	31 July 2023	½ × £14,200	7,100
			14,200
Balancing payment	31 January 2024	(£16,880 – £14,200)	2,680
Income tax and Class 4 NICs			16,880
Capital gains tax	31 January 2024		4,600

In addition, on 31 January 2024 the first POA of £8,440 (½ × £16,880) for 2023/24 is due.

(b) **Interest on underpaid tax**

	£		From	To
1st POA	7,100	x 3.25% x 1/12 = £19	31 January 2023	28 February 2023
2nd POA	7,100	x 3.25% x 1/12 = £19	31 July 2023	31 August 2023
Balancing payment	2,680			No interest as paid by the due date

31 Pat

(a) **Lifetime IHT payable by Pat**

Gift on 19 June 2014

- The gift is a PET
- No lifetime tax is due on PETs
- The PET utilises the annual exemptions for 2014/15 and 2013/14 b/f
- PETs are not cumulated when calculating lifetime IHT.

Gift on 14 May 2015

- The gift is an inter-spouse gift and is therefore exempt
- No IHT is payable during lifetime or on death
- The gift does not utilise any annual exemptions
- The gift can be ignored.

Other lifetime gifts

		CLT 20 Feb 2018	PET 6 July 2018
	£	£	£
Transfer of value		373,440	200,000
Marriage exemptions			(5,000)
Annual exemptions			
2017/18		(3,000)	
2016/17 b/f		(3,000)	
2018/19			(3,000)
Chargeable amount		367,440	192,000
NRB	325,000		
Gross CLTs in 7 yrs before this gift (20.02.11 – 20.02.18)			
(ignore the PET)	(Nil)		
NRB available		(325,000)	
Taxable amount		42,440	
Lifetime IHT			
£42,440 × 25%		10,610	
No IHT = PET			Nil
Paid by		Pat	
Due date		31.08.18	
Gross CLT to c/f (£367,440 + £10,610)		378,050	

(b) Death tax due in respect of lifetime gifts

Date of death   17 April 2022
Seven years before   17 April 2015

Gift on 19 June 2014
- As the gift is more than seven years before death, the PET is exempt
- No death IHT arises
- The PET is not cumulated when calculating the IHT on subsequent gifts.

Gift on 14 May 2015
- Inter spouse gift, therefore exempt.

Other lifetime gifts	CLT 20 Feb 2018		PET 6 July 2018	
	£	£	£	£
Gross chargeable amount per lifetime		378,050		192,000
NRB	325,000		325,000	
Gross chargeable gifts in 7 years before this gift				
20.02.11 – 20.02.18 (ignore PET)	(Nil)			
06.07.11 – 06.07.18 (include CLT, ignore PET)			(378,050)	
NRB available		(325,000)		(Nil)
Taxable amount		53,050		192,000
IHT at 40%		21,220		76,800
Less Taper Relief				
20.02.18 – 17.04.22 (4-5 years) (40%)		(8,488)		
06.07.18 – 17.04.22 (3-4 years) (20%)				(15,360)
		12,732		61,440
Less Lifetime IHT paid		(10,610)		(Nil)
IHT payable on death		2,122		61,440
Paid by		Trustees		Daughter
Due date		31.10.22		31.10.22

32 Graham

Estate computation

	£
Private residence	420,000
Less: Repayment mortgage	(140,000)
	280,000
Bank accounts	180,000
ISA	48,000
Car and chattels (20,500 + 14,000)	34,500
Life assurance policy (Note)	169,000
	711,500
Less: Funeral expenses	(5,400)
Income tax liability	(6,300)
Credit card bills	(1,280)
	698,520
Less: Exempt legacy to wife	(60,000)
Gross chargeable estate	638,520
Less: Nil rate band	(325,000)
Less: Residence nil rate band	(175,000)
Chargeable	138,520
IHT £138,520 × 40%	55,408
Due date of payment	31 January 2023

The tax is payable by the executors, but is suffered by the son and daughter.

Notes

(1) The life assurance policy proceeds actually received are included in the estate, not the surrender value.

(2) All of the nil rate band is available as Graham has not made any lifetime gifts.

(3) The residence nil rate band is available as the main residence is left to his direct descendants (i.e. his son and daughter).

33 Craig

Lifetime gifts

The gift to his daughter on 16 June 2017 is a PET, so there is no lifetime IHT payable.

As the gift is within seven years of the date of death, the PET becomes chargeable. The chargeable amount on death is calculated as follows:

	£
Value of gift	46,250
Less: Annual exemptions	
2017/18	(3,000)
2016/17 b/f	(3,000)
Revised chargeable amount on death	40,250

There is no IHT payable as the gift is covered by the nil rate band.

However, the nil rate band available to set against the death estate is £284,750 (325,000 – £40,250).

Estate computation

	Note	£
Main residence (446,000 – 120,000)	Note	326,000
London flat		400,000
Chattels and cars		61,000
Bank accounts		310,000
Shares		48,000
		1,145,000
Less: Funeral expenses		(7,650)
Income tax		(7,260)
		1,130,090
Less: Exempt legacy to wife		(726,000)
Gross chargeable estate		404,090
IHT payable on estate		
(£404,090 – £284,750) × 40%		47,736

Notes

(1) The interest-only mortgage is deducted from the value of the main residence.

(2) The residence nil rate band does not apply as the main residence is inherited by his wife rather than a direct descendant.

Answers to practice questions

34 ABC Ltd

ABC Ltd

(a) Corporation tax computation – year ended 31 March 2023

	£
Income	
Trading income	448,000
Interest income	24,000
UK property income	160,000
Chargeable gain	242,000
Total Profits	874,000
Qualifying charitable donations	(4,000)
Taxable Total Profits (TTP)	870,000
Dividend income	100,000
Augmented profits	970,000
Corporation tax liability (TTP × 19%) (£870,000 × 19%)	165,300

Due date 1 January 2024

Notes

Dividends received from non-group companies are not taxable income and so do not appear in the computation of TTP. They are, however, taken into account in determining the level of augmented profits.

The augmented profits are below the profit threshold of £1,500,000. ABC Ltd is not classed as a large company and so all its corporation tax is payable nine months and one day following the end of its accounting period.

35 DEF Ltd

A Instalments begin during the accounting period.

DEF Ltd: Corporation tax payments

Quarterly instalment	14 days after end of	Due date
1	6th month	14 December 2021
2	9th month	14 March 2022
3	12th month	14 June 2022
4	15th month	14 September 2022

36 GH Ltd

GH Ltd
Corporation tax computation – year ended 31 March 2023

	£
Income	
Trading income	226,000
Interest income (W1)	1,400
UK property income (W2)	19,200
Capital gains	
Net chargeable gains (see note)	Nil
Total profits	246,600
Qualifying charitable donation	(2,500)
Taxable Total Profits (TTP)	244,100
Corporation tax liability (TTP × 19%) (£244,100 × 19%)	46,379

Workings

(W1) Interest income

	£
Loan note interest receivable	7,200
Minus: Interest on underpaid corporation tax	(5,800)
Interest income	1,400

(W2) UK property income – Premium received on the granting of a short lease

	£
Premium received	60,000
Minus 2% × £60,000 × 34 years	(40,800)
Property income assessment	19,200

Notes

(1) The amount of loan note interest *actually* paid in the CAP is not relevant. Interest income is assessed on an accruals basis.

(2) Loan stock interest *payable* which is incurred for trading purposes is treated as an allowable deduction from trading income and is not deducted from interest income. The question gives the adjusted trading profits, therefore no further adjustment is required.

(3) The capital disposal in the period gave rise to a capital loss. Capital losses cannot be set against other profits. Capital losses can only be carried forward and set against future capital gains.

(4) Dividends received are not taxable income but, as they are from non-group companies, they will be taken into account in determining GH Ltd's augmented profits. Augmented profits determine whether a company is large for the purpose of paying corporation tax in instalments.

(5) Dividends paid are not an allowable expense and so have no effect on a company's corporation tax liability.

Answers to practice questions

37 IJ plc

IJ plc: Corporation tax computations	y/e 31 March 2022	p/e 30 June 2022
	£	£
Adjusted profit before capital allowances (£400,000 × 12/15 : £400,000 × 3/15)	320,000	80,000
Capital allowances	(67,640)	(14,910)
Trading income	252,360	65,090
Interest income (£150,000 × 6% : £150,000 × 6% × 3/12)	9,000	2,250
UK property income (£18,300 × 12/15 : £18,300 × 3/15)	14,640	3,660
Net chargeable gains (Second CAP: £62,500 – £22,600)	15,100	39,900
Total profits	291,100	110,900
Qualifying charitable donation	(4,500)	Nil
TTP	286,600	110,900
Dividend income	Nil	5,500
Augmented profits	286,600	116,400
Profit threshold (full limit : full limit × 3/12)	1,500,000	375,000

Corporation tax liabilities	£	£
£286,600 × 19%	54,454	
£110,900 × 19%		21,071
Due dates for payment	1 Jan 2023	1 April 2023

Working: UK property income assessment for the 15-month accounting period	£
Rents accrued: (£3,000 × 15 months)	45,000
Minus: Allowable expenses	
Estate agent fees (£300 × 15 months)	(4,500)
Insurance (£100 × 15 months)	(1,500)
Repairs	(16,000)
Accountants' fees	(4,200)
Replacement furniture relief	(500)
	18,300

Notes

(1) Interest income is assessed on an accruals basis.

(2) Loan note interest payable is an allowable deduction from trading profits and will have already been deducted in the adjusted profits figure given in the question.

(3) The conservatory extension is capital expenditure and not an allowable deduction from rental income.

(4) In a long period of account, UK property income is time-apportioned.

(5) Corporation tax is payable on the figure of taxable total profits (TTP). Augmented profits are only used to determine whether a company is large for the purpose of paying its corporation tax in instalments.

38 KL Ltd

(a)

KL Ltd: Trading income assessment – year ended 31 March 2023	£
Profit before taxation	202,640
Add Depreciation	109,880
Qualifying charitable donation	660
Gifts of champagne to customers	720
Gifts of decanters (cost in excess of £50 each)	1,155
Gifts to staff	0
Maintenance of plant and machinery	0
Extension of workshop (capital)	53,100
Rebuilding damaged chimney	0
Accountancy and audit fees	0
Legal fees in relation to breaching health and safety laws	950
Debt collection fees	0
Legal fees in relation to renewal of long lease	1,450
Legal fees re issue of new loan notes	0
Staff Christmas party	0
Interest on overdue tax	3,600
Pollution fine	16,000
	390,155
Minus Loan interest receivable	(13,560)
Profit on the disposal of a warehouse	(85,910)
Adjusted profits before capital allowances	290,685
Minus Capital allowances	(45,035)
Trading income	245,650

(b)

KL Ltd

Corporation tax computation – year ended 31 March 2023	£
Income	
Trading income	245,650
Interest income (see working)	9,960
Capital gains	
Chargeable gain	56,160
Total Profits	311,770
Qualifying charitable donation	(660)
Taxable Total Profits (TTP)	311,110
Corporation tax liability (£311,110 × 19%)	59,111

Working: Interest income	£
Loan interest receivable	13,560
Minus: Interest on overdue tax	(3,600)
Interest income	9,960

39 MN Ltd

MN Ltd: Trading income – y/e 30 September 2022	£
Profit before taxation	25,125
Add Alteration to floor to install display stands	1,460
Decoration	0
Re-plastering walls	0
Depreciation – vans and equipment (£2,800 + £750)	3,550
Amortisation of lease	120
Loss on sale of equipment	40
Accountancy	0
Breach of customs regulations and fine (£110 + £250)	360
Legal fees in relation to acquiring new lease	820
Debt collection	0
Trade subscription	0
Donation to police welfare fund	20
Entertaining customers	300
Gifts to customers	0
Royalties	0
Miscellaneous	0
	31,795
Minus Bank deposit interest	(160)
Dividend received	(40)
Allowable deduction for short lease (see working)	(90)
Adjusted profits before capital allowances	31,505
Minus Capital allowances	(460)
Trading income	31,045

MN Ltd - TTP statement – year ended 30 September 2022	£
Income	
Trading income	31,045
Interest income	160
Taxable total profits (TTP)	31,205

Working: Allowable deduction for short lease	£
Property income assessment on Turin plc	
Premium paid to Turin plc	12,600
Minus: 2% × £12,600 × 20 years	(5,040)
Property income assessment on Turin plc	7,560

MN Ltd: Trading income – y/e 30 September 2022	£
Annual allowable deduction against profit (£7,560 ÷ 21 years)	360
Allowable deduction for year ended 30 September 2022: (leased for three months of MN Ltd's CAP) (£360 × 3/12)	90

40   OPQ Ltd

(a)   D   £3,114

(b)

	True	False
The car costing £14,500 qualifies for a First Year Allowance of £14,500	√	
The car costing £12,500 qualifies for a writing down allowance of £750	√	
The car costing £12,200 must be kept separate from the main pool as there is private use by a director		√

Workings

OPQ Ltd - Capital allowances – y/e 31 December 2022		Main pool	Special rate pool	Total allowances
	£	£	£	£
TWDV b/f		22,000		
Acquisitions not qualifying for AIAs		12,200	12,500	
Disposals		(16,900)		
		17,300		
Writing down allowance: 18%/6%		(3,114)	(750)	3,864
		14,186	11,750	
Low emission car	14,500			
FYA (100%)	(14,500)			14,500
		Nil		
TWDV c/f		14,186	11,750	
Total allowances available				18,364

(c)   If the expenditure relates to items that can be added to the main pool, OPQ Ltd can claim **a super-deduction** of **£2,340,000** (£1,800,000 x 130%).

If the expenditure relates to items that belong to the special rate pool, OPQ Ltd can claim **an annual investment allowance** of **£1,000,000** and a **first year allowance** of **£400,000** ((£1,800 000 – 1,000,000) x 50%).

41   RS plc

RS plc
Corporation tax computation – y/e 31 March 2023   £

Income	
Trading income (working 1)	322,826
Interest income	700
Net chargeable gains	500
Total Profits	324,026
Qualifying charitable donation	(1,000)
TTP	323,026
Corporation tax liability (£323,026 × 19%)	61,375

Workings

(W1) Trading income

		£
Profit before taxation		344,685
Add	Salaries, wages and directors' remuneration	0
	Rates, electricity and insurance	0
	Travelling expenses	0
	Stationery, postage and telephone	0
	Legal fees in relation to rights issue of shares	3,150
	Legal fees in relation to collection of trade debts	0
	Qualifying charitable donations	1,000
	Staff Christmas party	0
	Contribution to Deeside Enterprise Agency	0
	Directors' relocation expenses	0
	Sundry expenses	0
	Repairs	0
	Audit and accountancy	0
	Royalties	0
	Loan note interest	0
	Depreciation	21,170
		370,005
Minus	Interest on Government Stock	(700)
	UK dividends received	(10,800)
	Gain on sale of shares	(4,700)
Adjusted profits before capital allowances		353,805
Minus	Capital allowances (working 2)	(30,979)
Trading income		322,826

Note – Dividends paid are not an allowable expense and so have no effect on a company's corporation tax liability.

(W2) Capital allowances

	£	Main pool £	Total allowances £
TWDV b/f		14,240	
Acquisitions **not** qualifying for AIAs			
Car		8,616	
		22,856	
Disposals (restrict to cost)		(750)	
		22,106	
Writing down allowance: (18%)		(3,979)	3,979
		18,127	
Acquisitions qualifying for FYAs			
Low emission car	27,000		
FYA (100%)	(27,000)		27,000
		Nil	
TWDV c/f		18,127	
Total allowances available			30,979

Note - Private use of low emission car by managing director is irrelevant.

42 TUV plc

(a) **B** £55,490

(b) **D** £19,661

Working: Investment building	£
Gross sale proceeds (November 2022)	95,000
Minus: Incidental expenses	(2,450)
Net sale proceeds	92,550
Minus: Allowable costs	
July 2002 (£28,000 + £1,460 + £2,000)	(31,460)
August 2006	(5,600)
Unindexed gain	55,490
Minus: Indexation allowance	
July 2002 to December 2017	
0.558 × £31,460	(17,555)
August 2006 to December 2017	
0.376 × £5,600	(2,106)
Chargeable gain	35,829

Note - Redecorating costs are not capital expenditure and are therefore not an allowable deduction in the capital gain computation.

Answers to practice questions

43 WXY Ltd

(a)

WXY Ltd: Chargeable gain on the disposal of the original office building	£
Sale proceeds (August 2022)	600,000
Minus: Cost (July 2004)	(220,000)
Unindexed gain	380,000
Minus: Indexation allowance	
July 2004 to December 2017	
0.457 × £220,000	(100,540)
Chargeable gain before rollover relief	279,460
Minus: Rollover relief (see working)	(219,460)
Chargeable gain – y/e 31 August 2022	60,000

The deferred gain of £219,460 becomes chargeable on the sale of the replacement office block: (expected in 2033).

Base cost of the replacement office building	£
Cost of new office building	540,000
Minus: Rollover relief	(219,460)
Base cost	320,540

Working

Is the asset a QBA for rollover relief purposes?	Yes
Has it been replaced with a QBA?	Yes
Has it been replaced in the four year qualifying period (15 August 2021 to 15 August 2025)?	Yes
Have all the sale proceeds been reinvested in a QBA?	No

Chargeable gain arising in y/e 31 August 2022 – Lower of:	£	£
(1) All the gain	279,460	
(2) Sale proceeds not reinvested in a QBA (£600,000 - £540,000)	60,000	
Rollover relief = £279,460 - £60,000		219,460

(b) If WXY Ltd was to purchase fixed plant and machinery instead of the smaller office building:

- Fixed plant and machinery is a depreciating QBA.
- WXY Ltd will still have a chargeable gain of £60,000 in the year ended 31 August 2022.
- £219,460 of the gain will be deferred, but not by deducting it from the base cost of the plant and machinery.

- The gain is held over (i.e. a separate record of the gain is kept) and becomes chargeable on the earliest of:
    (1) 10 years after the acquisition of the replacement asset (30 June 2032)
    (2) the date the replacement asset ceases to be used in the business
    (3) the date the replacement asset is sold.
- As WXY Ltd does not expect to sell the asset until 2033, the deferred gain will become chargeable on 30 June 2032.

44 Bonus issue

Chargeable gain on the disposal of Y plc shares	£
Gross sale proceeds	7,500
Minus: Cost (from pool working)	(1,600)
Unindexed gain	5,900
Minus: Indexation allowance (from pool working) (£2,090 – £1,600)	(490)
Chargeable gain	5,410

Share pool	Number of shares	Original cost	Indexed cost
		£	£
January 2009			
Purchase	1,500	2,000	2,000
July 2011			
Bonus issues (1 for 4)	375	Nil	Nil
	1,875	2,000	2,000
January 2023			
IA: from Jan 2009 to Dec 2017 £2,000 × 0.306			612
			2,612
Sale of shares	(1,500)	(1,600)	(2,090)
	375	400	522

45 Rights issue

Chargeable gain on the disposal of X plc shares	£
Gross sale proceeds	14,960
Minus: Cost (from pool working)	(6,050)
Unindexed gain	8,910
Minus: Indexation allowance (from pool working) (£9,162 – £6,050)	(3,112)
Chargeable gain	5,798

Answers to practice questions

Share pool	Number of shares	Original cost	Indexed cost
		£	£
January 2000			
Purchase	1,000	3,000	3,000
July 2004			
(1) IA: from January 2000 to July 2004 £3,000 × 0.121			363
(2) Purchase	600	2,000	2,000
	1,600	5,000	5,363
February 2008			
(1) IA: from July 2004 to February 2008 £5,363 × 0.132			708
(2) Rights issue (1 for 2) at £2 per share	800	1,600	1,600
	2,400	6,600	7,671
March 2023			
(1) IA: from February 2008 to December 2017 £7,671 × 0.303			2,324
			9,995
Sale of shares	(2,200)	(6,050)	(9,162)
	200	550	833

46 Takeover

There is no chargeable gain at the time of the takeover as no cash consideration is received.

Takeover consideration received by DE plc	Market value
	£
(10,000/5) × 10 = 20,000 ordinary shares in H plc at £3.80	76,000
(10,000/5) × 2 = 4,000 preference shares in H plc at £2.00	8,000
	84,000

S plc: Share pool	Number of shares	Original cost	Indexed cost
		£	£
August 2008			
Purchase	10,000	37,000	37,000
March 2013			
IA: from August 2008 to March 2013 £37,000 × 0.145			5,365
Balance at time of takeover	10,000	37,000	42,365

Allocation of original cost and indexed cost of S plc shares	Original cost	Indexed cost
	£	£
20,000 ordinary shares: (£76,000/£84,000) × £37,000 or £42,365	33,476	38,330
4,000 preference shares: (£8,000/£84,000) × £37,000 or £42,365	3,524	4,035
	37,000	42,365

H plc: Share pool	Number of shares	Original cost	Indexed cost
March 2013		£	£
Balance at time of takeover	20,000	33,476	38,330
March 2023			
(1) IA: from March 2013 to December 2017 £38,330 × 0.108			4,140
Balance at time of takeover	20,000	33,476	42,470
(2) Sale of shares	(10,000)	(16,738)	(21,235)
Balance carried forward	10,000	16,738	21,235

Chargeable gain on the disposal of 10,000 ordinary shares in H plc	£
Sale proceeds March 2023: (10,000 × £5)	50,000
Minus: Cost (from pool, see above)	(16,738)
Unindexed gain	33,262
Minus: Indexation allowance (from pool working) (£21,235 – £16,738)	(4,497)
Chargeable gain	28,765

47 FG Ltd

FG Ltd: Corporation tax computations	Year to 31 December 2021	Period ended 31 March 2022	Year to 31 March 2023
	£	£	£
Trading income	88,800	Nil	26,400
Interest income	10,000	10,000	10,000
Net chargeable gains	30,720	33,600	28,800
Minus: loss relief	129,520	43,600	65,200
– current loss-making CAP		(43,600)	
– carry back to previous 12 months	(129,520)		
– carried forward			(47,680)
Total Profits	Nil	Nil	17,520
Minus: Qualifying charitable donation	Lost	Lost	(2,400)
TTP	Nil	Nil	15,120

Working: Record of trading losses	£
Loss in CAP	220,800
Set off	
– in loss-making CAP	(43,600)
– in carry back CAP	(129,520)
Trading loss c/f and used in y/e March 2023	(47,680)

48 HI Ltd

(a) **HI Ltd: Corporation tax computations**

	Y/e 30 Nov 2020	P/e 31 Mar 2021	Y/e 31 Mar 2022	Y/e 31 Mar 2023
	£	£	£	£
Trading income	850,380	146,800	Nil	85,940
Interest income	10,680	3,560	10,680	10,680
Net chargeable gains	48,500	26,000	Nil	Nil
	909,560	176,360	10,680	96,620
Minus: loss relief				
– current loss-making CAP			(10,680)	
– carry back 12 months				
p/e 31 March 2021		(176,360)		
y/e 30 November 2020	(169,420)			
	740,140	Nil	Nil	96,620
Minus:				
Qualifying charitable donations	(1,170)	Nil	Lost	(1,170)
	738,970	Nil	Nil	95,450

(b) **Losses available to carry forward at 31 March 2023**

Record of trading losses	£
Loss in CAP	356,460
Set off	
– in loss-making CAP	(10,680)
– period ending 31 March 2021	(176,360)
– year ending 30 November 2020 (the balance of the loss) (which cannot exceed $^8/_{12} \times £909,560 = £606,373$)	(169,420)
Trading loss c/f	Nil

There is an allowable capital loss of £14,000 available to carry forward to the next CAP.

49 UK group

(a) Profit threshold for corporation tax payment purposes

Number of related 51% group companies = 5

C Ltd is a related 51% group company with D Ltd, E Ltd, F Ltd and G Ltd because it has a more-than-50% interest in each company.

The C Ltd group and B Ltd are not related 51% group companies as the shares in B Ltd are held by an individual rather than a company.

Profit threshold for C Ltd group   £1,500,000 ÷ 5   £300,000

(b) Identification of loss relief groups

Group 1: C Ltd, D Ltd, E Ltd, G Ltd

C Ltd has at least a 75% interest in D Ltd and E Ltd. G Ltd is included because the effective interest of C Ltd in G Ltd is also at least 75% (i.e. 90% × 90% = 81%).

F Ltd is not included in Group 1 because C Ltd does not have an effective interest of at least 75% in F Ltd. (The effective interest is 80% × 90% = 72%.)

Group 2: D Ltd and F Ltd

A separate loss relief group exists. D Ltd can be a member of more than one loss group.

(c) Use of F Ltd's loss

F Ltd will not want to claim relief against its current year profits as this would utilise £5,000 of the loss, achieve a tax saving of only £190 (£1,000 x 19%) and waste £4,000 of the qualifying charitable donation.

F Ltd should therefore surrender all its loss under the group relief provisions. F Ltd is in Group 2 and so can only surrender its loss to D Ltd. This will reduce the TTP of D Ltd to £78,000 (= £118,000 - £40,000) and save tax of £7,600 (= £40,000 × 19%).

(d) Corporation tax computations: with loss relief

	B Ltd	C Ltd	D Ltd	E Ltd	F Ltd	G Ltd
	£	£	£	£	£	£
Trading profit	260,000	80,000	120,000	24,000	Nil	10,000
Rental income	20,000		8,000	4,000	5,000	6,000
	280,000	80,000	128,000	28,000	5,000	16,000
Donations	(10,000)	(6,000)	(10,000)	(2,000)	(4,000)	(5,000)
TTP before loss relief	270,000	74,000	118,000	26,000	1,000	11,000
Group relief: From F Ltd			(40,000)			
TTP	270,000	74,000	78,000	26,000	1,000	11,000

Notes

As F Ltd is able to utilise its charitable donations against its own profits, they cannot be surrendered to other group members. This rule applies despite the fact that a loss relief claim by F Ltd would be made against its profits prior to the deduction of the charitable donations.

However, F Ltd could claim trading loss relief of £1,000 against its own profits by surrendering £39,000 of its losses to D Ltd first.

50 PQ group

All companies in the PQ Ltd group are members of the same gains group as PQ Ltd has at least a 75% interest in all companies. Transfers between group members therefore take place on a no gain no loss basis.

Year ended 31 March 2012: Intra-group transfer from C Ltd to A Ltd

	£
Deemed sale proceeds	307,320
(Ignore actual proceeds received: Use cost plus IA)	
Cost (July 2006)	(260,000)
IA on cost from July 2006 to July 2011	(47,320)
0.182 × £260,000	
Chargeable gain	Nil

Year ended 31 March 2023: Disposal by A Ltd outside the group

	£
Sale proceeds	500,000
Deemed cost	(307,320)
Unindexed gain	192,680
IA on deemed cost from July 2011 to December 2017	(47,635)
0.155 × £307,320	
Chargeable gain arising in A Ltd before considering rollover relief	145,045

As the office building is a QBA and PQ Ltd has purchased a QBA within a four-year time period (14 June 2021 to 14 June 2025). A group rollover relief claim can be made.

PQ Ltd has not reinvested all the sale proceeds. Therefore, a chargeable gain still arises in respect of the disposal of the office building, as follows:

Chargeable gain =

Lower of:	
(1) All of the gain	£145,045
(2) Sale proceeds not reinvested in QBAs (£500,000 - £480,000)	£20,000
Rollover relief claim = £145,045 - £20,000	£125,045

The chargeable gain will be chargeable on A Ltd unless an election is made to transfer the gain to another group company.

51 Deborah

(a) Compulsory registration

12 months ended	Workings	Taxable supplies
		£
31 August 2022	(12 × £6,000)	72,000
30 September 2022	£72,000 - £6,000 + £7,300	73,300
31 October 2022	£73,300 - £6,000 + £9,600	76,900
30 November 2022	£76,900 - £6,000 + £13,000	83,900
31 December 2022	£83,900 - £6,000 + £13,500	91,400

Deborah exceeded the £85,000 threshold on 31 December 2022.

She must notify HMRC by 30 January 2023 (i.e. 30 days after the end of the month in which the threshold is exceeded).

She must start to charge VAT from 1 February 2023 (i.e. the first day of the month following the end of the month in which the threshold is exceeded).

(b) Pre-registration input tax

Deborah will be able to recover the pre-registration input VAT incurred on the purchase of goods or non-current assets used for business purposes if still held at the date of registration and purchased within four years of registration.

She will also be able to recover the input VAT on services supplied to her in the six months before the date of registration.

52 WX Ltd

VAT return for the quarter ended: 31 March 2023

	£
Output VAT	
Standard rated sales (£201,230 × 1/6)	33,538
Input VAT	
Purchases of goods (£41,525 × 1/6)	(6,921)
Distribution expenses (£10,000 × 1/6)	(1,667)
Other expenses (£16,825 × 1/6)	(2,804)
Purchase of plant machinery (£35,000 × 1/6)	(5,833)
Impairment loss relief (not six months old)	(Nil)
Amount payable to HMRC	16,313

Due date: 7 May 2023 (must be paid electronically)

Notes

(1) Employment costs are outside of the scope of VAT.

(2) Input VAT on entertaining UK customers and the car is blocked.

Taxation – United Kingdom
(TX-UK) FA2022

Index

A

Accrued income scheme	52
Adjustment of profit	90
Amendments	278
Annual	
allowance	192, 195
exemption	296
investment allowance	110
Appeals	279
Appropriations of profit	92
Approved mileage allowances	69
Augmented profits	327
Average method	76

B

Badges of trade	86
Balancing	
adjustments	125
allowances	116
charges	116
Beneficial loans	75
Blocked items	414
Bonus issues	247, 365
Business asset disposal relief	251

C

Capital	
allowances	107
expenditure	94
gains tax	215
losses	222
Carry forward of trading losses	148
Cars	122
Cash	
basis	184
earnings	207
Civil Partnership Act 2004	31
Class	
1 NICs	206
1A NICs	211
2 NICs	213
4 NICs	213
Closing year rules	141
Company car	64
Compensation	235
Compliance checks	278
Connected person	221
Contract	
for services	56
of service	56
Current year basis	134
Chargeable	
accounting period	323
disposal	216
lifetime transfers	297

person	216
Charitable donations	344
Chattels	232
Child benefit income tax charge	34, 36
Choice of accounting date	143

D

Damaged assets	238
Deceased individual's estate	311
Deemed occupation	267
Default	
interest	422
surcharge	421
De-pooling election	125
Depreciating asset	257
Deregistration	409
Determination assessment	276
Direct taxation	5
Disallowable expenditure	93
Discovery assessments	280
Dividend	
income	24
nil rate band	24
Domicile	198
Donations	95

E

Early years' loss relief	159
Earnings period	207
Employer Payment Summary	289
Employment	
allowance	209, 210
income	55
Enhanced capital allowances	335
Enhancement expenditure	222
Entertaining expenses	80, 97
Errors	423
Executors	315
Exempt	
assets	216
benefits	61
gifts	295
income	14, 102
interest	16
supplies	402
Expensive accommodation	72

Exports	429
Extra-Statutory Concessions	6

F

Filing	
Corporation tax return	330
Income tax return	275
Financial Year	326
Fines	97
First year allowances	110
First-tier Tribunal	279
Fiscal year	12
Fixed rate adjustments	180
Fuel	68
Full Payment Submission	289
Functional test	109
Furnished holiday lettings	45

G

General Anti-Abuse Rule	9
Gift(s)	97
Aid	29
holdover-relief	261
Gilt-edged securities	242
Gilts	242
Give As You Earn	79
Group	
chargeable gains	396
loss relief	387
registration	409

I

Impairment losses	416
Imports	429
Income tax	
liability	28, 37
payable	28
Independent taxation	31
Indexation allowance	357
Indirect	
subsidiaries	387
taxation	5
Individual Savings Accounts	50
Inheritance tax	292, 310

Index

Input VAT	404, 413
Insurance	235
Integral features	119
Interest	
payable	95, 338
payments	16
receivable	337
International services	429
Intra-group transfers	397
Investors' relief	254
iXBRL tagging	331

J

Job-related accommodation	71

L

Large company	327, 328
Late payment interest	284
Leasing costs	96
Legal and professional fees	96
Letting relief	270
Lifetime allowance	196
Limited liability partnerships	175
List price	64
Living accommodation	71
Loan relationships	337
Long	
life assets	119
periods of account	129
periods of account	349

M

Main pool	114
Marriage allowance	18
Married couples	31

N

Nil rate band	314

O

Occupational pension scheme	190
Opening year rules	135

Output VAT	404, 412
Overlap profits	136

P

P11D	289
P2	287
P45	289
P6	287
P60	289
Part disposals	230
Partnership(s)	169
losses	176
PAYE	60
system	286
Payment dates for	
corporation tax	326
income tax	281
Payrolling of benefits	78
Penalties for late	
filing	
Corporation tax return	331
Income tax return	276
payment	283
Pension contributions	189
Personal	
allowances	17
withdrawal	17
representatives	315
Plant and machinery	109
Pool cars	68
Potential lost revenue	274
Potentially exempt transfers	296
Premiums	49
Pre-registration expenditure	415
Pre-trading expenditure	99
Private	
residence relief	266
use assets	127
Progressive taxation	3
Property	
business losses	382
income	340
losses	342
Proportional taxation	2
Provisions	94

Q

Qualifying	
business assets	256
Corporate Bonds	242
Quarterly instalments	327

R

Real time reporting	289
Reasonable excuse	275
Receipts basis	59
Record keeping	280, 332
Recovery of overpaid tax	278
Reduced-rated supplies	403
Regressive taxation	3
Related 51% group companies	327, 328, 384
Remoteness test	91
Rental income	40, 340
Rent-a-room relief	47
Reorganisations	250
Replacement furniture relief	42
Residence	197
nil rate band	317
Residual legatee	315
Revenue expenditure	94
Rights issues	248, 367
Rollover relief	256, 359
Royalties	95

S

Savings income	15, 22
Secondary contributions	206
Share identification rules	244, 361
Short	
lease(s)	49, 99
life assets	124
periods of account	128
Small gifts	295
Special rate pool	119
Specific legatees	315
Starting rate band	22
Statements of practice	6
Structures and buildings allowance	130
Subscriptions	95
Succession election	118

Super deduction	336

T

Takeovers	249, 368
Taper relief	306
Tax	
avoidance	8
code	287
evasion	8
point	415
year	12
Taxable	
income	12
supplies	402
total profits	324
Terminal loss relief	162, 379
Trading	
income	334
income	85
losses	146, 372
Transfer(s)	
as a going concern	410
between spouses	229
of value	292
Travel expenses	80

U

Upper Tribunal	279

V

Value Added Tax (VAT)	401
annual accounting scheme	425
cash accounting scheme	424
flat rate scheme	426
invoices	420
registration	405
returns	419
Van	69
Voluntary registration	408
Vouchers	77

W

Wasting
    asset   232
    chattel   232
Wedding gifts   295
Writing down allowances   110

Y

Year of assessment   12

Z

Zero-rated supplies   404

Printed in Great Britain
by Amazon